T0003194

GETTING MONETARY POLICY BACK ON TRACK

The Hoover Institution gratefully acknowledges the following individuals and foundations for their significant support of the ECONOMIC POLICY WORKING GROUP *and this publication:*

Lynde and Harry Bradley Foundation

John A. Gunn and Cynthia Fry Gunn

Preston and Carolyn Butcher

Sarah Page Herrick

Gail A. Jaquish

Koret Foundation

GETTING MONETARY POLICY BACK ON TRACK

EDITORS

MICHAEL D. BORDO
JOHN H. COCHRANE
JOHN B. TAYLOR

CONTRIBUTING AUTHORS

Anat R. Admati
Michael D. Bordo
James Bullard
Anusha Chari
Richard H. Clarida
John H. Cochrane
Steven J. Davis
Darrell Duffie
Sebastian Edwards
Barry Eichengreen
Niall Ferguson
Peter Blair Henry
Philip N. Jefferson
Martin Kornejew
Haruhiko Kuroda

Jeffrey M. Lacker
Mickey D. Levy
John Lipsky
William R. Nelson
Charles I. Plosser
Randal Quarles
Joshua D. Rauh
Condoleezza Rice
Paul Schmelzing
Moritz Schularick
Amit Seru
John B. Taylor
Volker Wieland
James A. Wilcox

HOOVER INSTITUTION PRESS
STANFORD UNIVERSITY   STANFORD, CALIFORNIA

hoover.org

Hoover Institution Press Publication No. 736
Hoover Institution at Leland Stanford Junior University,
Stanford, California 94305-6003

First printing 2024
30 29 28 27 26 25 24   7 6 5 4 3 2 1

Manufactured in the United States of America
Printed on acid-free, archival-quality paper

Library of Congress Cataloging-in-Publication Data
Names: How to Get Back on Track (Conference) (2023 : Hoover Institution on War, Revolution, and Peace), author. | Bordo, Michael D., editor. | Cochrane, John H. (John Howland), 1957- editor. | Taylor, John B., editor.
Title: Getting monetary policy back on track / editors, Michael D. Bordo, John H. Cochrane, John B. Taylor.
Other titles: Hoover Institution Press publication ; 736.
Description: Stanford, California : Hoover Institution Press, Stanford University, 2024. | Series: Hoover Institution Press publication ; no. 736 | Proceedings of the conference How to Get Back on Track held May 12, 2023 at the Hoover Institution. | Includes bibliographical references and index. | Summary: "Experts in economic policy debate the 2021 surge in inflation, why the Federal Reserve was slow to respond, and whether rule-like policy is the best approach to controlling inflation"—Provided by publisher.
Identifiers: LCCN 2023046345 (print) | LCCN 2023046346 (ebook) | ISBN 9780817926243 (cloth) | ISBN 9780817926267 (epub) | ISBN 9780817926281 (pdf)
Subjects: LCSH: Board of Governors of the Federal Reserve System (U.S.)—Congresses. | Monetary policy—United States—Congresses. | Inflation (Finance)—United States—Congresses. | LCGFT: Conference papers and proceedings.
Classification: LCC HG540 .H698 2024 (print) | LCC HG540 (ebook) | DDC 332.4/973—dc23 /eng/20231031
LC record available at https://lccn.loc.gov/2023046345
LC ebook record available at https://lccn.loc.gov/2023046346

CONTENTS

INFLATION TARGETING IN JAPAN, 2013–2023

CENTRAL BANK BALANCE SHEETS

FORECASTING INFLATION AND OUTPUT

TOWARD A MONETARY POLICY STRATEGY

LATIN AMERICAN INFLATION

PREFACE

Michael D. Bordo, John H. Cochrane, and John B. Taylor

On May 12, 2023, we convened for the annual Hoover Monetary Policy Conference. This year's conference was titled "How to Get Back on Track."

We met at a tumultuous time in monetary policy. Inflation surged starting in February 2021. When we met previously on May 6, 2022, the Federal Reserve had only begun to react, with its first 0.25% rate increase in March 2022. That conference was titled "How Monetary Policy Got Behind the Curve and How to Get Back." The central questions were why inflation had surged, why the Fed failed to forecast or perceive inflation when it happened, whether the Fed had made inflation worse by waiting so long to take action, and whether it would be necessary to sharply raise interest rates before inflation got out of control.

As always, an underlying question remained whether the Fed should follow a rule-like monetary policy, which balances the potential benefits of reacting to the perceived particularities of each situation versus the costs of misperceiving the situation and acting unpredictably.

Inflation peaked at 9% in the summer of 2022, while the Fed had only raised the federal funds to 1.25%. Inflation then eased, settling somewhat the question of whether interest rates must exceed past inflation for inflation to decline. The Fed continued to raise interest rates. By May 2023, the Fed had enacted a swift tightening cycle, reaching 5.00–5.25%, where the Fed "paused."

Meanwhile, inflation had eased further to just about equal to the level of the federal funds rate. Yet inflation was still high at 5%, and as such, far above the Fed's 2% target.

Was policy, therefore, back on track? What will it take to wring out the remaining inflation? What headwinds will the Fed face from a still unprecedentedly loose fiscal policy and the financial troubles epitomized by the spring 2023 bank failures? How did the Fed get inflation forecasts so wrong? How did it miss the plain-vanilla interest rate risk suffusing the banking system? How can both forecasting and financial oversight improve?

Looking forward, monetary policy and financial regulation clearly interact. As we met, many outside commentators worried that higher interest rates would lead to greater financial instability and argued for a pause unrelated to inflation and employment. Others, and many participants, felt that the Fed needed to raise rates further.

We met to discuss these issues.

Opening Remarks

The Hoover Institution's director and former secretary of state Condoleezza Rice opened the conference, reminding us of the global, historical, and geostrategic context of US economic issues. A new great-power competition is emerging with China, which is both more productive economically and more integrated in the global economy than the Soviet Union ever was. Technology continues to advance, bringing opportunities and dangers. Most of all, she asked, "What is happening in the international global order?" reiterating the view that the international economy is a positive-sum game, built on free trade, cooperative monetary and exchange-rate policies, and countries building their way out of poverty, including, spectacularly, 1.4 billion Chinese. China's turn to authoritarian expansion is provoking a reaction, including sanctions and restrictions on capital and trade with China. It also threatens to construct "artificial barriers to commerce based on a broad definition of national security."

Sage domestic economic policy is needed within the context of international cooperation. "Inflation and the great spending sprees of governments" undermine that cooperation.

Rice closed with a memorable contrast: Whatever one thinks of the policies, the international responses to the terrorist attacks of 9/11 and the 2008 Global Financial Crisis were quick and closely coordinated across countries. Every airport in the world now looks the same. But, "During COVID-19, for each nation it was *my* vaccines, *my* border restrictions, *my* travel restrictions, and *my* citizens." So, "We will have to contemplate over the next few years how we build or rebuild a sense of a common project for the international order."

Thirty-Year Anniversary of the Taylor Rule

The first session celebrated the thirtieth anniversary of John Taylor's 1993 "Discretion versus Policy Rules in Practice."[1] John Cochrane opened the session by putting the Taylor rule and this paper in historical and theoretical perspective. Taylor's paper was not the first to state the basic principle of the Taylor rule that interest rates should react aggressively to inflation. But the paper's vital contribution is in practice. By explaining how the Taylor rule is an important guide to practical monetary policy, this paper really put the Taylor rule on the map. And, of course, stressing the link of academic research to practice has been the hallmark of these conferences for over fifteen years.

The Taylor rule is a central contribution to economic theory. Our central banks control inflation via interest rate targets. Central banks do not control the money supply. The Taylor rule is the key element of all theories in which a central bank can control inflation via an interest rate target. The rule is beautifully robust: it is not the exact optimal policy in most theories, but it works very well in dramatically different economic theories, including Old Keynesian (ISLM), New Keynesian (DSGE), and fiscal theory. Its roots are empirical, however: Taylor showed how inflation performed well when central banks followed such a rule and badly when they did not.

Richard Clarida added perspective from the point of view of an academic and a central banker. (Clarida wrote classic articles showing how the Taylor rule works in New Keynesian models and showing how the conquest of inflation in the 1980s came with a shift toward Taylor-rule policy.[2]) Clarida also started with a historical perspective. He pointed out that in Milton Friedman's famous 1968 address, he had isolated the basic concepts of the natural rate of interest and unemployment (u-star and r-star) but did not make them part of his policy rule. Clarida noted how money supply control was briefly tried and failed—central banks now set interest rates, not money supplies. So "the time was right for something to fill the vacuum in central bank practice left by the realization that monetary aggregate targeting was not, in reality, a workable monetary policy framework. . . . There was a growing sense at the time that a simple, systematic framework for central bank practice was needed."

Clarida emphasized that the Taylor rule doesn't just recommend interest rates that respond to inflation but anchors that response at the natural rates of interest and unemployment or output. Understanding how the natural rate of interest has varied has proven to be an important challenge in applying Taylor rule ideas in real time. Clarida summarized some of his and other researchers' study of Taylor rules when both people and the Fed have to learn about shifts in natural rates and Fed behavior over time and pointed out that central banks typically respond to expected future inflation, not current inflation, as in the simplest version of the Taylor rule. Since inflation expectations are a function of many variables, the central bank can seem to respond to many different variables, though it really only responds to expected inflation. Clarida presented a nice graph showing that the Fed did follow a Taylor rule much more closely in the inflation-reducing 1980s than in the inflationary 1970s. Clarida went on to outline how thinking in terms of the Taylor rule quickly infused the study of interest rates and exchange rates, where expectations of future interest rates and Fed policy changes are central.

Clarida next reported on his experience at the Fed. Taylor rules are "ubiquitous in any economics literature in which macro factors and asset prices are objects of interest." Whether or not the Fed follows the rule, it is at least an important benchmark.

Finally, Clarida aimed straight at the central question: just how far off track has the Fed been? He presented simulations of the recent past that include real-time data, the Fed's assessment of r-star, the fact of the zero bound so the Taylor-rule interest rate might start below the achievable value, and an inertial component, recognizing how the Fed routinely adjusts interest rates slowly in response to inflation. Each of these considerations allows a delayed response to inflation. Clarida also includes quantitative easing (QE) operations in his view of monetary tightening: "By the fall of 2021, monetary policy rules I consult . . . were indicating that lift-off from the effective lower bound (ELB) was or soon would be warranted. In the event, the Federal Open Market Committee (FOMC) began to pivot in the fall of 2021 to end quantitative easing earlier than had been expected." In short, in Clarida's view, "The conditions the committee laid out in its September 2020 forward guidance for lifting off . . . were met by the December 2021 FOMC meeting, just three months after they were met by the balanced approached Taylor rule."

John Lipsky gave a market practitioner's point of view. He was chief economist for Salomon Brothers at the time he read Taylor's paper. Reading the paper and calculating that the federal funds rate was a bit more than a percent below the Taylor rule allowed Lipsky to correctly interpret Alan Greenspan's famously delphic remarks and see a big interest rate rise ahead: "My colleagues and I virtually ran around the trading floor yelling, 'The Fed is coming! The Fed is coming!'" And it did. Alas, the Salomon Brothers trading desks did not listen. They "lost copious amounts of money in their portfolios on a mark-to-market basis. As Salomon Brothers research analysts, we were mortified to realize that our bond trading colleagues simply hadn't believed our Fed analysis."

In 1994, however, long bond yields also moved up roughly in parallel with short-term interest rates, leading to a "wave of Treasury bond selling by traders seeking to control their duration risk." This time, Lipsky saw that policy was tighter than the Taylor rule prediction, allowing him to see that rates would decline.

In part, Lipsky told these stories to answer the question, how did the Taylor rule become the "Taylor rule?" Taylor himself did not use that name. At least in practitioner circles, Lipsky and his team's reports certainly get a lot of credit for the baptism.

Why did the Taylor rule spread so far and so fast? To Lipsky, "One key lesson from investment banking is that the right deal at the right time and the right price will be snapped up in a flash." The Taylor rule proved useful to understanding how the Fed will move interest rates, and so it spread quickly in financial circles in the 1990s. Except sadly, at Salomon Brothers, which, as Lipsky recounted, did not survive the bond market losses of the early 1990s.

Volker Wieland spoke next, with the particular viewpoint of an academic steeped in explicit quantitative models. Wieland started by noting how Taylor's 1993 paper, in fact, summarized a decade's worth of detailed academic research, including work by Taylor going back to the 1970s. The key contribution, and reason for its influence, was showing how "monetary macroeconomics has undergone a major transformation and this scientific progress has had important implications for policy ... It is time to recognize the huge progress in monetary macroeconomics, the advances in

New Keynesian modeling of real effects of monetary policy, and the design of feedback rules for stabilization policy with a wide impact on policy practice."

Wieland emphasized how in models and in practice, the Taylor rule is important to stabilize expectations of how policymakers will behave. If a bank follows a rule, you know what the bank will do. Here models give important insight into why that advice is so sage.

Wieland specializes in comparing models. He showed a surprising result: across several different medium-scale models, the Taylor rule works quite well. Also, the different models generate about the same responses to monetary policy shocks—deviations from the rule. Wieland showed that even computing optimal rules in different models leads to about the same result. There is one interesting exception, however. In rational expectations models, a first difference rule is often optimal, in which the Fed raises the interest rate from whatever it was before in response to inflation. Such a rule is disastrous in adaptive expectations models. The Fed is usually estimated to follow a rule with a great deal of such persistence. Whether it should do so remains an active research question and a frequent bone of contention in our conferences.

Wieland next presented an evaluation of history with a variety of sensible variations on the Taylor rule. He finds that policy should have been tightened more before the financial crisis. Rules called for negative rates in its aftermath, suggesting QE and other unconventional policies. But most rules suggested an earlier lift-off than 2016.

Turning to current events, Wieland showed how conventional measures showed an astonishing output gap during the pandemic. But was the fall in output a lack of demand or supply during a pandemic? Wieland pointed to recent epidemic-macro models that capture the common sense of the latter. More money doesn't do any good if the stores are shut down. The models produce only a small fall in inflation, as we saw, and only recommend a small interest rate decline.

In the event, the stimulus did produce inflation. Wieland pointed to explicit New Keynesian models that track the result. In Wieland's models, the Fed should also have reacted more promptly to inflation.

In the discussion, Harald Uhlig asked whether, with nominal rates about equal to year-on-year inflation, real interest rates are actually positive. David Papell highlighted the importance of inertial terms (whether interest rates react immediately or slowly to inflation) in empirical estimates and also in evaluating whether the Fed is or is not reacting as promptly as the Taylor rule recommends. Sebastian Edwards reminded us of the conundrum of 1994 and how much short-term rate rises result in higher long-term rates, and he asked what might be different across episodes. Andrew Levin pointed out that the Taylor rule has achieved economic immortality—in that we leave out the citation (1993) when we reference it, like the Modigliani-Miller theorem and the Black-Scholes formula. As a better measure of influence, he mentioned Google trends that show Taylor rule searches at an all-time high. He also related how John Taylor once had a business card with the Taylor rule on it and suggested that might have a lot to do with its popularity. Bring back business cards! Christopher Erceg asked whether, in light of our new understanding of just how important financial affairs are to monetary transmission, if perhaps a financial conditions index ought to be included in a monetary policy rule. Michael Boskin offered several reflections on Taylor's interactions with colleagues and students in producing and popularizing the rule and pointed out how a similar effort quickly produced a prescient estimate of the fiscal multiplier in 2009.

Brian Sack asked a simple but provocative question, if you could choose one variable to add to the Taylor rule, what would it be? Cochrane clarified that "none" is an acceptable answer, and indeed one point of the Taylor rule and the Fed's mandate is that the Fed should *not* pay attention to other variables. Wieland answered for inertial, lagged, or first-difference rules, which obviate the need to guess the natural (r-star) interest rate. Lipsky echoed, "None." Clarida added that the Fed should *drop* a variable: "It's so hard to measure potential output, [and] it can lead to such mischief." Cochrane agreed, endorsing a pure inflation or price-level target.

Financial Regulation: Silicon Valley Bank and Beyond

The second panel centered on financial regulation. The Silicon Valley Bank (SVB) failed in early 2023 from a simple run due to losses on long-term government bonds as interest rates rose. Now, the huge regulatory machinery seemed to have a failure on its hands comparable to the failure of monetary policy to perceive inflation. One wonders how the Fed and other regulators could have missed something so seemingly simple. Moreover, in the aftermath, monetary policy and regulation are now clearly linked. Must the Fed restrain interest rate hikes to keep banks afloat?

Anat Admati set the stage. She reminded us of the failures of Silicon Valley, Signature, and First Republic Banks, along with the larger failure of Credit Suisse. The latter is particularly salient as it was designated a systemically important financial institution (SIFI). It was quickly merged with UBS, creating a "monster SIFI in Switzerland, twice the country's GDP."

Admati noted that all of the failed banks were deemed well capitalized by their regulators. Banks fulfilled hundreds of thousands of rules but failed anyway. In the post-2008 burst of financial regulation, much effort was devoted to orderly liquidation, living wills, and the issuance of loss-absorbing securities (other than equity), such as convertible bonds, all to avoid too-big-to-fail bailouts. Yet, Admati pointed out that when the time finally came, "The authorities chose not to go to resolution and not to impose losses on 50 billion Swiss francs of TLAC [total loss-absorbing capacity] securities. . . . What happened to those promises that the TLAC will be there for failed banks?" Naturally, Admati, long a principled advocate for the simple answer of more common equity, opined: "We should also have market-based stress tests, which involve, for example, *the* market stress test, what I call 'raise equity!'"

Darrell Duffie started by focusing on liquidity. Yes, the failed banks were fundamentally insolvent in that the market value of their assets was less than that of their liabilities. But the sudden and unexpected run was part of their failure and points to deeper problems in current liquidity rules.

In experience and regulation, depositors leave slowly. More Signature and Silicon Valley deposits "left in a single day than the Fed's liquidity coverage ratio had anticipated would leave in an entire month." Once, it was impossible for everyone to get their money out in a day; long lines at the teller windows would slow things down. And now everyone has news instantly. (According to media reports, many SVB customers drained their accounts via cell phones from Jackson Hole, Wyoming.) Deposits are no longer "sticky," a warning against extrapolating past statistical experience too blithely.

If the rest of the banking structure remains the same and we rely on liquidity to avoid runs, something has to be fixed. Duffie first addressed one obvious solution: that all large uninsured deposits be backed by reserves at the Fed. If the quantity of large deposits remains unchanged, however, and banks do not pursue other forms of funding, this means trillions of additional reserves, and banks cannot use those deposits for other purposes, such as underwriting bond market trading activity.

Duffie then advocated a different approach to greater liquidity, with characteristic vision and clarity: rather than pile on liquid assets that banks must *hold*, instead make it easier for them to *get* liquidity in times of stress. For centuries, banks have stopped runs by borrowing against illiquid assets when under stress, including under the pre-Fed clearinghouse system. "Going back to the formation of the Federal Reserve System, a primary purpose of the Fed has been to provide crisis liquidity to banks as a lender of last resort. . . . Banks should have posted lots of their assets at the Fed's discount window to receive the liquidity they needed to cover fleeing depositors." Despite this longstanding tradition, the Dodd-Frank era took a different turn: "Under current regulations, lender-of-last-resort liquidity from the Fed does not count. . . . Currently, banks must be self-reliant in meeting these requirements."

Duffie emphasized that the point is not just that banks should be *able* to borrow more freely at the discount window but that such a contingent borrowing capacity should count in their ex ante liquidity requirements. Regulators must also allow them to use that borrowing ability in times of stress, not like the famous joke about regulations that require one taxi always to be present at the station or lifeboats to stay on the ship even as it sinks.

Randal Quarles was the vice chair of the Federal Reserve for supervision and chair of the Financial Stability Board through the fall of 2021. As such, he has been subject to political criticism over the Fed's role in the bank failures and the charge that regulatory changes under his guidance were responsible for the failures. He gave a detailed and eloquent account of how Fed regulation evolved and how the problems cropped up. He asserted that while SVB's run shows a deep regulatory failure, the changes in regulation were not responsible.

Quarles started with the Fed's Barr Memo analyzing the regulatory problems behind SVB's failure.[3] That report has "four key conclusions: 1) SVB's executive team failed to manage its risk. 2) The Fed's supervisory team failed to appreciate the extent of the vulnerabilities. 3) When they did recognize the vulnerabilities, they didn't do enough about them. 4) The Fed's lassitude was attributable to the regulatory tailoring project mandated by the Economic Growth, Regulatory Relief, and Consumer Protection Act of 2018. . . . Most of the Barr Memo's recommendations stem from the final conclusion," a view that has "now been quite widely discredited."

The first charge in the report is that banks like SVB were allowed to exclude losses on available-for-sale securities against regulatory capital. But there's a reason for that. Otherwise, banks have an incentive to stuff even more securities into the hold-to-maturity portfolio, which is never marked to market. In any case, "even if SVB had been required to hold capital against its AOCI [Accumulated Other Comprehensive Income] losses, it would still have been a very highly capitalized bank. . . . The AOCI rule would not have required SVB to raise a penny of capital." Hold-to-maturity rules are a problem, but not this problem.

The second charge is that regulatory tailoring excluded SVB from the capital stress test. However, SVB would have done fine under the Fed's Comprehensive Capital Analysis and Review stress test. Quarles again notes there is a central regulatory problem: the stress tests contemplate a severe recession; they contemplate interest rates falling, and they do not include an evaluation of funding stability. Again, Quarles reveals a deep problem: Why did the Fed not stress test banks for interest rate rises as it was preparing to raise interest rates? But even in such a test, which was conducted once under Quarles, SVB would have been fine, because most of its securities were in that hold-to-maturity portfolio.

Third, "The Tailoring Changes effectively excluded SVB from applying the net stable funding ratio (NSFR) and the most stringent version of the liquidity coverage ratio (LCR). But these changes, too, did not matter for SVB's ultimate resilience."

In sum, "the Barr Memo itself recognizes the weakness of the case that the Tailoring Changes and the supposed cultural shift were relevant to the failure of SVB." But, in our view, the conclusion is more damning for the essential regulatory structure, with or without tailoring. Hold-to-maturity assets hide mark-to-market losses. There is no rule linking the potential for plain-vanilla interest rate risk to spark depositor runs. Banks can fill the checkboxes of thousands of rules, and simple risks will remain.

Quarles went on to examine the claim that a shift in supervisory culture impeded supervision. He humorously compared the Barr Memo to an email he received from a French madwoman. But he went on to isolate the problem that remains: supervisors are overwhelmed with administrative responsibilities such as third-party vendor management and audit management, which though admittedly important, distract them from the core financial issues facing the bank.

So if it wasn't tailoring and it wasn't weak supervision, then what was it? Here, Quarles echoed both Admati and Duffie: neither regulators, nor rules, nor SVB management put two and two together in time, that large uninsured deposits might run much more quickly than historical experience suggested.

Here Quarles eloquently expanded on Duffie's suggestion. "For decades the Fed has been affirmatively eroding its core reason for being: providing liquidity to the banking system, especially in times of stress. The Fed's express mantra since the Great Financial Crisis has been that banks need to "self-insure" their liquidity needs. But . . . it simply isn't possible for a bank to rely solely on its own liquidity resources in a world where a very large percentage of bank liabilities are going to be highly runnable." Note that this view clashes a bit with Duffie's view (and Amit Seru's, as follows), that SVB was fundamentally insolvent, not just illiquid, but the larger point remains.

Amit Seru provided a contrasting view, focusing on insolvency rather than illiquidity—which both Quarles and Duffie actually agreed was the central problem in this case. No matter how generous the Fed had been, SVB simply did not have enough securities to borrow against to meet the depositor run. In a remarkable effort, "When the run at SVB occurred over that weekend last March, and SVB collapsed, we decided to stress test the whole US banking system of 4,800 banks." That this is possible for a small group of academics with public records and not routinely done by the Fed is an interesting observation. As Seru reported, the US banking system has $24 trillion in assets, $24 trillion in liabilities, including $9 trillion in uninsured deposits, and $2 trillion of equity. When Seru and coauthors mark assets to market, however—most are in hold-to-maturity portfolios or otherwise not marked to market, just like SVB's—they find about $2 trillion of losses—all the equity of the US banking system is wiped out. Seru and coauthors also found that banks had done very little hedging against interest rate risk, even though higher interest rates after a year of surging inflation ought to have been an obvious possibility, and hedging interest rate risk with swaps is easy and commonplace.

"If you thought that SVB was an outlier and special just because it has huge mark-to-market losses, there could be another five hundred banks that should have faced a similar kind of run as SVB. But they didn't." They did not largely because they had fewer uninsured depositors. But the risk remains.

One answer, of course: "A bank can sustain the stress if it has enough equity."

Seru also opined that regulators still mistake insolvency for illiquidity. The Barr Memo "mentions the word 'liquidity' in relationship to SVB a staggering 320 times. 'Solvency' is only mentioned once, which almost suggests it may have been a typo." Long-term government bonds are very liquid. The problem was simply that there were not enough to sell or borrow against at market prices to stem an uninsured depositor run. Finally, Seru pointed out that there is strong pressure for local regulators to go easy on important regional banks.

Looking ahead, Seru warned against repeating the Savings and Loan Crisis. Already, the Fed has extended deposit insurance to all deposits and is lending money against underwater assets at par rather than market value. But gambling for resurrection by allowing banks to take large risks with taxpayer money is a dangerous strategy. Instead, Seru argued for separating insolvent from solvent banks with a real market test.

In the long run, Seru stressed just what a failure of regulation this whole fiasco represents and that piling on more rules is not the answer: "Interest rate risk is in the first chapter of any finance textbook. And if four collaborators working two days over a weekend can do a stress test of the banking system as we did, it is unclear what the real issue is. I think the ultimate answer is, rather than trying to tweak this into an amazing physics laboratory-based experiment, we need to just realize there are limits to regulation and what regulators can do." The answer is equity. Banks lever up with insured deposits. Shadow banks, by contrast, with no deposit insurance or bailout expectations "end up taking a lot of equity. Why? Because these institutions and the market understand there's a lot of runnable risk in these institutions."

Bottom line: "I think in the long run, the answer is not liquidity or more liquidity requirements. . . . The answer is asking banks to have a significant amount of equity capital."

In the discussion, Admati pressed Quarles on whether the whole resolution planning effort was a waste, since regulators refused to use it for SVB and especially Credit Suisse. Quarles answered that, in analogy to military preparations, planning is essential even though the plans may end up not being used. Admati, Quarles, and Duffie agreed that, in the end, common equity is better than the TLAC, and all agreed that SVB and related failures were primarily about insolvency, not illiquidity.

Disinflation and the Stock Market

Peter Blair Henry presented his paper with Anusha Chari, "Disinflation and the Stock Market: Third-World Lessons for First-World Monetary Policy." Chari and Henry used evidence from a panel of twenty-one developing countries between 1973 and 1994, which included eighty-one disinflation programs involving the International Monetary Fund (IMF).

They used these experiences to get at central questions for the current US disinflation strategy: Will disinflation produce a soft or a hard landing? When do disinflations succeed, and when do they fail? Is the historical evidence different for large versus small inflations?

The hard landing issue goes back to the 1970s, when economists argued over the sacrifice ratio, just how much unemployment and lost output would be required to eliminate inflation. For some economists, the cost would be too large to bother trying to lower inflation. Others argued that disinflation could happen relatively costlessly if it accompanied a credible change in a regime that shifted inflation expectations.

To assess the economic impact of the disinflations from moderate inflation (above 10% per year), Chari and Henry assess stock market performance. If a disinflation is perceived to be successful, it will be reflected in higher equity valuations as an indicator of the net benefit of the disinflation program.

Chari and Henry find that for high-inflation episodes (above 40% per year), the net benefit of the disinflation programs is positive. But the net benefit is negative for moderate disinflations in their sample. This result resonates with the disinflation shock engineered by Paul Volcker in the United States from 1979 to 1982. It took some time before the Fed gained the credibility needed to restore price stability. The effects on the real economy were painful. On the other hand, that particular US episode differs from the average in Chari and Henry's sample in that inflation did come down quickly in 1982, and the stock market subsequently boomed.

Joshua Rauh offered comments. First, he questioned the timing of the disinflation episodes. In the high-inflation cases, during the time window that Chari and Henry used to measure the impact on stock prices, inflation was already declining. Whereas in the time window in the cases of moderate disinflation, inflation continued to accelerate. He then asked what happens to markets after the moderate-inflation countries start to cool.

Second, Rauh questioned the timing of the discount rate used to calculate the net present value of investment opportunities. Third, he pointed out that the sample of emerging-market countries with moderate inflations may be quite different from the United States today. Perhaps the experience of other advanced countries that successfully reduced inflation from moderate levels is more apt. Last, Rauh asked what happens to the distribution of wealth as real interest rates rise in the tightening episode.

John Cochrane, in the discussion, reflected on the positive experience of the early advanced inflation-targeting countries in reducing moderate inflation based on their achieving credibility. This agrees with Thomas Sargent's focus on a credible change in the fiscal, monetary, and microeconomic regimes in the cases of the successful German and Austrian decelerations from high inflation and the French from moderate inflation in the 1920s. Sargent's emphasis on the importance of gaining credibility was echoed by Andrew Filardo, Andrew Levin, Michael Bordo, and James Bullard. Perhaps Chari and Henry's empirical finding that high inflations are more successfully resolved than moderate inflations reflects more permanent institutional reforms needed to stop them. Several commenters asked about differences between the emerging-market experience in the sample versus advanced countries like the United States. Henry reminded us that we shouldn't ignore international and emerging-market experiences. Finally, Sebastian Edwards described how Chile recently achieved a soft landing based on its record of credible monetary policy.

Inflation Targeting in Japan, 2013–2023

Over lunch, Haruhiko Kuroda, former governor of the Bank of Japan, updated us on the Japanese situation. In his introductory comments, Kuroda explained that Japan adopted a 2% inflation target in 2013 yet undershot inflation for most of that time. Recently inflation has risen to 3–4%, in Kuroda's view, "almost wholly caused by the import price hike." Though "the 'no price increase and no wage increase' norm is changing (long-term inflation expectations are rising)," he was confident that 2% inflation would return soon.

Kuroda gave a quick history of Japan's monetary policy in the context of below-2% inflation, including the steadily increasing quantitative easing, negative interest rates, and long-term bond price target innovations. The recent inflation, though undesirable, has broken the long deflationary period and coincided with a large increase in employment. He closed, stressing the importance of the inflation target in the quest for long-term control of inflation.

Sebastian Edwards asked about Japan's policy of yield curve control, which directly targets both short- and long-term interest rates. Kuroda responded that directly targeting the price of long-term bonds, rather than buying fixed quantities, is "more effective and more transparent," especially to ordinary people. Beat Siegenthaler asked whether the inevitable interest rate normalization would cause financial impacts. Kuroda responded that households have substantial assets, so they stand to gain from higher interest rates, while firms and banks hold a large amount of cash. The greatest danger Kuroda foresees is that government interest costs on the 200% of GDP debt will rise substantially. Though Japan's debt is relatively long term, that maturity choice only buys five years or so of protection against interest rate increases.

Central Bank Balance Sheets

Niall Ferguson and Paul Schmelzing presented their paper, "Five Centuries of Central Bank Balance Sheets: A Primer." The paper presents a new comprehensive database on the balance sheets of seventeen advanced countries going back four hundred years. The authors use that data to measure the macroeconomic effects of central bank balance sheet expansions—buying securities in exchange for newly created money or central bank loans.

They thus provide a history-based perspective on the recent massive liquidity expansions by advanced country central banks during the Global Financial Crisis of 2007–9, the subsequent long zero bound, and the COVID-19 pandemic of 2020.

Schmelzing discussed the construction of their database. The authors delved into historical archives in several languages to produce central bank balance sheets that were consistent over time and comparable across countries.

Central banks expand balance sheets *in response* to events, so one needs a strategy to isolate the causal effect of the balance sheet expansion. Ferguson explained that they use an index of central bank governors' prior stance as either a hawk or a dove as an instrument to identify this causal effect. Ferguson and Schmelzing base this index on extensive narrative analysis of speeches, newspaper articles, and biographies to indicate bankers' stances before crises erupt. Hawks would then worry more about the moral hazard consequences of intervention, while doves would worry more about the deleterious economic and financial effects of not intervening. Based on this index as an instrument, Ferguson and Schmelzing calculate the average response of economic conditions to an unexpectedly large or small balance sheet expansion. The key result is that balance sheet expansions led to statistically significant higher money growth, real GDP, and inflation in the short to medium runs. These effects are followed by a statistically higher likelihood of another systemic financial crisis. Both economic impact and moral hazard occur in turn.

In his discussion, Barry Eichengreen praised their data collection effort but raised some fundamental questions about the empirical methodology. His first question was about the definition of a central bank used in their long historical database. It was unclear to him if every institution demarcated in the study as a central bank would satisfy a modern definition. His second question concerned the distinction made in the paper between financial, war-related, and "other" related balance sheet expansions. He presented a number of important historical examples where making such distinctions was difficult. He also posited that there was a major regime change in liquidity expansions after the Overend Gurney crisis of 1866 in London, when Walter Bagehot criticized the Bank of England for not providing sufficient liquidity to allay the crisis. This led to Bagehot's 1873 rule, which made the crucial distinction between liquidity and solvency in prescribing lender-of-last-resort operations. His reading of the paper was that the empirical results were driven by experience after Overend Gurney. Related to Bagehot's rule, Eichengreen also raised the issue of whether banks in crisis were forced to borrow at a penalty rate, as Bagehot advocated, or not, as is modern practice. Finally, he wondered whether the relevant policymaker in different institutional environments is the central bank governor, a committee, or the minister of finance.

In discussion, Jeffrey Lacker questioned the meaning of lender-of-last-resort actions used in the paper—whether it is discount lending to individual banks or open market operations providing liquidity to the economy as a whole. He also stressed that the paper did not distinguish between sterilized and unsterilized balance sheet expansion. Sterilized lending, as conducted during the Global Financial Crisis, did not expand the balance sheet yet had significant economic effects. (In a "sterilized" operation, the central bank lends money to a bank in trouble but reduces other sources of money supply at the same time.)

Andrew Levin followed up on Barry Eichengreen's comment that his reading of Walter Bagehot's book *Lombard Street: A Description of the Money Market* (1873) suggests that the agents responsible for lender-of-last-resort policy were a much larger group of experts than the central bank governor. Christopher Erceg asked whether longer-lived interventions created larger problems of moral hazard. Finally, Krishna Guha wondered whether the international monetary regime mattered in demarcating the effects of balance sheet expansions.

Forecasting Inflation and Output

Mickey Levy presented "The Fed: Bad Forecasts and Misguided Monetary Policy." The Fed—and most industry analysts—completely missed the rise to 8% inflation, both ahead of time and as it was happening. This is a major institutional failure for an institution whose first mandate is price stability, interpreted as a 2% inflation target. Why? How can the Fed do better? If such a large rise in inflation is unforecastable and its persistence unrecognizable, clearly, Fed policy procedures should change, but how? And why is the Fed not investigating this question?

James Wilcox, the session chair, started with a view that the Fed was late to recognize inflation due to a belief that the Phillips curve—linking inflation to unemployment—is quite flat. In recent history, large changes in unemployment have occurred with very little change in inflation. Elevating the Phillips curve to a central determinant of inflation then, the immense rise and sudden reversion of unemployment back to the low value of February 2020 (3.6%) should not have led to an inflation rate much different from the low February 2020 value; and observed inflation in the meantime must be the sort of transient supply shock noise that temporarily moves relative prices. Alternatively, or equivalently, "too much too late" might also result from underestimating how fast Phillips curves can shift.

Wilcox also addressed the question of why the Fed waited so long and here suggested that its new flexible average inflation targeting policy may be at work. Simply put, the Fed promised such slow responses, though in the positive direction only.

Levy analyzed the Fed's inflation projections in the quarterly Summary of Economic Projections (SEP). He finds that as inflation rose higher and higher, the Fed persistently projected inflation would fall back toward 2% while dramatically underestimating the rise in interest rates that would be required to achieve their inflation projections. He then analyzed the modeling, analytical, human, and institutional errors, including not heeding the important lessons from history behind those forecasts.

In Levy's summary, the SEP projections slowly incorporate observed inflation but always quickly decline back to 2%. Indeed, to our eyes, Levy's plot of Fed inflation forecasts comes down nearly perfectly to AR(1) reversion to 2%, no matter what history or current circumstances are. Levy also showed projections for the federal funds rate that never exceeded the projected inflation rate. On the view that high real interest rates are needed to quell inflation, the Fed always projected inflation to go away on its own. Comparing forecasts to what happened later, the Fed was overly optimistic on inflation, that it would recede rapidly toward 2%, and it significantly underestimated the federal funds rate that it would later raise to fight that inflation. Also striking is the "lack of dispersion of forecasts among FOMC members." How can everyone come to the same wrong answer so confidently?

Levy went on to consider the sources of the projection errors, admitting the exercise must be speculative. First, he considers analytical and conceptual errors. The Fed's modeling, both formal (the FRB-US model) and informal, pretty much ignored the impact of the "unprecedented fiscal stimulus," with "$5.1 trillion in additional deficit spending, over 27% of real GDP." In addition, that spending came with extreme monetary accommodation. The Fed effectively bought about half of the Treasury's new bond issuance.

Neither does the Fed pay any attention to monetary aggregates, as "M2 surged 40%."

The FRB-US model and informal thinking put strong and perhaps excessive weight on the Fed's ability to credibly manage inflationary expectations in the New Keynesian style. But Levy points out that to manage inflationary expectations, the Fed needs people to expect some action, not just more forward-guidance promises.

In sum, with a presumption that inflation would stay low, when inflation did rise, it didn't fit the Fed's model, and the Fed was quick to blame it on transitory factors. For example, Levy showed the December 2020 SEP, which projected inflation to decline sharply, while at the same time forecasting the unemployment rate to be materially below its estimate of the natural rate—while simultaneously estimating the appropriate policy rate below inflation. It doesn't add up in the standard Phillips curve thinking, so the projections must reflect quickly waning effects of some external shock.

Next, Levy considered institutional errors. In his view, the new "flexible average inflation targeting" strategic plan stands out like a sore thumb. It prioritized employment, favored higher inflation, and committed the Fed to stop raising rates preemptively, instead promising to allow inflation to exceed its target before reacting. All of these contributed to the policy errors of 2021–22. More charitably, one might say the strategic plan was a well-constructed defense against deflation, which proved to be a Maginot Line against the actual challenge that emerged. Levy also pointed to the lack of diversity, with no dissents in 2021, and then significant failures in risk management, including relying on the consensus forecasts without considering alternatives. The latter point is striking. The Fed's main mindset is to agree on a forecast and what policy is appropriate given the forecast. It spends relatively little effort, in an uncertain world, gaming out how it might respond if forecasts are wrong. Its time-based forward guidance provides an additional commitment to sticking to a forecast-based policy.

Levy encapsulated the discussion of the failed inflation response to the Fed's other recent institutional failure, neglecting simple interest rate risk in the banking system to the point of a run and series of bank failures. The Fed's delayed exit from zero interest rates, its misleading forward guidance provided by its projections, plausibly misled banks that had profited from slowly declining interest rates for decades, and the Fed's regulators, to underestimate the risk of higher interest rates. Higher rates really shouldn't have been a surprise, but they were, even to the Fed's stress testers, who had banks simulating interest rate *declines* in late 2022!

Steven Davis provided an excellent discussion, building on the paper to describe a central incentive problem. The Fed issues forecasts, but it also tries to shape expectations. The two efforts conflict. Like public health authorities, the Fed can be afraid to reveal its actual fears. Specifically, Davis proceeded from two widely shared views: First, "Expected inflation affects actual inflation." Second, "Fed projections influence expected inflation." If you accept those two propositions, then the Fed faces an incentive to distort the inflation projections. This incentive will not just infect verbal statements but will influence the Fed's choice, design, and the features of headline models, like the FRB-US. "There is a trade-off between the Fed's desire to meet near-term policy goals at least cost and the desire to preserve its credibility and reputation." Indeed, if Fed officials did not believe the soothing messages they were trying to convey, if there were visible evidence against that message, like model simulations, the messages would not be credible.

Davis emphasized that all these considerations come to a head at a time of uncertainty, such as the postpandemic inflation breakout. If there is some uncertainty about the cause of inflation and its likely persistence, if there is at least a plausible narrative that inflation comes from swiftly self-correcting supply shocks, if keeping expectations anchored is critical to a swift and costless (no Phillips curve shift) end to inflation, then the Fed would certainly not want to validate alternative narratives that would add to inflationary pressure. Davis added that the "flat Phillips curve" belief adds to the pressure. "If you approach the conduct of monetary policy through the lens of a Phillips curve and you further believe that economic slack has little impact on inflation, then monetary policy can materially influence inflation only through its impact on inflation expectations. It's either that or pray for favorable supply shocks." More generally, the flat Phillips curve leads to a mental model in which inflation is entirely driven by expected inflation. So, with that conceptual framework, trying to manipulate expectations becomes the entire focus of monetary policy.

Davis suggested some institutional reforms. First, clarify the inherent contradiction in making federal funds rate and inflation forecasts simultaneously. A forecast should be conditional on a policy rate, and an optimal policy conditional on a forecast. Second, the Fed needs more out-of-the-bubble, alternative-scenario, and risk management thinking. Davis suggested an annual conference that "highlights tail risks for monetary policy and central banking, advances nonstandard scenario analyses, considers emerging and latent threats to sound monetary policy, and draws lessons from historical episodes," largely featuring analysts outside the Fed. Third, "Separate business-as-usual forecasting from assessing recession risks, major inflation threats, financial crisis risks, and the implications of unprecedented shocks." They are indeed different conceptual exercises. And lastly, include historians.

In comments, Richard Clarida led off, pointing out that the missed forecasts and slow responses were common basically to all G10 countries. The problem is not Fed specific. He pointed out that private-sector economists shared the Fed's missed forecasts. All seventy-five economists surveyed by the *Wall Street Journal* missed the inflation breakout, "an epic forecast missed here." He reiterated that the Taylor rule, in his calculation, did not recommend much earlier tightening, and the new flexible average inflation targeting strategy less so. And he pointed out that inflation is easing worldwide, with interest rates below inflation, and that expectations do seem "anchored."

James Bullard also pointed out that the end of asset purchases began much before rate tightening. So "hawkish moves were being made." He also emphasized that we did not know at the time how swiftly the economy would recover from the pandemic, justifying some doveish caution: "[It was widely feared] that this was going to be the Great Depression."

Andrew Levin gave a good medical analogy about doctors giving patients bad news. He argued that greater preparation is in order, analogous to the point that the Fed should pay more attention to risks and less to the center of the forecast: "The problem the Fed is still facing now is they haven't clearly told the public, Congress, or the markets that the possibility [for substantially higher interest rates and persistent inflation] is still out there."

John Cochrane echoed the fact that the forecast mistakes were pervasive to central banks around the world, analysts, and markets. That means "conceptual problems are common to lots of people." He added a few conceptual problems to the list: Central bankers routinely ignore supply, and "demand and output are practically synonyms." If supply shocks are serious economics and not just a dog-ate-my-homework excuse, then "where is the team of central bank economists monitoring supply? They're not there. If there are going to be supply shocks, we needed such a team." On the Fed ignoring the massive fiscal stimulus, he noted the Fed seems to deliberately blind itself to fiscal policy to avoid seeming political. He criticized the use of the Phillips curve as a causal relation or a model in itself in thinking about inflation. He criticized expectations management. Expectations must be anchored by expected actions, not by speeches and expectations of more speeches. For example, people must expect the Fed to be ready to replay 1980 if necessary. The Fed is unwilling to say anything so harsh. Cochrane emphasized the need for risk management with military and sports analogies. There, people think about alternative scenarios and risk management. Finally, he noted that in the face of such a large institutional failure, an inquest or self-examination is necessary.

Jeffrey Lacker endorsed Steven Davis's view and made an analogy to old-fashioned paternalistic doctors who didn't tell you how sick you were. He offered that there was something like the risk-management approach in the early 2000s, but that fell out of favor with the SEP procedure. "The SEP was sort of built around trying to influence expected inflation, and I think it needs to be rebuilt now."

On the strange fact that stress tests did not ask about interest rate rises, he added, "The macroeconomic assumptions were vetted at the most senior levels. A perspective brought to bear on those assumptions was how it might get out and how it might reflect on what the Fed thought about what was going to happen," validating Davis's view. Davis's incentive problem extends to stress tests and explains why the Fed could not ask banks about their exposure to sharply higher interest rates.

Volker Wieland spoke in favor of SEP projections, noting that the European Central Bank does not produce them, and he has been arguing for them. "It's worse if the central bank is not transparent in this regard. The advantage of the SEP is that these individual forecasts are public. This allows criticism and makes the central bank somewhat vulnerable." He also stressed that even when making mild forecasts, talking about risks would lead central banks to prepare to address them.

Terry Anderson asked the eternal question, how does institutional change come about? Davis responded, praising the role of regional Feds in institutional and conceptual change.

Toward a Monetary Policy Strategy

The conference day ended with the traditional policy panel. James Bullard pointed to the huge fiscal stimulus as the central source of inflation. He argued, however, that "the fiscal stimulus is receding, and monetary policy has been adjusted rapidly in the last year to better align with traditional central bank strategy. Accordingly, the prospects for continued disinflation are good but not guaranteed."

To understand the fiscal-monetary impulse (large deficits, mostly monetized), he pointed out that "the spirit of the macroeconomic policy response to the pandemic was to err on the side of too much rather than too little . . . risking a high-inflation regime."

He also said that to analyze fiscal policy, it's important to study what government spending is used for. In this case, it was mostly transfer payments to individuals and businesses. That led to a "sharp increase in personal savings," as money temporarily piled up in bank accounts. Both the size and this nature of fiscal stimulus are "unprecedented in US postwar macroeconomics," so it's not surprising that previous experience missed the mark on its effects. He pointed to George Hall and Thomas Sargent's view at our last conference, that we should think of pandemic fiscal policy like a war financed by huge borrowing and money creation, often leading to sharp but temporary inflation, which devalues government debt, a form of capital tax.[4]

Thinking about inflation going forward, Bullard first showed a chart with several different measures of underlying inflation that are not receding as quickly as the more popular measures.

More optimistically, though, he presented an interesting and novel analysis of fiscal pressure on inflation, focusing on the personal savings rate. We can think of that somewhat informally as indicating how much pent-up cash is still lying around waiting to be spent and drive prices up. The large increase in personal savings during the pandemic fiscal transfers has reversed. But cumulative lower savings are still about half a trillion dollars less than the cumulatively higher previous saving: "Excess savings are diminishing but have not yet dissipated."

Bullard went on to evaluate current monetary policy. He stressed the importance of a credible regime and how a Taylor rule is most important to solidify expectations rather than to try to fine-tune long and variable lags. Evaluating policy with a wide range of plausible assumptions about Taylor rule coefficients and inflation measures, he found current policy close to a Taylor rule with no inertial elements. Yes, policy was slow to react, but the speed of the reaction and the fact that it was widely expected may make up for some of that slowness.

In sum, onetime inflation from a onetime warlike fiscal shock is petering out; we are returning to a pretty good previous monetary policy regime roughly following a Taylor rule, and "the prospects for continued disinflation are reasonably good."

Philip Jefferson started by announcing his appointment as vice chair of the Federal Reserve, which got a well-deserved ovation. He then jumped right in, thoughtfully challenging the premise of the conference title:

> The title of the conference, "How to Get Back on Track: A Policy Conference," is potent. Its intent and ambiguity are striking. First, the title presupposes that US monetary policy is currently on the wrong track. Second, the webpage for this conference advances a puzzling definition of the phrase "on track." How so? According to the Hoover webpage, "A key goal of the conference is to examine how to get back on track and, thereby, how to reduce the inflation rate *without* slowing down economic growth" (emphasis added). . . . Third, the definition of "on track" in the title contrasts with more commonplace definitions such as "achieving or doing what is necessary or expected," as offered by a standard reference such as the Merriam-Webster dictionary. My view is that this commonplace definition provides a more practical lens through which to assess real-world policymaking.

The standard Fed view of monetary policy is that higher interest rates lower aggregate demand, which reduces output and employment, and via Phillips curve logic, then slowly brings down inflation. The painless disinflations that come from a shift in monetary (and fiscal) policy regimes, giving a shift in the Phillips curve, are unusual events. "Without slowing down economic growth" is not the usual "track."

Jefferson proceeded to methodically lay out a case that the Fed is, as he sees it, "on track." After laying out contrasting measures of inflation, he said that he expects "slower consumer spending growth over the remainder of the year in response to tight financial conditions, depressed consumer sentiment, greater uncertainty, and declines in overall household wealth and excess savings." Most of all, he sees tighter financial conditions, though no crisis, on the horizon to depress demand. However, he acknowledged "that there is significant uncertainty" in both directions.

He thoughtfully evaluated monetary policy in terms of a few strategic principles:

> First, policymakers should be ready to react to a wide range of economic conditions with respect to inflation, unemployment, economic growth, and financial stability. The unprecedented pandemic shock is a good reminder that under extraordinary circumstances, it will be difficult to formulate precise forecasts in real time.

This is an important statement that came up several times at the conference: think in terms of how the Fed will react to events rather than commit to one policy based on the central tendency of the forecast. Of course, a Taylor rule is an explicit example of a policy that states a reaction to events rather than a firm course. It is a data-dependent rather than a time-dependent commitment.

Second, policymakers should clearly communicate monetary policy decisions to the public. Our commitment to transparency should be evident to the public, and monetary policy should be conducted in a way that anchors longer-term inflation expectations. Third—and this is where I am revealing my passion for econometrics—policymakers should continuously update their priors about how the economy works as new data become available. In other words, it is appropriate to change one's perspective as new facts emerge.

In sum, with unemployment at a record low of 3.4%, yet personal consumption expenditures (PCE) inflation already declining from 7% to 4.2%, with long and variable lags of current tightening still ahead, Jefferson closed with the view that we are well on track.

Jeffrey Lacker and Charles Plosser presented a contrasting view. Lacker started with a critique of Fed communication: "The gyrations in public perceptions of the Fed's likely policy course were the result of significant gaps in the FOMC's communications and could have been avoided." Lacker cited the phrase *sufficiently restrictive* and discussion over what it meant.

He recommended anchoring policy discussions with several rules as a way to enhance transparency. Moreover, Lacker emphasized that commitment to a rule provides needed anchoring: "Referencing systematic policy rules that are grounded in historical experience can be a constructive way for the Fed to communicate about the likely path of monetary policy." Lacker emphasized rules as a benchmark, not that policy should mechanically follow a rule, stating, "Such references would not constitute rigid commitments but would be more informative to markets and the public than the subjective, discretionary, 'trust me' approach that largely describes current practice."

He followed with a concrete example. We don't know what will happen to inflation over the next year. He calculated policy-rule responses to several plausible scenarios, and they are quite different.

A single number for forward guidance does not capture or communicate that reaction.

Plosser added comments on discretion versus rules, a broader sense of "on track" than just the level of interest rates. A rule, like a mandate, is a precommitment both to act and not to pay attention to items outside the mandate. The Fed has, however, resisted steps to limit its own discretion and has done so for many years, thus limiting its transparency and any ability to hold it accountable.

Why? One answer is the political pressures that the Fed is under. Since the 1951 Treasury-Fed Accord, the Fed has had independent control over its balance sheet. But the Fed's assets are no longer just Treasury debt. So political pressure can get really applied to the balance sheet, and now the Fed is heavily engaged in credit policy. Additionally, he said that we (and the Fed) are asking monetary policy to achieve too many goals, which are far beyond its reach.

Mickey Levy challenged Bullard's assumption that fiscal policy is back to normal after a onetime pandemic stimulus. Much of the pandemic money has not been spent, we still have trillion-dollar deficits despite a 3.4% unemployment rate, and entitlement programs are looming.

Charles Siguler asked about the money supply. M2 surged with the pandemic fiscal transfers but now has shrunk dramatically. Is that good news, and should the Fed go back to looking at the money supply? Bullard responded that while M2 did surge ahead of this inflation, it has not proved a reliable guide over longer time periods.

William Nelson asked whether the Fed bears some responsibility for financial turmoil, both from regulatory failures to spot interest rate risk in banks and from raising interest rates so quickly. He also asked panelists what they thought the neutral interest rate was. (Lacker responded that it depends on how you define neutral.)

Andrew Levin noted that the Bank of England seems to have more dissent, while the FOMC now seems to circle the wagons to offer a unified view and encourages more independent thinking and its expression. He went on to note that Bullard showed the Fed in the bottom of the comfortable zone, Jefferson thinking interest rates are just fine, and expressing a view that now the risks of 1970s inflation blowout are high. With that and a risk-management framework in mind, he asked just where each thought the right zone should be.

Krishna Guha noted that if the Fed's inflation projections are correct, even the Taylor rule will recommend a funds rate between 2.5% and 3% by the end of 2024, so maybe the muted market reaction to inflation is not incorrect. Then he asked how one might extend Taylor-rule thinking to include balance sheet and credit tightening along with the usual level of interest rates.

In response, Jefferson highlighted the importance of the dual mandate, but Bullard pointed out that inflation is a tax that hits hardest "the lowest segment of the population," so perhaps equity concerns should push one in a hawkish direction. Bullard and Lacker pointed out that credit is part transmission mechanism, not necessarily an independent policy lever.

Latin American Inflation

In his dinner speech, Sebastian Edwards discussed the progress that Latin America has made in recent decades in reducing endemic inflation, its lessons, and the Chilean miracle initiated by the Chicago Boys, which raised Chile from one of the poorest countries of the continent to becoming its superstar.

Edwards showed that the majority of Latin American countries experienced a dramatic drop from three-digit annual inflation fifty years ago to numbers comparable to the advanced countries today. He attributed this success to the market-friendly reforms, fiscal consolidation, and adoption of rules-based monetary policies stemming from the policy advice of the IMF and US (mainly University of Chicago) economists. The principal exceptions to this heartening story are Argentina, which has never solved its fiscal problem, and Venezuela, which functions under a harsh socialist regime.

Then, based on his new Princeton University Press book, *The Chile Project: The Story of the Chicago Boys and the Downfall of Neoliberalism*, he told the story of how in fifty years, Chile became the success story of Latin America. He described the role of the Chicago economists Milton Friedman and especially Arnold Harberger and his students—the Chicago Boys—in instigating this remarkable transformation from the high-inflation, dysfunctional, and planned economy under Salvador Allende to the institution of Chicago School reforms, including a massive reduction in tariffs, the liberalization of goods and factor markets, and fiscal and monetary stabilization.

He described some of the bumps in the road of reform—especially the major financial crisis of 1982—reflecting the decision in the 1970s to peg the Chilean peso to the US dollar during a period when US disinflation elevated the Chilean real exchange rate. He also discussed how the democratic regime that succeeded the Pinochet dictatorship in 1990 adopted and improved upon the blueprint laid out by the Chicago-trained economists. Indeed, much of the economic growth happened after Augusto Pinochet.

To Edwards, Chile is a good example of the fact that a central bank acting on its own doesn't control inflation. He then warned that the social unrest in Chile in 2019 and the leftward shift in the political regime currently pose a severe threat to Chile's continued economic progress.

Notes

1. John B. Taylor, "Discretion versus Policy Rules in Practice," *Carnegie-Rochester Conference Series on Public Policy* 39 (1993): 195–214. Amsterdam: North-Holland.

2. Richard Clarida, Jordi Galí, and Mark Gertler, "The Science of Monetary Policy: A New Keynesian Perspective," *Journal of Economic Literature* 37, no. 4 (December 1999): 1661–707; Richard Clarida, Jordi Galí, and Mark Gertler, "Monetary Policy Rules and Macroeconomic Stability: Evidence and Some Theory," *Quarterly Journal of Economics* 115, no. 1 (February 2000): 147–80.

3. Michael S. Barr, "Review of the Federal Reserve's Supervision and Regulation of Silicon Valley Bank" (which has become known simply as the Barr Memo), April 28, 2023, https://www.federalreserve.gov /publications/review-of-the-federal-reserves-supervision-and-regulation -of-silicon-valley-bank.htm.

4. George J. Hall and Thomas J. Sargent, "Financing Big US Federal Expenditures Surges: COVID-19 and Earlier US Wars," in *How Monetary Policy Got Behind the Curve—and How to Get Back*, ed. Michael D. Bordo, John H. Cochrane, and John B. Taylor (Stanford, CA: Hoover Institution Press, 2023), 253–91.

I

Introductory Remarks to the Conference

Condoleezza Rice

For thirteen years, the Hoover Institution's Monetary Policy Conference has impacted economic policy worldwide. It is fitting that this book, *Getting Monetary Policy Back on Track*, brings together academic talent to analyze the problems and develop a monetary policy strategy, because we are clearly in need of one.

Do we even know what track we're trying to get back on?

I was a young Soviet specialist with President George H. W. Bush when the Soviet Union collapsed and the Cold War ended. I was a national security advisor on September 11. Yet, I've never seen a more chaotic international environment than the one we are dealing with now.

There are multiple sources and reasons for this sense of chaos in the international system, and the tectonic plates are indeed shifting. There is the reemergence of great-power conflict. We haven't seen this in a major way since the end of World War II. Great-power conflict is different from other kinds of conflict, because while it involves a lot of military power, it brings with it a lot of economic power and the desire to reshape the international system, not just participate in it.

We had the conflict with the Soviet Union, but we forget that the Soviet Union was completely isolated from the international economy. It was a military giant, but it was also an economic and technological midget. In fact, no more than 1% of Soviet GDP was ever accounted for in international trade, and that 1% was almost completely due to commodities trading.

I call this a different kind of conflict than what we are seeing today. Now, the fundamental factors in the international system are a war in Europe and a no-longer-rising but risen China.

We are seeing technology have an extraordinary impact across the world. People are increasingly talking about the implications of generative AI, whether we know what we're talking about or not. The fact is that even AI leaders talk about the transformational nature of these frontier technologies. I was at a conference not too long ago where AI leaders were asking, "Are we moving too fast? Should we pause?"

I asked, "Why would you do that?"

The answer was a bit frightening—that the scale and power of these machines may be something we cannot control. I had thought that was only in *The Terminator* and science fiction. The AI leaders asked: "Will these technologies—quantum and AI and synthetic biology—be weapons of war?" I had to say, "Sadly, there has never been a major technology that did not become a weapon of war." Technology can have enormously great effects, but I wonder if the hazard of our penchant as humans for technology is that we are very good with knowledge but not with wisdom.

There's also the question of what is happening in global energy markets. Not only are countries trying to make a transition to a less carbon-dominated economy, but they are doing so at a time when energy security is a resurgent issue. This goes back to what we are learning in Europe—the European countries, particularly Germany, who have made themselves dependent on Russian energy find that's not a good place to be when President Putin's manipulation has made that energy supply unreliable.

There will be a major restructuring of energy markets. As an oil company director in the 1990s, I learned that the Russians have oil fields that are remote, old, and in need of Western technology. One of the results of the Ukraine war has been that the major producers of oil and gas with this technology—Exxon, BP, and others—have pulled out of Russia. I think there will be a decline in the Russian energy supply and its quality.

These factors of chaos—the rise of great powers, the advancement of technology, the changes in energy supply, and the expectations among populations of what their governments can and cannot do are raising questions: What is happening in the international global order? What is happening to the order we tend to take for granted?

After World War II, we created an order based on the view that the international economy should not be a zero-sum but a positive-sum game. Countries could build their way out of poverty by adhering to what became known as the Washington Consensus: having stable currencies through the International Monetary Fund, and free trade, initially through the General Agreement on Tariffs and Trade and later the World Trade Organization.

What's happening to the international order? I'll start with China and questions about its role in the international order. For years, we had an integrationist narrative about China—the idea to bring China into the international system rather than isolate 1.4 billion people who are creative and innovative. We made a bet that bringing them into the international order is better than keeping them out. For years, we tried to do just that.

I hesitate as a political scientist to blame things on one person, but in this case, I will say that there has been a dramatic change under Xi Jinping from his predecessors, Jiang Zemin and Hu Jintao. For one thing, China seems ready to assert itself as a great power. That means when Xi Jinping gives a speech saying that China is going to surpass the United States in frontier technologies like AI and quantum, people listen. It's not surprising that the global community reacts to the suggestion that China will use these technologies to fuel its own power and push countries like the United States out of international leadership. Therefore, we see the enactment of measures, including sanctions and restrictions on capital flows to

Beijing and back, that can be artificial barriers to commerce based on a broad definition of national security. This is different from the international order we thought we were building.

On globalization, we largely took for granted that it was a good thing. We need to recognize that globalization, for all of its benefits, did leave some people behind. For unemployed coal miners in West Virginia and steelworkers in Britain, populists' claim that globalization only benefited the elite resonated. To a certain extent, they weren't completely wrong. I often relate that in my classes at Stanford, where I teach at the Graduate School of Business, I will have a student with the following profile: born in Brazil, went to school at Oxford, first job was in Shanghai, now in business school at Stanford, and their next job will be in Dubai. But that is not the path for many people. Most people never live more than twenty-five miles from where they were born, and somehow, we've not been able to ensure they have the skills they need to have good prospects in a globalized economy. Their aspirations and prospects are different from someone who can easily move around the international system.

We're dealing with many moving parts in the international system, including inflation and the great spending sprees of governments in reaction to the COVID-19 pandemic, particularly in the United States. This is an important time to try to find what the track should be for monetary policy strategy, as we have the entire system moving around us.

As these changes are happening, we also see our international institutions, such as the Bretton Woods Institutions (the International Monetary Fund and the World Bank), sidelined in the face of significant challenges. This is in contrast to the period after September 11, when, within days of the attacks, we had a Security Council resolution that allowed us to track terrorist financing across borders. We had the Proliferation Security Initiative, in which ninety countries agreed to stop the shipment of suspicious cargo.

We harmonized travel restrictions extremely quickly. If you travel to Mexico City, Dallas, New York, or Paris, you will have the same experience at the airport—metal detectors and restrictions on carrying more than three ounces of liquid. Even with the Global Financial Crisis of 2008 to 2009, I'll never forget the G20 coming to the White House that November to lay out some principles, among them that nobody would try to take advantage of that moment.

The response of the international system to this latest set of problems has been very different than in September 2001 and November 2008. If you look today at what happened during COVID-19, the response was very different. During COVID-19, for each nation it was *my* vaccines, *my* border restrictions, *my* travel restrictions, and *my* citizens. Indeed, it's been the revenge of the sovereign state.

We will have to contemplate over the next few years how we build or rebuild a sense of a common project for the international order—to find a world that is more peaceful but also one that is more prosperous—based on coordination, collaboration, and the sense that we're all in it together.

THIRTY-YEAR ANNIVERSARY
OF THE TAYLOR RULE

2

The Taylor Rule at Thirty

Richard H. Clarida

It is a privilege to participate once again in this annual Hoover Institution Monetary Policy Conference. The theme of this year's conference is especially timely given sharp hawkish policy pivots since last year's Hoover conference by the Fed and other major central banks as they've tried to get back on track and ahead of the curve after presiding over the sharpest sustained surge in inflation in forty years. I will have something to say toward the end of my remarks about recent events and, specifically, the "get back to where you once belonged" theme, but my welcome assignment on this panel is to offer some thoughts on the Taylor rule (TR) at thirty, and I am honored and humbled to do so.

When John Taylor called in March to extend the invitation, I, of course, accepted on the spot, but being an economist, I also recognized that writing a paper and preparing remarks for a fifteen-minute presentation on the TR at thirty would be an exercise in constrained optimization. After all, that is less than one minute per year! It then occurred to me that I could perhaps organize my remarks not by chronology but instead by the many extensions of the original Taylor rule paper that have been developed over the past thirty years and applied across various fields in economics, including but not confined to monetary theory, macroeconometrics, international finance, asset pricing, and yes, the fiscal theory of the price level. But of course, the influence of the TR paper on each of these fields is vast—it does, after all, have thirteen thousand Google Scholar citations—and has stimulated so many papers and books that I am simply unable to survey today. Instead, if you permit me, I will draw on my remarks and papers presented at previous Hoover conferences to offer a certainly selective and unabashedly personal thirty-thousand-foot perspective on the Taylor rule at thirty.

Let me set the scene with a very brief—and certainly selective—review of the evolution over the past sixty years of professional thinking about monetary policy. I will begin with Milton Friedman's landmark 1968 American Economic Association presidential address, "The Role of Monetary Policy" (Friedman 1968). This article is, of course, most famous for its message that there is no long-run, exploitable trade-off between inflation and unemployment. And in this paper, Friedman introduced the concept of the "natural rate of unemployment," which we now call u^*. What is less widely appreciated—at least outside these walls—is that Friedman's article also contains a concise but insightful discussion of [Knut] Wicksell's "natural rate of interest"—r^* in today's terminology—the real interest rate consistent with price stability.

But while u^* and r^* provide key reference points in Friedman's framework for assessing how far an economy may be from its long-run equilibrium in labor and financial markets, they play absolutely no role in the monetary policy rule. Instead, he advocates his well-known K-percent rule, which proposes that central banks should aim for and deliver a constant rate of growth of a monetary aggregate. This simple rule, he believed, could deliver long-run price stability without requiring the central bank to take a stand on, model, or estimate either r^* or u^*. Although he acknowledged that shocks would push u away from u^* (and, implicitly, r away from r^*), Friedman felt the role of monetary policy was to operate with a simple quantity rule that did not itself introduce potential instability into the process by which an economy on its own would converge to u^* and r^*. In Friedman's policy framework, u^* and r^* are economic destinations, not policy rule inputs.

Of course, I do not need to elaborate for this audience that the history of K-percent rules is that they were rarely tried, and when they were tried in the 1970s and the 1980s, they were found to work much better in theory than in practice. Velocity relationships proved to be empirically unstable, and there was often only a very loose connection between the growth rate of the monetary base—which the central bank could control—and the growth rate of the broader monetary aggregates, which are more tightly linked to economic activity. Moreover, the macroeconomic priority in the 1980s in the United States, the United Kingdom, and other major countries was to do "whatever it takes" to break the back of inflation and to restore the credibility squandered by central banks that had been unable or unwilling to provide a nominal anchor after the collapse of the Bretton Woods System.

By the early 1990s, thanks to Paul Volcker, the back of inflation had been broken, and thanks to Alan Greenspan, the conditions for price stability had been achieved, and the time was right for something to fill the vacuum in central bank practice left by the realization that monetary aggregate targeting was not, in reality, a workable monetary policy framework. Although it was mostly unspoken, there was a growing sense at the time that a simple, systematic framework for central bank practice was needed to ensure that the hard-won gains from breaking the back of inflation were not given away by shortsighted monetary experiments that were poorly executed, such as had been the case in the 1970s.

That vacuum, of course, was filled by John Taylor with the classic 1993 paper, "Discretion versus Policy Rules in Practice." For this audience, and at this conference, I will not need to remind you of the enormous impact this single paper had not only on the field of monetary economics but also—and more importantly—on the practice of monetary policy. For our purposes today, I will note that the crucial insight of Taylor's paper was that, whereas a central bank could pick the "K" in a K-percent rule on its own, without any reference to the underlying parameters of the economy (including r^* and u^*), a well-designed rule for setting a short-term interest rate as a policy instrument should, Taylor argued, respect several requirements.

First, the rule should anchor the nominal policy rate at a level equal to the sum of its estimate of the neutral real interest rate (r^*) and the inflation target. Second, to achieve this nominal anchor, the central bank should be prepared to raise the nominal policy rate by more than one-for-one when inflation exceeds the target (the Taylor principle). And third, the central bank should lean against the wind when output—or, via an Okun's law relationship, the unemployment rate—deviates from its estimate of potential (u^*). In other words, whereas in Friedman's K-percent policy rule u^* and r^* are destinations irrelevant to the choice of k, in the Taylor rule—and most subsequent Taylor-type rules—u^* and r^* are necessary inputs. As [Michael] Woodford (2003) demonstrates theoretically, the first two requirements for a Taylor-type rule are necessary to be consistent with the objective of price stability. The third requirement—that monetary policy lean against the wind in response to an output or unemployment gap—not only contributes to the objective of price stability but is also obviously desirable from the perspective of a central bank like the Fed that has a dual mandate.

The Taylor approach to instrument-rule specification has been found to produce good macroeconomic outcomes across a wide range of macroeconomic models. Moreover, in a broad class of both closed (Clarida, Galí, and Gertler 1999; Galí and Monacelli 2008) and open economy (Clarida, Galí, and Gertler 2001 and 2002) dynamic stochastic general equilibrium, or DSGE models, Taylor-type rules can be shown to be optimal given the underlying microfoundations of these models. This in itself is a remarkable achievement. And when they are not strictly optimal, Taylor rules are very often found to be robust in that they produce near-optimal outcomes with modest information requirements on the full structure of the economy, as would a fully optimal rule. I said modest instead of minimal because, of course, using a TR in practice to set policy rates does require the central bank to take a stand on the key inputs of r^* and u^*. Another desirable feature of Taylor rules is that when embedded in DSGE models, a policy that respects the Taylor principle rules out multiple stationary equilibria for inflation. Also, DSGE monetary models with TR reaction functions are learnable (Bullard and Mitra 2002; Evans and Honkapohja 2003; Marcet and Sargent 1989) in the sense that linear least squares learning about the parameters of the model will eventually converge to the true unique RE (rational expectations) equilibrium. In some of my own research on what it means for monetary policy to be data dependent, which I began while on the Board of Governors of the Federal Reserve System, I've studied a DSGE plus TR setup where the central bank—and agents—use optimal Bayesian updating to learn about the unobserved level of long-run potential output. In the model, the level of potential output is subject to infrequent Hamilton-type regime switches between low and high. With this simple structure, the model under optimal Bayesian updating (with perceived laws of motion that equal actual laws of motion, period by period) features "perpetual" learning. An interesting result is that overconfidence can be very costly if the central bank incorrectly believes there can be no Markov switch in potential output.

Taylor's original paper was, of course, an exercise in both positive and normative economics. It not only wrote down what a good policy rule should look like, but it also made the case that Fed policy during the Greenspan disinflation more or less tracked such a rule (see figure 2.1).

Taylor's original formulation of the TR assumed that r^* was equal to 2% and that the Fed should aim to keep inflation at 2%. This was, of course, nearly twenty years before the Fed adopted a formal inflation target of 2% and at a time, 1993, when US inflation had last printed 2% twenty years earlier. Strikingly, over the

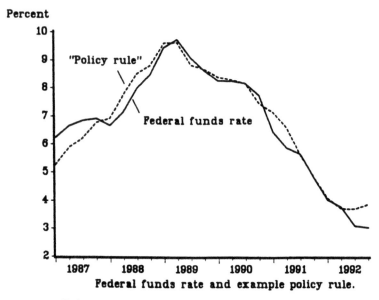

FIGURE 2.1. Federal Funds Rate and Example Policy Rule.
Fed policy during the Greenspan disinflation era more or less tracked the
policy rule.
Source: Taylor (1993). Reprinted with permission from Elsevier.

ensuing fifteen years, US inflation averaged 2%, the federal funds
rate averaged 4%, and the ex post real funds rate averaged 2%!

The finding that a Taylor rule could account for Fed policy during the early Greenspan years spawned its own research agenda
to formulate and try to identify in time series data empirical Taylor-
type rules that could account for broad swings in policy rates in
the US, Europe, and Japan (Clarida, Galí, and Gertler 1998 and
2000; Clarida and Gertler 1997). This literature also embedded
empirical "forward-looking" Taylor-type rules into a vector auto-
regressive (VAR) framework. In particular, if the policy is a function of expected inflation, and expected inflation, in turn, is a linear
function, the n variables in the VAR with m lags, so then under an
FLTR (forward-looking Taylor rule), the policy rate in the VAR
will be a function of the n variables with m lags. When staring at

the interest rate equation in a VAR, it may at first glance appear, as it did to us, to represent an ad hoc kitchen sink specification of a central bank reaction function. But look closer and think harder, and you see that the FLTR placed testable restrictions—actually cross-equation restrictions—on the reduced form coefficients in the policy rate equation in the VAR. Figure 2.2 is taken from Clarida, Galí, and Gertler (1998) and plots the FLTRs against the actual policy rates in the United States, Germany, and Japan during those halcyon days when Germany still had the deutsche mark, the Bank of Japan was worried that inflation was too high, and the zero lower bound (ZLB) was but a footnote. I vividly recall presenting an early version of this work at the [Deutsche] Bundesbank in 1996 with Otmar Issing in the audience. When I asked Otmar if the Bundesbank—which at that time still publicly explained their policy in terms of the quantity theory—was formulating policy with reference to the Taylor rule, he replied, "I won't concede it, but I don't dispute it."

The fact that Taylor-type rules can, away from the ZLB, empirically help to account for the mapping from macro data to policy rates means that they can be an essential input to asset pricing models of yield curves and currencies in academia and fixed income markets. Indeed, I first became aware of Taylor's 1993 paper not from an economics professor but from a bond trader who was using it to build yield curve models for Citibank! After all, bond yields reflect the expected path of short rates, and if central banks set short rates based in part on a Taylor-type rule, bond yields will embed the joint dynamics of inflation and output gap data as filtered by the Taylor rule (Ang and Piazzesi 2003). The same is true for exchange rates. Real exchange rates, for example, reflect in part the expected path of real short rate differentials, and if central banks set short rates based in part on a Taylor-type rule, then real exchange rates will embed the joint dynamics of inflation and output gap data as filtered by the Taylor rule (Clarida, Galí, and Gertler 2001; Clarida 2014; Engel and West 2006). In sum, Taylor

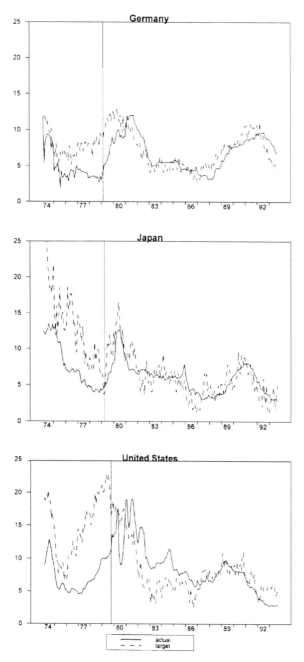

FIGURE 2.2. G3 Interest Rates: Target vs. Actual.
FLTRs plotted against the actual policy rates in the United States, Germany, and Japan indicate some correlation with the Taylor rule.

Source: Clarida, Galí, and Gertler (1998). Reprinted with permission from Elsevier.

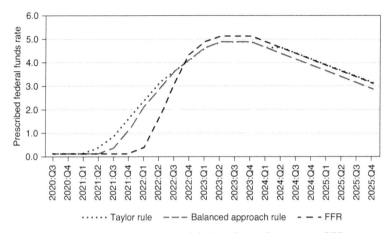

FIGURE 2.3. A Straightforward Way of Adding Policy Rules to the SEP. How using the inertial policy rules would have worked in the March 2023 SEP. Source: Papell and Prodan (2023).

rules are today ubiquitous in any economics literature in which macro factors and asset prices are objects of interest.

Turning now from theory and econometrics to policy in practice, Taylor-type rules are also, based on my experience, ubiquitous, at least in the briefing books staff prepare for Fed officials ahead of each monetary policy meeting, and are usually, but not always, featured in the Fed's semiannual *Monetary Policy Report* to Congress. Recent research from Papell and Prodan (2023) suggests a straightforward way that policy rules could be added to the Summary of Economic Projections (SEP) itself. Figure 2.3 shows how this would have worked in the March 2023 SEP using inertial policy rules, as are favored by many policymakers as a reference.

It is important to note how the policy paths are constructed. At each calendar date before June 2023, the policy rule paths are computed using actual data available to the Fed at dates before the most recent SEP, along with model-consistent values for the lagged policy rate (not actual policy rates) in the inertial rule.

As I explained at last year's Hoover conference and as is evident in the figure, certainly by the fall of 2021, monetary policy rules I consult, based on my research with Mark Gertler and Jordi Galí (Clarida, Galí, and Gertler 1999 and 2000)—for example, as highlighted in a presentation I delivered (virtually) to a Hoover seminar in January 2021 (Clarida 2021)—were indicating that lift-off from the effective lower bound was or soon would be warranted. In the event, the Federal Open Market Committee (FOMC) began to pivot in the fall of 2021 to end quantitative easing earlier than had been expected, commence rate hikes sooner than had been expected, signal a faster pace of policy normalization than had been previously projected, begin balance sheet normalization much sooner and at a much faster pace than was the case following the Great Financial Crisis, and to accelerate rate hikes to the fastest pace in forty years. Interestingly, the conditions the committee laid out in its September 2020 forward guidance for lifting off—that inflation had reached 2% and maximum employment had been achieved—were met by the December 2021 FOMC meeting, just three months after they were met by the balanced approached Taylor rule: the unemployment rate fell to 3.9% in December 2021 and as of at least August 2021, it was clear that under the Fed's own projections, inflation would more than average 2% over time.

There is much more to say, but I have now exhausted my fifteen minutes, so let me conclude by wishing the Taylor rule a very, very happy thirtieth birthday, and here's to many more.

References

Ang, Andrew, and Monika Piazzesi. 2003. "A No-Arbitrage Vector Autoregression of Term Structure Dynamics with Macroeconomic and Latent Variables." *Journal of Monetary Economics* 50, no. 4 (May): 745–87.

Bullard, James, and Kaushik Mitra. 2002. "Learning about Monetary Policy Rules." *Journal of Monetary Economics* 49, no. 6 (September): 1105–29.

Clarida, Richard H. 2014. "Monetary Policy in Open Economies: Practical Perspectives for Pragmatic Central Bankers." *Journal of Economic Dynamics and Control* 49 (December): 21–30.

———. 2021. "The Federal Reserve's New Framework: Context and Consequences." The Road Ahead for Central Banks, a seminar sponsored by the Hoover Economic Policy Working Group. January 13, Stanford, California, Webcast.

Clarida, Richard, Jordi Galí, and Mark Gertler. 1998. "Monetary Policy Rules in Practice: Some International Evidence." *European Economic Review* 42, no. 6 (June): 1033–67.

———. 1999. "The Science of Monetary Policy: A New Keynesian Perspective." *Journal of Economic Literature* 37, no. 4 (December): 1661–707.

———. 2000. "Monetary Policy Rules and Macroeconomic Stability: Evidence and Some Theory." *Quarterly Journal of Economics* 115, no. 1 (February): 147–80.

———. 2001. "Optimal Monetary Policy in Open versus Closed Economies: An Integrated Approach." *American Economic Review* 91, no. 2 (May): 248–52.

———. 2002. "A Simple Framework for International Monetary Policy Analysis." *Journal of Monetary Economics* 49, no. 5 (July): 879–904.

Clarida, Richard H., and Mark Gertler. 1997. "How the Bundesbank Conducts Monetary Policy." In *Reducing Inflation: Motivation and Strategy*, edited by Christina D. Romer and David H. Romer. University of Chicago Press, 363–412.

Engel, Charles, and Kenneth D. West. 2006. "Taylor Rules and the Deutschmark-Dollar Real Exchange Rate." *Journal of Money, Credit, and Banking* 38, no. 5 (August): 1175–94.

Evans, George W., and Seppo Honkapohja. 2003. "Adaptive Learning and Monetary Policy Design." *Journal of Money, Credit, and Banking* 35, no. 6 (December): 1045–72.

Friedman, Milton. 1968. "The Role of Monetary Policy." *American Economic Review* 58, no. 1 (March): 1–17.

Galí, Jordi, and Tommaso Monacelli. 2008. "Optimal Monetary and Fiscal Policy in a Currency Union." *Journal of International Economics* 76, no. 1 (September): 116–32.

Marcet, Albert, and Thomas J. Sargent. 1989. "Convergence of Least Squares Learning Mechanisms in Self-Referential Linear Stochastic Models." *Journal of Economic Theory* 48, no. 2 (August): 337–68.

Papell, David H., and Ruxandra Prodan. 2023. "Policy Rules and Forward Guidance following the COVID-19 Recession." Unpublished paper, University of Houston. Available at SSRN: http://ssrn.com/abstract=4083466.

Taylor, John B. 1993. "Discretion versus Policy Rules in Practice." *Carnegie-Rochester Conference Series on Public Policy* 39 (December): 195–214. Amsterdam: North-Holland.

Woodford, Michael. 2003. *Interest and Prices: Foundations of a Theory of Monetary Policy*. Princeton, NJ: Princeton University Press.

Woodford, Michael, and Carl E. Walsh. 2005. "Interest and Prices: Foundations of a Theory of Monetary Policy." *Macroeconomic Dynamics* 9, no. 3 (June): 462–68.

3

Naming the Taylor Rule

John Lipsky

Introduction

It is a great pleasure to participate in this terrific conference, and I feel honored to be included in such a great panel and to discuss a topic that is particularly important to me, that is, the Taylor rule on the occasion of its thirtieth anniversary.

Time is short, and my fellow panelists are renowned, so I will restrict my opening remarks to addressing a few critical but burning questions—ones I know you have wondered about for some time. First: How did the Taylor rule get its name? Second: How did a modest proposal contained in a paper delivered at an academic conference become known worldwide, seemingly instantaneously? And third: What happened to Salomon Brothers, and what did the Taylor rule have to do with it?

Taking the First Issue First: The Taylor Rule and Its Name

My guess is that you have never thought about this, and even if you had, you would have concluded: "Of course, John Taylor concocted it; why wouldn't it be called the Taylor rule?"

No matter, you've probably never wondered why everyone calls transparent cellophane adhesive tape Scotch Tape or why facial tissues are referred to everywhere as Kleenex. It turns out that Scotch Tape was developed by a fellow named Richard Drew, who allegedly had Scottish bosses.[1] With regard to Kleenex, let me assure you that you don't really want to know the advertising logic that went into creating the now iconic and ubiquitous brand name.

But think about it. All of you who know John Taylor (and I presume that's pretty much everyone here) know him well enough to be sure that he's about the last person on earth who would have named the Taylor rule the Taylor rule. Not his style, to say the least.

Here's the title page of the original paper (see figure 3.1) containing the rule that Taylor wrote for the Center for Economic Policy Research here at Stanford University.[2]

Did any of you attend the conference where it was first presented or read it when it was first published? Note the historical aspect of the cover page. The Center for Economic Policy Research (or CEPR) was then modestly housed at 100 Encina Commons. Yes indeed, that's the predecessor of today's Stanford Institute for Economic Policy Research (or SIEPR), located comfortably in the wonderful Gunn Building just across the way. Like the Hoover Institution, Stanford, and Silicon Valley, SIEPR has come a long way from CEPR in Encina Commons.

I did not attend the Carnegie-Rochester conference where the "Discretion versus Policy Rules in Practice" paper was first presented, but I did read it when it was published by CEPR. At the time, I was the newly appointed chief economist of Salomon Brothers.

To me, the monetary policy rule contained in the paper was—to mix metaphors—music to my ears. My Salomon Brothers economic research colleagues and I were convinced that the Federal Reserve's policy had veered off course by failing to tighten policy during the course of 1993, and Taylor's policy rule formulation provided another arrow for our quiver.

Here (in figure 3.2) you can see one formulation of the rule, arrayed in contrast to the actual federal funds rate. We made this

This work is distributed as a Policy Paper by the

CENTER FOR ECONOMIC POLICY RESEARCH

CEPR Publication No. 327

DISCRETION VERSUS POLICY RULES
IN PRACTICE

by

John B. Taylor
Stanford University

November 1992

Center for Economic Policy Research
100 Encina Commons
Stanford University
Stanford, CA 94305
(415) 725-1874

The Center for Economic Policy Research at Stanford University supports research bearing on economic and public policy issues. The CEPR Discussion Paper Series reports on research and policy analysis conducted by researchers affiliated with the Center. Working papers in this series reflect the views of the authors and not necessarily those of the Center for Economic Policy Research or Stanford University.

FIGURE 3.1. Title Page of the Original Paper Introducing the Taylor Rule. The origin story for the Taylor rule begins with an unpublished paper presented at an academic conference.
Source: Center for Economic Policy Research (now Stanford Institute for Economic Policy Research, or SIEPR).

argument about the federal funds rate a centerpiece of our annual economic and market analysis "Prospects for Financial Markets," published by Salomon Brothers in December 1993 with the title "Keeping Inflation Low in the 1990s."

In this report, we made the claim that the Fed had veered off course, citing Taylor's article, highlighting "a recent study indicating that until last year, the Fed's policy actions were consistent with an implicit 2% inflation target, but that its failure to hike

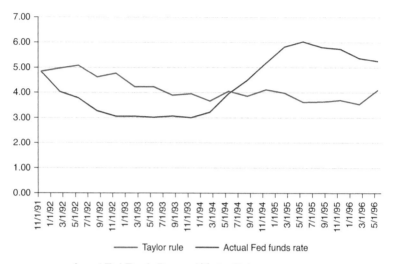

FIGURE 3.2. Actual Fed Funds Rate and Taylor Rule.
From too loose to too tight: Fed Policy Rates 1991–96.
Source: Taylor Rule Utility, Federal Reserve Bank of Atlanta (Atlantafed.org).

rates during the past year has called into question the stringency of the Fed's policy goals." And we footnoted this quote from the Carnegie-Rochester paper.

As far as we can ascertain, this is the first independent reference to Taylor's paper—at least outside of an academic context. Also, while the federal funds rate at the time was about 3%, we calculated that it should be realized at about 4.125% or so, utilizing the formulation in the conference paper to corroborate our claim.

Next up was Fed chair Alan Greenspan's Congressional Testimony of January 31, 1994.[3] Suffice it to say that what we at Salomon economic research heard the chair say was, "We are going to raise rates, and we are going to begin any minute now." In contrast, the press reports about the testimony—as were typical—reveled in telling everyone that you never could make head nor tail of the chairman's Delphic remarks. At Salomon Brothers, however,

TABLE 3.1. Fed Rate Hikes 1994–95: Engineering a Soft Landing.
The attempt to engineer a soft landing resulted in a terrible year for long-duration bonds as many traders were unprepared for the rate increases.

FOMC Meeting Date	Rate Change (bps)	Federal Funds Rate
February 1, 1995	+50	6.00%
November 15, 1994	+75	5.50%
August 16, 1994	+50	4.75%
May 17, 1994	+50	4.25%
April 18, 1994	+25	3.75%
March 22, 1994	+25	3.50%
February 4, 1994	+25	3.25%

Source: Federal Reserve Board.

my colleagues and I virtually ran around the trading floor, yelling, "The Fed is coming, the Fed is coming!"

Well, the Fed hiked the federal funds rate by 25 basis points on February 4, 1994, beginning a tightening cycle that would extend until February 1995, encompassing a rise in the federal funds rate from 3% to 6%. In other words, using the Taylor calculations, the Fed went from too loose to too tight in the space of about a year. Parenthetically, the core personal consumption expenditures (PCE) deflator was about 2.25% year over year in January 1994 and about the same rate a year later.

Even more unnerving—at least for financial market participants—was the accompanying bond market rout (see table 3.1). When Chair Greenspan spoke on January 31, the ten-year Treasury bond yield was 5.94%. It peaked on October 31 at 8.04%. In fact, precedent would have suggested that the Fed's first 50 basis points of tightening would have produced a bond yield backup of about half that magnitude or roughly 25 basis points.

In 1994, by contrast, ten-year bond yields backed up by nearly a full percentage point in response to the first 50 basis point rise in the federal funds rate. Traders' lack of experience with a Federal

Reserve tightening environment in the context of large holdings of mortgage-backed securities (MBS), and their negative convexity, set off a wave of Treasury bond selling by traders seeking to control their duration risk.

My Salomon Brothers economic research colleagues and I eventually became convinced that the Fed had overdone the tightening and that the bond market sell-off also was overdone. In the meantime, however, Salomon Brothers bond trading desks—especially the MBS traders—had lost copious amounts of money in their portfolios on a mark-to-market basis. As Salomon Brothers research analysts, we were mortified to realize that our bond trading colleagues simply hadn't believed our Fed analysis and were unprepared for the bond market consequences. I'll return to this theme a bit later.

As we subsequently built our case with regard to both Fed policy and bond market valuations, as my former Salomon Brothers colleague Robert DiClemente reminded me recently, we made our arguments based on comparing the actual federal funds rate to a "neutral" or "hypothetical equilibrium" rate, footnoting the Carnegie-Rochester paper every time. In making client presentations, we routinely would include what we referred to as Taylor rule calculations.

Finally, in mid-1995, we decided to summarize the burgeoning discussion regarding monetary policy rules in a compact form for our clients. The result was a monetary policy research paper, "Policy Rules Shed New Light on Fed Stance," which Salomon Brothers published in June 1995. In it, we introduced the topic in a generic fashion and highlighted a list of alternative policy rules, giving pride of place to the work of John Taylor and his rule. We then went on to emphasize the usefulness of what we called "Taylor's Rule." As far as we know, this was the first use in print of this personalized nomenclature, which since has become a universal practice.

Why Did the Taylor Rule's Fame Spread So Far and So Fast?

One key lesson from investment banking is that the right deal at the right time and the right price will be snapped up in a flash. I think (and at the time, probably hoped) that Salomon Brothers economic research had attracted some attention with our vindicated call on the Fed's belated tightening (this despite our trading colleagues' failure to believe us). We then spent a fair amount of time in 1994 arguing that the Fed was overdoing it, as was the yield backup in the Treasury bond market. Perhaps we gained a bit of street credibility, having called it both ways, as it were. And we consistently referred to the Taylor rule (by now using the name as a matter of course) as providing useful guidance.

In any case, other Wall Street economists quickly followed suit—that is, utilizing the Taylor rule as a basis for their analysis. They, along with some journalists and even some scholars, began to challenge central bankers to defend or explain their policy moves (or lack of same) by reference to the Taylor rule. Before you knew it, virtually everyone everywhere was using it. And even some skeptics—who tended to view its practical usefulness as a short-term artifact of "right place, right time" rather than something that would retain validity over time—seem to be coming back to utilizing the Taylor rule as a practical policy guide.

In investment banking terms, it was much more durable than simply the right deal at the right time. It continues to demonstrate its relevance thirty years on.

What Happened to Salomon Brothers?

I don't want to bore you with a detailed story. Suffice it to say that the firm's self-image as the world's preeminent securities trading firm simply didn't survive the 1994 trading losses. Remember that Lew Ranieri—the pioneer of the mortgage-backed bond market—was long gone (from Salomon Brothers), and John Meriwether and his original crew of proprietary traders—made famous by author Michael Lewis's book *Liar's Poker*—were by and large up in Greenwich (and London and elsewhere) doing business as Long-Term Capital Management, and still convincing investors that they possessed the Midas touch, at least until they didn't, but that came later.[4]

So what followed after the 1994 bond debacle wasn't pretty. In 1985, Salomon Brothers CEO John Gutfreund appeared on the cover of *Business Week* (then a big deal) with the caption, "The King of Wall Street." Imagine the implications of this title at a time when I doubt that the firm totaled more than two thousand five hundred employees, soup to nuts. Only a decade later—encompassing a few nontrivial missteps—the firm had lost momentum and didn't appear to have a viable long-term strategy. Along came Sandy Weill and Smith Barney, and then Citigroup.[5] And the rest is history.

If only Salomon Brothers's vaunted bond traders had paid attention in January 1994 to the message of the Taylor rule, even in its infancy, perhaps they still would be the "Kings of Wall Street." But we'll never know.

Thus, despite the 1993–94 prescience of the Salomon Brothers economics research team, the firm is no more. At the same time, the Taylor rule—that helped guide Salomon analysts and countless others right from its infancy—continues to thrive and hopefully will contribute to getting policy back on track everywhere, following a period of unprecedented challenges.

Notes

1. Scotch Tape was invented by Richard Drew, a 3M engineer, in 1925. The official story from the brand lacks specificity as to where the name came from. See Scotchbrand.com.

2. John B. Taylor, "Discretion versus Policy Rules in Practice," *Carnegie-Rochester Conference Series on Public Policy* 39 (1993): 195–214. Amsterdam: North-Holland.

3. US Congress, Joint Economic Committee. Testimony of Alan Greenspan, Chair of the Federal Reserve Bank. 103rd Cong., 2nd sess., January 31, 1994.

4. Michael Lewis, *Liar's Poker: Rising through the Wreckage on Wall Street* (New York: W. W. Norton & Company, 1989). Long-Term Capital Management L.P. was founded in 1994. The leveraged hedge fund went bankrupt in 1998.

5. Salomon Brothers was acquired by Travelers Group, which owned Smith Barney, in 1997. When Travelers Group merged with Citicorp in 1998, it became part of Citigroup, which used the name for its combined investment banking operations, Salomon Smith Barney. In 2003, the division rebranded as Citigroup Global Markets.

4

The Taylor Rule at Thirty: Still Useful to Get the Fed Back on Track

Volker Wieland

It is a great pleasure for me to celebrate the thirtieth anniversary of the famous Taylor rule with you at this conference. I can even say I was right there at its birth. At least, the first footnote of John Taylor's "Discretion versus Policy Rules in Practice" in the Carnegie-Rochester Conference Series states that helpful comments and research assistance were provided by Craig Furfine, Ben McCallum, John Williams, and Volker Wieland (see Taylor 1993a). Craig, John, and I were working as research assistants for John Taylor at the time.

Nowadays, I teach about policy rules in general and Taylor's rule in particular in my courses on macro and monetary policy. Typically, students have already heard about it. But many of them think that it is an exercise in description. Considering figure 4.1 (the original figure from Taylor 1993a), this is not surprising. Students see this as a reaction function estimated to fit the data on interest rates, output, and inflation in the late 1980s and early 1990s.

Yet, the coefficients of the policy rule are round numbers that do not look like estimates, and there are no standard errors reported. Upon reading the abstract or introduction of the article, it quickly becomes clear that the process of arriving at figure 4.1 was the other way around. Taylor used macroeconomic models to identify a type of feedback rule that performed well across a new class of models. Only then did he go on to compare a representative rule with actual Fed decisions.

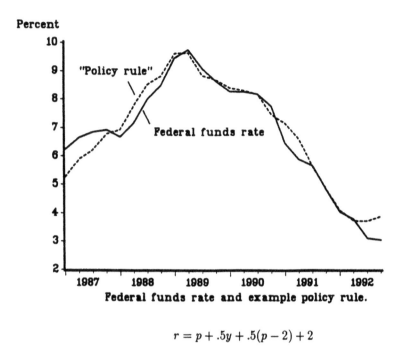

Federal funds rate and example policy rule.

$$r = p + .5y + .5(p - 2) + 2$$

where

  r   is the federal funds rate,
  p   is the rate of inflation over the previous four quarters
  y   is the percent deviation of real GDP from a target.

FIGURE 4.1. The Original Taylor Rule: John Taylor's Seminal Contributions. Figure from John Taylor's original paper, with definition of Taylor rule. Source: Taylor (1993a). Reprinted with permission from Elsevier.

The abstract explains this very clearly. Accordingly, "econometric policy evaluation research" had shown that "good policy rules typically call for changes in the federal funds rate in response to changes in the price level or changes in real income." Taylor's objective was to "preserve the concept of such a policy rule in a policy environment where it is practically impossible to follow mechanically any particular algebraic formula that describes the policy rule." He focuses on "a hypothetical but representative policy rule much like that advocated in (then) recent research" and explains that it closely approximates Federal Reserve policy during the preceding several years.

So, Taylor was coming from new research using the methods of rational expectations macroeconomics to deliver lessons and tools for practical policymaking. As to the sources for this research, the footnote in the photo of the abstract shown in figure 4.2 refers to the two books also shown.

Both of them were published in 1993. The volume edited by Bryant, Hooper, and Mann (1993), three former Federal Reserve economists, summarized a substantial body of empirical research with large multi-country models, one of them, the model of the G7 economies presented in Taylor (1993b). The latter is an early-generation New Keynesian model with rational expectations and nominal rigidities due to overlapping wage contracts. Taylor (1993a) distills lessons from this body of research in the form of a feedback rule for the federal funds rate that comes close to actual Federal Reserve decision making from 1988 to 1993.

But John Taylor's contributions to macroeconomics go far beyond the 1993 article and the book. In the late 1970s and early 1980s, he already built the foundations for this as well as subsequent research on economic policy evaluation. I will focus on a selection of three seminal contributions here. Each of them introduced a household name to monetary macroeconomics: Taylor contracts, Taylor curves, and the Fair-Taylor method.

"Aggregate Dynamics and Staggered Contracts," published in the *Journal of Political Economy* in 1980, laid the foundations for analyzing the real effects of monetary policy under rational expectations. Until then, rational expectations macro had pushed the line that only monetary policy surprises would change real GDP and employment. Taylor (1980) changed that by deriving the real effects of anticipated monetary policy under overlapping wage or price contracts. It was the key step toward the New Keynesian Phillips curve that is used today.

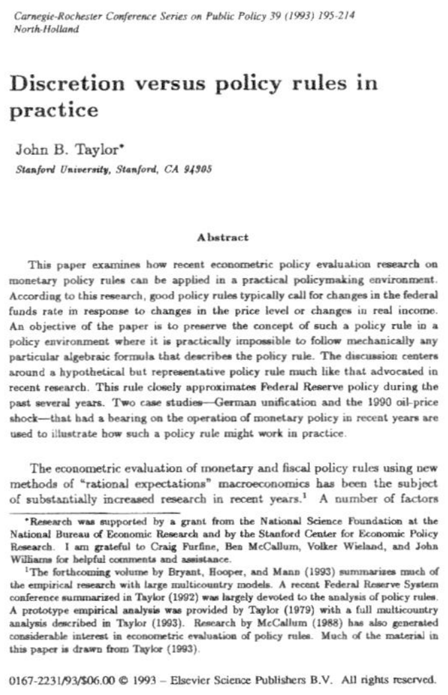

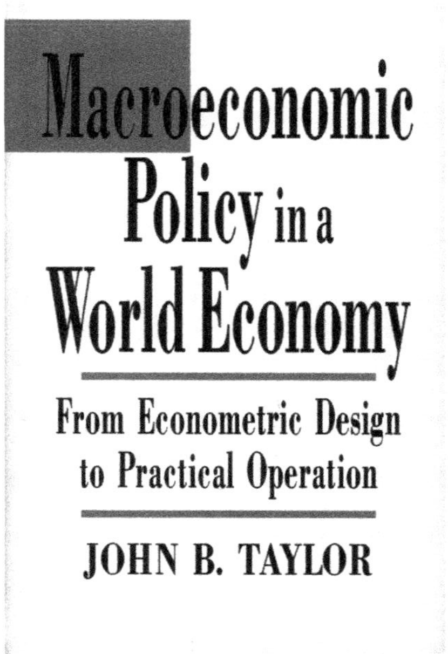

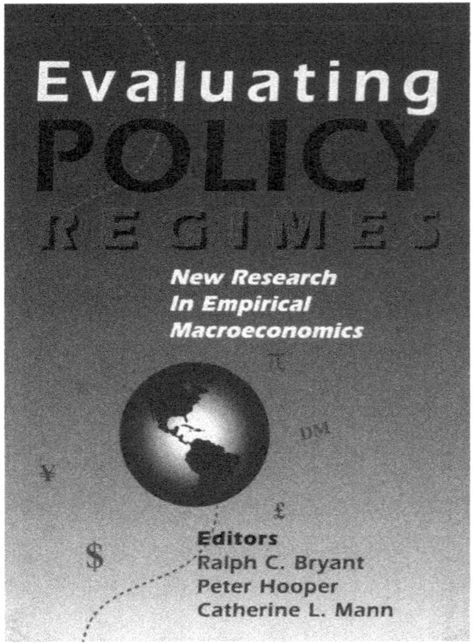

FIGURE 4.2. A Representative Rule Emerging from Macro Model Comparisons. Left to right: abstract page from Taylor (1993a), reprinted with permission from Elsevier; cover of Taylor (1993b), reprinted with permission from W. W. Norton; and cover of Bryant, Hooper, and Mann (1993), reprinted with permission from Rowman & Littlefield Publishing Group Inc.; permission conveyed through Copyright Clearance Center Inc.

In "Estimation and Control of a Macroeconomic Model with Rational Expectations," published in *Econometrica* in 1979, Taylor estimated a prototype macro model with rational expectations empirically and computed optimal policy rules. Taylor (1979) first reported so-called Taylor curves that showed the policy trade-off between the standard deviation of inflation and the standard deviation of the output gap.

Finally, "Solution and Maximum Likelihood Estimation of Dynamic Nonlinear Rational Expectations Models," published by Ray Fair and John Taylor in *Econometrica* in 1983, presented the tools for solving and estimating the new class of models. Together the three papers provided the necessary theoretical and methodological innovations that made the development of a new generation of practical policy models with rational expectations and nominal rigidities possible. Solving these models required the introduction of feedback rules for policy, because solving them involved computing the expectations of future policy decisions. Such rules still form an essential part of macro models and policy analysis today. They have become known as Taylor rules or Taylor-style rules.

Starting with Jan Tinbergen and Ragnar Frisch, who received the first Sveriges Riksbank Prize in Economic Sciences in Memory of Alfred Nobel in 1969 for "having developed and applied dynamic models for the analysis of economic processes," there have been a number of Nobel Prizes awarded for advances in macroeconomics and economic policy. The prize awarded to Milton Friedman in 1976 included the dedication "and for his demonstration of the complexity of stabilization policy." Robert Lucas was recognized in 1995 "for having developed and applied the hypothesis of rational expectations . . . and deepened our understanding of economic policy." In 2004, Finn Kydland and Edward Prescott followed with a prize for "the time consistency of economic policy and the driving forces behind business cycles." In 2011, the prize was given to Thomas Sargent and Christopher Sims "for their empirical research on cause and effect in the macroeconomy."[1]

Yet, as outlined above, monetary macroeconomics has undergone a major transformation and this scientific progress has had important implications for policy. Thus, in my humble opinion, it is time to recognize the huge progress in monetary macroeconomics, the advances in New Keynesian modeling of real effects of monetary policy, and the design of feedback rules for stabilization policy with a wide impact on policy practice. The lessons for rule-based policy, in particular, remain valid and highly relevant today. I would say it is time for a prize to be given "for modeling the linkages between the real and monetary sides of the macroeconomy and developing effective rules for stabilization policy."

Taylor Rules in Macro Models and Policy Practice

In modern macro models with rational expectations and nominal rigidities, households and firms behave in a forward-looking, optimizing manner. A model solution needs to account for endogenous policy reactions and determine expectations and policy jointly. These models typically include rules for monetary policy that respect the so-called Taylor principle, which states that the nominal interest rate changes more than one-for-one with inflation or inflation expectations—at least over the medium run. Similarly, these models include feedback rules for fiscal policy that stabilize debt-to-GDP ratios. Such a fiscal policy implemented via a tax or transfer rule allows monetary policy to achieve price stability.

Taylor (1993a) emphasized the case for rule-based policy. Rule-based policy is predictable and predictable policy is more effective because it exploits the expectations channel of policy transmission. To illustrate the power of the expectations channel, I ran two simulations in the Taylor (1993b) multi-country model using the Macroeconomic Model Data Base.[2] First, I consider a onetime surprise deviation ε from Taylor's original rule shown in equation (1).

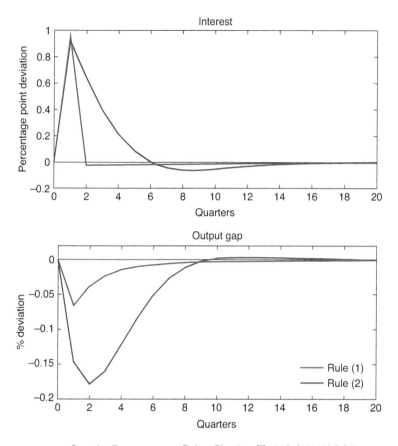

FIGURE 4.3. Impulse Responses to a Policy Shock in Taylor's (1993b) Multi-country Model.
Source: Macroeconomic Model Data Base, https://www.macromodelbase.com.

$$r_t = a_0 + 1.5p_t + 0.5y_t + \varepsilon_t \tag{1}$$

The size of the deviation is one percentage point. As a consequence, the federal funds rate (blue line in figure 4.3, top panel) rises for one quarter by about one percentage point and drops back down to the initial level by the second quarter. The impact on GDP is very small at little more than 5 basis points and remains short lived (blue line in figure 4.3, bottom panel).

Next, I add the lagged federal funds rate r_{t-1} to the rule with a reaction coefficient of 0.8, as shown in equation (2).

$$r_t = a_0 + 0.8r_{t-1} + 1.5p_t + 0.5y_t + \varepsilon_t \qquad (2)$$

As a consequence, the increase in the federal funds rate following the temporary deviation ε persists for a longer time (red line in figure 4.3, top panel). The interest rate returns to the initial level by the fifth quarter. While the initial deviation is unexpected, the subsequent endogenous persistence is predictable. Via the expectations channel, it contributes to an outsized effect on real GDP. The decline in GDP is about three times larger and longer-lasting than in the case without endogenous interest rate persistence (red line in figure 4.3, bottom panel), even though the peak of the interest rate is the same, and it declines only a bit more slowly.

In the 1990s and 2000s, monetary models were developed further to include more stringent microeconomic foundations. They became known under the acronym DSGE (dynamic stochastic general equilibrium) models. Still, these models assume rational expectations and include policy rules as well as nominal rigidities due to staggered wage and price contracts. The first medium-sized New Keynesian DSGE model for the US economy was developed by Lawrence Christiano, Martin Eichenbaum, and Charles Evans in 2001 and ultimately published in Christiano et al. (2005). This model was estimated by matching the impulse response of a monetary shock in the structural model to the impulse response of a monetary surprise in a vector autoregression (VAR) model. Smets and Wouters (2003 and 2007) proposed and applied Bayesian methods that proved much more practical for estimating such New Keynesian DSGE models.

Christiano et al. (2005) used a simple Taylor rule with interest rate persistence (equation 3) to conduct simulations of their model.

$$r_t = a_0 + 0.8r_{t-1} + 0.3p_t + 0.08y_t + \varepsilon_t \qquad (3)$$

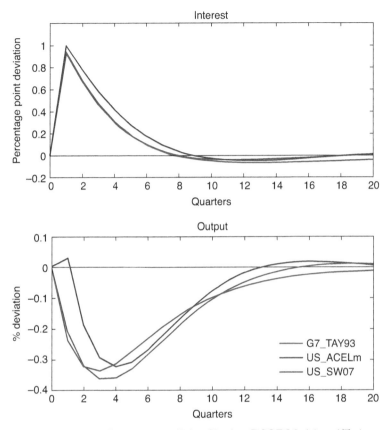

FIGURE 4.4. Impulse Responses to a Policy Shock in DSGE Models and Taylor. Simulation of monetary policy shock under rule (3) in three models: G7_TAY93 (model of G7 economies, Taylor 1993b); US_ACELm (version of model of US economy US_SW07, Christiano et al. 2005); Smets and Wouters (2007) model of US economy. Acronyms as in Macroeconomic Model Data Base.

Source: Macroeconomic Model Data Base, https://www.macromodelbase.com.

Interestingly, the effects of policy shocks in these New Keynesian DSGE models turned out to be very similar to the effects of such shocks in the multi-country model of Taylor (1993b). Figure 4.4 shows the impulse responses when the federal funds rate is set according to equation (3) in the Christiano et al. (2005), Smets and Wouters (2007), and Taylor (1993b) models.

In all three models, interest rates rise for a sustained period in response to the policy shock. This causes a reduction of about 35 basis points in real GDP within three quarters. Wieland et al. (2016) extended the comparison to consider many new macro-financial DSGE models that were developed after the Global Financial Crisis of 2007–9. These models include financial frictions in corporate investment financing, housing finance, and banking capital. Comparisons of monetary policy shocks in those models indicate somewhat sharper effects on economic activity than in the earlier generation of DSGE models. The Macroeconomic Model Data Base allows one to conduct many more model and policy comparisons of this type.

Taylor (1993a) puts great emphasis on the need for testing the robustness of policy rules across different models. This strategy for identifying useful policy rules was pursued in a large number of subsequent research contributions. Some examples to which I contributed include Levin et al. (1999 and 2003) and Taylor and Wieland (2012) for the United States and Orphanides and Wieland (2013) for the Euro area. Table 4.1, which reproduces table 4 from Taylor and Wieland (2012), indicates one of several possible approaches for achieving robustness—namely, model averaging.

We consider a standard ad hoc central bank loss function that includes the variances of inflation, the output gap, and the change in the federal funds rate. Then, we search for the rule that maximizes the average loss for the three New Keynesian models with rational expectations used in the simulation in figure 4.4. The optimization is carried out for 2-, 3-, and 4-parameter rules that respond to inflation, the current and preceding output gap, and the lagged interest rate. Optimized parameters are shown in table 4.1. Such 3- and 4-parameter rules typically perform better than 2-parameter rules. The coefficient on the lagged interest rate is slightly above unity. Thus, they are very close to first-difference

TABLE 4.1. Searching for Robust Policy Rules: The Example of Model Averaging.

Optimized Model-Averaging Rules

Objective: $\text{Min} \sum_{m \in M} \frac{1}{3}(\text{Var}(\pi_m) + \text{Var}(y_m) + \text{Var}(\Delta i_m))$;

Rules: $i_t = \rho i_{t-1} + \alpha \pi_t + \beta_0 y_t + \beta_1 y_{t-1} + \beta_\Delta \Delta y_t$

Set of Equally Weighted Models: $M = \{SW, TAYLOR, ACEL\}$	ρ	α	β_0	β_1	β_Δ
2-Parameter Rule (Gap)		2.75	0.52		
3-Parameter Rule (Gap)	1.05	0.41	0.23		
3-Parameter Rule (Growth)	1.09	0.20			0.76
4-Parameter Rule (Gap)	1.06	0.19	0.67	−0.59	

Source: Taylor and Wieland (2012).

or change rules. Yet, 2-parameter rules perform more robustly if one were to add models with backward-looking or adaptive expectations (see Cochrane et al. 2020). First-difference rules tend to induce explosive behavior in such models.

Moving to policy practice, I should note that the Taylor rule and other rules of this type almost immediately became part of regular briefing materials prepared for the Board of Governors and the Federal Open Market Committee (FOMC). Board researchers such as Glenn Rudebusch, Andrew Levin, Brian Madigan, John C. Williams, and Athanasios Orphanides right away engaged in research on Taylor rules. I joined them as a young Board economist and helped prepare a regular rules package from 1996 onwards. Far beyond the Fed, policy rules quickly became a standard tool to be presented to central bank decision makers around the world.

The Federal Reserve eventually introduced a policy rules section as a regular part of its monetary policy report. I think that is an excellent practice and would suggest the same for other central banks, such as the European Central Bank. Table 4.2 reproduces the prepandemic rules menu from the Fed's monetary policy report (see Federal Reserve Board 2020).

TABLE 4.2. The Fed's Prepandemic Rules Menu.

Taylor (1993a) rule	$R_t^{T93} = r_t^{LR} + \pi_t + 0.5\left(\pi_t - \pi^{LR}\right) + \left(u_t^{LR} - u_t\right)$
Balanced-approach rule	$R_t^{BA} = r_t^{LR} + \pi_t + 0.5\left(\pi_t - \pi^{LR}\right) + 2\left(u_t^{LR} - u_t\right)$
Taylor (1993a) adjusted	$R_t^{T93adj} = maximum\left\{R_t^{T93} - Z_t, 0\right\}$
Price-level rule	$R_t^{PL} = maximum\left\{r_t^{LR} + \pi_t + \left(u_t^{LR} - u_t\right) + 0.5(PLgap_t), 0\right\}$
First-difference rule	$R_t^{FD} = R_{t-1} + 0.5\left(\pi_t - \pi^{LR}\right) + \left(u_t^{LR} - u_t\right) - \left(u_{t-4}^{LR} - u_{t-4}\right)$

Notes: R_t^{T93}, R_t^{BA}, R_t^{T93adj}, R_t^{PL}, and R_t^{FD} represent the values of the nominal federal funds rate prescribed by the Taylor (1993a), balanced-approach, adjusted Taylor (1993), price-level, and first-difference rules, respectively.

R_t denotes the realized nominal federal funds rate for quarter t, π_t is the four-quarter price inflation for quarter t, u_t is the unemployment rate in quarter t, and r_t^{LR} is the level of the neutral real federal funds rate in the longer run that is expected to be consistent with sustaining maximum employment and inflation at the FOMC's 2% longer-run objective, π^{LR}. In the addition, u_t^{LR} is the rate of unemployment expected in the longer run. Z_t is the cumulative sum of past deviations of the federal funds rate from the prescriptions of the Taylor (1993a) rule when that rule prescribes setting the federal funds rate below zero. $PLgap_t$ is the percent deviation of the realized level of prices from a price level that rises 2% per year from its level in a specified starting period.

The Taylor (1993a) rule and other policy rules are generally written in terms of the deviation of real output from its full capacity level. In these equations, the output gap has been replaced with the gap between the rate of unemployment in the longer run and its actual level (using a relationship known as Okun's law) to represent the rules in terms of the FOMC's statutory goals. The rules are implemented as responding to core PCE inflation rather than to headline PCE inflation because current and near-term core inflation rates tend to outperform headline inflation rates as predictors of the medium-term behavior of headline inflation.

Source: Federal Reserve Board (2023).

The menu includes the original Taylor (1993a) rule and several variants. However, the Fed uses the unemployment gap in place of the output gap. It doubles the respective response coefficient from 0.5 to 1.0 to account for the smaller degree of variation in the unemployment gap. The so-called balanced-approach rule doubles that coefficient again, raising it to 2.0. The adjusted Taylor (1993a) rule simply keeps interest rates lower for longer after a period of negative rates. The price-level rule keeps Taylor's coefficients but replaces the inflation gap with a price-level gap, that is the deviation from a price-level trend. Finally, there is also a first-difference rule.

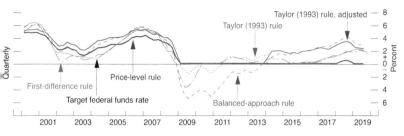

FIGURE 4.5. Federal Funds Rate Prescriptions from the Prepandemic Rules Menu.

Notes: The rules use historical values of core personal consumption expenditures (PCE) inflation, and the unemployment rate. Quarterly projections of longer-run values for the federal funds rate and the unemployment rate are derived through interpolations of biannual six-to-ten-year-ahead projections from Blue Chip Economic Indicators. The longer-run value for inflation is set to 2%. The target value of the price level is the average level of the price index for PCE excluding food and energy in 1998 extrapolated at 2% growth per year. The data extend through Q3 2019, with the exception of the midpoint of the target range for the federal funds rate data, which go through Q4 2019.

Sources: Federal Reserve Board (2020), from Federal Reserve Bank of Philadelphia; Wolters Kluwer, Blue Chip Economic Indicators; Federal Reserve Board staff estimates.

Interestingly, the rules in the prepandemic menu provided several useful signals to policy. This can be seen in figure 4.5, which reproduces the chart with historical federal funds rate prescriptions from the rules menu. First, the Taylor rule and two variants called for the Fed to raise interest rates earlier and faster ahead of the Global Financial Crisis in the years 2002 to 2005. This could have slowed down the housing boom that set the stage for the crisis (see Taylor 2007). Second, several of the rules called for lowering the federal funds rate into negative territory in 2009. This could be taken as a signal of the need for quantitative easing. In fact, the Fed initiated quantitative easing at that time. Third, the Taylor rule and some variants prescribed a substantial lift-off into positive territory by 2014, which is a good bit ahead of the tightening from the end of 2016 onwards. Raising rates earlier could have helped reduce the buildup of risks in the financial sector from the long period of low interest rates.

TABLE 4.3. The Fed's Postpandemic Rules Menu.

Taylor (1993a) rule	$R_t^{T93} = r_t^{LR} + \pi_t + 0.5(\pi_t - \pi^{LR}) + (u_t^{LR} - u_t)$
Balanced-approach rule	$R_t^{BA} = r_t^{LR} + \pi_t + 0.5(\pi_t - \pi^{LR}) + 2(u_t^{LR} - u_t)$
Balanced-approach (shortfalls) rule	$R_t^{BAS} = r_t^{LR} + \pi_t + 0.5(\pi_t - \pi^{LR}) + 2min\{(u_t^{LR} - u_t), 0\}$
Taylor (1993a) adjusted	$R_t^{T93adj} = max\{R_t^{T93} - Z_t, ELB\}$
First-difference rule	$R_t^{FD} = R_{t-1} + 0.5(\pi_t + \pi^{LR}) + (u_t^{LR} - u_t) - (u_{t-4}^{LR} - u_{t-4})$

Note: For variable definitions please see the note to table 4.2.

From COVID-19 to the Inflation Surge and How to Get Back on Track

Following the Federal Reserve's strategy review that was completed in August 2020, the rules menu was changed. The price-level gap version of the Taylor rule was dropped. Instead, a balanced-approach (shortfalls) rule was added. This rule implemented the newly adopted concept that the Fed would only respond to shortfalls from maximum employment. Hence, the rule reacts when the unemployment rate exceeds the estimate of the long-run natural rate but not when it falls below that estimate. Table 4.3 and figure 4.6, respectively, show the Fed's postpandemic rules menu and the resulting federal funds rate prescriptions (see Federal Reserve Board 2023).

Figure 4.6 focuses on the years 2017 to 2023. There are two major events driving the federal funds rate prescriptions—the start of the pandemic in 2020 and the surge of inflation from 2021 onwards. As a result, the Taylor prescriptions dropped deeply into negative territory in 2020 and then quickly rose to high positive levels in 2021, reaching about 7% by 2022.

The pandemic caused a deep but short-lived recession in the first half of 2020. GDP declined by about 10% in the first two quarters of the year and quickly recovered after that. The unemployment rate rose from 3.5% in February 2020 to 14.7% in April 2020. By the

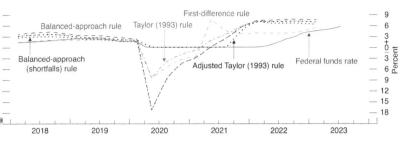

FIGURE 4.6. Federal Funds Rate Prescriptions from the Postpandemic Rules Menu.

Notes: The rules use historical values of core personal consumption expenditures inflation, the unemployment rate, and, where applicable, historical values of the midpoint of the target range for the federal funds rate. Quarterly projections of longer-run values for the federal funds rate and the unemployment rate used in the computation of the rules' prescriptions are derived through interpolations of biannual projections from Blue Chip Economic Indicators. The longer-run value for inflation is set to 2%. The rules' prescriptions are quarterly, and the federal funds rate data are the monthly average of the daily midpoint of the target range for the federal funds rate.

Sources: Federal Reserve Board (2020), from Federal Reserve Bank of Philadelphia; Wolters Kluwer, Blue Chip Economic Indicators; Federal Reserve Board staff estimates.

end of the year, it returned to 6.7%. The resulting unemployment gap is huge. Accordingly, the Taylor (1993a) rule in the Fed's chart called for a federal funds rate of −8.5% and the balanced-approach rule for a rate of −17% in the second quarter of 2020. For comparison, the output gap calculated by the Congressional Budget Office dropped to −11% in the second quarter of 2020. Hence, a Taylor rule computed based on such output gaps would also have called for a deeply negative federal funds rate.

Since negative rates are not possible on this scale, this could be interpreted as a call for massive quantitative easing and fiscal support. And this is indeed what happened. Purchases of government debt and other assets boosted the Fed balance sheet from about 20% to 35% of GDP. Furthermore, the Trump and Biden administrations implemented fiscal transfers—in particular, to the unemployed—on a scale never seen before.[3] Personal current transfer receipts rose from \$3.2 trillion to \$5.6 trillion, a 70% increase in the second quarter of 2020, and again from \$3.8 trillion to \$6 trillion in the first quarter of 2021 (a 60% increase). In parallel and partly as a consequence, US personal income rose from \$19 trillion in the first quarter of 2020 to \$20.5 trillion in the second quarter (a 7.6% increase) and from \$19.8 trillion to \$22.1 trillion in the first quarter of 2021 (an 11.6% increase). Essentially, these fiscal interventions were money financed. The same occurred in other advanced economies. The governments issued debt, but central banks bought up the debt, issuing money instead and thereby increasing their balance sheets. Thus, there was a major money-financed stimulus in the United States and other advanced economies.

Interestingly, the unprecedented deep recession and output gap did not cause a comparable drop in the inflation rate into negative territory. In the United States, inflation measured by the consumer price index (CPI) or personal consumption expenditures index (PCE) briefly fell to about half a percentage point in the first half of 2020. Then it rose again and reached 5.7 % (PCE) and 6.7% (CPI) by the end of 2021. The Russian attack on Ukraine in February 2022 and the ensuing energy crisis only added more fuel to the fire that had started before. At this point, one may well ask whether the expansionary monetary and fiscal interventions were not excessive. Similarly, one may question whether the huge resource gaps were plausible indicators of the actual divergence of aggregate demand and aggregate supply in 2020, given that they used trend-based measures for the supply side.

It is important to recognize that the pandemic had a similar impact on aggregate demand and supply. As consumers and workers feared infection with COVID-19, they reduced contact-intensive consumption and work hours. Employers shut down contact-intensive production to avoid the spread of the pandemic at the workplace, dismissed workers, or let them work from home if possible. Governments implemented lockdowns to further reduce the risk of infections. Consequently, both demand and supply of contact-intensive goods and services moved in lockstep, first sharply down and then back up. These behavioral responses are also embedded in the new class of epidemic-macro models. Such models incorporate the dynamics of a pandemic in a DSGE framework with forward-looking and optimizing households and firms. A new model database developed by a team led by Mathias Trabandt and myself allows for the simulation and reproduction of many of these models.[4] Here, I use the New Keynesian macro-epi model of Eichenbaum, Rebelo, and Trabandt (2022) to simulate the impact of an epidemic on the output gap, inflation, and interest rates under a Taylor rule. Figure 4.7 shows the outcomes given the initial spread of infections and parameterizations of the model authors. The x-axis for each panel represents the timeline in weeks. To lower the risk of infection, consumers and workers reduce consumption and work hours. GDP declines by about 8%, similar to the 2020 recession. As the infected recover and the spread of the pandemic ends, consumption and hours worked rise again quickly.

Interestingly, inflation only declines by a little more than half a percentage point. This is rather surprising given the deep recession of more than 8% of GDP relative to the steady-state level of GDP. However, this corresponds rather well with the actual impact of the COVID-19 pandemic on inflation in 2020. The reason is that aggregate supply declines almost as much as aggregate demand. The relevant gap is defined in the model as the difference between the so-called flexible-price level of GDP, that is, the level of economic output that would be realized if the price level were completely flexible. It differs from actual GDP in the model due to price rigidities arising from staggered wage and price contracts. The middle-right panel shows both measures together

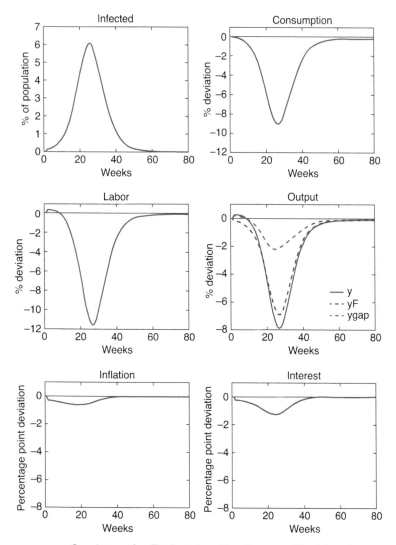

FIGURE 4.7. Simulation of an Epidemic in a New Keynesian Epi-Macro Model.
Source: Epidemic-Macro Model Data Base, https://www.epi-mmb.com.

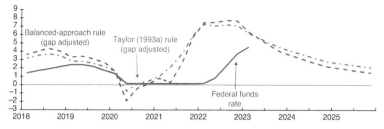

FIGURE 4.8. Taylor Rule with Adjusted Pandemic Output Gap and FOMC Projections.
Source: Author's calculations.

with the resulting output gap, which falls to about −1% at the depth of the recession. This output gap is included in the Taylor rule. Hence the prescribed interest rate cut is little more than one percentage point.

From the perspective of the analysis with the macro-epi model, the resource gap used in the Fed's rule menu during the coronavirus pandemic should be adjusted to better reflect the largely parallel movement of demand and supply. Figure 4.8 replicates two of the rules from the Fed's menu with the unemployment gap in 2020 adjusted by a factor of one-eighth. The rules are then projected forward for the remainder of 2023 to 2026 using the FOMC's projections for inflation and the unemployment rate.

The two rules still prescribe a monetary policy easing in 2020. The federal funds rate prescriptions briefly turn negative at −1% and −2%, respectively. This can still be interpreted as a call for quantitative easing at the time of the recession. Yet, it is much less pronounced than in the chart shown in the Fed's monetary policy report. The federal funds rate prescriptions quickly return to positive territory. In 2021, the prescribed federal funds rates rose quite rapidly along with inflation. The main driver is the Taylor principle embodied in both policy rules. The central bank needs to tighten interest rates more than one-for-one with inflation or inflation expectations to bring inflation back under control.

Importantly, the rules clearly signaled the need to tighten policy well ahead of the Fed's decision to increase the federal funds rate in spring 2022. Again, the Taylor rule proved its usefulness as a guidepost for monetary policy. If the Fed had responded to the rise of inflation earlier than it did, it could have spread the tightening over a longer period. This might have made it easier for the financial sector to adjust to higher interest rates, for example, by allowing banks more time to strengthen capital and liquidity positions and to account for potential losses due to asset price reversals. Thus, the financial sector could have been better positioned to weather the troubles we observed in spring 2023.

At this point, the federal funds rate prescriptions shown in figure 4.8 have been stabilizing at a high level thanks to the slowdown in inflation. Since the summer of 2022, the Fed has moved rapidly, bringing the federal funds rate closer to the rule's prescriptions. Additional tightening may still be necessary, as the trend change in headline inflation is not yet reflected in core inflation.

Looking forward, the FOMC projections for inflation and unemployment rates indicate that Taylor rule prescriptions could soon decline. Of course, this depends on whether the US economy proceeds along the path predicted by these projections. Importantly, the speed of decline also depends on the long-run projections for inflation and interest rates that signal FOMC members' perspectives on steady-state growth and real interest rates. At this point, the relevant estimate of the long-run real interest rate, the so-called r-star, embodied in the FOMC projections remains rather low. The median is 0.5%. If the economy returns to a higher trend growth path, the equilibrium real interest rate could well be higher. In this case, such Taylor rule projections would not decline as far, as figure 4.8 suggests.

In sum, even after thirty years, the Taylor rule remains a very useful guidepost to help the Fed get back on track, and it is encouraging that the Fed keeps including such policy rules in its official communications.

References

Adjemian, Stéphane, Houtan Bastani, Michel Juillard, Frédéric Karamé, Ferhat Mihoubi, Willi Mutschler, Johannes Pfeifer, Marco Ratto, Normann Rion, and Sébastien Villemot. 2022. "Dynare: Reference Manual, Version 5." Dynare Working Papers, Centre pour la recherche économique et ses applications (CEPREMAP).

Bryant, Ralph C., Peter Hooper, and Catherine L. Mann, eds. 1993. *Evaluating Policy Regimes*. Washington, DC: Brookings Institution.

Christiano, Lawrence, Martin Eichenbaum, and Charles Evans. 2005. "Nominal Rigidities and the Dynamic Effects of a Shock to Monetary Policy." *Journal of Political Economy* 113, no. 1 (February): 1–45.

Cochrane, John H., John B. Taylor, and Volker Wieland. 2020. "Evaluating Rules in the Fed's Report and Measuring Discretion." Chapter 5 in *Strategies for Monetary Policy*, edited by John H. Cochrane and John B. Taylor, 217–58. Stanford, CA: Hoover Institution Press.

Eichenbaum, Martin, Sergio Rebelo, and Mathias Trabandt. 2022. "Epidemics in the New Keynesian Model." *Journal of Economic Dynamics and Control* 140 (July): 1–19.

Fair, Ray, and John B. Taylor. 1983. "Solution and Maximum Likelihood Estimation of Dynamic Nonlinear Rational Expectations Models." *Econometrica* 51, no. 4 (July): 1169–85.

Federal Reserve Board. 2020. *Monetary Policy Report*, February.

———. 2023. *Monetary Policy Report*, July.

Levin, Andrew, Volker Wieland, and John C. Williams. 1999. "Robustness of Simple Monetary Policy Rules under Model Uncertainty." In *Monetary Policy Rules*, edited by John B. Taylor, 263–318. Chicago: University of Chicago Press.

———. 2003. "The Performance of Forecast-Based Monetary Policy Rules under Model Uncertainty." *American Economic Review* 93, no. 3 (June): 622–45.

Orphanides, Athanasios, and Volker Wieland. 2013. "Complexity and Monetary Policy." *International Journal of Central Banking* 9, no. 1 (January): 167–204.

Smets, Frank, and Raf Wouters. 2003. "An Estimated Stochastic Dynamic General Equilibrium Model of the Euro Area." *Journal of the European Economic Association* 1, no. 5 (September): 1123–75.

———. 2007. "Shocks and Frictions in US Business Cycles: A Bayesian DSGE Approach." *American Economic Review* 97, no. 3 (June): 586–606.

Taylor, John B. 1979. "Estimation and Control of a Macroeconomic Model with Rational Expectations." *Econometrica* 47, no. 5 (September): 1267–86.

———. 1980. "Aggregate Dynamics and Staggered Contracts." *Journal of Political Economy* 88, no. 1 (February): 1–23.

———. 1993a. "Discretion versus Policy Rules in Practice." *Carnegie-Rochester Conference Series on Public Policy* 39: 195–214. Amsterdam: North-Holland.

———. 1993b. *Macroeconomic Policy in a World Economy: From Econometric Design to Practical Operation*. New York: W. W. Norton.

———. 2007. "Housing and Monetary Policy." In *Housing, Housing Finance, and Monetary Policy*, proceedings of Jackson Hole (Wyoming) Economic Policy Symposium hosted by the Federal Reserve Bank of Kansas City, September.

Taylor, John B., and Volker Wieland. 2012. "Surprising Comparative Properties of Monetary Models: Results from a New Model Database." *Review of Economics and Statistics* 94, no. 3 (August): 800–816

Wieland, Volker, Elena Afanasyeva, Meguy Kuete, and Jinhyuk Yoo. 2016. "New Methods for Macro-Financial Model Comparisons and Policy Analysis." In *Handbook of Macroeconomics 2*, edited by John B. Taylor and Harald Uhlig, 1241–319. Amsterdam: Elsevier.

Notes

1. All quotes found at Nobel Prize website, https://www.nobelprize.org /prizes/lists/all-prizes-in-economic-sciences.

2. This software tool and model archive, which contains more than 150 macroeconomic models is described in Wieland et al. (2016) and available from https://www.macromodelbase.com.

3. Starting in March 2020, the Coronavirus Aid, Relief, and Economic Security Act (CARES Act) provided onetime Economic Impact Payments of up to $1,200 per adult for eligible individuals and $500 per qualifying child under age 17. The payments were reduced for individuals with adjusted gross income (AGI) greater than $75,000 ($150,000 for

married couples filing a joint return). For a family of four, these Economic Impact Payments provided up to $3,400 of direct financial relief. Two subsequent rounds of such payments followed in December 2020 and March 2021. See US Department of the Treasury, "Policy Issues" at https://home.treasury.gov, accessed July 22, 2023.

4. The Epidemic-Macro Model Data Base is available at https://www.epi -mmb.com. Epidemic dynamics introduce a crucial nonlinearity in the macro-epi model. Hence the simulations require a nonlinear solution method. The macro-epi model database uses a version of the Fair and Taylor (1983) method that is implemented in the Dynare model solution software (see Adjemian et al. 2022, 72; and Dynare website, https://www .dynare.org).

GENERAL DISCUSSION

JOHN COCHRANE (INTRODUCTION): That was wonderful. Thanks to Condi [Rice] for reminding us that we're lucky to study easy questions like inflation and bank runs.

This is the panel on the Taylor rule at thirty, celebrating John [Taylor]'s 1993 paper "Discretion versus Policy Rules in Practice."

Disclaimer: John didn't want us to do this. This was Mike Bordo's idea, my enthusiastic second, and John's reluctant, "Okay, if you guys really have to." John's a very modest guy, but we can't not celebrate this moment.

What is the Taylor rule? If inflation rises one percentage point, central banks should raise interest rates by about 1.5 percentage points, and if the output gap rises one percentage point, they should raise interest rates a half a percentage point. Like all great ideas, this one had precursors. Knut Wicksell wrote a book in the 1890s with something like that idea in it, in complicated German prose. The Bank of England long raised interest rates to defend the gold standard. Bennett McCallum showed in 1981 how interest rates that rise more than one-for-one with inflation solve a multiple-equilibrium problem of rational expectations models, and that principle was well embedded in New Keynesian models by the early 1990s. John had already contributed to that. But this paper is what really made the Taylor rule important and brought it to life.

What's important about the Taylor rule? First, the previous nearly universal doctrine was that the central bank cannot and should not target interest rates. In his famous 1968 AEA [American Economic Association] address, Milton Friedman said that the economy is unstable under an interest rate target. Try it, and inflation will blow up. Target money growth. [Thomas] Sargent and [Neil] Wallace, in 1975, wrote that an interest rate target will lead to indeterminacy, sunspots, and multiple equilibria.[1] Target money growth instead.

But the Fed and other central banks don't target money growth. They target interest rates and have done so for decades.

How does our world work? Well, the Taylor rule, raising interest rates more than one-for-one with inflation, repairs both Friedman's and Sargent and Wallace's problems. In these theories, the Taylor rule leads to an economy that is both stable and determinate. The Taylor rule was the central ingredient that we need to add to all preexisting theories to even talk about central banks that target interest rates, which our central banks do. So it was a great theoretical advance.

The Taylor rule is also, and perhaps primarily, empirical. John's 1993 paper was primarily about empirical and historical work. John noticed that in periods like the 1980s, with good macroeconomic performance, interest rates hewed pretty closely to the Taylor rule, while in periods like the 1970s, with recessions and inflation, interest rates did not respond as much to inflation. Many others refined these observations. Rich Clarida is here, and he, Jordi Galí, and Mark Gertler wrote a very famous paper showing, by careful regressions, that when the Fed started following a Taylor rule in the 1980s, the inflation got much better.

John's 1993 paper really brought the Taylor rule from theory and from an empirical characterization to a prescription. It was not just, this is how the Fed has behaved when times have been good, but how the Fed should behave. The crucial part is the second part of the title, "in practice." John showed in simple terms how the Taylor rule should work.

A deeply important feature of the Taylor rule is that it is robust. It is not just the optimal rule in a particular model or class of models, and thus dependent on that model's particular assumptions. In fact, the Taylor rule is not optimal in most models. Most models have complicated optimal rules but very different rules across models. The Taylor rule, by contrast, is pretty darn good in all models. Old-fashioned IS-LM models? The Taylor rule is pretty darn good. New Keynesian rational expectations models, which are totally different? The Taylor rule is still pretty darn good but for totally different reasons. I now do fiscal theory of the price level, a third category of model. Guess what? Though fiscal theory is a totally different model, the Taylor rule is pretty darn good, again.

Is the Taylor rule a "rule?" Well, it's sort of a rule and sort of not a rule. One of the great calumnies that John has had to fight against for thirty years is that he says, "Just replace the Fed with a computer." No. One of the most important and unsung parts of John's advocacy of the rule is his view of how it should be used and implemented. It's not a mechanical rule. It's a strategy. It's a benchmark. It gives the Fed accountability and predictability. It helps communication. Sure, deviate from the rule, but explain why and when you will come back to the rule. People think that economics is hard because of the equations. They're wrong. Translating the equations and adapting them to practical policy advice is the hard part. John's advocacy of the rule as part of a realistic monetary policy strategy is, I think, one of his greatest contributions and that of the 1993 paper.

But yes, it is a "rule" in that it's there to help guide expectations. We all understand that inflation is quiet when people know what to expect of the Fed. If we live in a society with stable institutions and know what to expect of the future, things are much better today. I think this is the general point and might summarize what Condi was just saying about foreign policy.

So it is a "rule" in that sense. The Taylor rule replaces a money-growth rule or a gold standard as a way of telling people, over

the long run, what the Fed is going to do. It's also precommitment. Milton Friedman had the great analogy of a shower where
you turn on the water and it gets too hot, then you turn it off
and it gets too cold. That's discretion. And a lot of John's point
was that rules, rather than discretion, are a "rule" in the sense
they precommit the Fed to do things that it might not want to
do ex post.

A rule is like a mandate. As you know, the Fed has a mandate:
pay attention to inflation and employment. These happen to be
pretty much the things in the Taylor rule—employment statistics and John's output gap work in just about the same way. A
mandate tells the Fed the things it should pay attention to but
also all the things the Fed should not pay attention to. Limited
scope is vital for an independent agency in a democracy. The
Taylor rule does much of the same, quantitatively. Yes, focus on
inflation and output. But ignore the hundreds of problems that
occupy Fed officials and tempt them to economic and financial
fine-tuning or micro-planning.

The Taylor rule is, of course, amazingly influential. Andy
Levin remarked that it has achieved the final measure of economic immortality: like the Modigliani-Miller theorem or
Black-Scholes formula, you refer to the Taylor rule without the
date following the name. And that's why we're here. The Taylor
rule is at the heart of all monetary economics that talks about
central banks with interest rate targets, which is how our central
banks do things. It's at the heart of all our current understanding
and doctrines of how central banks should operate when they're
doing things well. And we come together once a year to remind
central banks of that fact.

But it's not an eternal verity, not quite yet ready to be carved in
marble on the front of the Hoover Institution next to $MV = PY$.
How do we use the Taylor rule today? How does its advice
adapt to different shocks—financial, fiscal, real, pandemic, trade

shocks—different conditions and an evolving economy—low real interest rates, changing measures of natural unemployment or potential output, the zero bound, and so forth? How quickly should the interest rate follow the rule—how "inertial" should the rule be, and how much should it weight the previous [federal] funds rate? How do we interpret evolving history and experience? We are here again today to debate active research questions, not just to once a year say, "Fed, follow the Taylor rule!"

So with that preamble, let's go. I think I'll take it in the order we've got here. Rich [Clarida], why don't you go next, and then John [Lipsky] and then Volker [Wieland]?

* * *

COCHRANE: Great job, panelists. We have time for questions. We'll take two or three questions and then give quick responses so that everyone gets a chance.

HARALD UHLIG: Harald Uhlig from the University of Chicago. The relationship between the Taylor rule and the federal funds rate right now is very interesting. Let me make a back-of-the-envelope calculation. Inflation is around 5%, and the federal funds rate is around 5%. That means that the real rate is currently around zero. This strikes me as considerably below a neutral level. Of course, one may wish to appeal to interest rate smoothing, as you showed, Richard [Clarida]. Still, when Paul Volcker fought inflation in the early 1980s, he chose to set the funds rate to a much higher number. Of course, if one follows a policy of raising the federal funds substantially now, I can see inflation coming down and, therefore, the nominal interest rates coming down eventually. But I am wondering whether in order to get back on track, we need to first raise the federal funds rate considerably more than where it currently stands. And it looks to me like the Taylor rule tells us that we ought to do that.

DAVID PAPELL: I'd like to highlight the differences between, on the one hand, inertial and noninertial rules and, on the other hand, Taylor rules and balanced-approach rules. With both Rich Clarida's results for inertial rules and Volker Wieland's results for noninertial rules, there is not much difference between Taylor rules and balanced-approach rules. While the difference between the two rules was important after 2009, what is important now is the difference between noninertial and inertial rules. At the time of lift-off from the effective lower bound in March 2022, the prescriptions with the inertial rules were about 200 basis points above the actual federal funds rate while the prescriptions with the noninertial rules were about 800 basis points above the actual rate.

As of March 2023, while the prescriptions with the noninertial rules were still about 250 basis points above the federal funds rate, the prescriptions with the inertial rules were actually 25 basis points below the rate. The large gaps with inertial rules are completely gone. As Rich Clarida showed, the Taylor rule prescriptions are very close to the federal funds rate projections for 2023 and equal to the projections in 2024 and 2025.

COCHRANE: Let's take responses quickly. We have current policy, real rates are still negative, why is inflation going down, and accounting for where is the Fed in real-time inertial versus noninertial rules?

RICHARD CLARIDA: I'll be very quick. The practice is typically to think about policy options in the inertial space, both because that describes past history pretty well—that was my work twenty years ago—and also because it has some desirable properties in a lot of models, because you basically get the bond market to do your work for you.

But you're right. It makes a big difference initially in terms of measuring how far behind the curve the central bank is, and this is crucially dependent on what is the benchmark rule. I'll just leave it at that.

VOLKER WIELAND: As Harald said, if you use an ex-post short-term real interest rate, we're just at zero. So that doesn't seem like that much, and would call for raising it more. If you instead plug in a near-term inflation forecast, say market based or the Fed's forecast, you're in positive territory. In terms of risk management, the bigger risk right now is not to have inflation come down. The relevant measure is core inflation. Core inflation is about 5.5% in the United States and also in the euro area. But the difference between the US and the euro area is that headline inflation is still higher in the euro area, and core inflation hasn't declined. In the US, there has been some decline followed by stagnation of core inflation. So I think right now policymakers should really look at core inflation.

In Frankfurt, I keep referring to the Fed positively, because the ECB policy rate is still at 3.25% while we also have 5.5% core inflation. And now with the banking stress, it's harder to raise policy rates. So the ECB is even further behind. At the ECB, they shouldn't be talking about pausing. In my view, they need to get up to 4 or 5%.

It is interesting to compare the current situation to 1973 by aligning the attack on Ukraine with the Yom Kippur War in 1973. That was the attack on Israel and the oil embargo. When you do that, you'll find that in the period before the start of the war, policy was much more expansionary in the current episode. That is because in 2021, inflation was rising, while interest rates were kept constant. Thus, real rates fell in 2021. Yet in 2022, there was a very sharp rise in the nominal rate, which brings the real rate back to at least zero. Policy is much more reactive in the current episode than in 1973–74, not in terms of the level but in terms of the steepness of the rate rise.

COCHRANE: Sebastian, you're next.

SEBASTIAN EDWARDS: Sebastian Edwards. That was very interesting. I assign a number of John [Taylor]'s works to my students. And every year since 2009, the piece they like the most is a little book called *Getting Off Track*. So John was worrying about that since that time. And in it is the famous graph that shows that the Fed got behind the curve, and that generated the construction boom and made the crisis much worse.

But then [Alan] Greenspan went out and said, "Well, that's the conundrum." And we did hike rates eventually. And nothing happened to the ten-year rate, which is really the one that matters as a transmission mechanism. So many people. And many of my students at the time were saying, "Well, maybe the Taylor rule is still a nice rule. But since there is a conundrum, which is here to stay because of the saving gluts or whatever, the Taylor rule has lost its power." And now we see that the rate has gone up by—the federal funds rate—by almost as much as at that time, 500 basis points. And there's no conundrum. The ten-year has gone up by 300 basis points. Right? So what's the difference between now and then, and why? So that's what I think is an interesting question and would like to take advantage of this great panel to have some comments on that.

COCHRANE: Andy Levin.

ANDREW LEVIN: I'm Andrew Levin from Dartmouth College. I just want to add a couple of facts to the really great comments by the panelists. John Cochrane has mentioned Google citations. I think what marks a truly monumental work is the point at which people don't even bother to include the citation. It's sufficient to simply say "the Taylor rule," and everyone knows what you're talking about. So those references to the Taylor rule aren't even counted as Google Scholar citations.

For example, in 2007, the Dallas Fed held a conference in honor of John Taylor. Don Kohn, who was at the time the vice chair of the Federal Reserve, gave a talk entitled "Taylor Rules Rule." And at that time, we used a Google search and found that tens of millions of web pages contained the phrase "Taylor rule." At this point, about fifteen years later, I'm guessing that the tally is probably "billions and billions," kind of like McDonald's hamburgers.

In fact, Google now has a feature called "trends," which indicates that the trend in searches for the phrase "Taylor rule" is now at an all-time high. That's really remarkable, because lots of Nobel Prize–winning papers have been influential for a decade or two and then kind of faded away, whereas John Taylor's work continues to rise in importance.

Now, elaborating on John Lipsky's comments, it's essential to remind everyone about John Taylor's business card. In the 1990s, John Taylor had the Stanford Business Card Office add the Taylor rule to the back of his business cards. And so every time he would meet with people in the private sector, you know, he'd flip over the card and give a brief explanation of the Taylor rule. And that played a significant role in its rapid dissemination. Indeed, those business cards should be kept in mind in documenting the history of the Taylor rule.

COCHRANE: Chris Erceg.

CHRISTOPHER ERCEG:[2] This was a very interesting panel. There's clearly a lot of interest in how monetary policy should respond to financial conditions. Last fall, we saw that financial conditions eased despite very tight monetary policy, which was somewhat surprising, and subsequently have seen some tightening of financial conditions, especially in the last couple of months. So with that in mind, I was wondering about your perspectives on a spread-adjusted Taylor rule. The difference would be that relative to the original Taylor rule, monetary policy would ease preemptively if financial conditions tightened and credit spreads rose in order to insulate output and inflation from the shock. Thanks.

COCHRANE: While the microphone makes it over to that side of the room, I would summarize: We have a conundrum. Should Taylor rules pay attention to long-term interest rates, which reveal inflation expectations, or interest rates with default spreads in them, which of course are what matter for borrowing? And have interest rates lost their power to do much these days?

CLARIDA: Okay, I'll jump in quickly. Excellent points. I've had many—thought a lot about them. I get nervous, and especially after my time with the Fed, I get nervous about getting too high frequency on the r-stars, you know, because in my mind, in [Michael] Woodford model's r-star changes every second, right? So I like to have, in my own mind, think of an anchor, for communication. I do agree that you can't take a stand on a neutral policy rate even in a steady state unless you have a view on the equilibrium term. Because no one borrows at the federal funds rate except people who shouldn't, right? But everybody who borrows does so at five, ten years and so, you know, I would get nervous about the term-*premium move* today. Let's change policy, but having a view of what is the steady-state anchor, you do. And then that gets into the conundrum situation. Right?

So, the conundrum was, we did this on the federal funds rate, but the steady-state term premium is lower, and I think that is relevant. To me, you want to put it in a real model, but at some sense in a steady-state condition that the term premium is higher, you can get by with a shorter riskless short rate, because the term premium is doing some of your work and vice versa. One thing with expected inflation, it's a little bit easier than it was when we started. There is a TIPS [Treasury Inflation-Protected Securities] market. Your real-rate interest rates on a TIP now are 1.8%. So yeah, Michigan Survey, Survey of Professional Forecasters. We can start with market-based real rates and they are 1.8% right now.

COCHRANE: Brian Sack and then Mike Boskin.

BRIAN SACK: Hi, I'm Brian Sack, no affiliation at the moment. So I want to ask a question, and it's been covered here a little bit. I understand the advantages of the Taylor rule are its simplicity and its robustness. But if you could choose one variable to add to your policy rule, I'm curious what it would be. I think some of the other questions maybe provide some potential answers— from Sebastian, maybe it's term premia or longer-term interest rates; from Chris, maybe it's the financial conditions index–type measure. But more broadly, are those what you would add, or would you add something else?

MICHAEL BOSKIN: I just wanted to add a few reflections, and then second the question about credit conditions, or ask you to go a little bit deeper into that. But I was really appreciative of his former students talking about its intellectual history, because the Taylor rule didn't come out of nothing. Actually, John's thesis advisor was T. W. Anderson, a very famous time-series statistician, who also taught economics. And so from early on, he was interested in this interaction of econometric estimation, dynamic model solution, and policy evaluation.

I think it's also worth mentioning that he had an association with Alan Greenspan when he was in New York and had conversations with him. He had long conversations with Milton [Friedman], which turned into arguments about what the proper rule was, and so on. He also wrote a very important chapter in the Economic Report of the President when he was on the CEA [Council of Economic Advisers], which, as I understand it, was the first mention that monetary policy should be rules based. That was the formulation we came up with, it wasn't whether it was a specific rule but whether it should be anchored in a rule. And we got feedback from the Fed when we circulated the chapter that wasn't complimentary, but we included it anyway.

I then would add, he wrote a very prominent principles book and started teaching simple macroeconomics in Econ 1 with an embedded monetary policy rule. And I think that was really, really important, because most of macroeconomics was done—here's what's going on, now the Fed will do something. There was no interaction at all. And I thought that was really important. I used that book when I taught Econ 1 some years ago, and it was, I think, a big teaching breakthrough.

There are many things I could go on about, but I think it's really important to emphasize that this has been a continuum, and the Taylor rule—as tremendously important as it is, and by the way as deserving of a Nobel Prize—I think it's important to realize this, what he's done continuing in that, and continues to teach, continues to do research. The one part I want to emphasize that hasn't been mentioned, coming primarily from the fiscal side myself, is that John, John Cogan, and Volker wrote an important paper, remarkable in real time, they estimated the government expenditure multiplier coming from the 2009 stimulus of about 0.6. That's exactly the number that Valerie Ramey came up with a decade later in an exhaustive meta-analysis of all the research that had been done in the years following, which she called the renaissance of fiscal research. So they nailed it in real time, which is very, very impressive.

COCHRANE: Thank you, Mike. I guess we have to close, so we'll do a lightning round. If you get to add one variable to the Taylor rule, which would it be? And "none" is also an acceptable answer!

WIELAND: I think it does make sense to include first-difference rules in the menu of rules, even if they're not as robust. So that would be adding the lagged interest rate. Because if you do that, then you don't need a view of where the long-run equilibrium is, which can also lead you off track.

JOHN LIPSKY: And my answer is: none. But please let me add two thoughts. First, apologies, I didn't mention the card. However, the main point is that the Taylor rule became so prominent so quickly not via advertising but because it was so powerful conceptually and so useful practically. Almost immediately, everyone started asking each other to use it as a benchmark. The speed of its spread was incredible and essentially unprecedented, in my experience. I would also like to add that it seems we're still grappling with how to interpret the effects of the imposed economic shutdown in response to the pandemic. At this time, goods prices in the United States are increasing on the margin by less than 2% at an annual rate. Rent is a problematic measure; we know the data are backward looking. If anybody's in the property market, they know that rents and house prices at present are going down, not up. The real crux of the matter right now is to try to understand the labor market data. It appears that the labor share of GDP has been declining. In that case, how are wages causing inflation? And many indicators, including the TIPS market, suggest that wage pressures are expected to fade away, essentially on their own. I think most analysts don't agree with that expectation. Just parenthetically, most analysts and most models haven't had a very good recent run with regard to their forecasts of inflation, among other things. So, we'll see.

CLARIDA: I'll shake it up. I would drop a variable. It's so hard to measure potential output, it can lead to such mischief. Clarida, Galí, Gertler said you can do very well if you just focus on getting r-star right and getting inflation right.[3] If we knew the output gap, of course, you can put it in, but we don't. And as I said, it can lead to mischief. So I would just drop it.

COCHRANE: An inflation target! All right. Thank you very much. We'll move on to the next panel.

Notes

1. Thomas J. Sargent and Neil Wallace, "'Rational' Expectations, the Optimal Monetary Instrument, and the Optimal Money Supply Rule," *Journal of Political Economy* 83, no. 2 (April 1975): 241–54.

2. The views expressed in this discussion are those of the author and do not necessarily represent the views of the IMF, its Executive Board, or IMF management.

3. Richard Clarida, Jordi Galí, and Mark Gertler, "The Science of Monetary Policy: A New Keynesian Perspective," *Journal of Economic Literature* 37, no. 4 (December 1999): 1661–707.

FINANCIAL REGULATION:
SILICON VALLEY BANK AND BEYOND

5

Silicon Valley Bank and Beyond: Regulating for Liquidity

Darrell Duffie

Thanks for the opportunity to speak with you all today about what we have learned from recent banking failures. First, however, I want to add my congratulations to John Taylor on the thirtieth anniversary of the Taylor rule.

As Professor Anat Admati emphasized in her presentation, we have learned a lot of lessons in the last couple of months about weaknesses in the regulation and supervision of banks. The failures of post-financial-crisis regulation and supervision of banks pretty much cover the gamut. These are quite disappointing and implicate regulatory frameworks for failure resolution and capital sufficiency. In the area of capital requirements, we saw failures of stress testing, disclosure, and accounting—the entire capital regime. Let's just stipulate, as Professor Admati has, that this was a solvency crisis.

However, I want to focus on what has been revealed by recent events about weaknesses in liquidity regulation. This is not to suggest that liquidity was the cause of the failure of these banks. The cause was insufficient capital. However, as shown in figure 5.1, which appeared in the Federal Reserve's May 2023 *Financial Stability Report*, we've also learned that depositors at large banks are likely to flee from a bank much more quickly now than they have in prior bank runs. You can see on this chart, for each of the largest bank failures of recent decades, the largest one-day deposit outflows. In the cases of Signature Bank and Silicon Valley Bank [SVB], more

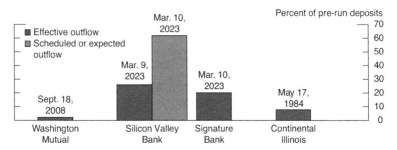

FIGURE 5.1. One-Day Deposit Outflows during Several Large Bank Failures. In the case of Silicon Valley Bank, more deposits left in a single day than the Fed's liquidity coverage ratio (LCR) rule had anticipated would leave in an entire month.

Source: *Financial Stability Report*, Board of Governors of the Federal Reserve, May 2023.

deposits left in a single day than the Fed's liquidity coverage ratio (LCR) rule had anticipated would leave in an entire month. What has changed the speed with which uninsured or large depositors might run, and what can the Federal Reserve do about this?

According to analysis released last week by Jason Goldberg, senior equity research analyst of Barclays, over the previous decade, there has been a huge increase in online banking and an even larger increase in mobile banking.[1] For just three large US banks, the number of mobile banking customers increased from about twenty million to roughly 120 million over the last twelve years. That's remarkable. Aided by other technology, including social media such as Twitter [X], large wholesale depositors are now connected to one another and to the news, while digital banking technology gives them the ability to move their money nearly instantly. And this is exactly what we saw at SVB and Signature Bank. People are not lining up outside the banks as they were in past classic bank runs.

Consider the hypothetical bank whose assets and liabilities are depicted in figure 5.2. This is not intended to represent any particular bank. This bank has a large amount of wholesale deposits, essentially uninsured, as well as some insured deposits and other

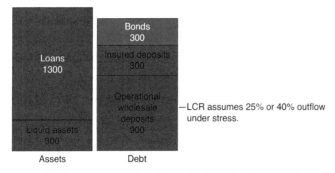

FIGURE 5.2. A Weakened Bank That Meets the Liquidity Coverage Ratio Rule. Balance sheet quantities for a hypothetical weakened bank that meets the LCR rule.

Source: Author's calculations.

liabilities. This bank is meeting the liquidity coverage ratio because, in current regulations, it's assumed that even over a thirty-day period, depending on details that we won't cover today, either 25% or 40% of these wholesale operational deposits are at risk of fleeing the bank. So, this bank seems not to require much liquidity coverage under current standards. But I showed you a moment ago (in figure 5.1) that perhaps 40% or 60% of wholesale deposits could leave in a single day. So something about liquidity regulations should be fixed.

Going forward, for the case of a solvent but weakened bank, how much liquidity, and what forms of liquidity, will be judged adequate to prevent a destructive bank run?

Banks currently meet a large part of their liquidity coverage requirements by stocking up on high-quality liquid assets (HQLA). But suppose we get much more realistic about how much coverage is required for wholesale large uninsured depositors. If we assume, as I would, that a large depositor would leave essentially instantly, then one needs roughly 100% coverage of the wholesale uninsured depositors. Some of you might find that shocking. Do we really need to zoom from about 25% liquidity coverage to 100%? There are people here today from the private sector. If one of you learned today that a bank at which you are keeping your firm's uninsured deposits is at risk, what fraction of your deposits would you choose to leave in the bank? And how many of you might be left out of the news of that event? Well, I think the answer is pretty clear. If it were me, I would almost instantly move all of my deposits. Realistic liquidity coverage for these depositors would be close to 100%. Some of you knowledgeable pragmatists in the audience might say, "That's ridiculous, because it would trap in the banking system an enormous quantity of high-quality liquid assets, which, for most of the time, are completely idle and unuseful."

An example of the negative impact of trapped HQLA occurred in September 2019 when large banks were unwilling to let go of their Federal Reserve deposits to quell a serious liquidity problem in wholesale funding markets. Overnight interest rates in Treasury repo markets went up by nearly 1,000 basis points intraday. On the JPMorgan Chase earnings call that immediately followed this crisis, CEO Jamie Dimon was asked by an analyst why he didn't invest JPMorgan Chase's enormous Federal Reserve balances into repos (repurchase agreements) to earn those high interest rates. That form of arbitrage would probably have brought the repurchase agreement market from crisis back to normalcy. In his response, Dimon referred specifically to liquidity regulations requiring large banks to cover all their intraday liquidity needs—not merely over thirty days—with their own resources.[2] The most popular liquidity source for meeting these requirements is Federal Reserve deposits. In effect, an enormous quantity of Federal Reserve deposits is now trapped by regulation. Figure 5.3 illustrates that, for adequate liquidity coverage, trillions of dollars of uninsured deposits in the US banking system would need to be covered by high-quality liquid assets, including Federal Reserve deposits. That's just not realistic—unless the Fed increases the size of its balance sheet even further.

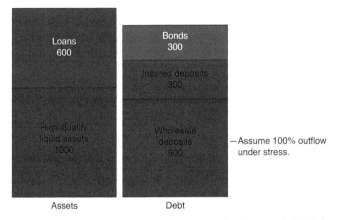

FIGURE 5.3. A Bank That Covers Realistic Deposit Outflows with HQLA.
A large quantity of HQLA is trapped on a hypothetical bank's balance sheet.
Source: Author's calculations.

What regulatory change would satisfy my suggested need to radically increase liquidity coverage while allowing for a much more realistic and useful approach for satisfying the liquidity resources needed by banks? Going back to the formation of the Federal Reserve System, a primary purpose of the Fed has been to provide crisis liquidity to banks as a lender of last resort (LOLR). In the sort of crisis that we have seen over the past two months, banks should have posted lots of their assets at the Fed's discount window to receive the liquidity they needed to cover fleeing depositors. But that was not the case. Under current regulations, lender-of-last-resort liquidity from the Fed does not count toward meeting a bank's regulatory liquidity needs. Currently, banks must be self-reliant in meeting these requirements.

That mistake has been picked up by a number of others, including my copanelist today, Randal Quarles, and Bill Nelson and in a speech he gave some years ago.[3] This approach of including LOLR support toward meeting regulatory liquidity requirements, depicted in figure 5.4, has been tried in some countries but not in the United States. This regulatory approach should be pushed forward in the

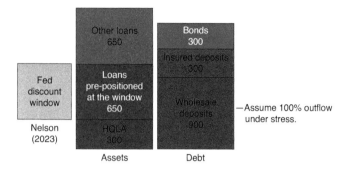

FIGURE 5.4. Proposed Higher Liquidity Coverage.
The illustrated bank ties down fewer high-quality liquid assets to meet a realistic assumption on deposit outflows by also relying on the Fed for liquidity support, pre-positioning some of its less-liquid assets at the Fed's discount window. However, access to the discount window does not count toward liquidity coverage requirements in the current regulatory framework.
Source: Author's calculations.

United States so that banks can cover the liquidity needs imposed by their depositors and, at the same time, not tie down so many high-quality liquid assets that those liquid assets are not available in sufficient quantity when needed elsewhere.

The Financial Stability Board released two reports in the last eighteen months that favorably evaluate post-financial-crisis banking regulation. However, in a quiet part of one of those reports, there is a discussion of problems associated with the "usability" of high-quality liquid assets. This brings to mind Charles Goodhart's telling of the parable of the "last taxi at the taxi stand."[4] As I'm sure almost everybody in the audience knows, this is the story of a weary traveler who has arrived at the train station and is now looking for a taxi to go home. By analogy, taxis represent high-quality liquid assets. The traveler thanks his good luck that there is indeed a taxi at the stand—but only one—and he requests a lift home. However, the taxi driver says, "No, I'm sorry, but we're required by regulation to ensure that there is always at least one taxi left at the stand in case someone arrives needing a ride." The passenger says, "Well, I'm here and ready to go home." But the taxi driver says, "No. Rules are rules; I can't take you, because there would then be no taxis left at the stand." Using this analogy, you can see that trapping a large quantity of high-quality liquid assets serves no useful purpose and involves significant costs.

The discount window is not the Fed's only source of last-resort lending. The Federal Reserve recently put a standing repo facility (SRF) in place, which could also be a useful source of liquidity for banks under stress. So far, however, many banks have not signed up for access to the SRF, and the SRF has rarely been used except in testing. My guess is that many banks haven't signed up for the SRF because that involves some costs, whereas they are not allowed to count access to the SRF toward their liquidity coverage requirements.

Thank you very much for the chance to speak with you today.

Notes

1. Jason M. Goldberg, "US Large-Cap Banks: Jason Goldberg's Bank Brief | Volume 20," Barclays Equity Research, May 2023. Totals are for Bank of America, JPMorgan Chase, and Wells Fargo.

2. Emily Barrett and Alex Harris, "Dimon Says Regulation Limited JPMorgan from Calming Repo Market," Bloomberg.com, October 15, 2019.

3. William Nelson, "Recognizing the Value of the Central Bank as a Liquidity Backstop," Staff Working Paper 2017-1, The Clearing House, January 2017.

4. Charles Goodhart, "Liquidity Risk Management," Banque de France, *Financial Stability Review*—Special Issue on Liquidity, no. 11 (February 2008): 3.

6

Silicon Valley Bank: What Happened? What Should We Do about It?

Randal Quarles

On March 10, 2023, the California Department of Financial Protection and Innovation seized Silicon Valley Bank (SVB), a state-chartered commercial bank headquartered in Santa Clara, California, with over $209 billion in assets, and appointed the Federal Deposit Insurance Corporation as receiver. On March 9, depositors of the bank had withdrawn over $40 billion of the bank's $175 billion in deposits during the course of a few hours, and on the morning of March 10, the bank and its regulators had information that the bank would lose another $100 billion in deposits before the end of the day, requiring an emergency closure. It was the second-largest bank failure in American history.

In the months since, the search for explanations has been wide ranging. There have been multiple congressional hearings, think tank white papers from across the ideological spectrum, learned commentary from a score of academics and former policymakers, and a 102-page memo from the banking system's chief regulator, Michael Barr, vice chairman for supervision of the Board of Governors of the Federal Reserve System (the "Barr Memo").[1] The analyses have been comprehensive and often quite technical, covering capital regulation, liquidity rules, and supervisory practice, and the resulting policy recommendations have been extremely varied and often highly political, from increasing the limit on deposit insurance to as much as $50 million per account to increasing capital requirements across the system by as much as 25%—recommendations that have often been quite similar to positions held by their proponents long before the failure of Silicon Valley Bank.

Lost in this surfeit of denunciation and policy entrepreneurship is a very simple story that ought to be familiar to us: well-meant but ill-calibrated and highly stimulative fiscal policy engenders serious and stubborn inflation, which causes a category of financial institutions that have particularly interest-rate-sensitive assets and highly mobile liabilities to come under great liquidity pressure as the value of their assets falls, and the cost of their liabilities rises, pressure that is exacerbated when the Fed takes sensible steps to bring that inflation under control. That was the fundamental story of the savings and loan associations in the United States: President Lyndon Johnson's "guns and butter" policy drove substantial deficits, leading to high inflation, which monetary policy was slow to contain. During the Great Inflation of the 1970s, inflation rose from about 1% in 1964 to more than 14% in 1980, driving down the value of the thirty-year mortgage assets of the country's savings and loan associations (S&Ls) and increasing their cost of funding. Many S&Ls, in turn, tried to salvage their position by taking additional risk, which ended up worsening their situation when the Federal Reserve finally began an aggressive response, driving the economy into a recession that led to large credit losses on that additional risk.

Although the assets in question are different, and the process is playing out over a couple of years rather than a couple of decades, this is almost exactly the story of SVB and the other banks that failed in the spring of 2023. Three waves of COVID-19 stimulus in 2020 and 2021, followed by the Infrastructure Investment and Jobs Act and Inflation Reduction Act in 2021 and 2022, put almost $7.5 trillion of stimulus into the economy in a little more than two years, triggering generationally high inflation, which the Fed at first accommodated and is now responding to with a generationally robust interest rate policy. As we think about lessons learned from this latest episode, we should keep this fundamental fact firmly in mind: the most important teaching of SVB is "Don't do that again." Massive fiscal irresponsibility has severe and inescapable consequences, not least for the financial system.

Almost none of the analyses of the SVB failure, however, emphasize or even mention this fundamental cause of the failure. Instead, they focus on the regulation and supervision of the entities that failed, although these are clearly secondary issues given the overwhelming importance of the sudden and self-inflicted inflationary surge. The most prominent of these analyses is the Barr Memo, which lays out a road map for a regulatory response based on four key conclusions:

1. SVB's executive team failed to manage its risk.
2. The Fed's supervisory team failed to appreciate the extent of the vulnerabilities.
3. When they did recognize the vulnerabilities, they didn't do enough about them.
4. The Fed's lassitude was attributable to the regulatory tailoring project mandated by the Economic Growth, Regulatory Relief, and Consumer Protection Act of 2018 and a contemporaneous change in supervisory culture at the Fed, which reduced standards and promoted a less assertive approach.

Given that the first three conclusions are both fairly obvious and fairly nonprescriptive, most of the Barr Memo's recommendations stem from the final conclusion: the regulatory changes and supervisory approach of the prior administration reduced standards that would otherwise have prevented the bank's failure, calling for a rapid reversal of these changes.

The fundamental conclusions of the Barr Memo have now been quite widely discredited. Other governors of the Federal Reserve Board have said that they had no input to the memo and did not agree with it—that it is simply the preexisting policy agenda of one governor.[2] Pat Parkinson, the civil servant who headed the supervisory staff at the Fed during the regulatory response to the Great Financial Crisis, has said that the memo's conclusions are not supported by the facts.[3] An independent working group chaired by former FDIC chair Sheila Bair—no fan of the 2018 regulatory changes—has said that those changes were nonetheless not relevant to SVB's failure, which was driven by other factors.[4] Barney Frank, the former congressman and sponsor of the Dodd-Frank Act and longtime regulatory hawk, has said that the regulatory changes of 2018 "had no impact" and that "they did not stop supervising banks."[5] And the Fed chairman himself has stated in congressional testimony that, contrary to the Barr Memo, he did not think there had been a cultural shift in supervision at the Fed.[6] It is, however, worth reviewing the Barr Memo's conclusions in some detail, because an understanding of *why* the memo's recommendations miss the mark can help sharpen the focus on what recommendations might, in fact, be helpful in the future.

First, consider the regulatory changes cited by the Barr Memo as "impeding effective supervision." In 2018, Congress enacted the Economic Growth, Regulatory Relief, and Consumer Protection Act (EGRRCPA), which raised the general threshold for the application of the strictest capital and liquidity standards from $50 billion in assets to $250 billion in assets. The Federal Reserve implemented this law in November of 2019 through the issuance of the so-called "tailoring rule," which established four categories of firms based on various indicators of risk and applied a sliding scale of regulatory stringency to those four categories, with the strictest standards reserved for the riskiest firms.[7] The effect of the EGRRCPA, as implemented by the tailoring rule, was to change certain of the capital and liquidity rules that would otherwise have applied to Silicon Valley Bank as it grew rapidly after 2019, passing the pre-2018 $50 billion threshold (the "Tailoring Changes").

Barr claims that the Tailoring Changes contributed to the failure of SVB, but a close examination of the relevant changes shows that this cannot be true. Consider first the changes in capital regulation. The relevant rule here is the so-called "AOCI opt-out" (where AOCI stands for Accumulated Other Comprehensive Income), to which Barr attaches great significance. The AOCI opt-out is quite technical but not conceptually difficult. Banks hold debt securities in two main categories: "available for sale" (or "AFS") and "held to maturity" (or "HTM"). HTM securities are those that the bank has acquired with the firm intention and ability to hold until they mature. As a consequence, changes in the market value of HTM securities are not recorded in the financial statements, as they could be misleading: an increase in market value is irrelevant for a security that will never be sold in the market (or so the thinking behind the accounting treatment goes), and showing that increase as an improvement in the firm's balance sheet would be deceptive; the same holds true, although in the reverse direction, for decreases in value. AFS securities, on the other hand, are held precisely so that they *can* be sold in the market (whether to make a trading profit or to cover a liquidity need) and therefore are marked to market periodically, and the changes in value are collected in an account entitled "Accumulated Other Comprehensive Income," or "AOCI."

Since 2013, the largest banks have been required to hold capital against changes in the AOCI account, but no bank holds capital against changes in the value of HTM securities, because there are no changes in the accounting value of HTM securities—they are held at par until maturity and never marked to market. Given the potential for abuse in moving securities back and forth between AFS and HTM status, the accounting guild—especially since some actual abuses in the late 1990s and early 2000s—is very rigid about preventing any securities characterized as HTM from ever being sold. The consequence for a firm selling even one HTM security is generally that all that firm's HTM securities must now be marked to market, which is widely viewed as so draconian an outcome as to effectively prohibit any such sale.

The above accounting treatment of AFS and HTM securities is not unique to banks and was not altered by the Tailoring Changes. It should be immediately apparent that it creates a strong incentive for a firm to move securities from the AFS category to the HTM category, where that can colorably be done because marking the AFS securities to market can result in a volatile balance sheet. This incentive is especially strong for banks because of the regulatory capital consequences of changes in the value of the AOCI account—a bank can greatly reduce its capital volatility, and even in some cases its overall capital requirement, by putting as many of its liquid assets as possible into the HTM category. But at the same time, as banks have an especially strong incentive to make this move, that move is especially dangerous for banks, because it increases the liquidity fragility of the institution: some of the bank's most liquid assets (Treasuries and agency securities) get placed into a category that precludes their sale in the event of a liquidity need.

As a consequence, when the Fed first implemented the Basel III capital standards in the US in 2013 (in a regulation crafted by Governor Daniel Tarullo at a time when every member of the Board of Governors but one had been appointed by a Democratic president), the Fed ameliorated this incentive by allowing banks with less than $250 billion in assets and $10 billion in cross-border exposures—which is 99% of all US banks—to make a onetime, "use it or lose it" election to opt out of the requirement to hold capital against changes in the AOCI account. The Fed did this knowing that it meant that capital regulation itself would not capture certain aspects of interest rate risk.[8] The consciously adopted approach—in order to avoid the worse problem of creating a strong incentive to increase illiquidity—was to focus on supervision and stress testing of interest rate risk rather than capital regulation for that particular issue.

In that context, the Tailoring Changes relevant to AOCI do not appear in any way consequential for SVB. SVB had less than $250 billion in assets, and banks with less than $250 billion in assets have always been exempt from holding capital against changes in AOCI, even after the implementation of the relevant rules under Dodd-Frank in 2013.[9] Equally important, however, even if SVB had been required to hold capital against its AOCI losses, it would still have been a very highly capitalized bank—with a Common Equity Tier 1 (CET1) capital ratio of over 10%, well above the 7% minimum. The AOCI rule would not have required SVB to raise a penny of capital.

One could argue that banks of SVB's size shouldn't have been exempt from holding capital against AOCI losses—but (a) that wasn't a result of the Tailoring Changes; (b) it didn't change SVB's capital adequacy; and most important, (c) the Tarullo Fed's concern about the incentive for moving securities to the HTM category was certainly borne out by SVB. Even without the AOCI capital incentive, it had a far larger amount of securities in the HTM category than held as AFS, and it was public concern about interest-rate-driven losses *in the HTM securities* that triggered the run that brought down the bank.[10] Had SVB been subject to a requirement to hold capital against AOCI, it likely would have moved even *more* securities into the HTM account, resulting in an even more fragile institution when the run began.[11] In other words, not only did the Tailoring Changes not make any difference for SVB, the performance of SVB under stress is evidence that the Tailoring Changes' expansion of the AOCI opt-out to even larger firms than SVB was, in fact, a sensible, stability-enhancing adjustment.

But if the capital changes were not relevant, perhaps the liquidity changes were. The Tailoring Changes effectively excluded SVB from applying the net stable funding ratio (NSFR) and the most stringent version of the liquidity coverage ratio (LCR).[12] But these changes, too, did not matter for SVB's ultimate resilience.

The NSFR is perhaps the easiest. The NSFR seeks to mitigate the liquidity risks of firms by requiring them to maintain a minimum level of stable funding to support their assets, funding commitments, and derivative exposures over a one-year time horizon. The Barr Memo itself notes that SVB would have met the requirements of the full NSFR.[13] In other words, even though the Tailoring Changes had exempted SVB from the NSFR, the firm still met those requirements, and even meeting those requirements did not protect the firm against failure.

The LCR is somewhat more interesting. The LCR seeks to strengthen firms' short-term resilience to funding shocks by requiring them to hold a minimum amount of high-quality liquid assets to meet total net cash outflows in a thirty-day stress period. In the absence of the Tailoring Changes, SVB would have become subject to the full LCR requirements, and the Fed estimates that SVB would have needed an additional $8 billion in high-quality liquid assets to comply with the full LCR as of December 2022.[14]

But this would have been easy for SVB to do, and doing so would not have changed SVB's liquidity profile at all. Indeed, part of the problem with SVB's banking model was that its focus on venture capitalists and their start-up portfolio companies created relatively few traditional financing opportunities, leaving the bank to invest the deposits that it gathered in low-risk, highly liquid securities. As of the end of 2022, the bank had almost 60% of its assets in liquid securities, more than double the average for banks of its size. Indeed, over half of its assets were Treasury and agency securities. Had the bank shifted the composition of that liquid portfolio mildly away from agencies and mildly toward Treasuries, the bank would easily have come into compliance with the full LCR. Yet, it would still have had the same interest rate risk and fundamental liquidity position—which would not have been sufficient to withstand the March run.

Given the weaknesses of the regulatory analysis, the claims of the Barr Memo that have gained the most attention have been those regarding a supposed "shift in supervisory culture" at the Federal Reserve that resulted in a "less assertive stance" of SVB's examiners: less willingness to raise supervisory concerns, longer delays in examination processes, more timidity in enforcement.[15] These claims, however, are the weakest of the memo. The memo itself notes that "there was no formal or specific policy" that promoted this supposed change in culture,[16] nor does it cite communications that directed a weaker stance. It simply states that a limited number of anonymous, mid-level examiners in San Francisco, on the opposite side of the continent from Washington, "felt" something was different.[17] The only concrete example offered of the basis for this impression is bizarrely self-referential: supervisors in San Francisco developed a memorandum of understanding with Silicon Valley Bank around information technology in 2021 but subsequently dropped the matter on their own accord, because they "felt" it would not be pursued—without ever asking anyone in Washington about it, let alone sending it to Washington for review or hearing from anyone in Washington that it should be dropped.[18] The Barr Memo supplies no other examples or evidence.

Those feelings flew in the face of repeated communication from Washington from 2017 onward that supervisors were expressly *not* to weaken supervision but to reduce the bureaucracy around supervision and focus on what was most important.

During 2018 and 2019, the Federal Reserve's vice chair for supervision held town halls at every Federal Reserve Bank that included the entire examiner corps expressly to say, "We need to make supervision more assertive on the things that really matter and avoid being distracted by what doesn't." That message was entirely consistent with messages from the heads of supervisory agencies around the world, urging international best practices on examiners. Andrea Enria, for example—the chair of the European Central Bank's Supervisory Board—has introduced a new supervisory framework designed to allow examiners to focus on the true strategic priorities and key risks for each bank, concentrating efforts where they are most needed. And he expressly notes that such an approach does not mean "less supervision, or a 'light touch' approach, but rather more focused and impactful supervision, homing in on the most material risks."[19]

The Barr Memo's claims about supervisory culture also fly in the face of the actual supervisory practice, evidenced by the supporting materials released in connection with the Barr Memo. Rather than demonstrating a timid approach directed by political instruction that overrode the supervisors' best instincts, the materials themselves show a quite athletic supervisory stance that was, however, diffused across too broad a range of administrative compliance minutiae and not focused on the items that really mattered.

A long-term problem with the culture of bank supervision—not merely at the Fed, but especially evident there—is a focus on process and governance rather than on actual evidence of risk. This problem has persisted for decades. As long ago as 2009, in the aftermath of the Great Financial Crisis, the Federal Reserve Bank of New York issued a "Report on Systemic Risk and Bank Supervision" concluding that the Fed should move away from focusing on banks' general administrative processes and instead identify and make a priority of the key risks for a bank and focus on remediating those actual risks.[20]

The actual risks at SVB were obvious and long-standing. SVB had constructed a government securities portfolio with a high degree of interest rate risk, it had a highly concentrated deposit base, and it lacked a clear liquidity strategy should those highly concentrated deposits move out of the bank quickly. A properly focused supervisory strategy—in line with the repeated instructions of the vice chair for supervision to focus on what was most important—would have required the bank to reduce its interest rate risk, increase its liquidity, and reduce its deposit concentration. The Barr Memo asserts that the supervisors did not do this, because they were intimidated into passiveness by the culture fostered in Washington. The evidence, however, shows that this is almost exactly the opposite of what happened.

For example, at the end of 2022, SVB had thirty-one "matters requiring attention" (MRAs) and "matters requiring immediate attention" (MRIAs) open.[21] MRAs and MRIAs are communications from a bank's examiners to its management or board of directors identifying deficiencies in a bank's practices or financial condition that the supervisory agency expects to see addressed. MRAs and MRIAs are not mandated by—or even referred to in—law or regulation but are simply supervisory conventions that have grown up over time. They have become, however, the principal mechanism for the execution of the supervisory process.

Thirty-one open MRAs and MRIAs are obviously a lot; it was almost three times the average number for banks of SVB's size. This does not suggest a timid or passive supervisory team. Far from it—this team was quite willing to tell SVB what they believed the bank needed to do. But the great bulk of these communications had nothing to do with the most important problems at SVB. Three-quarters of them were routine administrative matters such as vendor management, password management, board effectiveness, Bank Secrecy Act compliance, systems development methodology, and steps for keeping track of laptops. All are very worthy but not existential. A small handful of the open items dealt with liquidity risk or interest rate risk—but almost all of those were MRAs, not MRIAs. For example, the sole item dealing with interest rate risk was an MRA (not an MRIA) about their interest rate risk models, not anything dealing with their actual, obvious interest rate risk itself. Of the twelve MRIAs (requiring the most urgent action), ten of them dealt with something other than liquidity risk, none of them dealt with interest rate risk, and the two dealing with liquidity risk were focused on process, not actual risk.

Moreover, even among this welter of process checklists, the Fed established no priorities as to which were related to the most important matters. The sole effort to establish priorities was in designating some supervisory communications MRIAs rather than MRAs, and as noted above, almost all of the MRIAs would have distracted SVB from focusing on concrete actions to ameliorate actual, evident risk, and the Fed did not anywhere indicate that any MRIA was more important than any other. It is a basic truth of project management that when everything's urgent, nothing is.

Finally, the Barr Memo mentions in several places that an emphasis on due process in the supervisory function stymied assertive action and led to supervisors pulling their punches.[22] This assertion does not comport with the memo's own evidence, as noted above. But even more important, it cannot be the case that supervisors must be allowed to ignore due process if they are to do their jobs effectively. Due process is simply the requirement that governments act transparently, consistently, and fairly. If the supervisory cadre at the Fed believed their jobs required them to be opaque, arbitrary, and unjust, there is a much bigger cultural problem than simply the overemphasis on process and governance and the failure to prioritize risks. An assertive, rigorous supervisory function is perfectly consistent with the principles of due process, and the Fed—together with its bank regulatory cousins—must learn to accommodate these principles and maintain its effectiveness. It is not a particularly hard thing to do, but even if it were, it is the bare minimum requirement of governmental action in a democracy. In the past, supervisors have not had to worry about their actions being challenged, given the reluctance of traditional banks to sue their supervisors and because of the historical deference of the judiciary to the financial regulatory agencies. Both of those factors are changing. There are many new entrants to the banking system who are not traditional bankers, and they will not feel the traditional bankers' reluctance to call out overreaching behavior. And the judiciary has clearly signaled that it will no longer simply defer to an agency's own interpretation of the limits to its action.[23] If the Fed's supervisors continue to chafe at complying with due process—as the Barr Memo suggests that they are—then many of their actions will not survive contact with the modern judiciary. They will be found to be a farrago of inappropriate end runs of the Administrative Procedure Act and congressionally unauthorized resolution of major questions.

This cultural focus on "governance and controls" rather than actual risk, accompanied by an equally culturally driven failure to establish priorities among the long list of MRAs and MRIAs that the Fed had insisted that SVB focus on, may possibly have contributed to SVB's failure.[24] It certainly didn't help. But those are very different problems than the supposed passivity engendered by a culture of laxity emanating from Washington. Not only has that conclusion been disavowed by other Fed governors, including the chairman, but the Barr Memo's own supporting materials demonstrate that the supervisors of SVB were anything but lax; they were just urgently insisting that SVB focus on the wrong things.

Indeed, the Barr Memo itself recognizes the weakness of the case that the Tailoring Changes and the supposed cultural shift were relevant to the failure of SVB. In its summary conclusions, the memo states that "higher regulatory and supervisory requirements may not have prevented the firm's failure," which is Fed-speak for "*would* not have prevented the firm's failure," a conclusion that is inescapable in light of the above analysis.[25]

It is also an entirely unsurprising conclusion, given the purpose of the original post-2010 regulatory reforms and of the subsequent Tailoring Changes. The express purpose of the original regulations was not to prevent all bank failures but to create a system resilient enough that any bank could fail. And, accordingly, the thesis of the Tailoring Changes was not that no bank could fail after making them (because the hypothesis was that any bank could fail even before the changes), but rather that we could make moderate changes to the framework that would make the system more efficient and less costly, without changing the fundamental resilience of the system or the likelihood that any particular bank would fail. The facts of the collapse of SVB certainly support that thesis. Reasonable people can differ with the calibration of the Tailoring Changes or argue that Congress should not have authorized them at all. But SVB is not evidence for that view—to the extent it is evidence of anything, it is evidence that the Tailoring Changes were well calibrated not to change any expected outcome under stress.

If the Tailoring Changes were not at fault for SVB's failure, and if the cultural shift in supervision was a mirage, does that mean there are no regulatory or supervisory changes we ought to make? On the contrary, I believe that there are some significant questions we can study that can lead to some important regulatory and supervisory refinements that are the true lessons of SVB, though they are not the key takeaways of the Barr Memo.

Generally, the explanations of unexpected events that do not require everyone involved to be either a crook or a moron are the ones that are the most illuminating (although often not the most politically popular). But if we hypothesize that SVB's management was generally competent and that the supervisors of the bank were experienced and alert, what would explain their failure to address these existential issues?

The most surprising element of the entire SVB episode—and one that I believe explains more than anything else the behavior of the bank's management and its supervisors—is that the uninsured depositors at SVB behaved much differently than decades of experience had led all of us to believe that they would. This is my hypothesis for why both competent bank managements and smart, experienced supervisors would not have set their hair on fire over the potential risks at SVB. They saw the risks developing—who could not? But they also saw that the bank was funded overwhelmingly by its core business depositors and therefore believed they had time to get the bank's financial position in order, because there would not be a run. History has shown that banks were unstable when funded by short-term wholesale funding, deposits from other financial institutions, or by brokered deposits acquired from noncustomers, but when funded by their core depositors—even large uninsured depositors, so long as they were business customers of the bank—that funding would be relatively stable. Business customers have a web of interactions with the banks at which they keep their deposits: the bank may handle the firm's payroll and cash management; there will be loans to the firm and to its executives; the bank may manage investment and retirement products for the firm; the bank may provide the business credit cards to the firm's employees on preferential terms, and so on. It takes quite a bit to upset those relationships and trigger a core business depositor to move its business elsewhere. They certainly don't move because of something the CEO read at lunch on Twitter [X].

Except that these deposits did, and did so at speed. As I noted at the outset, on Thursday, March 9, SVB experienced a deposit outflow of almost $42 billion, and over $100 billion was in the queue to leave the bank on March 10. Let's consider this in comparison to past bank failures. The largest bank failure in US history was the failure of Washington Mutual (WAMU), which experienced a large deposit run, ostensibly triggered by the failure of Lehman Brothers on September 15, 2008, before the Office of Thrift Supervision seized it on September 25, 2008. Over the course of that ten days, WAMU lost $16.7 billion in deposits, averaging $1.67 billion per day and totaling about 11% of its total deposit liabilities.[26] This was considered a massive run, requiring closure. SVB's $142 billion over two days was over forty times as large per day and amounted to over 80% of SVB's total deposits.

Yet SVB had been almost completely funded by core business depositors. Over 90% of its deposits were uninsured, but virtually all of those were core business deposits, and the significant majority of those were operational deposits of nonfinancial companies. Because of the long historical record of how such deposits behave, the relevant liquidity regulations assign a relatively low probability of outflow to such liabilities and, thus, a relatively low liquidity requirement against them.[27] Similarly, bank managements and supervisors would expect that the liquidity needs of a bank funded by such deposits would be reasonably moderate. With those expectations, even a fairly severe asset-liability mismatch would be a problem that everyone might reasonably believe could be addressed over an extended period of time.

Those expectations turned out to be misplaced. The key question is why: was it because they were depositors of a particular type? Or because they were depositors at a particular time?

By depositors of a particular type, I mean that the business model of SVB resulted in a deposit base that was highly concentrated in a particular economic community: venture capitalists, their portfolio start-up companies, and the entrepreneurs running them. This is a particularly interconnected community famously subject to fads, enthusiasms, and herd behavior.[28] As the slowing economy put pressure on many of the tech firms in this fraternity, leading to a gradual but steady drawdown of deposits over 2022 because of the cash needs of the businesses, this led some of them to look at the financial position of their common bank, which they had not had particular reason to examine before. Some of them, most prominently Peter Thiel, withdrew their deposits and advised their portfolio companies to do the same—news that spread rapidly through this relatively close-knit group, a fact that many believe cascaded into an unprecedented bank run.[29]

Alternatively, these depositors' unexpected behavior may not have been a function of their community but of their century. On this account, the news that prominent depositors were withdrawing their deposits from SVB spread rapidly, not so much because the community was close knit and thus all the members of the community knew this was happening, but because we all knew this was happening when the withdrawers posted their views on Twitter. SVB was posted about on Twitter roughly two hundred thousand times on the day before it failed, many of those posts coming from executives stating they were pulling their funds from the bank and recommending others do so as well.[30] Many have reasonably hypothesized that "in the social media age, the psychological behavior around a bank run ... may be amplified and go viral quicker than bank officers and regulators can successfully respond."[31]

Depending on which of these two explanations is true—or most dominantly true—regulators and supervisors would need to emphasize differing responses. If the first (depositors of a particular type) predominated, then it would be reasonable for regulators and supervisors to place much more of a premium on depositor diversification than they have in the past: creating financial incentives, or administrative requirements, to reduce the concentration of deposits from a small number of individuals as well as individuals in the same industry or even geography, and to reduce the amount of uninsured deposits. Supervisors and bank managements have long emphasized asset diversification as essential to a stable bank; a similar effort on deposit diversification would be the logical flip side.

If the second (depositors in the twenty-first century) predominates, then the problems for the typical small regional or large community bank in the United States are much deeper. It is not uncommon for uninsured deposits to be well over half the total deposits at such a bank, and if that funding is now considered to be unstable, a bank would have to hold permanently high levels of high-quality liquid assets (HQLA) to be able to cover that potential liquidity need. Given the large number of such banks in the

United States and the importance of the lending they do in supporting small businesses and job creation in the economy, requiring a major shift in assets from credit extension to HQLA would lead to a material reduction in the ability of the US banking system to support growth in the real economy.

This problem would be especially severe in the United States, because of the insistence that banks must be prepared to self-insure their liquidity needs entirely. In evaluating a bank's liquidity resilience, the Fed—unlike many of its peer central banks around the world—does not give a bank any credit for its ability to obtain liquidity by borrowing from the central bank. Most central banks require a certain sturdy amount of HQLA at the bank as the first layer of liquidity resources but then also include a calculation of available central bank borrowing as a second layer. The Fed, by contrast, looks only at the HQLA currently on a bank's balance sheet. The HQLA includes actual reserves held at the Fed but does not include a bank's potential borrowing from the discount window or use of the Fed's standing repo facility or other potential Fed borrowing as available to satisfy a potential liquidity need.

The Fed's reluctance to give a bank credit for central bank borrowing access in assessing its liquidity resilience is a serious disincentive for banks to prepare themselves to use that access. It is well known that on the day before its failure, SVB was scrambling to get collateral released from the Federal Home Loan Bank of San Francisco and delivered to the Fed in order to support substantial Fed borrowing and that it was unable to complete this process before the bank was seized.[32] This is unsurprising, because the Fed had given the bank no incentive to prepare for such borrowing—and, indeed, had provided a significant disincentive, as the potential lending would not count toward SVB's liquidity requirements, and the securities delivered as collateral to support such lending would not be available to support other liquidity sources that *would* receive immediate credit.

This is a result of deliberate Fed action, ill judged though well meaning. For decades, the Fed has been affirmatively eroding its core reason for being: providing liquidity to the banking system, especially in times of stress. The Fed's express mantra since the Great Financial Crisis has been that banks need to "self-insure" their liquidity needs. But we had a system in the United States where banks had to self-insure their own liquidity in the nineteenth and early twentieth centuries, and it proved to be wildly unstable—in large part precisely because banks had to self-insure their own liquidity. It simply isn't possible for a bank to rely solely on its own liquidity resources in a world where a very large percentage of bank liabilities are going to be highly runnable.

Addressing this issue is the core reason for the Federal Reserve's creation. It is why we don't call it the Bank of the United States or the Federal Central Bank—it was created to be a central *reserve* from which liquidity could be supplied to those parts of the banking system that needed it from those parts that were in surplus.

But if regional banks' core business deposits are found to be more unstable in the future due to modern methods of communication and increasingly frictionless bank technology, then this stance of the Fed will have to change. SVB had over 90% of its funding from uninsured business deposits, and while that was an outlier, a very large number of banks have 50% or 60% of their deposits in uninsured accounts. A bank that had to treat these deposits as entirely runnable in calculating its internal liquidity needs would need to dramatically restrict its lending in favor of holding larger amounts of HQLA, becoming something closer to a glorified government money market fund. This would either reduce the overall amount of financing support provided to the real economy or drive ever larger amounts of credit provision into the more opaque and less regulated private credit markets, and probably both.

While the principal lesson of SVB is that overly generous fiscal policy—even in the pursuit of worthy public purposes—will have inescapable consequences for the financial system, there is a lesson for regulatory and supervisory policy as well. It is not, however, a more restrictive capital regime, or ever larger amounts of self-insured liquidity, or a more assertive but unfocused supervisory regime, but rather a rethinking of the misguided undermining of the Fed's core liquidity mission that we have been engaging in for quite some time, and a creative reinvigoration of its role as the financial system's central lender. This will require a reorientation of Fed policy, as well as a robust educational effort: banks must learn to integrate Fed borrowing into their general funding practices, and politicians and the public must learn that the use of this credit is not a scarlet letter but instead one of the most important public benefits for which the Fed was created. In today's world of social media and online banking, this may well be the only way to maintain the benefits of our highly diversified banking system.

Notes

1. Michael S. Barr, "Review of the Federal Reserve's Supervision and Regulation of Silicon Valley Bank," Board of Governors of the Federal Reserve System, Washington, DC, April 2023 (hereafter, "Barr Memo").
2. See, for example, Governor Michelle Bowman, "Responsive and Responsible Bank Regulation and Supervision," speech at the Salzburg Global Seminar on Global Turbulence and Financial Resilience: Implications for Financial Services and Society, Salzburg, Austria, June 25, 2023.
3. Jeremy Newell and Pat Parkinson, "A Failure of (Self-) Examination: A Thorough Review of SVB's Exam Reports Yields Conclusions Very Different from Those in the Fed's Self Assessment," BPI.com, May 8, 2023.
4. "Supervision and Regulation after Silicon Valley Bank," Center for Financial Stability, forthcoming.
5. Zachary Warmbrodt, "Barney Frank Blames Crypto Panic for His Bank's Collapse," *Politico*, March 13, 2023.
6. Capital Account Substack, June 21, 2023 (https://www.capitolaccountdc .com/p/sec-takes-a-stab-at-assessing-swap), recounting Chair [Jerome] Powell's testimony before the House Financial Services Committee:

"Democrat Nydia Velazquez brought up the Fed's recent SVB report, which detailed a 'cultural shift' under former vice chair for Supervision Randal Quarles that led to less aggressive oversight. She asked Powell whether he was aware of the change, and if he discussed it at the time with Quarles.

"The Chairman responded that he wouldn't characterize what happened during Quarles' tenure as a 'cultural shift.' Powell added that Quarles prioritized having staff focus on 'the most important issues' instead of being distracted by less pressing matters."

7. Prudential Standards for Large Bank Holding Companies, Savings and Loan Holding Companies, and Foreign Banking Organizations, 84 Fed. Reg. 59,032, November 1, 2019.

8. See the transcript of the Fed's open Board Meeting adopting the Basel III capital standards (https://www.federalreserve.gov/mediacenter/files/open-board-meeting-transcript-20130702.pdf) and Governor Jeremy Stein's question on pp. 30–33: "The question I have is, however, if we leave this AOCI filter in place, we're left in a situation where there's really no regulatory capital device in place that attempts to capture interest rate risk. The staff's response was: So, from the overall standpoint, what we are advising firms and have instructed our supervisory staff to do is to continue to be vigilant in their pursuit of interest rate risk management. . . . It just remains as a task for us as supervisors to be vigilant as rates increase or change in this environment, to follow up with firms as they implement appropriate changes to their strategies so we don't invariably fall behind."

9. The Tailoring Changes also raised the threshold of cross-border exposures that would require holding capital against AOCI from $10 billion to $75 billion, and on the day it failed, SVB had $14 billion in cross-border exposure. But this excess was neither relevant to SVB's failure nor important to its business—had SVB remained subject to the pre-2018 AOCI rule, it would simply have kept its cross-border exposures below $10 billion and would still never have been subject to the AOCI capital requirement.

10. Christiaan Hetzner, "SVB Collapse Highlights $620 Billion Hole Lurking in Bank Balance Sheets," *Fortune*, March 10, 2023.

11. One could, of course, try to address the incentive to move securities into HTM by requiring capital to be held against HTM securities rather than by reducing the amount of capital to be held against AFS securities. While

worth considering in light of the SVB failure, it will require close analysis to be sure that all the potential unintended consequences of such a move have been considered. The accounting profession has repeatedly reconsidered the general rule for HTM securities over the years and repeatedly concluded that changes in the value of such securities should not be recognized in the financial statements. In any event, any deficiency in the capital treatment of HTM securities was certainly not a result of the Tailoring Changes.

12. This statement is a mild oversimplification. SVB passed the asset threshold at which it became subject to the NSFR in June of 2021, but under the applicable transition rules, SVB had a grace period during which it could prepare to comply, and that grace period had not expired by the time the bank failed. Similarly, SVB would have been subject to a more stringent version of the LCR in the absence of the Tailoring Changes, but only because its cross-border exposures were $14 billion, and the Tailoring Changes had raised the threshold for application of the full-strength LCR from $10 billion to $75 billion of cross-border exposures. But just as in the analysis of the AOCI opt-out above, that relatively small excess cross-border exposure was not relevant to SVB's liquidity needs nor important to its business, and in the absence of the Tailoring Changes, SVB would simply have kept its cross-border exposure below $10 billion and the full LCR would never have applied. For ease of exposition, however, we can posit that the Tailoring Changes resulted in an exemption from these two rules and show that application of the rules still wouldn't have mattered for SVB's ultimate resilience.

13. See Barr Memo, 88.

14. See Barr Memo, 88.

15. Barr Memo, 11.

16. Barr Memo, 11.

17. Barr Memo, 11.

18. Barr Memo, 11.

19. Andrea Enria, "A New Stage for Banking Supervision," a keynote speech at the 22nd Handelsblatt Annual Conference on Banking Supervision. Frankfurt am Main, March 28, 2023.

20. David Beim and Christopher McCurdy, "Report on Systemic Risk and Bank Supervision," Federal Reserve Bank of New York, August 2009.

21. Barr Memo, 28.

22. See, e.g., Barr Memo, iii.

23. See, e.g., Sackett et ux. v. Environmental Protection Agency et al., 598 U.S. ___ (2023) (https://www.law360.com/articles/1682992/attach ments/0); Axon Enterprise, Inc. v. Federal Trade Commission et al., 598 U.S. 175 (2023).

24. Although we should always keep in mind that given the high inflation created by two years of excessive fiscal stimulus, even the deftest supervisory intervention and management response would have been hard pressed to keep SVB sustainable.

25. Barr Memo, iii.

26. Office of Thrift Supervision, "OTS Fact Sheet on Washington Mutual Bank," September 25, 2008.

27. William Nelson, "Update on SVB's LCR," March 27, 2023.

28. Hadrien Comte, "FOMO, or the Mimetic Desire Theory Leading to Herd Behavior in Venture Capital," Medium.com, March 25, 2021.

29. Christopher Hutton, "SVB Collapse: Peter Thiel's Role Scrutinized as Spark of Bank Run," *Washington Examiner*, March 13, 2023.

30. Kali Hays, "SVB Is the First Social Media Bank Run in History," *Business Insider*, March 13, 2023.

31. Jonathan Yerushalmy, "The First Twitter-Fueled Bank Run," *The Guardian*, March 16, 2023.

32. See, e.g., "Improving the Government's Lender of Last Resort Function: Lessons from SVB and Signature Bank," Bank Policy Institute, April 24, 2023.

7

What We Can Learn about Financial Regulation from Silicon Valley Bank's Collapse and Beyond

Amit Seru

Thank you, John Taylor, for the opportunity to speak today, and congratulations on the thirtieth anniversary of the Taylor rule. I probably disagree somewhat with the rest of the conference panelists on some of the aspects being discussed. In the rest of the talk, I will move beyond anecdotes and beyond Silicon Valley Bank (SVB). I will use data to describe what I see as the core problem in what happened to SVB and to other banks during the recent monetary tightening cycle. Then I will talk about what I see as the short-term diagnosis and solution before discussing the long-term solution to this problem. There'll be a lot of common themes with what Darrell Duffie and Randal Quarles have already said. But the way I think about these things is a bit different, and that will be reflected in my solutions to the problem. So here it goes.

Figure 7.1 illustrates the failures in the US banking system over the past two decades. One can see the large failures in the 2007 financial crisis, such as Washington Mutual. More recently, when the turbulence in the banking sector started in mid-March of 2023 with SVB, the rhetoric was that SVB's problems were unique because it had very high uninsured leverage relative to other banks.

My frequent collaborators (Erica Jiang, Gregor Matvos, and Tomasz Piskorski) and I had been studying the structure of bank liabilities—in particular, the uninsured leverage of banks—for some time and naturally found this issue interesting.[1] Uninsured leverage

Bank failures, 2001–23

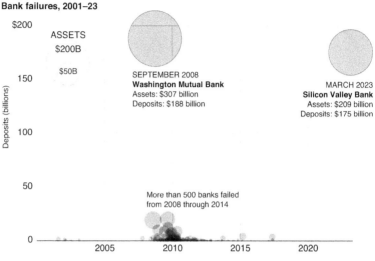

FIGURE 7.1. Bank Failures in the United States over the Last Two Decades.

Note: Figures for assets and deposits are estimates.

Source: Federal Deposit Insurance Corporation. Reprinted with permission of the *Wall Street Journal*, copyright © 2023 Dow Jones & Company, Inc. All Rights Reserved Worldwide. License number 5658940219616.

is interesting, because uninsured depositors are, well, "uninsured." This makes this form of debt more sensitive to information than insured debt. In other words, this type of debt is more "run prone." And if a bank has a lot of uninsured leverage, negative shocks to the asset side could lead to fragility. So when the run at SVB occurred over that weekend last March, and SVB collapsed, we decided to stress test the whole US banking system of 4,800 banks. In other words, we asked, what did the increase in interest rates over the monetary tightening from Q1 2022 to Q1 2023 do to the market value of the banks' assets, and what did it mean for the banks' solvency, given the structure of their liabilities? (Jiang et al. 2023a)

So to give you a sense, we are talking about SVB on this panel, but looking beyond that one bank's situation. Here is the entire US banking system: $24 trillion of assets held in securities, loans, and so on (see figure 7.2).

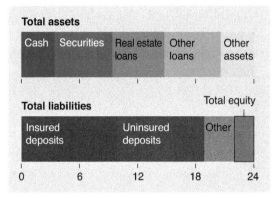

FIGURE 7.2. Between the Balance Sheets.
The aggregate balance sheet of US banks as of Q1 2022 (in trillions).
Source: Jiang et al. (2023a).

But what's interesting is that when you look at $24 trillion of liabilities, there are $9 trillion of insured and $9 trillion of uninsured deposits. A side note: in mid-May 2023, the data suggests that uninsured deposits had decreased to $7 trillion. This makes sense since, as you can imagine, some uninsured deposits left the banking system during the recent turbulence in the banking sector.

There is also $2 trillion in equity, which is a very important number in the aggregate. That's the capital in the banking system that we usually talk about. Now, why is this number important to remember? Because we took the assets of the banking system and marked these assets to their market values. Since interest rates went up, the value of fixed-rate-long-dated assets went down. So what did we find? We found that marking to market would lead to the banking system having $2 trillion of losses. I want to emphasize that this is not just the marking to market of securities. We also marked to market loans since we have details on the maturity structure. At the same time, it is also worth noting we are talking about securities such as Treasuries and the other liquid assets that banks invest in, like residential mortgage-backed securities (RMBS). So this is not the typical, "Hey, there are these long-term illiquid loans that banks have invested in, and banks have a special ability to invest in these illiquid, but positive, NPV loans." Here we have a collection of liquid and safe securities the banks invested in. Loans of the "typical" type are not really that big a part of a bank's mark-to-market exercise. But these safe and liquid securities all went down in market value when interest rates rose over the last year. And we ended with $2 trillion of mark-to-market losses across the banking system.

Recall that the aggregate equity in the banking system is $2 trillion. The losses, when compared with equity, tell you that there might be a few banks that could be underwater. When you look at the entire distribution, this is how it looks for the 4,800 banks in the system (see figure 7.3).

The average loss here is around 10%, so about $2 trillion on $24 trillion, roughly. If you look at the vertical line—that's basically where SVB is in terms of its mark-to-market losses. If you thought that SVB was an outlier and special just because it has huge mark-to-market losses, there could be another five hundred banks that should have faced a similar kind of run as SVB. But they didn't.

And we know why. I want to remind everyone that around the time the turbulence in the banking sector started, there was some discussion that maybe these mark-to-market losses would not be realized, because banks do a lot of hedging. But if you look inside the banks and ask how much hedging is going on, the answer is not a lot (see figure 7.4).

One simple way to look at how much hedging is going on is to look at the duration of assets a bank has after it does its hedging. There are two distributions of the duration of assets of banks in figure 7.4. One (orange) depicts the duration of bank assets before the monetary tightening, and the other (black) is the duration of assets during the monetary tightening. And what you see is, on average, you're talking about a duration of four or five years after hedging. Thus, whatever interest rate hedging the bank is doing, this tells you there is not a lot of hedging going on. If there were a lot of hedging,

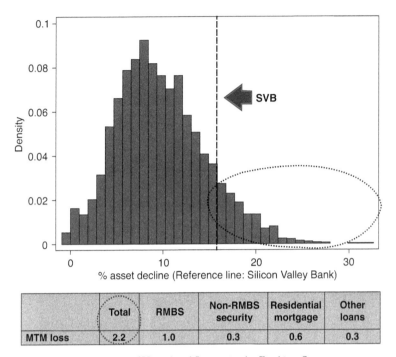

FIGURE 7.3. Distribution of Unrealized Losses in the Banking System. Based on our analysis (as of the end of Q1 2023), substantial unrealized losses may exist throughout the banking system.
Source: Jiang et al. (2023a).

this number would be close to zero in both distributions. So those mark-to-market losses we computed over the monetary tightening, even though they're unrealized, are still with the banks.

Many banks had losses that were larger than SVB's. So why did we see a run in the case of SVB? And what does it tell us about the solvency of other banks? The answer has to do with uninsured leverage. Figure 7.5 depicts how the uninsured leverage in the system looks across banks.

The vertical line again here is SVB. And if you look at SVB now, you can see why its run happened. It had very high uninsured leverage and was, in fact, in the top percentile of banks when looking at the distribution of uninsured leverage.

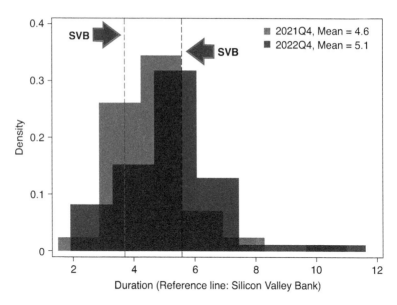

FIGURE 7.4. Not as Much Interest Rate Hedging in the Banking Sector as You'd Think.
The duration of assets for banks that report these in their disclosures.
Source: Jiang et al. (2023b).

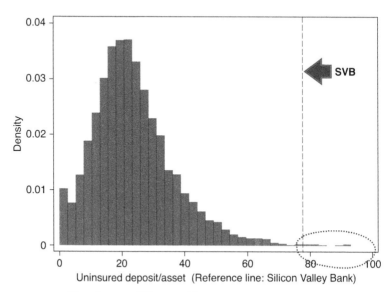

FIGURE 7.5. Distribution of Uninsured Leverage across US Banks.
Based on our analysis, SVB was an outlier in terms of its uninsured leverage.
But there are quite a few other banks with similar uninsured leverage as SVB.
Source: Jiang et al. (2023a).

Now how do we think about uninsured leverage and how it contributes to a possible run on a bank? Is it just that venture capitalists (VCs) are talking to each other, triggering a run, as in the case of SVB? If so, will a policy banning VCs from social media mean everything will be fine in the future? That's where economics comes in and tells us how to think about this.

Uninsured deposits are runnable. They are sensitive to information. But when do such depositors run? Well, uninsured depositors run if enough of them think other uninsured depositors will run. In other words, there could be multiple equilibria depending on the beliefs about how many other uninsured depositors would be running. There could be a "good" equilibrium where given some losses, uninsured depositors do not run because other uninsured depositors would not run. Alternatively, there could be a bad run equilibrium where depositors would have beliefs that enough uninsured depositors would run.

And so, how do we want to take this and figure out how much fragility is in the system? Well, one thing we can do is to take an extreme view and say 100% of uninsured depositors get spooked by the mark-to-market losses of a bank and run. We can ask what would happen to a bank in that scenario. This exercise can give you some sense of who the potentially insolvent banks in the system might be if one looked at what the value of equity might be after uninsured depositors withdraw all their money. In other words, we are looking at "turbulence" on the asset side due to mark-to-market losses versus "flight risk" due to uninsured depositors. Here is what that looks like (see figure 7.6).

Figure 7.6 shows the distribution of banks in the system that would be insolvent. That is, this plots banks whose equity would be underwater. The y-axis plots losses, and the x-axis shows the amount of runnable uninsured leverage the banks have. The size of the bubble tells you how big the bank is. So, the biggest bank has over a trillion dollars of assets. There is SVB there, but it's not an

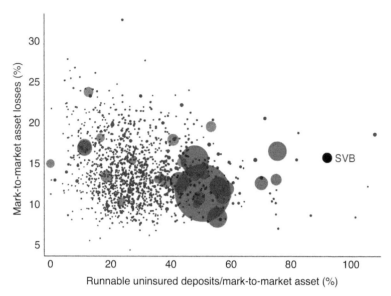

FIGURE 7.6. Uninsured Leverage and Unrealized Losses ("Flight Risk" versus "Turbulence").
A plot of the full set of "insolvent" banks. A bank is considered insolvent if the mark-to-market value of its assets—after paying all uninsured depositors—is insufficient to repay all insured deposits. On the x-axis is a measure of "flight risk." On the y-axis is a measure of "turbulence."
Source: Jiang et al. (2023a).

outlier. There are several other banks of similar or even larger size than SVB in the system that would be insolvent under the extreme view. Put another way, in this extreme scenario, this is basically the whole distribution of all the banks in the system. There are two distributions here; orange is before the tightening, and black is after the tightening (see figure 7.7).

If you look at the equity in the system, the banking system was well capitalized before the monetary tightening (the orange distribution is where the mean and the whole distribution are well above 0%). And then, after the tightening, assuming that all the uninsured depositors run, you see from the other distribution that several banks have equity below 0%. What that means is that the

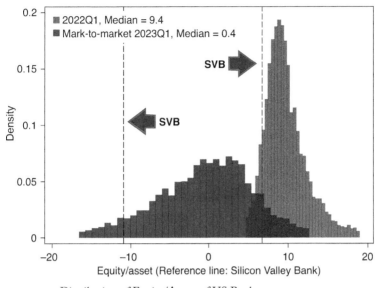

FIGURE 7.7. Distribution of Equity/Assets of US Banks.
Prior to the monetary tightening, the banking system was well capitalized,
based on the orange distribution of the chart. The black distribution illustrates
that after the tightening, the equity at several banks was underwater.
Source: Jiang et al. (2023a).

equity of these banks is underwater. So when I showed you those
bubble plots before and said a lot of banks are insolvent, this is
the distribution that supports that statement since it shows several
banks could, in fact, potentially be insolvent.

How should we then think about this? Is this only showing
up because we took the extreme view of all uninsured depositors
running in a bank? Is this the right way to think about it? Kind of,
because it depends on what type of equilibrium we have in mind.
Note that this setting is not the classic "Diamond-Dybvig" model
of bank runs. Those runs are liquidity runs; they are not solvency
runs. A solvency run, which applies to our situation, is different.
It happens when the interest rate rises sufficiently such that there
is a significant unrealized loss to assets. That's the first condition
that has to be true. Enough uninsured depositors have to think

that other uninsured depositors will run because of the losses they see. Recall that the unrealized mark-to-market losses due to an increase in interest rates are based on assets (such as Treasuries) that are liquid. When these two conditions hold, we could end up in a "bad" equilibrium, as we saw in the case of SVB and First Republic (and other regional banks). When this occurs, the bank then has to go to the market and take those securities and loans and sell them to satisfy these uninsured depositors. Those unrealized mark-to-market losses become realized. This prompts more depositors to withdraw, and we get a self-fulfilling run.

Are there conditions that make such runs more of a possibility? Well, it happens if banks have lower equity capital. Such banks have a limited ability to absorb the losses (see figure 7.8).

If there were enough equity, that would alleviate the concerns of uninsured depositors that the bank might not have enough of a buffer to absorb its losses. The fundamental thing here, therefore, is that a bank can sustain the stress if it has enough equity.

But leaving that aside, what will also be true is that a bank will face more of a solvency run if it has a higher proportion of uninsured depositors. The reason is, as discussed before, a solvency run will depend on how many other uninsured depositors will be running. We considered an extreme version earlier where all uninsured depositors ran, but we can really consider different scenarios. So that's what figure 7.8 does. On the x-axis in both charts are different scenarios regarding the proportion of uninsured depositors running, ranging from zero to 100%. The chart on the top plots the number of insolvent banks on the y-axis (i.e., banks with underwater equity under the scenario on the x-axis on uninsured depositors). The chart on the bottom reflects the assets (in trillions) at risk of such a run for different scenarios. I want to highlight the two numbers in red. Assuming half the uninsured depositors run, we have about two hundred banks potentially underwater, and $300 billion of assets with these banks are at risk.

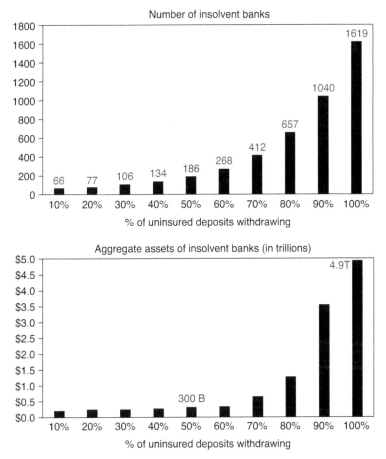

FIGURE 7.8. Where Are Self-Fulfilling Solvency Runs Possible?
Based on our analysis and model, when interest rates rise, solvency runs are
more likely in banks where equity capital is low and where a substantial proportion of uninsured depositors provide funding to the bank.
Source: Jiang et al. (2023a).

But of course, if we take a more stressful scenario, the equilibrium
is different, and you can pretty quickly get higher numbers that
are worse for the banking system.

Since this session is about SVB and beyond, what about the role
of regulators in all this? Well, regulators, as has been mentioned,
have diagnosed this problem as a liquidity problem. The "Barr

Memo" on the situation at SVB mentions the word "liquidity" in relationship to SVB a staggering 320 times.[2] "Solvency" is only mentioned once, which almost suggests it may have been a typo. More seriously, as I have already stated, this is not the traditional illiquidity of assets issue that prompts a lender-of-last-resort intervention to prevent a "bad" bank run. We are talking about the most liquid assets banks hold that have fallen in value. Yet, we saw the central bank intervene in dramatic ways. SVB suddenly became systemic overnight.

Yes, there was bad management, and the board of directors is the usual scapegoat. But I actually think something else is going on, which has not been talked about much. That is the political economy of regulatory enforcement. As you might know, regulation and its enforcement in the banking sector are pretty complex. If you look at all the midsized banks—and actually not just midsized, pretty large banks now—like SVB and First Republic Bank, they are regulated by multiple regulators—state and federal—with overlapping jurisdictions. Why is the fact that multiple regulators oversee these banks important?

Because political economy comes into enforcement when you have state and federal regulators. In a study ten years ago, we pointed out that there is a huge amount of inconsistency in the enforcement of straightforward rules (see figure 7.9). What does that mean? For much of the banking system in the US, federal and state regulators regulate a given bank in rotation. One finds that these regulators never implement the same rule for a given bank in the same way. The state regulators tend to be too soft on the bank. Why? Because it's "too big to fail" in their local economy.

The white vertical zone in figure 7.9 indicates when state regulators are in charge of enforcement at a bank, and the gray zone is when federal regulators are in charge of the same bank in rotation. This is how SVB and First Republic Bank were regulated. What is plotted is the CAMELS rating, which is everything a bank lives

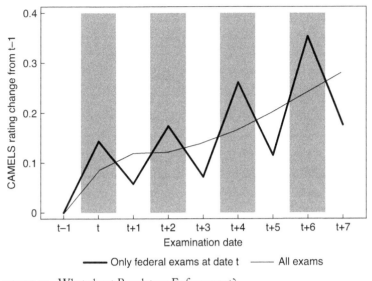

FIGURE 7.9. What about Regulatory Enforcement?
Based on our analysis, banks such as SVB (and First Republic), which are regulated under dual regulators in rotation, face potentially inconsistent enforcement of regulation.
Source: Agarwal et al. (2014).

and dies for.[3] A good rating—a smaller number—implies good things for the banks, such as approvals to acquire. And a bad rating—a higher number—means bad things are happening for the bank since it is deemed unsafe, such as higher FDIC deposit insurance premiums. And what does this tell you? Whenever the federal regulator comes in, they raise the CAMELS rating. When the states come in, they undo it and make it easier for the bank. Why? Because, for example, a bank like SVB is pretty important to a state regulator, given its importance to the local economy. It is possible that might have prompted the state regulators to look away from the brewing problems at both SVB and First Republic Bank.

And that gets me to the last couple of things I want to mention, which are beyond SVB. So we've already seen SVB is not an outlier. The question is, is this really a "tech phenomenon" occurring only to banks in California and maybe on the East Coast? (see figure 7.9). The answer is not really. If you look at the chart I showed you about insolvent banks and ask what deposits in the US across regions are at risk, this is how the map looks (see figure 7.10).

The map demonstrates that the problems are not confined to banks in Silicon Valley. The market has not been blind to all this. You can see how the market reaction has been to the regional banks across the country. The equity value of these banks is pretty depressed. And it's telling you loud and clear that a bunch of banks in the system are potentially insolvent. We can try giving these banks a lifeline with liquidity from the government as we did with First Republic Bank. But these banks are, in fact, insolvent.

So what next? The Fed has extended the deposit insurance to uninsured deposits. We have the Bank Term Funding Program established by the Fed that buys at par, even though the assets are underwater. All of this has been useful in the short run to alleviate short-term risks. But because there are many potentially insolvent banks, we need to worry about scenarios similar to what happened in the early 1980s during the savings and loan crisis. That crisis resulted in similar short-term help from the government and incentivized many insolvent institutions to gamble for resurrection.

Put simply, what we saw during the savings and loan crisis was that a bunch of insolvent banks took inordinate and imprudent risks when their liability side was protected by the government—not too dissimilar to what we are seeing now.

So what is the right way to ensure we do not fall into the same trap? In the short run, we've got to figure out a "market test" to separate insolvent banks from solvent but illiquid banks. The idea that we are going to just keep pumping in taxpayer money to save all the banks, many of which are insolvent, is inefficient. A few of my colleagues at Stanford University (Peter DeMarzo and Arvind Krishnamurthy), as well as my collaborators on the referenced study (Erica Jiang from the University of Southern California,

Share of deposits at risk of impairment (%)

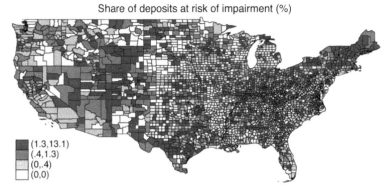

(1.3,13.1)
(.4,1.3)
(0,.4)
(0,0)

FIGURE 7.10. Beyond SVB? A Look at the Geographic Distribution of
"Deposits at Risk."
Based on the analysis, the extent to which deposits in banks are at risk (darker
colors convey more bank deposits are at risk).
Source: Jiang et al. (2023a).

Gregor Matvos from Kellogg School of Management, and Tomasz
Piskorski from Columbia University), wrote a proposal following
the analysis that we had done. The idea is that the banks should
promptly raise equity or other private or public capital. This will
reduce fragility and provide a real market test to identify truly solvent but illiquid banks from insolvent ones. This is something that
Anat Admati, who is moderating the panel, wrote a long time ago
in a proposal with other collaborators as well.

If banks can't raise equity right now for various reasons, at least
the regulators need to come out and do a stress test so that the
market can get a sense of which banks are solvent and which are
insolvent. This will also help regulators craft a plan to consolidate
or merge insolvent banks.

And what about the long run? The rhetoric coming from regulators includes the message that careful regulations are needed
to address complex, unanticipated, and unprecedented risks. Last
time I checked, interest rate risk is in the first chapter of any
finance textbook. And if four collaborators working two days over

a weekend can do a stress test of the banking system as we did, it is unclear what the real issue is. I think the ultimate answer is, rather than trying to tweak this into an amazing physics laboratory-based experiment, we need to just realize there are limits to regulation and what regulators can do. Both because these regulators have their biases and blind spots as well as deal with a political economy of enforcement. And I think the right answer is right in front of our eyes. Here is an example from a $10 trillion mortgage market in the US (see figure 7.11).

What I have plotted is how much mortgage lending financial institutions are doing. That's the x-axis. And the y-axis is how much equity they have in their capital structure. The orange line

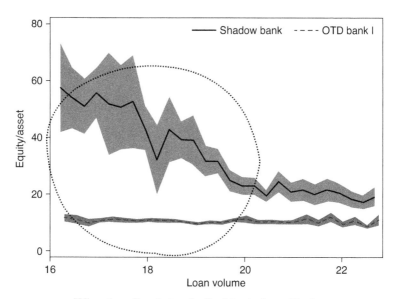

FIGURE 7.11. What about Regulating the Bank in the Long Run?
More equity capital is the least costly way to ensure the financial system remains stable while providing adequate intermediation services. The black line plots the equity-to-asset ratio of shadow lenders (i.e., nondepository institutions) providing mortgages to US households. The orange line plots the equity-to-capital ratio of traditional banks providing the same service. The lending volume of various institutions is on the x-axis, and the y-axis plots the equity-to-assets ratio.
Source: Jiang et al. (2020).

is for traditional deposit-taking banks. Remember, banks have a huge amount of government-backed insured liability structure. And the dark black line represents the shadow banks or nonbanks, which are largely funded by uninsured debt. When an institution is funded by so much uninsured debt, what does the market do? Well, these institutions end up taking a lot of equity. Why? Because these institutions and the market understand there's a lot of runnable risk in these institutions. Thus, these institutions provide the same amount of services that banks provide. But they have significantly more equity capital than traditional banks to account for the higher runnable risk of uninsured debt that they have. So I think in the long run, the answer is not liquidity or more liquidity requirements. Nor is the answer additional regulators or regulations. The answer is asking banks to have a significant amount of equity capital. And that's where I'll end it.

References

Agarwal, Sumit, David Lucca, Amit Seru, and Francesco Trebbi. 2014. "Inconsistent Regulators: Evidence from Banking." *Quarterly Journal of Economics* 129, no. 2 (May): 889–938.

Jiang, Erica Xuewei, Gregor Matvos, Tomasz Piskorski, and Amit Seru. 2020. "Banking without Deposits: Evidence from Shadow Bank Call Reports." National Bureau of Economic Research Working Paper 26903 (March).

———. 2023a. "Monetary Tightening and US Bank Fragility in 2023: Mark-to-Market Losses and Uninsured Depositor Runs?" National Bureau of Economic Research Working Paper 31048 (April).

———. 2023b. "Limited Hedging and Gambling for Resurrection by US Banks during the 2022 Monetary Tightening?" Social Science Working Paper 4410201 (April 3).

Notes

1. Erica Jiang is a professor of finance and business economics at the University of Southern California Marshall School of Business. Gregor

Matvos is a Howard Berolzheimer Chair in Finance at the Kellogg School of Management, Northwestern University. Tomasz Piskorski is the Edward S. Gordon Professor of Real Estate in the Finance Division at Columbia Business School.

2. On April 28, 2023, the Federal Reserve Board released its "Review of the Federal Reserve's Supervision and Regulation of Silicon Valley Bank" report. Vice Chair for Supervision Michael S. Barr led the review.

3. The CAMELS rating system is used to assess a bank's overall condition. It is an acronym for capital adequacy, assets, management capability, earnings, liquidity, and sensitivity.

GENERAL DISCUSSION

ANAT ADMATI (INTRODUCTION): Last evening, John Taylor quoted Secretary [George P.] Shultz, saying that governments should set the rules and then let the markets work. So I'm going to say the obvious. Markets can't operate without rules, just like sporting events, driving on the roads, or building buildings—they all need rules. And rules constrain somebody. I should also note the obvious, and I am sure Secretary Shultz knew, that enforcement of rules is part of the issue, and that the rules are useless without effective enforcement. So when we talk about rules and how well they work, we have to talk about how they're designed and how they're enforced. That is the topic of this session.

There are many governments in the world again, using the word "government" here, as opposed to the word "rule." When a government sets a rule, like a US federal government, oftentimes it's done through the legislature and then it is called a law, an act, or a statute. Then you have the dreaded word "regulations," which is also a government rule, except it's often an agency of the government that writes the details and then might engage in enforcement. So the difference between laws, acts, statutes, and regulations is only technical. All are rules, and all need to be enforced by somebody. That's just the basics.

In the case of banking, enforcers might include the Department of Justice, if rule violations involve crimes, and all sorts of regulatory agencies involved in enforcement. Some of them engage in supervision and examinations in the process. Enforcement involves actions by the enforcer if a rule is broken to create consequences and deter future rule violations. Often the devil is in the details. Therefore, a lot of lawyers are always involved when rules are written and enforced, and there are the courts hovering over this process.

This policy conference is about central banks, and a lot of what we talk about here is monetary economics. It's very rare that we have a discussion on regulations. But the rules actually matter to central banks, and central banks actually play a big role. First of all, central banks need the private-sector banks in order to transmit their policies. They need a stable banking system. And secondly, central banks are often involved in the regulation, in writing the rules, in enforcing the rules, and in supervision. In the US, there are many federal and state regulators.

In addition to this, and importantly, central banks are serving as lenders of last resort. So they actually play a role in private markets by buying assets and lending to private-sector institutions. And that role has expanded in the last fifteen years, certainly during the financial crisis, and certainly during COVID—we already heard some of that—and again in the recent situation that evolved or came into the open in March, which is why we're here today discussing this topic.

Current events set the stage for this panel. We had three banks sizable enough to really deserve a lot of news coverage fail in the US—all over $100 billion, two of them over $200 billion, and two of them in this area. It was Silicon Valley Bank [SVB]. Then it was Signature Bank on the same weekend in mid-March. And it was then more recently First Republic Bank, right here. Meanwhile, in Switzerland, Credit Suisse, one of the thirty— now twenty-nine—global systemically important financial institutions [SIFIs], was sort of forced into marriage with another SIFI, UBS, creating a monster SIFI in Switzerland, twice the country's GDP. What happened there is another issue related to regulation. Because one of our panelists was the chair of the Financial Stability Board, we note that banking regulations involve other international bodies, like the Basel Committee on Banking Supervision, etc. It's important to talk about the global banks as well as the local banks in every jurisdiction. In the US on this issue, one of our biggest SIFIs, JPMorgan Chase, which already violated the law about having more than 10% of deposits in the US (together with Bank of America, by the way), bought First Republic Bank recently from the FDIC [Federal Deposit Insurance Corporation], serving as the bank's receiver and entering a loss-sharing agreement.

This is the background. I will just mention three points of fact that I hope come out of the discussion by our panelists or come out in the questions afterward. First, the supervision and enforcement of the rules. The banks that failed in the US were supervised by different agencies. SVB was supervised by the Federal Reserve as a bank holding company. Signature and First Republic were supervised by the FDIC, and there were state regulators, but they weren't that involved. All these banks received high CAMEL ratings, namely the ratings that the supervisors gave, including about this thing called "capital," a piece of the regulation that I know well about. So they were considered "well capitalized," as was also claimed by FINMA [the Swiss Financial Market Supervisory Authority] about Credit Suisse right before it failed. The question arises: How can we have well-capitalized institutions fail within a very short amount of time, and should we rethink the definition of "well capitalized" so that it can be more reassuring? In particular, and relevant to these three US banks, or at least two of the three US banks, the risk that they took that ended up leading to their demise was interest rate risk, which is of course relevant for monetary economics and this monetary policy conference. The capital rules, however, tend to ignore interest rate risk. Risk weights only take into account credit risk, not interest rate risk and accounting measures may also obscure them.

Regulators also run stress tests, which raises another question about how much they took reasonable scenarios into account, and how much they used accounting rules, which do not recognize losses on held-to-maturity assets. We're going to hear more about this later.

I just raised the question of what it means to be well capitalized, and how a well-capitalized bank can default or go into insolvency very shortly after being well capitalized, and whether it would be useful to have the definition of "well capitalized" in the rules such that violating it does not mean you're basically at insolvency, that there is time to intervene before insolvency, for prompt corrective action, which is a principle of the regulation. And whether we should also have market-based stress tests, the one I call "raise equity." Those who fail to raise equity are clearly insolvent.

In 2014, Mark Carney, who chaired the Financial Stability Board—before Mr. [Randal] Quarles took the job—declared that the "too big to fail" problem is solved through the use of total loss-absorbing debt, so-called TLAC [total loss-absorbing capacity]. Supposedly, TLAC investors will absorb losses in the resolution of nonviable banks without disruption or need for bailouts. Yet in Switzerland—and the Swiss were among those cheering for TLACs—the authorities chose not to go to resolution and not to impose losses on 50 billion Swiss francs of TLAC securities. They did wipe out some 17 billion in "alternative tier one capital." We have to wonder, therefore, what happened to those promises that the TLAC will prevent bailouts. Clearly, Swiss regulators were afraid to send Credit Suisse to resolution and impose losses on TLAC holders.

On this topic, one issue has to do with cross-border resolution. One of the reasons the Swiss authorities did not trigger is that, as the Financial Stability Board report *Key Attributes of Effective Resolution Regimes* notes, the huge wish list that would make cross-border resolution work is simply not going to happen. It involves collaborations across countries and trusting other countries for "single points of entry" resolution to allocate losses of global banks that are systemic in multiple jurisdictions, like Credit Suisse was and JPMorgan definitely is systemically important in multiple jurisdictions. We have to confront the question of whether it is okay in a market economy to have institutions that cannot actually fail. I will now turn to our panelists, Darrell Duffie first, then Randal Quarles, and then Amit Seru.

Thank you very much.

*   *   *

ADMATI: Fortunately, I don't have to say as much, because Amit Seru articulated some of what I would say. It was not just a liquidity problem. I agree with other panelists that because we have central banks, we don't necessarily need "self-funded liquidity," but I want to add that we *do* want and we need *self-funded solvency*. And that's what it's about, really.

Credit Suisse also had a run. The cause of its insolvency wasn't interest rate risk, but still the reason for the run was concerns about insolvency. Credit Suisse has been on the edge for three years, managed to have bad business, bad management, and just not a viable business model in parts of its operation. It finally caught up with them and they became nonviable. That's why they needed all the support to make the takeover by UBS happen. We did not hear anything about being too big to fail from the panel. So I can take the liberty of asking, especially Mr. Quarles, what he thinks about Credit Suisse.

RANDAL QUARLES: So, Credit Suisse has triggered a lot of discussion about resolution structures and resolution planning, with the theme being, "So, was all of that work on resolution planning a complete waste?" It was very hard, very expensive work, and it seems to have been completely ignored. But after talking with a number of the regulators who were involved in the Credit Suisse-UBS merger, I take it as an example of what I, at least, always expected would be the end result of the resolution structuring and resolution planning effort, which would be to prove [General] Dwight Eisenhower's maxim as he prepared for D-Day: plans are useless, but planning is essential. And that was the theme that I've heard, at least from a number of the folks who were involved in that process, which was: we had a lot of plans as to how Credit Suisse could be resolved. And having them was, in fact, very useful when it came time to figure out exactly what we were going to do. But it should never have been expected that we were going to take one of those plans off the shelf and implement it—whether it was bail-in or the TLAC, or any other plan—exactly as expected. We had thought through a number of the dynamics in different situations, and it was very helpful to have done that. So, you know, I probably would have resolved it in a different way. But I don't think it demonstrates that if you're going to have something like Credit Suisse-UBS, that's an indication that the official sector has thrown all of that resolution planning work in the trash. It's exactly what we should have expected to be the result of that effort.

ADMATI: I'm going to connect the two cases here by just asking the following, because Amit Seru was talking about equity and I talk about equity. What is it that makes TLACs debt better than equity for the purpose of absorbing losses? When you need to trigger it, when you need to go into resolution, couldn't you avoid the entire trouble of triggering resolution if, instead, the bank had issued equity *instead* of TLAC, which is debt to absorb losses? This is the kind of question I've been asking for about fifteen years and have never gotten an answer to, so I'm trying again to ask this question, asked from society's perspective.

QUARLES: Well, if you're directing that to me, I've never been the world's biggest fan of TLAC. So maybe you should direct that to someone else on the panel.

ADMATI: Okay.

DARRELL DUFFIE: I'm with Randy on this issue.

ADMATI: Okay. Good. I hope you agree that equity dominates debt for loss absorption.

DUFFIE: I want to repeat what I said in my opening remarks. This was not a liquidity crisis. It was a solvency crisis.

ADMATI: But then your balance sheet didn't have equity, and you only talked about liquidity. We can talk about trapped liquidity, but capital is not "trapped." The issue is the funding mix. If you have sufficient loss absorption through equity, then you can take risks. That's how Silicon Valley operates in general—not the Silicon Valley Bank, but the place, Silicon Valley. A lot of equity in the tech sector, and if they fail, it's not a big problem for society.

I think Mike Boskin wants to ask a question here.

MICHAEL BOSKIN: I have two questions, but I want to make an observation, because it was mentioned: You spoke about the political economy, the regulation, and the knowledge of the regulators. Back when we were cleaning up the savings and loans and banks, I asked the four regulatory agencies, what was the experience level, the distribution of experience levels, of the examiners, and a very large fraction had never been through a large, deep recession. Now, nobody under sixty has been through a big increase in inflation in their working life. So that's a wrinkle in this. It probably has something to do with the delay and inertia.

The second point I wanted to make was, back then, banks were extending 70–75% of credit. And nonbanks [involved in] the credit markets may have [accounted for] a quarter or a little more. Now that's flipped. And so my first question is, how does that affect your thinking, not just about prudent regulation of an individual bank but how does it impact prudent regulation of the system embedded in this larger credit system? And second is if we're thinking about capital for the overall banking system rather than for each individual bank and its potential— Apple's basically becoming a bank. And back then we were trying to change things, we were trying to get the Fed to go along with letting Walmart become a bank, for example, to get more heavily capitalized institutions into banking. And [the Fed] resisted that. And by the way, we also tried to push the idea of unifying the regulators, something outside the Fed. And the Fed deeply resisted us (getting back to the last panel), because they said we needed the information from our regulation and supervision to conduct monetary policy. So just a couple of observations, two questions about how's the big shift in where credit is coming from in the economy, and about other sources of capital rather than the current individual banks raising capital.

ADMATI: Anybody want to take you there? Let's take another one from [Michael] Bordo.

MICHAEL BORDO: My question is for Darrell Duffie. An anecdote from history that might be relevant was an article by [economist] Phillip Cagan presented at a [1963] conference on the hundredth anniversary of the National Banking System. One of his explanations for why the National Banking System did not prevent banking panics was the high reserve requirements placed on the different categories of banks, to solve the problems of the preceding free-banking era when there were few reserve requirements. What happened was that the panics were worse during the national banking era, and the reason Cagan gave was that it was because the banks believed that they could not dip into their required reserves.

ADMATI: One more behind him, and then we'll answer. I think we don't have time for a lot, but we can continue.

WILLIAM NELSON: Thank you. I'm Bill Nelson from BPI. So in the mid-1950s, during one of the Fed swings away from the discount window, when they were trying to actively encourage institutions not to use the discount window, they created and used a combined capital and liquidity metric, in which basically assets were lined up by liquidity, and liabilities were lined up by runnability. And your capital was evaluated as some measure at sort of fire-sale prices to the extent that it was needed. I don't know if that's exactly the right approach needed now, but I'm wondering if you all see this as attractive—some kind of combined liquidity capital test?

ADMATI: Okay, let's go quickly here. And then there are a few other questions I want to get to maybe Jeffrey Lacker? Or do you want to answer?

QUARLES: Let me take the bank-nonbank question. Obviously, nonbanks have been a huge factor in many of the recent stresses, certainly during both COVID and the Great Financial Crisis. The Fed has had to develop a number of ad hoc mechanisms to provide liquidity to the whole financial system outside of the banking system, given how large the nonbank sector is. Clearly, if you were designing the Federal Reserve today instead of in 1913, it would not occur to you to say that its authorities and focus should be solely on the banking system. Instead, the Fed would be the central flywheel of an integrated financial system. And we should regularize that. We should acknowledge that nonbanks are an important, integral, and totally appropriate feature of the financial system. The Federal Reserve has a totally appropriate mandate to provide liquidity for the financial system, and connected with that it should have a totally appropriate regulatory and supervisory mandate over that nonbank system as well. And we should just absolutely rationalize that, because we are effectively trying to impose it in each period of stress on the fly, ad hoc, with limited and unclear authority, and having really not thought through the full implications of trying to do that in an integrated way.

ADMATI: Darrell?

DUFFIE: I do think there's an issue about whether the central bank should also be the banking supervisor. In Canada, the Bank of Canada does not regulate banks. That's done by the Office of the Superintendent of Financial Institutions. The United Kingdom has gone back and forth on who does bank supervision. That responsibility is definitely up for grabs. When Axel Weber, former head of the Bundesbank, was asked, "What about doing bank supervision?" he replied, in effect, "No, we don't want to do that, because we don't want that conflict of interest. We want to focus on monetary policy."

For the United States, I think it deserves a lot of study before one just goes ahead and proposes a separation of bank supervision and the central bank, but it should be an issue that is up for discussion in terms of costs and benefits.

Michael [Bordo], on your question about the national banking era, absolutely, yes. I referred in my prepared remarks to Charles Goodhart's last-taxi analogy, regarding the cost of trapped high-quality liquid assets [see chapter 5]. Gary Gorton has a related paper on the national banking era and the financial instability caused by trapped liquidity at that time. Gorton has brought that forward into modern liquidity regulations and explained that this is not a good idea. As you can tell from my remarks, I'm all in favor of having a central bank serve its intended role as the lender of last resort, so as to provide financial stability. Notwithstanding the very good points that Amit and Anat have made about—

ADMATI: —insolvent banks.

DUFFIE: The importance of starting with capital is that the issues of liquidity for solvent banks are important. The Fed is not legally permitted to lend to insolvent banks.

ADMATI: But it is.

DUFFIE: And on this last idea of combining liquidity and capital regulations that Bill Nelson raised, I definitely believe that banks should be given an incentive to raise their capital by being given a trade-off between required liquidity and required capital so that we end up with the situation that Amit described, in which bank shareholder capital at risk does not end up putting us into a—I think you called it—physics laboratory in which we're trying to titrate all of these complicated liquidity regulations. Just make it simple. Provide an incentive for banks to raise enough equity capital that these liquidity considerations drop into the background.

ADMATI: Or maybe cancel liquidity regulation altogether.

AMIT SERU: Let me just say one thing related to nonbanks. Michael, I think your point is very relevant, because nonbanks have a large market share now across many sectors. At the same time, we have 4,800 banks. And I think that there is a lot of political economy that drives how big nonbanks can become, in what sectors, and in what parts of the country. The political economy that drives why we have so many banks in every state and in the country is also what explains why nonbanks aren't an even larger part of the economy—despite banks having a very clunky business model. That's what I take from all of what I am hearing.

JAMES BULLARD: Jim Bullard, St. Louis Fed. I would like to make two points. The first is about the insolvency issue. This is based too much on mark-to-market accounting. Sure, if you had that, you'd have a different system. But this was all set up to not do mark-to-market accounting. There was a good reason for that. Interest rates can fluctuate for a variety of reasons. You don't want to reevaluate the capital in all these institutions and have a crisis on your hands whenever interest rates increase. So there's a good reason to say that maybe it is set up wisely.

My second point is about the distinction between insured and uninsured deposits. The uninsured deposits should be managed by somebody. There should be private insurance for that or some other arrangements. If you talk to bankers, there do appear to be other arrangements behind those so-called uninsured deposits. So they aren't as runnable as they appear. That's why SVB probably was a quirky institution. These other banks that have deposits that look like they're uninsured are really not in the same situation. I think the issue is more subtle than it's being portrayed by the panel here.

ADMATI: Okay, we were a little bit over time. Maybe one other question and then final, quick remarks.

HARALD UHLIG: Harald Uhlig from the University of Chicago. The time inconsistency of regulation really concerns me here. We thought there could be uninsured deposits, and now we have learned that they're all insured. We thought we should only lend to illiquid but solvent institutions. That is the Bagehot principle, which the Fed is supposed to abide by. But now we are also bailing out the insolvent banks. The government was supposed to intervene beyond that only for systemically important banks. But in April, the US Treasury Department, Federal Reserve, and Federal Deposit Insurance Corporation announced a systemic risk exception for Signature Bank, which is rather small. So it seems to me that there is always a taxpayer put at the end. When we design regulation, we have to think really, really hard about what regulators do at the end when the house is on fire, and that their promise not to do something beforehand is likely to be broken when the crisis is there.

ADMATI: Okay, final comment. I would just say to Amit, with regard to inconsistent regulators, that all the federal regulators gave high ratings to these banks, all of them, so that makes you pause.

QUARLES: So I'll take up Jim's challenge. I do think that we should recognize a difference between an institution that has assets that will in fact, cover its liabilities if they can be held to maturity (which is why they put them in a hold-to-maturity account), compared to an institution that has assets with significant credit losses. In thinking about the provision of liquidity, the central bank should consider that institution differently than an institution that has a huge credit loss in its loan portfolio that is much more difficult to resolve. The Fed did try to address that in the terms of the BTFP [Bank Term Funding Program] by lending against the hold-to-maturity securities at par rather than at a discount. That is irregular in the Fed religion and in traditional central banking practice. But, I think it is reasonable to think about how to regularize and institutionalize that approach for securities with no credit risk that will only recognize a loss if they must be sold in a liquidity squeeze.

ADMATI: By the way, when interest rates go up, depositors also want higher interest rates. So the assumption that the debt is going to stay where it is when it is the short-term debt is also questionable, I would say.

DUFFIE: On mark-to-market accounting, it's difficult to do with regulatory capital accounting, but we do also have stress tests that can emulate the effect of mark-to-market accounting for purposes of ensuring adequate capital. And, agreeing with Amit, it's kind of weird that an interest rate shift of 400 to 500 basis points, which the Fed itself was implementing, had important implications for bank solvency that deserved greater attention. Whether you mark the assets to market or not, a stress test for that sort of shift in rates was an obvious thing for the Fed to have done before the Fed got well into its interest rate rise.

SERU: So just one last thing, which is related to the comment that Jim made. But before I do that, I note that I fully agree with what Harald [Uhlig] was saying—inconsistency in regulation driven by political economy is the core issue here. Back to Jim's point, when the accountants pushed for hold-to-maturity accounting for banks the way they did after the Global Financial Crisis in 2007, there was some discussion about looking at the structure of liabilities and whether the banks are solvent when allowing banks to pick this sort of accounting. The whole idea that a bank is allowed to pick some assets that can be "held to maturity" makes sense when the banks are solvent and perhaps facing a temporary illiquidity issue that they might avoid. Moreover, banks that are allowed to pick hold-to-maturity accounting for some assets don't have significant runnable liabilities like uninsured depositors, since there might be no bank in the long run if there is a run. Somewhere along the way, we did the hold-to-maturity accounting but we completely forgot about allowing this for banks that are solvent and do not have runnable liabilities. This policy definitely needs to be fixed in my view, going forward. To Jim's second point, I think while SVB was special, it is not that special relative to many other banks, as I showed in my presentation.

ADMATI: Well, we are past time, so thank you all very much for attending.

DISINFLATION AND THE STOCK MARKET

8

Disinflation and the Stock Market: Third-World Lessons for First-World Monetary Policy

Anusha Chari and Peter Blair Henry

Introduction

With monetary policymakers having fallen behind the curve on their price stability mandate, there is much to learn from history about whether Federal Reserve officials can quickly, and at low cost to employment and output, reduce inflation to their stated target. There are two opposing schools of thought.

The first, call it the Sacrifice Ratio (SR) School, says that the journey back to stable prices will be painful and protracted, as it was during the Volcker disinflation of the late 1970s and early 1980s, because reducing inflation requires a short-run fall in output in accordance with the Phillips curve (Ball 1994; Fischer 1988; Gordon 1982; Okun 1978).

An opposing school of thought consists of financial market participants who have been parsing Federal Reserve chairman Jay Powell's speeches since the 2022 Jackson Hole Economic Symposium in the hope of extracting signals about a future pause in interest rate hikes and a willingness to cut rates if necessary. This school holds that this time is different, claiming that a Powell-led Fed, unlike Volcker's, will be able to restore price stability in short order and at a modest cost to the economy. In seeking support for its claim, the This Time Is Different (TTID) School might look for comfort in Sargent (1982), who documents that credible shifts in the monetary and fiscal policy regimes of Austria, Germany, Hungary, and Poland during episodes of hyperinflation in the aftermath of World War I: (a) rapidly stabilized these countries' price levels, and (b) inflicted little cost on their employment and output.

The trouble with the TTID view, however, is that: (1) there has been no change in US fiscal policy—the federal deficit as a percentage of GDP was 5.4% in 2022, will be 5.3% in 2023, and is forecast to climb, on average, through 2033 (Congressional Budget Office 2023); and (2) even after raising the federal funds rate at a record-setting pace, it is not clear that monetary policymakers, having let the inflation genie out of the bottle in the first place, have met the Sargent (1982) standard of a credible regime shift. Furthermore, both the SR and TTID views suffer from a small sample problem. It is difficult to infer how long and costly the current US disinflation path will be by comparing it to the only previous attempt in US history to actively engineer a disinflation on the order of magnitude of the one currently underway.

In contrast to the focus that both schools of thought place on the Volcker episode, this paper uses the historical experience of developing countries' attempts to actively engineer disinflation as a set of quasi-laboratory experiments to address the following question: will the Fed be able to achieve a rapid, low-cost return to 2% inflation? By exploiting the richness of the developing country data—eighty-one disinflation programs: fifty-six directed at reducing "moderate" inflation, twenty-five directed at reducing "high," and spread across twenty-one developing countries between 1973 and 1994—our paper concludes that a soft landing by the Fed is unlikely. In the process of drawing that conclusion, the paper makes two contributions.

First, by assembling a dataset of fifty-six disinflation programs directed at reducing "moderate" inflation—defined by Dornbusch and Fischer (1993) and Fischer (1993) as double-digit inflation of less than 40%—the paper provides more statistical power than the single Volcker episode. It is tempting to dismiss developing countries as too dissimilar to the US to provide a useful comparison. But the median level of peak inflation during the fifty-six developing country disinflation programs, 15%, was similar to peak inflation in (a) the Volcker era (11%) and (b) the United Kingdom, United States, and European Union in 2022. The current bouts of inflation in advanced economies, and the earlier episodes of inflation in developing countries, have parallel origins: large, spending-driven fiscal deficits. Further similarities include a context of foreign wars, oil-price spikes, and other shocks. Because the paper also assembles data on twenty-five disinflation programs directed at reducing "high" inflation—defined, by Easterly (1996) and Bruno and Easterly (1996), as inflation greater than 40% per year—it also provides more high-inflation episodes than Sargent's (1982) sample of four countries.

The second contribution is methodological. It uses stock market data from twenty-one developing countries to provide a cost-benefit analysis of disinflation. It conducts this analysis because the central issue about disinflation is not how costly it is in the short run but whether the costs of disinflation, if any, are outweighed by the longer-run benefits (Henry 2002). Policymakers presumably do not attempt to reduce inflation unless it is in the interest of the countries they serve to do so. However, if the net present value of disinflation is positive, there is no clear articulation of this point in the literature. For instance, the SR school measures the short-run cost of reducing inflation as the sum of undiscounted output losses over some horizon.[1] This approach assumes that there are long-run benefits to disinflation without making them explicit in a cost-benefit calculation. SR-based analyses, therefore, do not tell us whether the benefits of disinflation outweigh the costs.

In contrast to the exclusive previous emphasis on costs, by also accounting for the potential benefits, our stock market analysis of disinflation highlights the fundamental issue of net present value.

A country's aggregate share price index is the present value of the expected future profits of its publicly traded firms. Changes in stock prices, therefore, reflect revised expectations about future corporate profits and the discount rate at which those profits are capitalized. Contractionary measures taken to reduce inflation may raise discount rates and reduce profits in the short run. But the reduction in inflation may increase future profits, because reducing inflation: (a) raises productivity, and (b) may also reduce discount rates (e.g., equity risk premia) by reducing the variance of expected future profits. The percentage change in the stock market in response to the announcement of a disinflation program removes the temporal dimension of the analysis by collapsing the entire expected future stream of disinflation costs and benefits into a single summary statistic: the present value of the expected net benefits of the program.

Using standard event-study regressions (e.g., MacKinlay 1997), we estimate the average cumulative abnormal return (CAR), measured in real US dollars, associated with attempted disinflations of high versus moderate inflation. Figure 8.1 conveys the three central results. First, in real dollar terms, the average CAR associated with anticipated disinflation across the twenty-five high-inflation episodes is positive and large—44%. Second, the average CAR associated with anticipated disinflation across the fifty-six moderate-inflation episodes is negative and large—minus 24%. Third, the 68-percentage-point difference between the two sets of CARS is statistically as well as economically significant. The three central results persist after controlling for external and domestic factors and regardless of whether the left-hand-side variable in the regressions is in real dollar returns or real local currency returns. Bluntly stated: on average, the stock market views reducing high inflation as a positive net present value event while it regards attempts to reduce moderate inflation as destroying value.

Constructed using data on all of the developing countries between 1973 and 1994 that (a) had a disinflation program and

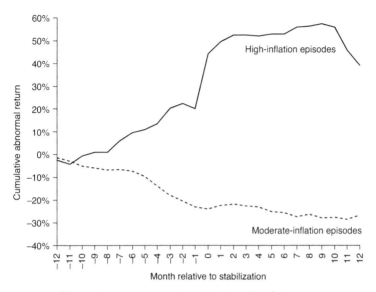

FIGURE 8.1. The stock market responds positively to disinflation programs directed at high inflation and negatively to those directed at moderate inflation. Source: Authors' calculations.

(b) also had a stock market, figure 8.1 does not capture the universe of developing-country disinflations, but it comes close and therefore suggests that reducing high inflation is, in general, a very different proposition than reducing moderate inflation. Said differently, figure 8.1 signals that we cannot easily extrapolate lessons from high-inflation episodes—where inflation was rapidly reduced at little apparent cost—to moderate-inflation scenarios. Starting with a description of the data in the following section, the rest of this paper grapples with the relevance of figure 8.1 and the accompanying institutional details for the challenges currently facing the Fed.

Data and Descriptive Findings

Data construction involves two steps—sample selection and assembly of the raw data, namely: stock prices, dates of disinflation programs, and classification of the level of inflation at the time each program was implemented. The sample includes all countries that (1) have publicly available stock market data and (2) have undertaken at least one disinflation since their stock market data became readily available. The twenty-one countries that satisfy both criteria are: Argentina, Brazil, Chile, Egypt, India, Indonesia, Israel, Jamaica, Jordan, Kenya, Mexico, Nigeria, Pakistan, Peru, the Philippines, South Africa, South Korea, Thailand, Turkey, Venezuela, and Zimbabwe.

Stock Markets

The principal source of stock prices is the International Finance Corporation's (IFC) Emerging Markets Data Base (EMDB). Stock price indices for individual countries are the dividend-inclusive, US dollar-denominated IFC Global Indices. For most countries, EMDB's coverage began in December 1975. For others, coverage started in December 1984. For countries where the IFC does not provide stock market data, we use the stock price index given in the IMF's [International Monetary Fund] International Financial Statistics (IFS). Each country's US dollar-denominated stock price index is deflated by the US consumer price index (CPI), which comes from the IFS. All data are monthly. The consumer price index for each country also comes from the IFS. Returns and inflation are calculated as the first difference of the natural logarithm of the real stock price and CPI.

Disinflation Dates

We use two sources to identify the implementation month and year of each of the eighty-one disinflation programs. The first source is Calvo and Végh (1999). They identify the best-known programs in the literature on inflation stabilization. The second source is the Annual Reports of the International Monetary Fund (IMF 1973–1994). We use these reports to construct a time series of the months in which each of the twenty-one countries effectively announced their intention to stabilize inflation (i.e., engineer a disinflation) by signing an official agreement with the IMF.

IMF programs typically call for current account stabilization in addition to disinflation. The dual objectives of these programs do not introduce important biases into the dating procedure. The macroeconomic targets in IMF programs are generated by the IMF's financial programming model, which is based on the monetary approach to the balance of payments (Agénor and Montiel 1996, 423; Mussa and Savastano 2000, 101). Under the monetary approach, balance of payments problems stem from an excess supply of money, with the monetization of the government deficit seen as the proximate cause of the excess supply. The IMF requires that countries reduce both the fiscal deficit and the growth rate of the money supply to stabilize their current accounts. The prescription for stabilizing the current account is, therefore, tantamount to a traditional disinflation program.

Including the IMF programs of Mexico in 1995, the Asian Crisis in 1997, Russia in 1998, and Brazil in 1999 would strengthen the central findings, because stock prices collapsed during the months leading up to the signing of the relevant agreements, all of which were implemented during moderate inflation. Nevertheless, we exclude these episodes from the sample for two reasons. First, the synopsis of IMF-sponsored disinflation programs outlined in the preceding paragraph does not provide an accurate description of the Mexican, Asian, Russian, and Brazilian episodes. These IMF agreements were not triggered by inflation crises per se, but rather financial crises, the proximate cause of which was country balance sheets whose assets and liabilities were misaligned to both maturity structure and currency denomination (Dornbusch 1999). Second, as part of these agreements, the IMF imposed major structural and institutional reforms in addition to insisting on its traditional short-run stabilization objectives (Feldstein 1998).

Inflation Classification

Turning to the classification of inflation episodes, as in Bruno and Easterly (1998) and Easterly (1996), we define high-inflation episodes as those where twelve-month inflation was greater than 40% during each of the twenty-four months leading up to and including the month in which policymakers implemented the disinflation program. We define moderate-inflation episodes analogously: those with twelve-month inflation between 10 and 40% during each of the twenty-four months leading up to and including the month in which policymakers implemented disinflation.

The online data appendix provides extended information about the eighty-one disinflation programs. Here is a summary. Fourteen of the eighty-one programs correspond to the beginning of Calvo and Végh (1999) disinflation episodes. Two of the fourteen Calvo and Végh episodes coincided with IMF agreements: Mexico in 1977 and Argentina in 1991. All fifty-six attempts at reducing moderate inflation had IMF sponsorship. Thirteen of the twenty-five attempts at reducing high inflation had official IMF sponsorship. Chile is the only country in the sample that successfully stabilized both high inflation and then, a decade later, moderate inflation. Jamaica had the most IMF agreements, eleven. Finally, seventeen of the twenty-five high-inflation episodes occurred in Argentina and Brazil.

Given the outsized presence of Argentina and Brazil, it is natural to ask whether figure 8.1 is sensitive to the classification of "high" inflation defined as 40% or greater. Table 8.1 compares stock price responses to disinflation under two alternative classifications. The first alternative divides the eighty-one episodes into two groups of roughly equal size by descending order of inflation when the

TABLE 8.1. The median stock price response to disinflations directed at high inflation exceeds the median stock price response to disinflations directed at moderate inflation.

	Bruno and Easterly Classification		Two-Way Numerical Split		Three-Way Numerical Split		
	High	Moderate	High	Moderate	High	Moderate	Low
Number of episodes	25	56	40	41	27	27	27
Median inflation	118	15	77	11	116	26	10
Median stock price change	16	1	14	1	15	11	1
Number negative	6	25	11	20	7	10	14
P-value	0.01	0.25	0.01	0.5	0.01	0.12	0.65

Source: Henry (2000).

disinflation program was initiated: high inflation (forty cases) and moderate inflation (forty-one cases). This two-way split is particularly useful, because it creates a superset of the high-inflation episodes not dominated by Argentina and Brazil. The second alternative divides the episodes into three groups of equal size: high inflation (twenty-seven cases), moderate inflation (twenty-seven cases), and low inflation (twenty-seven cases).

Table 8.1 divides the eighty-one stabilization episodes into three groups based on levels of average inflation prior to announcement. The first grouping corresponds to the Bruno and Easterly (1998) classification of high versus moderate inflation; the second simply divides the total sample into two groups of equal size: high and moderate inflation. The third comparison splits the sample into three groups of equal size: high, moderate, and low inflation. The first three rows provide summary statistics for each grouping: the number of episodes, the median inflation rate, and the median stock price response for the high and moderate categories under each inflation classification scheme. The fourth row reports the number of episodes for which the stock price change over the two-month-announcement window is less than the median (country-specific) two-month stock price change. The last row reports the two-sided *p*-value of observing at most the corresponding number of stock price responses to stabilization below the median (country-specific) two-month percentage change in the stock price.

The first three rows of table 8.1 report summary statistics for the number of country episodes, the median inflation rate, and the median stock price response for the high and moderate categories under each inflation classification scheme. In keeping with the spirit of presenting raw data in the previous two rows of the table, the third row presents information on raw, unadjusted stock returns instead of abnormal returns. Accordingly, instead of reporting information on cumulative returns over the twelve-month pre-disinflation window of $[-12, 0]$, where the discrepancy between cumulative returns and cumulative abnormal returns might be large, the table reports cumulative returns over the two-month window, $[-1, 0]$.

The last row of table 8.1 reports the two-sided *p*-value of observing, at most, the corresponding number of cumulative two-month returns below their country-specific, median cumulative two-month returns. Under all three inflation classification schemes, the sign tests are significant at the 1% level for the high-inflation episodes but they are never significant for the moderate-inflation episodes. The consistency of the sign tests across the three classification schemes suggests that the differential responses of the stock market to programs directed at reducing high versus moderate inflation indicated by figure 8.1 are not overly sensitive to the classification of high inflation as that exceeding 40%.

Descriptive Differences and Case Studies

Turning from issues of classification sensitivity back to broader themes of the disinflation episodes, one fact leaps out from the data: countries that attempt to reduce moderate inflation to low inflation (single digits) rarely succeed. Of the fifty-six stabilization programs directed at reducing moderate inflation between 1973 and 1994, only five worked.

At first blush, the rate at which governments successfully stabilized high inflations, eight of twenty-five, also appears low. But this low success rate is driven almost entirely by the seventeen attempts in Argentina and Brazil, fifteen of which failed. Of the six countries outside Argentina and Brazil that tried to stabilize high inflation, only Mexico and Peru needed more than one attempt—two each—to do so. In other words, beyond Latin America, all the countries in the sample that attempted to stabilize high inflation succeeded on their first try.

In short, countries have found it harder to reduce inflation from moderate to low than they have to reduce it from high to moderate. The reality that, even with official IMF sponsorship and financing, countries succeeded in reducing moderate inflation to single digits less than 10% of the time casts doubt on the view that the Fed will be able to engineer a quick return to its 2% inflation target.

Indeed, figure 8.2 tells a sobering story in this regard. The figure plots annualized monthly inflation during successful stabilizations of high inflation (solid line, left-hand-side) and moderate inflation (dashed line, right-hand-side scale). The graph indicates that high inflation comes down more quickly than moderate inflation. On average, high inflation falls from 120 to 20%—well within the Dornbusch and Fischer (1993) moderate-inflation range—in fifteen months. In contrast, it takes thirty-six months to reduce moderate inflation to the low-inflation threshold of 10%. The reality that high inflation falls to one-sixth its prestabilization level in fifteen months, whereas moderate inflation takes three years to recede by half, strongly suggests that moderate inflation is more persistent.

Moderate inflation may be more persistent than high inflation for structural reasons. It is also possible that moderate inflation

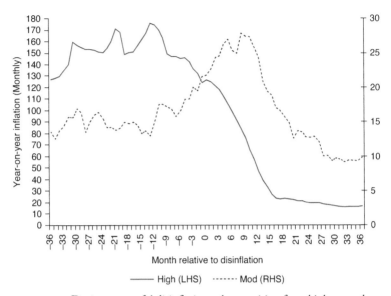

FIGURE 8.2. During successful disinflations, the transition from high to moderate inflation is swifter than the transition from moderate to low inflation. Source: Authors' calculations.

only appears more stubborn because governments facing high inflation implement cold turkey strategies, whereas those facing moderate inflation take a gradualist approach. Chile's experience, for example, reveals that the journey from moderate to low inflation can take years.

Following a decade of little progress toward achieving stable prices, in September 1990—with annual inflation in excess of 20%—the country's central bank announced that it would adopt an official target for annual inflation and tighten monetary policy as necessary to achieve it. The first target, set for the period of December 1990 to December 1991, was 15 to 20%, with the central bank reducing the annual target by 1.5 percentage points each year from 1991 to 2001. By publicly articulating an explicit goal and putting its credibility at stake, Chile's central bank reduced inflation to 8.2% by 1995 and kept it in the single digits through 2021.

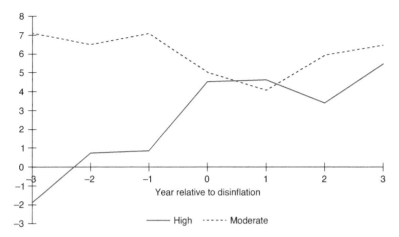

FIGURE 8.3. Growth slows during successful disinflations from moderate inflation to low inflation but rises during disinflations from high to moderate inflation. Source: Authors' calculations.

Moving beyond Chile to the broader developing world, did the longer period of time it took to reduce moderate inflation compared to high inflation have attendant consequences for output? Figure 8.3 addresses the question by plotting, in disinflation time, the average annual growth rate of real GDP for the eight episodes in which countries successfully reduced high inflation to moderate—Argentina, Brazil, Chile (1978), Israel, Jamaica, Mexico, Peru, and Turkey—versus the five episodes in which countries successfully reduced moderate inflation to low: Chile (1990), Egypt, Indonesia, Kenya, and South Korea. The time path of real GDP growth during the two types of disinflation episodes differs in three important ways.

First, during disinflation from moderate to low levels of inflation, there are output losses. On impact, between years −1 and 0, the only country in which growth does not decline is Kenya, and the average growth rate of GDP across the five countries falls by 2 percentage points. Looking over the entire disinflation horizon, the average growth rate of GDP during the post-disinflation period, years 1 to 3, is 5.5%, or 1.4 percentage points lower than the 6.9% growth rate of GDP in the pre-disinflation period, years −3 to −1.

Second, there are output gains during disinflation from high- to moderate-inflation levels. On impact, between years −1 and 0, growth increases in five of the eight countries, and their average GDP growth rate rises by 3.7 percentage points. Turning to the entire disinflation horizon, the average growth rate of GDP during the post-disinflation period, years 1 to 3, is 4.5%, or 4.6 percentage points higher than the negative 0.1% growth rate of GDP in the pre-disinflation period, years −3 to −1.

Third, the change in output associated with disinflation from high levels of inflation is 6.0 percentage points (4.6 minus negative 1.4) larger than the change in output associated with disinflation from moderate to low levels of inflation.

The output losses associated with successful disinflations of moderate inflation in developing countries documented here are consistent with the advanced country experiences of Ireland and Spain chronicled by Dornbusch and Fischer (1993). Ireland's disinflation began in 1982, and unemployment rose from 9.5% to more than 17% between the early 1980s and 1987. Spanish authorities initiated their disinflation in 1977, and "Spanish disinflation, like the Irish, involved a long, hard slog" (Dornbusch and Fischer 1993), with the Spanish unemployment rate rising by almost 10 percentage points before inflation declined to single digits in 1985. Dornbusch and Fischer (1993) conclude: "The countries that successfully disinflated to low inflation . . . Ireland and Spain—did so at a significant cost to output."

The experiences of Ireland and Spain, taken together with the five developing country episodes, paint a picture of output and employment during successful disinflations from moderate to low levels of inflation that is very different from the behavior of output and employment during successful disinflations from high levels of inflation. Nevertheless, defining a disinflation program by its outcome, namely a successful reduction of the inflation rate, may deliver biased estimates of the true effect of disinflation on growth (Calvo and Végh 1999). In a world where people are rational and forward looking, one ideally wants an *ex ante* measure of the effect they expect that the program will have on short- and long-run growth. The stock market view of disinflation, to which we now return, provides—with important limitations—just such an *ex ante* measure. It allows us to use the power of all eighty-one episodes to determine the expected impact of all disinflations, not just those that succeeded.

Regression Estimates

We analyze the difference in stock market reactions to disinflations depicted in figure 8.1 by running regressions of real dollar stock returns on control variables and two sets of disinflation dummies— one for the high-inflation episodes and another for the moderate-inflation episodes. Before proceeding to the results, there are four important caveats.

First, the variance of stock returns is not constant across countries, so we correct all standard errors for heteroscedasticity. Second, although there are 3,595 observations of monthly stock returns, common shocks can affect all twenty-one countries, so the observations may not be independent; we control for common shocks by using proxies for the world business cycle. Third, in addition to controlling for common world shocks, we also control for non-disinflation-related country-specific economic reforms. Fourth, all estimations include country-specific dummy variables.

Benchmark Specifications

Keeping the four caveats in mind, the following panel regression provides a benchmark specification for evaluating the magnitude and statistical significance of the cumulative abnormal twelve-month change in the stock market in anticipation of disinflation:

$$R_{it} = \alpha_i + \gamma_1 HIGH_{it} + \gamma_2 MOD_{it} + \varepsilon_{it} \qquad (1)$$

The α_i in equation (1) are country-specific dummies. $HIGH_{it}$ is a dummy variable for disinflation programs implemented during high inflation. $HIGH_{it}$ takes on the value 1 for country i in each of the months from −12 to 0, where 0 is the month during which the disinflation program is implemented.

Given market efficiency, the country's aggregate share price index will change only in response to new information. Specifically, when the market first learns that the government will implement a disinflation program at time 0, prices will jump up or down in reaction to the news. Because there can be no anticipated jumps in asset prices, absent any additional new information, the share price index will continue drifting in the same direction as the initial jump, until time 0, when the market reaches its new equilibrium price. After time 0, there will be no more changes in the aggregate share price index. Because we do not have precise information on when governments first announced (vs. implemented) the disinflations, we use a twelve-month, pre-implementation window to reflect the likelihood that market participants learned that the disinflation programs would be put in place before they were actually implemented.

The coefficient on $HIGH_{it}$, γ_1 measures the average monthly abnormal return in months −12 through 0 across all countries that implemented disinflation programs during high inflation. Multiplying γ_1 by twelve gives the average CAR attributable to the anticipated disinflation of high inflation. Similarly, γ_2, the coefficient on MOD_{it}, measures the average monthly abnormal return during the twelve-month window preceding disinflation programs that were implemented during moderate inflation.[2] Multiplying γ_2 by twelve gives the average CAR attributable to the anticipated disinflation of moderate inflation. Similarly, $12^*(\gamma_1 - \gamma_2)$ gives the average difference between the stock market response to the disinflation of high versus moderate inflation.

Table 8.2 presents the results. The entry in row 1 of column (1a) indicates that for the benchmark regression, the coefficient on *HIGH* is 0.04, meaning that the average CAR for high-inflation episodes is 48%. The entry in row 2 of column (1a) indicates that the coefficient on *MOD* is −0.015, so the average CAR for moderate-inflation episodes is negative 18%. Since $\gamma_1 - \gamma_2 = 0.055$, the average difference between the high and moderate CARs is 66 percentage points. The third row of table 8.2 is labeled "*HIGH>MOD?*" A "Yes" in this row means that an F-test rejects the restriction $\gamma_1 = \gamma_2$, indicating that the point estimate of γ_1 is significantly larger than the point estimate of γ_2. Thus, the entry in row 3 of column (1a) indicates that the cumulative 66-percentage-point differential between the two stock market responses is statistically significant. To control for external factors, we follow Calvo and Végh (1999) and Fischer, Sahay, and Végh (2002) by adding the growth rate of OECD industrial production and the level of real LIBOR as right-hand-side variables in the benchmark specification. The results reported in column (2a) of table 8.2 indicate that after controlling for external factors, the coefficients on *HIGH* and *MOD* are largely unchanged, and the difference between the coefficient on *HIGH* and *MOD* is still 0.055 and statistically significant.

Next, we extend the Fischer et al. (2002) set of right-hand-side variables by controlling directly for a host of domestic economic policy changes that often coincided with attempted disinflations. Using the policy events in Henry (2000), we construct five dummy variables to control for the effect of the following changes: stock market liberalization, trade liberalization, privatization, debt rescheduling, and national elections. These variables, denoted *SML*, *TRADE*, *PRIV*, *DEBT*, and *ELECTION*, control directly for the possibility that the stock market may increase more in anticipation

TABLE 8.2. The stock market responds positively to disinflations directed at high inflation and negatively to disinflations directed at moderate inflation.

	Panel A: Real Dollar Returns			Panel B: Real Local Currency Returns		
	(1a)	(2a)	(3a)	(1b)	(2b)	(3b)
HIGH	0.040*** (0.016)	0.040*** (0.016)	0.042*** (0.016)	0.040*** (0.016)	0.040*** (0.016)	0.040*** (0.016)
MOD	−0.015*** (0.005)	−0.015*** (0.005)	−0.017*** (0.005)	−0.010** (0.004)	−0.010** (0.004)	−0.011*** (0.004)
HIGH>MOD?	Yes***	Yes***	Yes***	Yes***	Yes***	Yes***
OECD		−0.022 (0.026)	−0.022 (0.026)		−0.044* (0.024)	−0.044* (0.024)
LIBOR		−0.002*** (0.008)	−0.002*** (0.008)		−0.000 (0.001)	−0.001 (0.001)
SML			0.039 (0.026)			0.031 (0.027)
TRADE			−0.014 (0.024)			−0.015 (0.024)
PRIV			−0.039 (0.047)			−0.030 (0.046)
DEBT			0.000 (0.011)			0.008 (0.010)
ELECTION			0.035* (0.021)			0.029 (0.021)

Notes: The table presents estimates of the average stock market response to the stabilization of high versus moderate inflation. The left-hand-side variable is real monthly stock returns. The estimation procedure is Ordinary Least Squares (OLS). Heteroskedastic consistent standard errors are reported in parentheses. The number of observations is 3,595. All regressions include a constant and twenty country-specific dummies (not shown). Levels of statistical significance are indicated by asterisks: *** 1%; ** 5%; * 10%. *HIGH* is a dummy variable that takes on the value 1 in each of the twelve months leading up to and including the month a stabilization program directed at reducing high inflation is implemented. *MOD* is a dummy variable that takes on the value 1 in each of the twelve months leading up to and including the month a stabilization program directed at reducing moderate inflation is implemented.

Source: Authors' calculations.

of reducing high inflation, because disinflations of high inflation are accompanied by other country-specific policy changes that also have a positive effect on stock prices.

We construct the non-disinflation-related reform variables in an entirely analogous fashion to the disinflation dummies. For example, Argentina liberalized its stock market in November 1989. Thus, November 1989 is month 0 for this particular stock market liberalization, and the variable *SML* takes on the value 1 in each of the twelve months from November 1988 to November 1989. Again, note that the dummy variable for each of these country-specific economic reforms is "on" only when these reforms coincide with a disinflation program. Thus, the correct interpretation of the reform coefficients is that of an average monthly effect on the stock market conditional on there also being a disinflation program underway. The results reported in column (3a) of table 8.2 indicate that after controlling for contemporaneous domestic policy changes as well as external economic fundamentals, the coefficients on *HIGH* and *MOD* are, again, largely unchanged. The difference between the coefficients on *HIGH* and *MOD* increases slightly to 0.059 and remains statistically significant. The general lack of significant coefficients on the non-disinflation reform variables may indicate that news of other reforms is of minor importance during periods of disinflation (Dornbusch 1992).

Finally, in addition to controlling for external and domestic factors, we also perform a parallel set of regressions using real local currency returns. We do this because in high-inflation countries, the rate of depreciation of the nominal exchange rate may not keep pace with inflation. If inflation exceeds the rate of nominal depreciation, then the currency is appreciating in real terms, which means that the real dollar value of the stock market may become artificially inflated. To see if this is the case, we re-estimate regressions (1a) through (3a) using real local currency returns instead of real dollar returns as the left-hand-side variable. The results, displayed in columns (1b) through (3b), are almost identical to the previous regressions in which the left-hand-side variable is real US dollars.

Interpretation

The estimates in table 8.2 confirm three central facts: (1) the net present value of reducing high inflation is positive; (2) the net present value of reducing moderate inflation is negative; and (3) both economically and statistically, the net present value of reducing high inflation is significantly larger than the net present value of reducing moderate inflation.

The second fact raises the question, why do countries do it if the expected net present value of reducing moderate inflation is negative? One reason is that the alternative is worse. Moderate inflation tends to rise (Ha, Kose, and Ohnsorge 2019). Rising moderate inflation runs the risk of becoming high inflation, and high inflation: (a) has negative consequences for productive activity and (b) rapidly erodes the purchasing power of people who cannot protect their incomes against inflation.

The caution required to interpret the negative stock market reaction to disinflation programs directed at moderate inflation highlights certain limitations of the stock market analysis. First, stock price responses measure the change in real wealth, not utility gains per se, and a shock that drives down stock market valuation may actually increase utility. For example, an increase in expected future productivity can decrease stock market value if the attendant rise in discount rates outstrips the valuation impact of greater expected future dividends (Lucas 1978). Nevertheless, welfare improves.

More generally, the stock market is not the economy, and a cost-benefit analysis of current and expected future gains to shareholders is not the same as a cost-benefit analysis of current and expected future output. The observation, for instance, that shareholders benefit from eliminating high inflation does not necessarily imply that nonshareholders (i.e., the majority of workers) are also better off. If eliminating high inflation increases capital's share in GDP, then stock prices may rise with no change (or even a fall) in expected future output. As we have seen, eradicating high inflation is associated with aggregate output gains. It does not appear to be zero sum, but the reality that disinflation may have distributive consequences has important implications for moderate-inflation scenarios.

For example, if stabilizing moderate inflation increases labor's share in GDP, workers' income may rise even though stock prices fall. In this case, shareholders and owners of capital more broadly, might prefer to live with moderate inflation than endure the devaluation of assets required to bring about low inflation, while wage earners (i.e., labor) would prefer disinflation. This potential for distributive conflict under moderate-inflation scenarios may provide important clues as to why attempts to reduce moderate inflation so often fail. Resolving these issues is beyond the scope of the paper, but the distributive conflict that flows from the initiation of disinflation programs directed at moderate inflation may explain why financial market participants in the US are so eager for the Fed to pause rate hikes, even as the wider US population wants much lower inflation.

Beyond the Stock Market

Turning from the stock market and the Fed back to inflation, something remarkable occurred during the 1990s. The set of nations classified by the IMF as emerging-market and developing economies (EMDEs) saw their average annual inflation rates decline from 89.4% in 1994 to 8.5% in 2000. The average inflation for these countries remained in the single digits until 2022. Per the earlier discussion about the 1990s emerging-market financial crises and IMF programs (in the section Data and Descriptive Findings:

Stock Markets), we cannot identify, with confidence, discrete dates after 1994 on which EMDEs initiated proper disinflation programs. We do not attempt, therefore, to replicate our stock market analysis for the post-1994 data. The post-1994 decline in inflation is nevertheless relevant for two reasons.

First, the speed with which inflation fell is consistent with the evidence we presented that demonstrates, quite apart from the numerical levels themselves, high and moderate inflation are very different phenomena (see Descriptive Differences and Case Studies above). Average inflation fell quickly from high in 1994 to moderate (39.2%) in 1995, whereas it takes an additional five years to decline from moderate to low. The persistence of moderate inflation for the universe of EMDEs is consistent with the sluggish speed of disinflation in the subset of five countries in the pre-1994 sample that successfully reduced inflation from moderate to low levels.

Second, and shifting the focus once again from short-run questions about speed and cost to the fundamental issue of whether the long-run benefits of disinflation outweigh the costs, the following points are worth noting about the world after 1994. For the universe of EMDEs that successfully reduced inflation from high to moderate, the average growth rate of GDP in the ten-year post-disinflation period was 2.6 percentage points higher—4.2% versus 1.6%—than it was in the previous ten-year period (Chari, Henry, and Reyes 2021). For the universe of EMDEs that eventually reduced inflation from moderate to low, the average growth rate of GDP in the ten-year post-disinflation period was 1.47 percentage points higher—5.52% versus 4.05%—than it was in the previous ten-year period (Chari, Henry, and Reyes 2021). These numbers are subject to the caveat (in Descriptive Differences and Case Studies above) about evaluating disinflation programs based on ex post growth, and the point applies with special force because of the litany of non-disinflation-related reforms undertaken by EMDEs in the 1990s (Chari and Henry 2014). Nevertheless, US lawmakers would do well to take notice of these developing country facts.

Conclusion

US inflation has declined from its forty-year high in 2022. Yet it remains above the Fed's 2% target, and throughout the current disinflation, US financial markets have been ignoring a simple reality. There is no historical precedent for a painless return from moderate to low inflation.

Former Fed chairman Paul Volcker's war against double-digit inflation in the late 1970s and early 1980s was not unusual. In fact, it was the norm—part of a wider, recurring phenomenon at a time when "Third World" nations struggled to reduce inflation. Of the fifty-six developing countries that tried to reduce inflation from levels similar to that where the US began its current journey, only five succeeded, and it took them an average of three years to reduce inflation to single digits.

It is possible that developing countries struggled with disinflation, not because moderate inflation is structurally different from high inflation, but because developing country policymakers lacked the credibility of their advanced economy counterparts. As emphasized by Sargent (1982) and Cochrane (2023), however, the joint commitment of fiscal and monetary policy to price stability is a key determinant of credibility, and the collapse of UK gilt prices in October 2022 bore distinct similarities to past emerging-market fiscal crises. And while US Treasuries have yet to be subjected to deep skepticism about the federal government's commitment to the debt, with American monetary policy having gone astray, it is not obvious the Fed possesses the credibility required for a swift return to 2% inflation.

Whether in advanced economies or the developing world, no team of policymakers has ever executed an immaculate reduction of inflation from moderate to low akin to what we have seen in the vanquishing of high inflations past. Ironically, the stock market, which in the US has been yearning for signs that interest rates will not remain higher for longer, actually provides the strongest evidence that a quick return to the Fed's target is highly unlikely. Policymakers—and financial markets—ignore this lesson at their own peril.

References

Agénor, Pierre-Richard, and Peter Montiel. 1996. *Development Macroeconomics.* Princeton, NJ: Princeton University Press.

Ball, Laurence. 1994. "What Determines the Sacrifice Ratio?" In *Monetary Policy*, edited by N. G. Mankiw, 155–93. Chicago: University of Chicago Press.

Blanchard, Olivier Jean. 1999. *Macroeconomics.* Upper Saddle River, NJ: Prentice Hall.

Bruno, Michael, and William Easterly. 1996. "Inflation's Children: Tales of Crises that Beget Reforms." *American Economic Review* 86, no. 2 (May): 213–17.

———. 1998. "Inflation Crises and Long-Run Growth." *Journal of Monetary Economics* 41, no. 1 (February): 3–26.

Calvo, Guillermo, and Carlos Végh. 1999. "Inflation Stabilization and Balance of Payments Crises in Developing Countries." In *Handbook of Macroeconomics*, edited by John B. Taylor and Michael Woodford, 1531–614. Amsterdam: North-Holland.

Chari, Anusha, and Peter Blair Henry. 2014. "Learning from the Doers: Developing Country Lessons for Advanced Economy Growth." *American Economic Review* 104, no. 5 (May): 260–65.

Chari, Anusha, Peter Blair Henry, and Hector Reyes. 2021. "The Baker Hypothesis: Stabilization, Structural Reforms, and Economic Growth." *Journal of Economic Perspectives* 35, no. 3 (Summer): 83–108.

Cochrane, John H. 2023. *The Fiscal Theory of the Price Level.* Princeton, NJ: Princeton University Press.

Congressional Budget Office. 2023. *The Budget and Economic Outlook: 2023 to 2033* (February). https://www.cbo.gov/publication/58946.

Dornbusch, Rudiger. 1992. "Lessons from Experiences with High Inflation." *World Bank Economic Review* 6, no. 1 (January): 13–31.

———. 1999. "After Asia: New Directions for the International Financial System." *Journal of Policy Modeling* (Elsevier) 21, no. 3: 289–99.

Dornbusch, Rudiger, and Stanley Fischer. 1987. *Macroeconomics.* New York: McGraw Hill.

———. 1993. "Moderate Inflation." *The World Bank Economic Review* 7, no. 1 (January): 1–44.

Easterly, William. 1996. "When Is Stabilization Expansionary?" *Economic Policy* 11, no. 22 (April 1): 65–107.

Feldstein, Martin. 1998. "Refocusing the IMF." *Foreign Affairs* (March/April): 20–33.

Fischer, Stanley. 1988. "Real Balances, the Exchange Rate, and Indexation: Real Variables in Disinflation." *Quarterly Journal of Economics* 103, no. 1 (February): 27–49.

———. 1993. "The Role of Macroeconomic Factors in Growth." *Journal of Monetary Economics* 32, no. 3 (December): 485–512.

Fischer, Stanley, Ratna Sahay, and Carlos A. Végh. 2002. "Modern Hyper- and High Inflations." *Journal of Economic Literature* 40, no. 3 (September): 837–80.

Gordon, Robert J. 1982. "Why Stopping Inflation May Be Costly: Evidence from Fourteen Historical Episodes." In *Inflation: Causes and Effects*, edited by Robert E. Hall, 11–40. Chicago: University of Chicago Press.

Ha, Jongrim, M. Ayhan Kose, and Franziska Ohnsorge. 2019. *Inflation in Emerging and Developing Economies: Evolution, Drivers, and Policies.* Washington, DC: The World Bank.

Henry, Peter Blair. 2000. "Stock Market Liberalization, Economic Reform, and Emerging Market Equity Prices." *Journal of Finance* 55, no. 2 (April): 529–64.

———. 2002. "Is Disinflation Good for the Stock Market?" *Journal of Finance* 57, no. 4 (August): 1617–48.

International Monetary Fund (IMF). 1973–1994. Annual Reports of the Executive Board.

Lucas, Robert E. 1978. "Asset Prices in an Exchange Economy." *Econometrica* 46, no. 6 (November): 1429–45.

MacKinlay, A. Craig. 1997. "Event Studies in Economics and Finance." *Journal of Economic Literature* 35, no. 1 (March): 13–39.

Mankiw, N. Gregory. 1997. *Macroeconomics*, 3rd ed. New York: Worth Publishers.

Mussa, Michael, and Miguel Savastano. 2000. "The IMF Approach to Economic Stabilization." *NBER Macroeconomics Annual 1999* (vol. 14), edited by Ben S. Bernanke and Julio J. Rotemberg, 79–128. Washington, DC: National Bureau of Economic Research.

Okun, Arthur M. 1978. "Efficient Disinflationary Policies." *American Economic Review* 68, no. 2 (May): 348–52.

Sargent, Thomas. 1982. "The Ends of Four Big Inflations." In *Inflation: Causes and Effects*, edited by Robert E. Hall, 41–97. Chicago: University of Chicago Press.

Notes

1. See, for example, Blanchard (1999), 368; Dornbusch and Fischer (1987), 528; Mankiw (1997), 352.
2. We also estimated the regressions using a market-adjusted regression specification, that is, regression (1) with world stock returns as right-hand-side variables. The results are virtually identical, so we present the more parsimonious mean-adjusted specification.

DISCUSSANT REMARKS

Joshua D. Rauh

Thank you very much, as I lower the microphone here. I was at a dinner last night, and I was sitting next to Art Laffer. And we stood up—I had been arguing with him about something a little bit—and he said, "I like your . . ." and I heard a word. I thought he said, "attitude."

And I said, "Okay."

He replied, "Did you hear what I said?" It turned out he'd said *altitude*, "I like your altitude." So he and I have a similar altitude. Peter Blair Henry and I have different altitudes.

Well, first of all, thanks very much to John Taylor. Congratulations on the thirty years of the Taylor rule, and it's an honor to have the opportunity to discuss this paper by Anusha Chari and Peter Henry on disinflation in the stock market. I'm not a macroeconomist. I'm not a monetary economist. I am a finance economist, and my research expertise is on fiscal policy, although I do a lot on valuation and discounting. Hopefully, through that lens, I'll be able to say something useful.

But the first thing I'll just say is I really enjoyed reading this paper and learned a lot from it, and I recommend that you all read it as well. One can learn a great deal from this technique of looking at other countries that have gone through attempts at disinflation and what has happened to markets when they've done so.

Essentially, the paper asks us: if we're going to get from here to there, where *here* is the US experiencing moderate inflation and *there* is the Federal Reserve's 2% target, what should we expect the stock market to do based on the experience of other countries?

Since Henry did a great job describing the paper and its results, I won't go through too much detail about it. But it's a study of twenty-one countries and eighty-one disinflation programs. That means that a number of these countries have multiple disinflation programs. And it uses a finance event-study methodology.

One of the things I'm going to talk a little bit about is the chosen timing—in other words, the chosen event window. The event begins with a time zero for the event that is twelve months prior to the announcement of an intention to stabilize inflation or to engineer disinflation by signing an official agreement with the International Monetary Fund (IMF). The idea is that there is some foresight into this disinflationary attempt that's going to happen. And then, the outcome is the twelve-month stock return. So we're looking at a time period that is from a year before the actual signing of the official agreement, or formal announcement, up until the date of that event. And the key sample split—as Henry described—was looking at cases where inflation was high, defined as greater than 40% over the time period, or twenty-four months to one month before the announcement of the disinflationary attempts. And then the moderate cases are those where inflation was in the 10 to 40% range during that two-year period.

Here's a graphical representation of the results as I see them if we take out the lines going over time and just look at a histogram (figure A). And I put up coefficients here on real dollar returns and real local currency returns from the regressions.

Henry didn't have much time to talk about this, but they're actually quite similar. For the high-inflation countries, you get a 48% increase in stock market values over the measured time period. Same for the real local currency returns. For the moderate inflation, the hit that Peter measures from implementing the disinflation is lower in the real local currency return setting, which I thought was interesting. If we think about what might be going on in currencies, really, we think that the disinflation should be strengthening

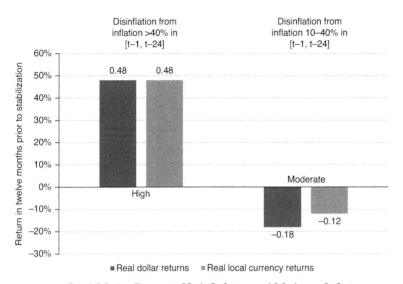

FIGURE A. Stock Market Return in High-Inflation and Moderate-Inflation Scenarios.

Note: Real dollar and real local currency returns of countries experiencing either high or moderate inflation in the period leading up to the announcement of a rate change by the central bank.

Source: Anusha Chari and Peter Blair Henry, "Disinflation and the Stock Market: Third World Lessons for First World Monetary Policy," National Bureau of Economic Research Working Paper 31129, April 2023.

the currencies. So my intuition would have suggested that you might have expected better dollar returns. But perhaps the difference isn't that significant. I suggest the authors say more about the effect of the disinflation on currencies in this setting.

Most of the paper emphasizes results in dollar returns, so I'm going to focus on that. The first comment is on timing. The paper is essentially looking at the stock market returns over this time period, twelve months to zero months. These are the returns that are measured in the regression. During this time, we see that the high inflation is already coming down. So there's some effect happening in anticipation of the formal announcement of the program. There could be real actions also happening in the run-up to that formal signature. The reason I highlight the range, though, is that it does appear that in the high-inflation episodes, the time period over which the authors are measuring stock returns is one where the inflation is already coming down. In contrast, in the moderate episodes, it's a time period where the inflation is actually continuing to accelerate. That's one kind of setting that we have to be aware of as we think about what's going on with the stock market in each of these instances.

The graph that Henry actually showed extends out so you can see what's going on in the stock market after the main period that's in the regressions. It extends it out for another six months. The stock market is pretty flat at that point. But that's the time period where the moderate-inflation countries are still seeing increases in inflation. A natural question that I had when looking at that was: what happens to markets after the moderate-inflation countries start to cool?

And another point they came up with in the presentation is, as Henry mentioned, there are only five cases defining a successful exit from a moderate inflation—getting below that 10% threshold. But these are countries where we're seeing an increase in inflation first and then a decrease in inflation. It does come down, although it's also going up during the time period where the authors are measuring the market returns. It'd be helpful to understand what was going on if the authors would present a few different windows of stock market behavior that might allow us to kind of understand the context of what's going on with inflation in these two sets of sample countries.

My second comment is on valuation. Why do we think the stock market should behave or react to disinflationary attempts by the central bank or by the government? Let's think about the valuation of the stock market as being a present-discounted value of expected free cash flows. I'm going to just use unlevered enterprise value and ignore leverage for now. So the standard valuation equation is:

$$\text{Unlevered } EV_0 = \sum_{t=1}^{\infty} \frac{E_0[FCF_t]}{(1+r_{A,t})^t}$$

The discount rate $r_{A,t}$ is going to be a risk-free rate plus a risk premium, where each cash flow is discounted by a point of the yield curve that is matched to that cash flow. What happens to this discount rate during disinflations? As a direct result of central bank monetary policy, we can say the short-term risk-free rate increases, and there may be effects farther out the yield curve as well, either due to the expectations hypothesis or the possibility of quantitative tightening. If discount rates increase, stock market values decline. In addition, the expected free cash flow is going to change as fewer investment opportunities are positive on a net present value basis (NPV). That is the finance analog to the macroeconomic point that Henry was making—the idea that lower growth, lower macroeconomic growth, is going to mean lower profits. In terms of investment opportunities that might have had positive NPV at a lower discount rate, these are now no longer positive NPV and are not going to create value for the firm.

We can explain the results by thinking that in cases of high inflation, the inflation per se might be very, very detrimental to the real cash flows that the firm is going to experience. When we have inflation above 40%, that would certainly create actual, real problems for the firm due to uncertainty about the future path of prices. In contrast, moderate inflation per se might not be that detrimental to real free cash flows. If inflation is expected, and at 2%, versus expected, and at 10%, if it's all expected, there's no economic model that's going to distinguish between those two scenarios. But when inflation is very high, these higher levels of inflation, also in practice, reflect considerable uncertainty about future inflation. If risk and uncertainty about inflation increase as the level of inflation increases, then I think the results in the paper are understandable through this framework.

For example, let's make an assumption that the average duration of the cash flows in the valuation is ten years. And for the sake of illustration, let's say the real yield goes up from 0.0 to 1.5%, similar to the path followed by the medium-term real yields recently. That would be reflected in a 14% decline in the valuation of the stock market. So this is one way to motivate the results of the paper.

How high do real yields actually have to go in order to fight moderate inflation or to bring moderate inflation back down to the target levels? Or put another way, since they don't always succeed, how much do central banks actually need to increase real yields during times when they are trying to get out of moderate inflation or trying to get out of high inflation? And, of course, they don't usually have as much impact on this medium to longer end of the yield curve. They're looking at the shorter end of the yield curve. But the valuation impact might be more on these longer horizons. What is going on with this medium to long-term end of the bond market is going to be very relevant to what we actually see happening in the stock market.

As table A shows, if we go from, say, a 0% to a 10% real yield, we're now entering the realm of countries that might be looking at very big swings. That would be a 61% decline in the value of the stock market, and again this is how I would conceptualize the results in the paper.

In order to understand the results even better, I thought it might be useful to go and look at a few countries that I just picked

TABLE A. Effect of Changes in Real Yield on Valuation.

Valuation Impact for *Dur*=10		dEV(0) versus			
10yr Real Yield	$1/(1+r)10$	0%	1.5%	3.0%	5.0%
0%	1.000				
1.5%	0.862	−14%			
3.0%	0.744	−26%	−14%		
5.0%	0.614	−39%	−29%	−17%	
10.0%	0.386	−61%	−55%	−48%	−37%

Note: The impacts of a decline in real yield on an investment with a given initial real yield ranging from 0.0 to 10.0% and a duration of ten years.

Source: Author's calculations.

at random out of the sample in the paper and to try to look at just how much the real yield actually did go up in these countries. Or at least see what the range of real yields is? This can be seen in figure B.

Since I didn't have the data on the exact episodes of when these inflationary episodes occurred, I can't really do something exact where I say, "Okay, in India, there was an inflation-fighting episode, and the real yield went up from 0.0 to 5%." But I can see that in India, it was around 0% around ten years ago. And that was a time when inflation was quite high, and those real yields went up to about 5% in part in order to bring that inflation down. In Brazil, you can see a similar pattern where, for a while, real yields are near zero. But preceding the time when inflation also seems to be coming down, real yields come up a lot. There, the maximum ten-year real yield was about 4.6% over this time horizon. Turkey, a country that I think in recent years, we'd say they're experiencing high inflation, actually gets cut off, because it spikes up too much above the chart. But the maximum real yield over the episodes that the authors are looking at in this paper is 11.25%. So the real yield had to go up to over 10% in order to take care of inflation, or at least to address inflation. In Mexico, the real yield topped out at about 6.5%.

If real valuation yields have to go up from, say, 0.0 to 5% or 10% to fight moderate inflation, is 18% a large effect, or would I really even have expected it to be even larger? Here is one hypothesis. Perhaps what is actually going on is that it would have been larger. Or maybe it actually is true that it is beneficial for managers of the cash flows of a company not to have to worry a lot about moderate inflation spiking up into very, very high inflation, and this is dampening what would be an even larger negative valuation impact.

My overall suggestion for the paper is to say more about these valuation impacts, including some of the ranges of where the rates (the valuation yields) might be going and what their expected impact on the market would be.

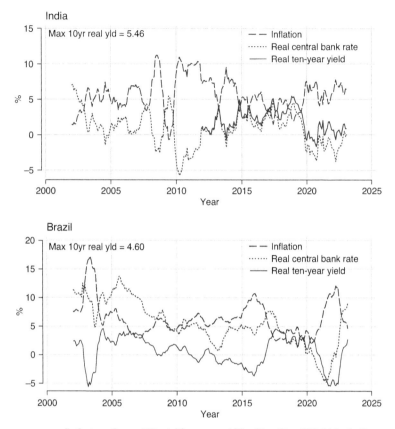

FIGURE B. Inflation, Central Bank Targets, and Ten-Year Bond Yield in India, Brazil, Turkey, and Mexico.

Note: Inflation rate, central bank target rate, and real ten-year yield on government bonds for India, Brazil, Turkey, and Mexico, 2002–23.

Sources: Bank for International Settlements; OECD; Eurostat.

My third comment is to ask whether these countries are valid comparisons? Henry addressed this to some extent, but I think we might want to discuss it a little bit more. Is the US more comparable to a low-inflation situation than a moderate-inflation situation? We never broke 10%. The kind of G7 countries that Henry mentioned were in the 9 to 11% range. That's the very low end of what you're calling in the paper "moderate inflation." And I wonder

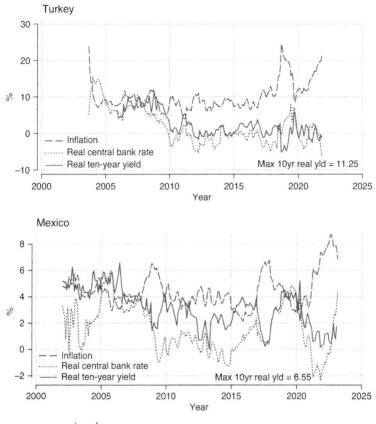

FIGURE B. *continued*

whether one could draw a circle around countries that addressed, say, 5 to 15% inflation, and maybe that might be informative for what we might expect from the US. Also, I'm wondering whether the US history of cooling inflation in the 1980s is relevant. We, in contrast to most of the sample countries, did have a successful episode of bringing down inflation. So maybe that is going to bring more confidence in the Fed's ability to actually do it, which will require less dramatic increases in these valuation yields and will hit the stock market maybe a bit less.

Part of what we might be seeing in this paper is a reflection of the fact that in economic models, the cost of expected moderate inflation is just not that high. So presumably, the reason the Fed is fighting moderate inflation is to demonstrate credibility in being able to respond quickly to unexpected inflationary shocks. It was painful that inflation went up from bumbling along the 2% level to suddenly being at 10%. And so this is the reason, presumably, to say, "Okay, now we're in this moderate-inflation realm, we're going to fight this." We're not just going to say, "Well, now you're going to live with 10% inflation going forward." By setting the precedent that they can respond quickly to unexpected inflationary shocks, the Fed can limit the damage to those unexpected inflationary shocks.

One final comment I want to mention on the redistribution question. Hanno Lustig—who I see in the audience—has done a lot of work on how the lowering of interest rates has impacted income and wealth distribution. Much of this inflation fighting is intimately linked to raising real interest rates, and much of the valuation factors in the stock market are about how those increases in real rates are affecting the longer end of the yield curve and hence the appropriate valuation discount rates for stocks. It may, therefore, be that going in reverse is going to have the opposite effect on wealth distribution. I think that's a valuable point to bring into the paper.

GENERAL DISCUSSION

WILLIAM NELSON (INTRODUCTION): All right, everyone, now turning to the next session, where we're going to be discussing "Disinflation and the Stock Market: Third-World Lessons for First-World Monetary Policy," by Anusha Chari and Peter Henry. So, Peter is the Class of 1984 Senior Fellow at Hoover, a senior fellow at Stanford's Freeman Spogli Institute for International Studies, and dean emeritus of Stern. Being a dean emeritus sounds like a great job, actually.

PETER BLAIR HENRY: It's much easier than being dean.

NELSON: I encourage you all to read the bios in the program for both of our presenters, which are extraordinarily impressive. Among other things, Peter was a college finalist in a slam dunk competition. So that's something we have in common actually. [*Laughter*] So, you're to speak for twenty-five minutes. I'm sorry, I should have introduced myself. I'm Bill Nelson. I'm the chief economist at the Bank Policy Institute.

And for our discussant, Josh Rauh is the Ormond Family Professor of Finance at the Stanford Graduate School of Business, as well as a senior fellow at Hoover. And Josh, you have twenty minutes to present your discussion.

I wanted to just say, Peter, I thought this was just a remarkably clear and compelling paper. Very much on topic. It draws on—as you all will shortly hear—it draws on emerging-market-economy experiences to help inform a very pressing current policy debate here in developing countries of how costly it is to fight inflation, using eighty-one new episodes. The bottom line being that it's easier to reduce high inflation, over 40%, than it is moderate inflation, and with the clear implication that the Fed should drive inflation up by 40% before commencing to reduce it. [*Laughter*] But a more serious implication, of course, is one that I think the FOMC [Federal Open Market Committee] should have, could have learned from over the last couple of years, that things aren't always necessarily going to go the way you expect them to go. And this could be a tough, tough slog. Don't just base your communications and plans on your baseline outlook. So with that, I'll turn it over to you.

*   *   *

NELSON: Peter, would you like to respond?

HENRY: Thank you, Josh [Rauh], for the helpful comments. I agree with everything you said. In particular, your point about distinguishing between the cash flow and discount rate effects is particularly important. I would love to have done it for the time period in question. The trouble is that because of high inflation, the bond market data for a lot of these countries in the 1970s and 1980s is not wonderful. But I'm still hoping that one day I'll actually be able to do something significant to address your observation, because it's an important point. Other than that comment, I really want to allow the audience to jump in, because Josh did a great job discussing the paper.

NELSON: All right. So, maybe I'll take the moderator's privilege here and ask my first question. I was actually going to ask something about debt overhang. But the lawyers looked into it, and evidently, Darrell [Duffie] has a pretty-solid-lock copyright on some questions about debt overhang. So I'll turn to another question, which is: In your paper, the regression results that you report for all of the episodes left me wondering, is there a difference? Were the results different when you look at the successful episodes versus the unsuccessful episodes? I could actually see it going in either direction. But I was curious.

HENRY: It's a good question. I didn't include those results, but I do have them, and the picture's not qualitatively different. It's slightly different, but not in a way that changes the thrust of things.

NELSON: So how much time do we have now? Does anybody know? So I saw John [Cochrane]'s hand jump up and then Andy [Filardo]. Maybe after John. What's that? Sebastian [Edwards]? We'll take those three questions.

JOHN COCHRANE: I have two quick questions. First, there's nothing like saying, "There is no episode" to lead one to scratch one's mind about episodes. Two come to mind. One is [Thomas] Sargent's "Methods of Poincaré and Thatcher."[1] Poincaré faced a moderate inflation but was stopped by the same mechanisms as the Germans and Austrians. A credible change in regime stopped inflation cold without any output loss. The second is the inflation-targeting countries that aren't in your sample because they're more advanced countries. New Zealand, Israel, Canada, and Sweden all stopped inflation in its tracks with no recession. Again, they implemented a credible and durable change in regime—fiscal, monetary, and microeconomic growth-oriented regimes. So it does seem like it's possible even for moderate inflations.

But that echoes your first comment. Is the US headed to this kind of disinflation? It doesn't look to me that we are headed to a credible change of fiscal, monetary, and microeconomic regime. So I would agree with that. That brings up a suggestion: You have the data to tell us why some attempted stabilizations worked and some didn't work. I suspect I know the answer. I suspect Sebastian's going to tell us more about that at dinner. When the central bank tries to go it alone, and the country doesn't solve the underlying fiscal and microeconomic growth problems, inflation stabilization doesn't stick or comes with big output losses. And maybe even the central bank isn't really committing itself to stabilization. But when there is a committed durable fiscal, monetary, and microeconomic reform, it does work.

NELSON: Andy?

ANDREW FILARDO: This is a really great paper, but my recollection is that over the past two decades after your sample ends, the disinflationary experiences among emerging-market economies and small, open, advanced economies were quite different from those in your study. We saw economies move from a 5%–10% inflation range—with a few starting above 10%—to below 5%. Those disinflationary episodes in general went fairly smoothly, and stock market returns were generally strong. Overall, those central banks would say that their disinflations were welfare improving. So the more recent central banking history may give you a somewhat different and richer set of implications than those emphasized in the paper.

Having said that, I don't think that the more recent disinflationary examples suggest that the Fed has an easy disinflationary challenge going forward. During the disinflations, central banks started from a place of low competence in their ability to target inflation and built up credibility. Notably, many achieved success by announcing intermediate inflation targets. They didn't move from almost 10% inflation to sub-5% in one fell swoop. Many did it in steps. I was a little skeptical at the time that they'd be able to achieve a moderate disinflationary path, but they did. Now the Fed has lost its inflation-targeting credibility, many are skeptical that the Fed can quickly disinflate down to 2%. Moreover, I think the Fed is understating to the public its true sense of how confident it is that it can rapidly restore price stability. If the Fed were to announce intermediate inflation targets, learning from the example of the earlier moderate inflation reductions, the Fed might be more likely to succeed and be more credible.

NELSON: Professor Edwards?

SEBASTIAN EDWARDS: This is a superinteresting paper, which I have not read. So many of the questions maybe are answered in the paper, the issues I'm going to raise. But first a question. You ended in 1994. So, Peter, that reminded me of our very dear Ronald McKinnon, and his repression in financial markets. During most of your period, many of these countries didn't have a well-functioning stock market, maybe some of them didn't even have a stock exchange. So I think that emphasizing the stock market as a methodological issue, as Joshua [Rauh] pointed out, is a great thing, but we'd have to look at every one of these countries. So, if one were to do what Joshua did, looking at the recent episodes, you looked at Turkey, Mexico, and two other countries. Chile just did it. Right. Inflation in Chile, it was announced two days ago, it's 9.9%. And it was 14%. So it went from moderate to a successful one. And the stock market is going up. But it's going up because there's one dominant stock in the index, which is SQM [Sociedad Química y Minera], which is the number-one or number-two lithium producer in the world. And this has to do with EVs [electric vehicles]. And there's also the political issue that I'm going to talk about tonight [see chapter 15]. So I think that probably the paper has more details. That's very important.

The second point is something that Joshua brought up, which is the exchange rate. And the two groups of countries have very different approaches to exchange rates. And if you define the attempts as IMF [International Monetary Fund] programs, most of the time the IMF asks for a devaluation up front. Right? But the magnitude of the devaluation is very different across countries. And I think that is something that should be taken into account, or tell us what you guys did about that.

And the final point is that I think that you can reinterpret your results. It's less controversial now than it used to be, but as an evaluation of IMF programs, what you're telling us is that out of eighty-one programs, only eight plus five worked out, or eight plus two, no, five plus two, so only seven out of eighty-one. So it's a pretty negative result relative to the effectiveness of IMF programs, and I wonder what you think about that?

NELSON: So maybe we'll answer those questions, and then we'll take another round. So, Peter?

HENRY: Thanks for all the comments. In the interest of time, I won't go into great detail, but let me just say a few things.

So, John, thanks for mentioning the Poincaré and Thatcher episodes. I'll go back and look at those. I don't remember Dornbusch and Fischer talking about the Thatcher episode, but I'll go back and investigate. And similarly with the New Zealand and Canada episodes as well.

Let me tie together two comments—the question about the low-inflation regime we've seen in emerging economies and Sebastian's point about 1994. The reason I broke the sample in 1994 is that starting in 1994, most of the IMF programs we saw in emerging-market and developing economies—really as Dornbusch has pointed out in his work, and I think Sebastian is talking about this as well—were really related to financial crises rather than inflation crises. And so for some methodological reasons, I take a different approach, but your point is very well taken. In a separate paper that Anusha [Chari] and I wrote with Hector Reyes, who's a PhD student here at Stanford as part of the PhD Excellence Initiative, that I mentioned at the outset of my presentation. In that paper, it's called "The Baker Hypothesis" and was published in the *Journal of Economic Perspectives* in 2021, we show that a big part of the acceleration in growth that happens in emerging and developing economies, post-1994, is because in 1994, we see inflation dropping like a stone in the emerging-market and developing economies.[2] Starting from an average that's close to 40% per year in the early 1990s, it falls radically in 1994–95. And then it's basically in single digits until 2021. And so the bigger message, which I should have emphasized here, is that getting rid of inflation has been a boon to growth in emerging-market and developing economies. But there are important political economy questions related to Sebastian's point about how effective the IMF is in getting countries to stay the course, particularly in moderate-inflation cases. Because we know that, again, from the data, once you get to moderate inflation, there are a lot of benefits. But the transition path there can be quite hard, and again to Sebastian's point, the IMF doesn't seem to actually add much value.

To Sebastian's point about the methodological challenges, the exchange rate and so forth, I didn't mention them very much in the talk, but we have addressed those issues. And even in the high-inflation cases, where there were a lot of exchange-rate-based stabilizations, controlling for all those things, the results still go through.

But I do think that the broader question a lot of folks have alluded to in terms of thinking about the relative effect of discount rates versus cash flows is vital, but also really digging in more deeply into what was it about the fiscal side that didn't happen in the unsuccessful cases. It is important to understand, more generally, what happened in the country—Jamaica, where I'm from, with the most failed IMF programs—there were eleven failed IMF programs in the sample. I was in Jamaica in 2017, when Christine Lagarde went there to have a major IMF conference, because Jamaica had finally successfully completed an IMF program. So why is it that for eleven straight programs over the course of forty years, you fail, you fail, you fail. And then suddenly, you actually get a successful program. I do think that's worth digging into, and it's probably, dare I say it, a book or something. I'm looking at my colleague John Cochrane. He's written a fantastic book, but it's taken him quite a long time to complete it. I'm not sure I have the same amount of temerity he does. But let me stop there.

NELSON: Jim [Bullard] and Mike [Bordo] and Andy [Levin], and the gentleman in the back there whom I don't know.

JAMES BULLARD: Jim Bullard, St. Louis Fed. I love this paper. I've been an advocate of the Sargent school, which says that maybe you can get a soft landing out of this. There is a famous paper by Goodfriend and King called "The Incredible Volcker Disinflation."[3] It argues that the reason the Volcker disinflation was costly was that Volcker had to earn credibility. There's some learning going on, and initially it's not credible. Volcker had to prove credibility, and this caused a big disruption in the economy. The alternative to that is if you have more credibility, then you have a better chance of achieving a soft landing and an immaculate disinflation. I think the modern Fed has a lot more credibility than Volcker had going into the big inflation in the early 1980s. So I think we have more chance of success because of that.

There's also a paper that takes that across countries, by Gibbs and Kulish.[4] They have a model that has learning and time-varying credibility. The costly disinflations were the ones that were not credible, and the less costly disinflations were the ones that were more credible. They've got estimates on that across countries. Gibbs and Kulish have a different sample than what you have here: I think more post-1994. I also like the emphasis on trying to look at equity pricing as a way to get a metric on whether the disinflation was costly or not.

NELSON: Okay, there's an emphasis now on being concise, because we're a few minutes over time. But, Michael, I'm told we have about five minutes for more questions. Okay.

MICHAEL BORDO: I wish to amplify on John Cochrane's remarks. My research with Pierre Siklos for a Bank of Chile conference in 2019 showed for a large panel of emerging countries, which goes back to the period discussed in this paper, that emerging-market countries that adopted inflation targeting [IT] did much better in reducing inflation and improving their real economies compared to countries that did not adopt IT. We also showed that it took time for successful emerging-market economies that adopted IT to earn the credibility necessary to successfully restore price stability.

ANDREW LEVIN: Really great paper. Following up on what Mike said, we wrote a Hoover working paper that was published last year in the *IMF Economic Review*, and it noted what we call the "quiet revolution in monetary policy."[5] The paper is focused on low-income countries. So it's focused on countries with even lower incomes than the tabulation for emerging-market economies. It's been dramatic over the last twenty-five years how most low-income countries have succeeded in bringing inflation down not just to single digits, but in most cases to below 5%. Now that includes sub-Saharan African countries as well as countries in Central Asia and Southeast Asia. And the reason I want to emphasize this is that it builds on the same legacy that we discussed this morning, John Taylor's legacy of systematic monetary policy frameworks with a clear policy strategy. And I would say that over the last twenty years, the IMF has been remarkably effective in providing ongoing technical assistance to help many of these low-income countries implement monetary policy frameworks that have been quietly successful year after year. So I would urge Peter to extend the sample to the more recent period and to incorporate those countries into the analysis.

NELSON: And the gentleman in the back in the blue shirt and the brown jacket, and then who had his hand up first.

PETER BLAIR: Hi, Peter Blair, Harvard and Hoover. I just wanted to commend the use of data from developing countries to understand macroeconomic policy in the United States. I think it's a huge conceptual leap, and one that brought me into the profession, because I think oftentimes, development economists and macroeconomists view developing countries a bit cynically in terms of saying, "How can we provide them with microinterventions," whether it's bed nets or something like that. But what you're really saying is that we can learn lessons from those countries. And I think you've quite rightly foregrounded that in the presentation. I hope that it's very foregrounded in the paper and that for all of us in the audience here, as we teach students, that we bring that lens. That there are policy experiments happening around the world, macroeconomic policy experiments, not just in developed countries but in developing countries, that we can learn from.

NELSON: One last question.

JOHN GUNN: Hi. I just gotta say something about John Taylor. This is not about the Taylor rule. I don't quite understand it. This guy over there, when he was under secretary of the Treasury for international affairs from 2000 to 2004, went to Iraq and set up at the central bank with a number of Iraqis. And that central bank has had one devaluation in the last twenty years, and it just got reversed. And the currency went up against the dollar. And the country is booming. And so it's just a . . . it's another version of the Taylor rule.

NELSON: Any final comments, Josh and Peter? No? Thanks very much.

HENRY: Lastly, I'll say, I think appropriately connecting to John Gunn's point, John Taylor's had an enormous impact, obviously, even on inflation targeting, and I think the point is well taken. I certainly hope the Fed has enough credibility to get us back to 2% quickly and painlessly. My suspicion is that it's going to be harder than people realize. And I think the biggest measure of that is frankly, right now, the difference between where the Fed thinks rates are going to be and where the market thinks rates are going. But the lesson in emerging economies is deep. And inflation targeting was a big part of it. My only point here is that the Chilean example specifically was a more gradual approach that was taken, as part of a broader strategy. And Fed officials have made it clear they want to get inflation down to 2% quickly. And so that's where I think we're looking at a different scenario, but as my fourteen-year-old son likes to say, time will tell.

Notes

1. See, e.g., Thomas J. Sargent, "Stopping Moderate Inflations: The Methods of Poincaré and Thatcher," chapter 4 in *Rational Expectations and Inflation* (Princeton, NJ: Princeton University Press, 2013), 111–58.
2. See *Journal of Economic Perspectives* 35, no. 3 (Summer 2021): 83–108.
3. See M. Goodfriend and R. G. King, "The Incredible Volcker Disinflation," *Journal of Monetary Economics* 52, no. 5 (July 2005): 981–1015.
4. See C. G. Gibbs and M. Kulish, "Disinflations in a Model of Imperfectly Anchored Expectations," *European Economic Review* 100 (November 2017): 157–74.
5. Alina Carare, Carlos de Resende, Andrew T. Levin, and Chelsea Zhang, "Do Monetary Policy Frameworks Matter in Low-Income Countries?" *IMF Economic Review* (published online October 26, 2022).

INFLATION TARGETING IN JAPAN, 2013–2023

9

Inflation Targeting in Japan, 2013–2023

Haruhiko Kuroda

Japan started targeting 2% inflation in 2013 and continued to do so until 2023. And yet, the 2% inflation target has not yet been achieved in a sustainable and stable manner. The current inflation of 3–4% is almost wholly caused by the import price hike and will slow down to less than 2% by the middle of fiscal year (FY) 2023. However, the "no price increase and no wage increase" norm is changing (long-term inflation expectations are rising), and further labor supply increases are unlikely, because female labor participation is already higher than in the United States. Therefore, by continuing accommodative monetary policy so that firms can continue to raise wages by around 3%, the 2% inflation target will be achieved in a sustainable and stable manner in the near future.

Adoption of the 2% Inflation Target

The Bank of Japan adopted the 2% inflation target in January 2013, when it also agreed to the Joint Statement of the Government on Overcoming Deflation and Achieving Sustainable Economic Growth, in which the bank committed to achieving the 2% inflation target "at the earliest possible time" by executing monetary easing. This agreement was made before I joined the bank in March 2013.

Quantitative and Qualitative Monetary Easing (QQE)

Actually, the Bank of Japan was under continued deflation since 1998 and introduced quantitative easing (QE) in 2001, expanded it step-by-step in 2003–6, and began to include long-term Japanese government bonds (JGBs) as well as commercial paper, corporate bonds, and exchange-traded funds (ETFs) between 2008 and 2013. But deflation persisted with low growth and high unemployment (see table 9.1).

So, in April 2013, the Bank of Japan substantially expanded QE by doubling the purchase of JGBs and the monetary base to achieve the 2% inflation target "at the earliest possible time, with a view to achieving it in two years." The bank called this quantitative and qualitative monetary easing (QQE).

The initial reaction from the economy was significant: economic growth recovered and the stock market rebounded, while the consumer price index (CPI) inflation rate reached 1.4% by the spring of 2014. However, the increase in the consumption tax rate from 5 to 8% in April 2014, along with still sluggish wage increases, made personal consumption deteriorate, leading to a declining CPI inflation rate. So, in October 2014, the Bank of Japan expanded the QQE by substantially increasing its JGB purchases with longer-term maturities and committing to a higher increase in base money.

However, oil prices, which had been around $100 per barrel, declined toward $50 in 2015 and reached less than $30 in early 2016, reducing the CPI inflation rate to zero. The situation required the bank to further strengthen monetary easing (see table 9.2).

TABLE 9.1. Inflation, Growth, and Unemployment in 1998–2012.

	Inflation Rate	Growth Rate	Unemployment Rate
1998–2012 average	−0.3%	+0.6%	4.6%

Source: Statistics Bureau, Ministry of Internal Affairs and Communications, Japan.

TABLE 9.2. Inflation, Growth, and Unemployment in 2013–15.

	Inflation Rate	Growth Rate	Unemployment Rate
2013	+0.4%	+2.0%	4.0%
2014	+1.1%	+0.3%	3.6%
2015	0.0%	+1.6%	3.4%

Source: Statistics Bureau, Ministry of Internal Affairs and Communications, Japan.

QQE with Negative Interest Rates

To further lower the entire yield curve, in January 2016 the Bank of Japan decided to introduce the negative interest rate policy (NIRP) by imposing a –0.1% policy rate on one of the three tiers of demand deposits at the bank while it further lengthened remaining maturities of JGB holdings. The bank certainly learned from the experience of NIRPs utilized by the European Central Bank and other European central banks so as not to undermine financial intermediation by the banking sector.

QQE with Yield Curve Control

Thereafter, considering unstable international financial markets and weakening emerging-market economies, in July 2016 the Bank of Japan decided to expand the QQE by increasing its purchase of ETFs and declared it would make a comprehensive examination of the QQE regarding the negative interest rate. Then, in September 2016, after the comprehensive examination, the bank introduced the yield curve control (YCC)—accompanied by new forward guidance to continue the monetary base increase until the 2% inflation target was achieved—and widened operational tools. The CPI inflation rate recovered toward 1%, although because of the consumption tax rate increase from 8 to 10% in October 2019, inflation (excluding its direct impact on prices) slowed down slightly (see table 9.3).

TABLE 9.3. Inflation, Growth, and Unemployment in 2016–19.

	Inflation Rate	Growth Rate	Unemployment Rate
2016	−0.3%	+0.8%	3.1%
2017	+0.5%	+1.7%	2.8%
2018	+0.9%	+0.6%	2.4%
2019	+0.6%	−0.4%	2.4%

Source: Statistics Bureau, Ministry of Internal Affairs and Communications, Japan.

TABLE 9.4. Inflation, Growth, and Unemployment in 2020–23.

	Inflation Rate	Growth Rate	Unemployment Rate
2020	−0.4%	−4.3%	2.8%
2021	−0.2%	+2.1%	2.8%
2022	+2.3%	+1.0%	2.6%
2023	+3.1%*	—	2.6%*

* March 2023
Source: Statistics Bureau, Ministry of Internal Affairs and Communications, Japan.

Then in early 2020, the world economy was seriously affected by the COVID-19 pandemic, which reduced supply as well as demand, becoming mired in negative growth and deflation. Japan was no exception. By 2022, the pandemic became less severe and the world economy started to recover. But then the war in Ukraine erupted in February 2022, which raised energy and food prices enormously, resulting in extremely high inflation, the highest in the last forty years. Again, Japan was no exception (see table 9.4).

Inflation Targeting in Japan, 2013–23

As I said at the outset, although the current CPI inflation rate is 3–4%, it will slow down to less than 2% by the middle of FY2023. However, the important fact is that the fifteen-year deflation has been overcome with substantial employment and wage increases. Based on the significant improvement in the economy, we can now

TABLE 9.5. Hourly Wage Increase and Total Wage Increase, 1998–2012 vs. 2013–22.

	Hourly Wage Increase	Wage Increase
1998–2012 Average	–0.4%	–0.9%
2013–22 Average	+1.1%	+0.5%

Source: Statistics Bureau, Ministry of Internal Affairs and Communications, Japan.

TABLE 9.6. Employment, Employment Income, and Corporate Income.

	Employment*	Employment Income**	Corporate Income**
2012	62.6	251.7	47.2
2022 (Oct–Dec, annualized)	67.3	296.8	82.2

* million employees; ** trillion yen

Source: Statistics Bureau, Ministry of Internal Affairs and Communications, Japan.

envisage the 2% inflation target being achieved in the near future (see tables 9.5 and 9.6).

I am sure that without the clear 2% inflation target and strong commitment by the Bank of Japan, we could not have overcome Japan's persistent deflation. At the same time, with various shocks coming from inside as well as outside of Japan, and above all, with the aftermath of fifteen years of deflation—i.e., the resulting entrenched deflationary mindset (the new "norm")—achieving the 2% inflation target within a reasonable time span has been difficult. Having said that, I must emphasize that there appears to be no other policy framework, other than inflation targeting, for achieving price stability, which is the main mandate and objective of any central bank.

GENERAL DISCUSSION

JOHN TAYLOR (INTRODUCTION): Before we have our lunch, we're going to have a wonderful speech by the former governor of the Bank of Japan, my good friend Haruhiko Kuroda. And I have to say, there's been no more fun for me in working with central banks than to spend some time at the Bank of Japan. It's a real treat. If you ever have a chance, go and do that. You learn so much about different ways to do policy. But we're interested in what's happening in Asia and Japan, and we can't wait to hear your talk. So welcome, and thanks so much for being here.

* * *

SEBASTIAN EDWARDS: One of the controversial tools used in this process of bringing this inflation to an end was the YCC [yield curve control]. And when I teach monetary policy and the Taylor rule, and I go and teach Japan, my students say, how can you attempt to be successful without creating great distortion fixing and targeting both the short-term and longer-term interest rates? So could you comment a little bit on that?

HARUHIKO KURODA: Yeah. I think we call it yield curve control with QQE [quantitative and qualitative monetary easing]. So the basic structure and nature of the QQE continue, and then with a negative policy rate, coupled with a ten-year JGB [Japanese government bond] rate target at around 0%, we introduced YCC. Why did we change from simple QQE to QQE with the yield curve control? The main concern was, of course . . . maybe two things. One, targeting the amount of the JGB purchase, and the asset purchase program, of course, had some strong impact on market expectations and so forth. But at the same time, you can imagine that depending on overseas financial market conditions, and so on and so forth, even if you continue to make an 80-trillion-yen JGB purchase every year, the long-term interest rate may fluctuate somewhat. So, we thought that by targeting the ten-year JGB rate at around 0%, we could fix the strings of monetary easing more than the simple QQE.

The second point is because [the] 80-trillion-yen JGB purchase, and so on and so forth, may be understood by financial market people, but ordinary households and ordinary company managers do not understand what 80 trillion yen is. Better to say that we will target the ten-year JGB rate at around 0%. That could be more transparent, understandable, and make the QQE more effective.

So, we introduced YCC, and of course, it is somewhat unusual. Many central banks adopted some kinds of QE [quantitative easing] after the Lehman crisis, but none of them adopted yield curve control, except for the Australian Reserve Bank. The Bank, of course, introduced a minus or quite low short-term policy rate but never intended to target long-term interest rates. That is true, that it is somewhat unusual, but we thought it was more effective and more transparent and could be good. And, of course, that could make JGB market people less happy or unhappy. That is true. But we still think that this YCC was appropriate and will continue to be appropriate until the 2% inflation target is achieved in a stable manner.

BEAT SIEGENTHALER: Thank you very much. Beat Siegenthaler, Rokos Capital. The market is debating a lot about what could happen once the system is unwound. And we're seeing in the US, and this morning we discussed about, what can happen when you have years and years of a lot of liquidity in the system, and then how once you withdraw it, rates go up. You see an impact there. Now, in Japan, I'm wondering how dangerous is it going to be when eventually monetary policy will be normalized. And how disruptive could it turn out to be? Thank you.

KURODA: I think once the 2% inflation target is achieved in a sustainable and stable manner, the Bank of Japan would start normalization, meaning raising the policy rate and, of course, gradually reducing asset purchases, and so on and so forth. Now, then, there would be various impacts on the financial sector, households, companies, and also the government.

Now, as far as the household sector is concerned, you may know that Japanese households have about 60% of GDP equivalent debt, mainly housing purchase debt. But at the same time, Japanese households hold something like 2,000 trillion yen in financial assets, which is roughly four times GDP. So, even if interest rates are raised, that could affect some households that have significant amounts of housing loans, and so on. But households, generally speaking, would benefit from rising interest rates, because they hold a huge amount of bank deposits.

Ordinary companies after the Lehman crisis reduced total debt, but now they increased their debt beyond the level that prevailed before the Lehman crisis, now about 120% of GDP. But Japanese companies and firms hold something like 60% of GDP equivalent cash. And the former finance minister [Tarō] Asō always criticized Japanese companies—why do they have such huge amounts of cash instead of raising wages or increasing investment? So, firms have enough liquidity, and even if monetary situations tighten and the interest rate rises, no major impact is likely.

Now, Japanese financial institutions, they have substantial capital bases, and also liquidity is quite abundant. And by the way, in Japan, the deposit insurance scheme is quite interesting. On the one hand, there is some upper limit for ordinary deposits, but demand deposits without interest payments would be insured without limits. So, the entire amount of the demand deposits without interest payments will be insured by the deposit corporation. And also, FSA [the Financial Services Agency] has been making various stress tests on megabanks as well as local banks, and they found that they have enough capital. There's enough liquidity. And so even if the interest rate goes up and monetary conditions become tighter, I don't think the banking or financial sector would be affected seriously.

The only entity that will be significantly affected by the monetary normalization is the government. Government has more than 200% of GDP equivalent debt. By the way, when I was vice minister of finance around 2000, at that time the Japanese government's national debt burden in terms of interest payment was about 10 trillion yen. And the current budget shows the interest payment by the government is only 8 trillion yen, while the stock of government debt increased more than triple. And yet the interest payment declined. That means that if the monetary situation is normalized, the interest rate would rise. Eventually, the Japanese government's interest payment burden would experience more than a threefold increase. So, from 8 trillion yen to 30 trillion yen. Quite huge, of course. Not instantly, but it will take five, six years, because the average maturity of JGBs outstanding is, I think, seven or eight years, including ten-year, twenty-year, and thirty-year JGBs. So roughly in five years, more than half or nearly two-thirds of JGBs would mature. So in the next five years or so after monetary normalization, the government debt burden will increase substantially. I have been telling the government this is the case. They know, but I don't know whether politicians understand the situation.

TAYLOR: Thank you.

CENTRAL BANK BALANCE SHEETS

10

Five Centuries of Central Bank Balance Sheets: A Primer

Niall Ferguson, Paul Schmelzing, Martin Kornejew, and Moritz Schularick

Introduction

Central bank balance sheets have played a prominent role in response to the past decade's financial and public health upheavals, and they have been a focus of this conference series in previous years. In a bid to shield households and financial markets from the most severe economic strains, both the response to the Global Financial Crisis (GFC) of 2008–9 and the more recent response to the COVID-19 pandemic of 2020–22 featured large-scale asset purchases and the extension of significant amounts of liquidity to the financial sector. In these times of financial stress, major central banks chose to deploy balance sheet resources as their preferred tool to contain market volatility and prevent real economy spillovers (Cochrane 2022).

A growing literature seeks to understand the effects of such central bank interventions and to assess their potential to mitigate current and future economic shocks (Gertler and Karadi 2011; Wu and Xia 2016; Smets and Potter 2019; Bernanke 2020). However, the pre-2008 experience of using central balance sheets as a policy tool has barely been studied. Our paper is the first to provide historical data aggregating trends, drivers, and the full range of policy precedents associated with using central bank balance sheets (FKSS 2023). We undertake these analyses based on a new dataset that reconstructs central bank balance sheets for advanced economies over multiple centuries using primary and secondary sources, on an annual basis, including the full breakdown of asset and liability components for many episodes.

Why is such a long-run historical view useful for both policy-makers and researchers? We argue that, given the rarity of large macroeconomic and financial shocks, only a long-run approach yields a sufficient sample size across different types of shocks and across different macroeconomic environments. While long-run chronologies for various financial "tail events" exist in the litera-ture, the history of central bank interventions has not been studied systematically. A longer view allows for a comprehensive study of the effects of balance sheet operations, including lender-of-last-resort interventions.

Conventional wisdom assumes that central banks' utilization of their balance sheets was limited prior to the 1970s. This is partly due to the emphasis on the interest rate as the primary operational tool in the treatises by Walter Bagehot ([1873] 1962) and others in the late nineteenth century, and partly due to central banks' supposedly "pas-sive" mandates (Sayers 1957; Volcker 2004; Carlson and Wheelock 2015; Shafik 2016). However, it can be shown that time and again, central banks have deployed their power to create liquidity in bids to insulate economies from disasters. While such deployments first began to be linked to geopolitical shocks during the seventeenth and eighteenth centuries—occurring with increasing regularity during wars and revolutions—it can be shown that the trigger for central bank liquidity support gradually, but consistently, shifted towards financial crises. Not only the frequency of tail events but also the readiness of central banks to offer liquidity support changed over time. In particular, central banks' sensitivity to financial crises rose sharply over the twentieth century and, after the Great Depression, increasingly became a systematic response to financial distress.

The long-run historical data we compiled for FKSS (2023) allow for the study of the effects of central bank liquidity support during financial crises. Building upon the classic paradigm of public runs on bank retail deposits (Diamond and Dybvig 1983), recent scholarship has placed liquidity at the heart of theories rationalizing financial turmoil (Caballero and Krishnamurthy 2008; Brunnermeier 2009; Acharya and Skeie 2011; Ashcraft et al. 2011; Bolton et al. 2011; Gertler and Karadi 2011; Guerrieri and Shimer 2014; Benmelech et al. 2016; Del Negro et al. 2017). Stress events associated with uncertainty about asset returns can spiral into a collective flight to liquid assets, i.e., central bank reserves and close substitutes, to meet unexpected shortfalls in returns and cash flows. Unless the monetary authority meets the elevated desire to hold liquidity in these situations, the shock will be transmitted beyond the financial system, fueling potentially severe real economic downturns.

Are the alleviating effects of crisis liquidity support large enough to dominate other possible general-equilibrium side effects? The recent literature is mostly skeptical. Using a sample of about eighty countries, Bordo et al. (2001) posited that banking crises since the late nineteenth century were, on average, associated with larger GDP losses when accompanied by open-ended liquidity support—a finding confirmed by, among others, Honohan and Klingebiel (2003), who showed that public liquidity support was associated with longer crises, larger output losses, and slower growth in sectors dependent on external finance.[1] Adverse selection effects and moral hazard can increase banks' risk-taking (Drechsler et al. 2016a; Behr and Wang 2020), financial frictions can foster credit misallocation (Bleck and Liu 2018), and the monetary authority risks being trapped by excess liquidity (Benmelech and Bergman 2012; Acharya et al. 2022). Yet large parts of the existing literature suffer from a potential endogeneity bias, because support will scale with crisis severity. We are the first to disentangle the effects of crisis severity and liquidity provision by proposing and implementing a novel identification strategy to estimate the causal effects of central bank liquidity support.[2] The FKSS (2023) identification strategy is based on a narrative assessment of a central bank governor's beliefs prior to the outbreak of a banking crisis, relying on a detailed analysis of historical sources. It is well known that politicians and other policymakers can be sorted according to relatively stable economic ideologies. Recent research has established close links between the personal beliefs of political decision makers, relative economic preferences, and aggregate economic outcomes (Gohlmann and Vaubel 2007; Mishra and Reshef 2019; Monnet and Puy 2020; Malmendier and Wachter 2022). Financial commentators also routinely group current central bank governors into "hawkish" and "dovish/pragmatic" policy categories based on their assessment of their public statements (Kuttner and Posen 2010). In the same way, past central bank governors can be classified according to their policy beliefs over time.

In FKSS (2023), we utilize the extensive records of debates, speeches, and statements to locate each governor in the context of the ideological climate of his time but prior to a financial crisis, classifying governors as either "doves/pragmatists" or "hawks." To do so, we propose an algorithm that ranks governors' relative economic and financial preferences across six major variables. We argue that one of the defining features of "hawks" is that they consistently express concern about moral hazard dynamics and prioritize price stability, whereas "doves/pragmatists" consistently downplay moral hazard concerns and reject an active leaning against asset price bubbles.

Preexisting ideological beliefs of central bank governors correlate closely with central bank actions during crises. Dovish governors were 36% more likely to expand their central bank's balance sheet in a crisis, indicating that monetary policy reactions corresponded to governors' beliefs formed before the crisis. This provides us with an instrument to identify exogenous variation in crisis liquidity support and circumnavigate the inherent endogeneity entangling monetary policy and the macroeconomy. Importantly, such beliefs are uncorrelated to other factors driving any acute crisis. It is, in theory, possible that the anticipation of dovish crisis management could encourage financial risk-taking ex ante, but this only raises the bar for finding positive macroeconomic effects of central bank liquidity injections.

In FKSS (2023), we show for the first time that central bank liquidity support regularly cushioned the effects of financial crises throughout the modern history of advanced economies. Using governors' beliefs as a statistical instrument, we estimate that a central bank balance sheet expansion of at least +15% during the first or second year after the onset of a financial crisis bolstered real GDP over the subsequent three years relative to the counterfactual. This stabilization was generally achieved without runaway inflation, whereas crises without support were often followed by protracted deflation. In the FKSS (2023) data, liquidity support seems effective in the form of lender-of-last-resort (LLR) action with Bagehot-style private asset purchases operations rather than through supporting public borrowing with intervention in government bond markets. These results are consistent with the hypothesis that risk absorption by the public sector matters in stimulating private-sector activity.

Thus, we can corroborate and generalize the case-study findings of Richardson and Troost (2009) and Benmelech et al. (2016), who evaluated particular liquidity provisions during financial crises. The results are also robust to factoring in differences in central bank independence and controlling for the fiscal policy reaction to crises.

Finally, we present evidence that these positive short-run effects come with an important caveat. Hawkish central bank governors often invoke moral hazard before and after the outbreak of a banking crisis. In FKSS (2023), we show that such concerns have merit. Central bank liquidity support in crises is associated with a rising probability of future financial crises. If central banks refrained from using their balance sheet to support markets in the previous crisis, episodes of renewed excessive risk-taking were much rarer.

Previous Literature

First, FKSS (2023) adds to the extensive literature on LLR operations. In the classic accounts by Thornton ([1802] 1939) and Bagehot ([1873] 1962), LLR policy works through lending by the central bank to illiquid but solvent private institutions against good collateral at high ("penalty") interest rates. Our measure of liquidity interventions based on central bank balance sheet expansions complements the policy chronologies of Calomiris (2011) and Bindseil (2019).

More specialized recent literature has investigated the impact of unconventional monetary policy (Bernanke et al. 2004; Gagnon et al. 2011; Joyce et al. 2011; Engen et al. 2015; Sims and Wu 2021), with big-picture contributions by Bernanke (2020) and Bailey et al. (2020). The literature has offered positive evaluations of large-scale asset purchases as they appear to have succeeded in reducing financial market uncertainty, lowered borrowing costs for households and sovereigns, and meaningfully raised inflation.[3]

The structure of this summary paper is as follows. In the next section, we present snapshots of how the size of central balance sheets has fluctuated over time, with reference to four case studies included in FKSS (2023). Then we turn to a discussion on the finding in FKSS (2023) that central bank balance sheets have responded to multiple types of macroeconomic shocks over the past four hundred years. From there, we focus on financial crises and studies of the suggestions in FKSS (2023) on the effects of central bank liquidity supply. Our conclusions follow.

Central Bank Balance Sheet Data since 1600: Case Studies

In FKSS (2023), we assembled data covering seventeen advanced economies. For some of these, we were able to trace de facto central bank data as far back as 1600. Here we summarize long-term trends for four selected central bank balance sheets that are among the components in this new data set. FKSS (2023) presents historical data on both de jure national central banks and their de facto predecessor institutions. These institutions could be privately owned (as the Bank of England was prior to 1946) or publicly owned, as long as they were recognized as occupying a de facto position as a "bank among banks" or had a de facto monopoly on note issuance or government financing. The institutional organization of central banks varies across advanced economies, even in modern times. FKSS (2023) includes early modern data such as the public banks of Naples, the Bank of Amsterdam, and the Bank of the United States. In the nineteenth century, comparatively modern institutions such as the Bank of Finland (from 1813), the Royal Bank of Prussia (from 1817), and the Banco de San Fernando/Banco de España (from 1830) enter the stage. From 1870, we have data from the national central banks in Belgium, Finland, Norway, and Portugal, to give historical central bank balance sheet data for seventeen of the most advanced economies.

International Long-Term Trends: Four Case Studies

FKSS (2023) combines these new balance sheet series for modern and early modern central banks with associated macroeconomic and financial time series, including nominal GDP, total private assets, and government debt. The data suggest that, while central bank balance sheets relative to output have indeed reached unprecedented levels in the early twenty-first century, they are by no means exceptional in size relative to total private assets or the stock of government debt. Importantly, we show that central bank balance sheets provided meaningful amounts of elasticity even under the classical gold standard and did not move closely in tandem with any particular output or financial variable.

Bank of England, 1700–2020

Figure 10.1 shows the Bank of England's assets as a share of GDP, for which we utilize data presented in Dimsdale and Thomas (2017). We observe that the inception period of central banks in the seventeenth and eighteenth centuries saw sharp growth in this measure, followed by international dispersion during the second half of the eighteenth century, mainly driven by the international wars during this time. A key change set in with the Napoleonic Wars in the early nineteenth century. For the subsequent eighty years, aggregate central bank assets-to-GDP ratios varied in tight ranges, both across countries and across time, rarely surpassing 15% of GDP, even during costly macroeconomic and financial shocks such as the Crimean War (1853–56) or the 1857 and 1866 financial crises. But from the 1880s, there was a renewed growth of aggregate central bank assets relative to output, partly induced by new ideas about central banking, such as those of Bagehot ([1873] 1962), which triggered monetary policy reforms, notably in the UK (Calomiris 2011).

Figure 10.1 shows total central bank assets relative to GDP for the UK between 1700 and 2016 based on Dimsdale and Thomas (2017) and current GDP estimates at market prices via Broadberry et al. (2015). Britain has served as a key case study for financial-institutional modernization and the emergence of a centralized public financial system.[4] World War II and the post-2008 expansion stand out here on a historical scale, but we note that pre-GFC, all-time records were not, in fact, set during 1939–45, but rather during the early years of the Bank of England, following its 1694 foundation.

The British case is the first where we can directly associate expansion events with active emergency interventions. As early as 1711, the Bank of England expanded its asset base to counter a financial crisis, explicitly engaging in exchequer bill purchases,

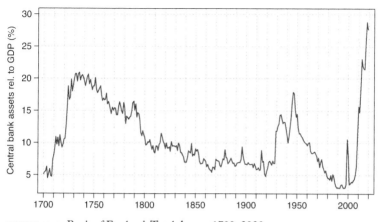

FIGURE 10.1. Bank of England, Total Assets, 1700–2020.
Note: In percent of current UK GDP (contemporary borders).
Sources: GDP data via Dimsdale and Thomas (2017) and underlying sources.

partly financed by a special GBP 45,000 Treasury loan. This is the first confirmed case of an early "asset purchase program" undertaken explicitly to "revive confidence in [exchequer] bills." That the operation could be deemed a success was determined with reference to the fall in exchequer discount rates from 3% in early January 1711 to 0.75% by the end of the month (Scott 1912; Hill 1971).[5] Next, while initially remaining agnostic during the summer of 1720, standing apart, the Bank eventually agreed to mobilize substantial amounts of balance sheet resources via the 1722 Act (at GBP 4.02M no less than 6.95% of total 1722 UK public debt outstanding, or 5.5% of 1722 GDP) to help restructure the South Sea Company in exchange for stock. This is visible in our series as a sharp acceleration in assets-to-GDP over 1721–22, a clear case of the balance sheet being driven by an active liquidity provision in the face of mounting fears of financial disaster (Clapham 1958, 84). Figure 10.1 shows sharp asset expansions beginning around the time of the South Sea Bubble, with total Bank of England assets relative to GDP reaching a peak of 24% by 1735, illustrating the fact that early central banks were able to provide substantial liquidity volumes even under gold standard regimes, and were initially not bound to target real economic activity.[6]

Repeatedly, it can be documented how the Treasury opted to utilize the Bank of England's balance sheet resources instead of imposing regular taxes. This is key evidence that the size of the central bank balance sheet can serve as a major variable in the growing "state capacity" literature, quite distinct from the "tax ability" on which scholars overwhelmingly focus. The Duke of Newcastle frequently co-opted the Bank to anticipate regular tax revenues, particularly during the Seven Years' War, as chronicled in detail by Browning (1971). In other words, we can associate both active asset purchases and financial stability operations with balance sheet expansions as early as the eighteenth century. After this initial expansion, the British record is remarkable for the near-undisturbed reduction in assets-to-GDP until the eve of World War I. Over the period 1700–1870, the average total assets-to-GDP ratio stands at 12.2%—a figure very close to both modern twentieth-century averages and the long-run averages for privately owned central banks operating in centralized public finance regimes.

Riksbank, 1668–2020

Next, figure 10.2 displays the Riksbank's total assets as a share of Swedish GDP, 1668–2020, based on recently released data (Fregert 2014). Sweden—in contrast to the British case—serves as an example of a historical laggard in the development of public finance. From its inception, the Swedish central bank was formally under public (parliamentary) ownership.[7] Public ownership did not preclude substantial active central bank balance sheet expansions relative to GDP, however. Once again, large asset expansions can be linked directly to the motivation to reduce liquidity risks in financial markets. In the Swedish case, the most dramatic increase in total assets over the very long term was between 1750 and 1765, when

FIGURE 10.2. Riksbank, Total Assets, 1668–2020.
Note: Total assets of the Riksbank, as a percentage of current Swedish nominal GDP.
Sources: Fregert (2014); Edvinsson (2014).

the share surged from below 20% to a record 49.8% in 1759. The backdrop was the Seven Years' War, with the costly Pomeranian campaign almost exclusively financed by rapid Riksbank note issuance. The erosion of silver prices and heavy bank runs in Stockholm during the 1740s eventually triggered a suspension of convertibility by 1745 and a period of floating currency in Sweden (Heckscher 1954; Fregert and Jonung 1996). We can speak of a major liquidity provision operation that sought simultaneously to calm currency markets and underpin demand for government debt.[8]

Another sharp rise in assets-to-GDP occurred during the Napoleonic Wars, with peak assets-to-GDP levels in 1809 reaching 21.7%. This provides another example of active asset purchases. While both publicly and privately owned institutions were utilized during war efforts, the Riksbank case confirms that a public ownership model was more susceptible to co-optation by the political executive. By contrast, Bank of England assets were virtually flat relative to GDP during 1795–1810. As in the British case, however, the general evidence confirms that the Swedish executive utilized the Riksbank balance sheet as a substitute for tax impositions.

"As it took time to collect the new taxes . . . the Bank was used in a way that circumvented the Parliament's instructions against further government borrowing" (Fregert and Jonung 1996, 461). No fewer than seven times prior to World War I, the Riksbank used its balance sheet to assist the financial sector during periods of stress, in 1811, 1815, 1857, 1876, 1890, 1897, and 1907.[9] Well before Bagehot's formalized LLR principles, the Riksbank—like its counterpart in London—thus repeatedly saw its balance sheet expand for both emergency liquidity provision and active asset purchases, even under gold standard constraints. The English and the Swedish cases saw central bank balance sheet co-optation by the political executive well before the inflection points posited in the literature.

Public Banks of Naples, 1587–1808

Figure 10.3 displays the total nominal assets of the public banks of Naples, as reconstructed by Balletta (2008) and as discussed there and in Costabile and Nappi (2018) and Balletta et al. (2018). The Kingdom of Naples was a Spanish possession from 1559, apart from brief periods as a republic (1647) and under Austrian rule (1714–35). It was, therefore, more politically and economically aligned with Spain than with northern Italy. Balance sheet expansions for the public banks of Naples are highly correlated with local tail events. We observe rather tepid growth in the initial phase, sharp volatility around the infamous 1622 and 1702 financial crises, as well as around the 1656 Naples Plague, and sustained expansion of total assets from circa 1715 until 1806, when Naples lost its independence to Napoleon.

Bank of Amsterdam, 1610–1819

Finally, figure 10.4 displays the total nominal assets of the Bank of Amsterdam, a privately owned institution regarded as a leading

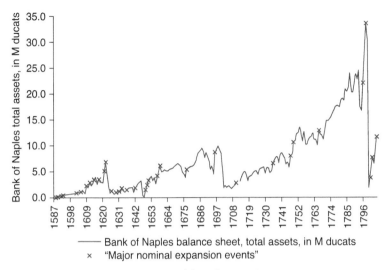

FIGURE 10.3. Public Banks of Naples, Total Assets, 1587–1808.

Note: Balance sheet data in total nominal terms (million Neapolitan ducats).

Source: Data via Balletta (2008).

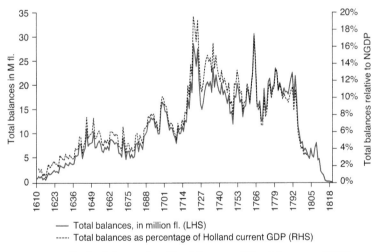

FIGURE 10.4. Bank of Amsterdam, Total Assets and Total Assets-to-GDP, 1610–1819.

Note: Balance sheet data is in million Dutch Guilder (left axis) and relative to Holland GDP (right axis).

Sources: Van Dillen (1934); Van Zanden and Van Leeuwen (2012).

early central bank, and assets relative to GDP (RHS), with annual total assets data sourced from Van Dillen (1934). The Netherlands was often considered the "safe asset provider" prior to the Glorious Revolution, and therefore the actions of the Bank of Amsterdam reverberated well beyond the political borders of Holland. We observe that its total assets reached around Guilders 15M near the end of the seventeenth century, or close to 10% of Dutch GDP. The measure peaked around the time of the South Sea Bubble, when assets reached around 20% of GDP, as Amsterdam was the destination of substantial amounts of capital flight. With the Napoleonic Wars, the Bank was restructured, and De Nederlandsche Bank (DNB) took over its functions. The DNB's asset data in FKSS (2023) are based on primary sources in the Dutch archives.

As in the case of Naples, we can associate early modern balance sheet expansion events closely with a variety of tail events, including wars (1665, 1674, and 1810) and financial crises (1720 and 1763). The elasticity of the bank's balance sheet in absolute terms and relative to Dutch output is striking, and this was continued during the nineteenth century by the DNB.

One observation based on our examples is that bullion standard regimes did not necessitate static balance sheets relative to output. Conversely, the floating era (when balance sheet sizes were freed from any remaining gold coverage ratios) did not unleash an acceleration of central bank asset growth. Both absolute and relative assets (assets-to-GDP), in other words, evolved opportunistically in response to crisis events rather than in compliance with the "rules of the game."

Stylized Historical Facts and Summary Statistics

In FKSS (2023), we present a variety of aggregate global balance sheet data sets, including central bank assets relative to GDP over centuries, assets relative to total financial assets, and assets relative to the stock of government debt. Generally, the variation in annual growth rates of central bank balance sheets was substantial across all historical episodes, suggesting that balance sheets were, in principle, able to behave elastically, even under the constraints of the classical gold standard. FKSS (2023) determines the precise policy motivation and event context for each central bank balance sheet expansion, defining a "major balance sheet expansion" as an individual country-year during which total nominal central bank assets grew by at least 15% year-over-year (YOY). However, all our key conclusions are robust to other cutoffs or real-term expansion measures. Over the period 1600–2020, 742 country-years fulfilled the 15% nominal asset expansion criterion (out of 7,157 total country-year observations). Across all central banks over time, annual balance sheet growth exceeded +15% YOY for around 16.3% of country-years pre-1870 (23.7% post-1870).[10]

Table 10.1 analyzes the distribution of annual balance sheet fluctuations across polity and central bank ownership types. We observe that privately owned central banks had lower balance sheet sizes relative to GDP and lower major expansion frequencies under both republican and monarchical political regimes. Interestingly, publicly owned central banks had similar absolute balance sheet sizes relative to GDP and similar expansion frequencies in both

TABLE 10.1. Balance Sheet Size and Expansion Frequency by Polity and Central Bank Type, 1600–2020.

Balance Sheet Size (% of GDP)	Republic	Monarchy	Expansion Frequency (% Country-Years)	Republic	Monarchy
Privately owned	5.4	12.2	Privately owned	4.7	0.6
Publicly owned	9.8	10.9	Publicly owned	6.0	7.6

Note: The table displays central bank balance sheet size relative to GDP (left panel) and central bank balance sheet expansion frequency (right panel), defined as country-years with nominal total asset growth of at least 15% year-over-year, as a share of total observation years.

Source: See FKSS (2023) for the full list.

republics and monarchies. Therefore, it appears that the ownership structure associated with central banks might be a more relevant constraint on balance sheet dynamics than the political system per se, though that issue requires more careful study.

Different Categories of Balance Sheet Expansions

Previous literature has offered some guidance on how to distinguish between different central bank balance sheet drivers, classifying types from the operational side. According to Bindseil (2004), central bank balance sheet expansions can be a function of (a) currency issuance; (b) a foreign exchange operation; (c) an investment of own funds; (d) liquidity assistance; or (e) a monetary policy operation.

FKSS (2023) distinguishes four main underlying macro shock categories that have led to major balance sheet expansions (as defined above), all of which have historically been associated with the operational responses in Bindseil (2004).[11] The first three represent instances where either public- or private-sector stress prompted an active deployment to the central bank balance sheet with the intention of reducing short-term liquidity or refinancing risks—in other words, a "safety net" function. We add a fourth, residual category: actions that were not intended to reduce short-term risk premia or refinancing stress but exclusively reflected transactional or operational fluctuations.[12]

- *Financial crisis*: FKSS (2023) uses this category to denote those country-years primarily associated with financial market volatility to which the central bank responded. Existing chronologies provide a robust picture of several types of volatility in this context, including stock market crashes, bank runs, systemic liquidity shortages, or other threats to the systemic health of the private financial sector. Our classification concentrates on the standard banking crisis chronologies in Reinhart and Rogoff (2009), Schularick and Taylor (2012), and Baron et al. (2021) rather than on sovereign debt or currency crises to capture more narrowly traditional LLR events. We count eighty-three country-year events in this category—mainly representing private-sector recourse to the safety net—of which forty-seven were in the post-2007 period. The average country-year in this category saw a 44.6% annual balance sheet expansion.[13]

- *War or revolution*: FKSS (2023) uses this category to denote country-years that were primarily related to major geopolitical events, during which either rising military spending led to requests by fiscal authorities to monetize ensuing deficits or domestic political uncertainty motivated policymakers to monetize fiscal outlays, or provide private-sector liquidity.[14] War and revolutionary events are identified based on long-run military history chronologies (Clodfelter 2017). Over the long run, this category constitutes by far the most important one: there were 142 country-year events in this category since 1588, of which thirty-nine occurred during World War I and forty-seven during World War II. The average country-year in this category saw a 50.8% balance sheet expansion.

- *Pandemics or natural disasters*: This is a category with limited pre-2020 significance, because in no previous pandemic was there anything resembling the fiscal and monetary response to that seen in 2021–22.[15] The sample for this category is therefore comparatively small (n=19), and—except for the 1656–58 pandemic in Naples, in response to which the viceroyalty launched a grain purchase program (Fusco 2007)—restricted to the most recent central bank policy actions over 2020–21. Country-years in this category have, on average, so far seen a 48% balance sheet expansion.

How has the relative importance of these expansion types changed over time? Figure 10.5 addresses this question by showing rolling probabilities of major central bank balance sheet expansions, by the three broad event types, since 1600. The spikes in the rolling probability over centuries are associated with major political and financial shocks, with concerted balance sheet expansions first jumping significantly during Louis XIV's wars from the 1670s.

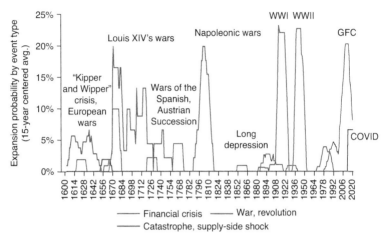

FIGURE 10.5. Rolling Central Bank Balance Sheet Expansion Probabilities, by Crisis Type, 1600–2020.

Notes: Balance sheet expansion events are defined as +15% year-over-year total nominal asset growth. Probabilities are shown as fifteen-year centered averages of realized "major" expansion events.

Source: FKSS (2023).

Clearly, the drivers of central bank balance sheet expansions have undergone fundamental shifts over the long run. Geopolitical and financial crisis events account for six out of ten of all balance sheet expansions, but the relative importance of the two main drivers has undergone a substantial shift, partly due to changing event frequencies.[16] While almost half of all balance sheet expansions in the pre-1870 era (48.5%) can be linked to wars, revolutions, or other geopolitical events, such motivations have become rare in the post-1945 world. In turn, more than 40% of all central bank balance sheet expansions after World War II were linked to financial crises, whereas the share was less than 15% in the years prior to 1870 and remained of secondary importance even during the interwar period.[17]

Figure 10.6 ranks the largest nominal total asset expansions across all central banks on the YOY basis in the FKSS (2023) sample.[18] The Bank of Japan (BoJ)'s 1883 balance sheet expansion (+728% YOY) by far exceeds all other events over five centuries of

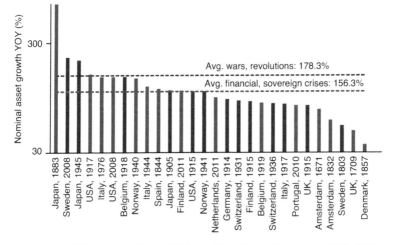

FIGURE 10.6. The Largest Nominal Balance Sheet Expansion Events, 1600–2020. Notes: Largest YOY nominal total asset balance sheets expansions. Y-axis in log scale. Source: FKSS (2023).

data—though it was a "technical expansion" that is explained by the inception of the BoJ in 1882 rather than specific financial or geopolitical crises (though there remained some legacy macro effects from the Seinan Civil War of 1877, see Shizume 2020). However, a number of twenty-first-century annual events also make it into the "all-time top ten," including Sweden 2008 (+230%) and US 2008 (+151%). By type, interestingly, we observe a relatively even distribution of extremely large nominal balance sheet expansion years across both geopolitical distress (average expansion: 178.3%) and financial distress (average expansion: 156.3%).

The Macroeconomic Effects of Liquidity Support during Crises

Throughout their history, we can find instances in which central banks sought to mitigate financial distress by expanding balance sheets to keep markets liquid. As the financial sector grew in economic importance—and with it, the cost of systemic distress—such interventions became more frequent, as we saw in the previous section. The benefits and side effects of such liquidity injections have long been the subject of scholarly debate, but consensus is elusive to this date. Systematic and reliable empirical quantification has been undermined by an inherent identification problem: How to measure the effects of interventions on crisis developments if the intervention itself endogenously depends on factors that shape crisis severity?[19]

FKSS (2023) proposes an empirical strategy to estimate the macroeconomic effects of central bank liquidity injections by isolating a variable in the central bank's reaction that is arguably exogenous to the acute crisis situation: The central bank governor's economic policy orientation prior to the crisis. We argue that the decision to use the central bank balance sheet and provide liquidity to struggling financial intermediaries depends crucially on the governor's economic beliefs and ideology. The latter has evolved over decades of life experience prior to, and thus independent of, any given crisis—though, of course, previous crises have contributed to that experience. Variations in liquidity injections caused by governors' beliefs can therefore be argued to be exogenous to other factors shaping crisis trajectories. To that end, we develop a new measure of central bank governors' beliefs.

Ex Ante Central Bank Governor Beliefs

A relatively new body of literature has explored the impact of personal attitudes and individual preferences of economic policymakers, their formation through particular experiences or formative life episodes (e.g., the "impressionable years" hypothesis), and their subsequent impact on decision making and macroeconomic variables (Gohlmann and Vaubel 2007; Mishra and Reshef 2019; Monnet and Puy 2020; Malmendier and Wachter 2022; Bordo

TABLE 10.2. Central Bank Governor Attributes, by Ideology.

	Hawks	Doves/Pragmatists
Crisis observations	29	47
Age at crisis	58	61
Treasury experience (share)	27.6%	40.4%
Political party membership (share)	17.2%	36.2%
Financial sector experience (share)	51.7%	31.9%
Pre-appointment crises	2.22	1.57
Avg. inflation experience	3.03%	4.35%

Notes: Central bank governor attributes prior to appointment or banking crisis. "Party Political Experience" counts either official political offices held prior to appointment (e.g., senator) or position within a national political party (e.g., press secretary) but not passive party memberships. "Pre-appointment crises" counts panics on the BVX basis between the birth year and the appointment year for the respective governor. "Avg. inflation experience" measures the average of the annual change in the CPI [consumer price index] from the respective governor's birth year to the final year prior to the banking crisis outbreak, with the CPI sourced via the "JST database."
Source: FKSS (2023).

and Istrefi 2023). It is increasingly understood how individuals' past occupational, educational, and other biographical experiences shape long-lasting economic preferences. For instance, individuals who experience a recession during the ages of eighteen to twenty-five have distinct lifelong political and economic beliefs (e.g., Aksoy et al. 2022).

We built on insights from this literature, using evidence of stated (publicly available) personal policy preferences to classify central bank governors as either "doves/pragmatists" or "hawks." We developed a classification algorithm that incorporates information available to the public immediately prior to the outbreak of a banking crisis and allows for the fact that governors may have undergone ideological shifts during their careers. FKSS (2023) focuses on advanced economy central banks during financial tail-event years across the seventeen countries since 1870, using the crisis coding in Baron et al. (2021), referred to as BVX.

The algorithm to classify governors builds on existing methodologies. It incorporates qualitative and quantitative information across six main economic variables, the first four of which designate the key categories: moral hazard (the most relevant variable), full employment, economic growth, price stability, exchange rate stability, and income inequality.

We then studied a wide range of primary and secondary historical material to trace governors' attitudes across these categories and to establish a ranking of economic preferences for each. Whenever central bank governors were publicly worried about asset bubbles, speculative excess, or loose lending standards, or when they used other catchphrases indicating at least an implicit preference to curb such exuberance, we took it as a hawkish signal. Together with price stability concerns, the evidence of worry about moral hazard received the highest relative weight in determining hawkishness.

Dovish governors typically either did not comment at all on moral hazard, price stability, and excessive risk-taking concerns or did so in a manner that ranked them as relatively less important than the goals of fostering employment or promoting economic growth, the two variables that receive the highest weight in our "doves/pragmatists" classification. A negative dovish signal is established when a governor cautions against a rigid interpretation of price stability mandates or downplayed risk-taking concerns. FKSS (2023) reaches a final classification verdict once the minimum criteria regarding source consistency, evidence on the person's actual decision authority, and ex ante timing for the evidence are all met.

Importantly, the governor coding approach in FKSS (2023) does not depend on taking a position on whether or not political parties or governments were influencing monetary policy.[20] The exceptions are instances where the central bank was not de facto independent (for instance, Germany during the 1930s). To assess such influences, FKSS (2023) either codes the Treasury leaning (in obvious cases) or, for the more recent period, benchmarks our classifications against one of the most recent and widely used "central bank independence" (CBI) indices (Garriga 2016). When we exclude all "weakly independent" central banks, our main results continue to hold.[21]

How does this classification algorithm work in practice? The following contours illustrate the interplay between governors' beliefs about emergency liquidity and moral hazard on the one hand and the broader context of output, price, and exchange rate preferences on the other:

- During the pre-1914 period, central bank governors remained widely indebted to the British debate between "banking" and "currency" schools. Amid a worldwide deflationary environment emphasizing monetary cooperation according to the "rules of the game," governors engaged in controversies surrounding the merits of bimetallism. Looming over all other policy delineations was the "real bills" controversy, which "hawks" generally interpreted as ruling out open-ended bank liquidity support (Green 1988; Dimand 2020). Governors were also shaped by the major British banking crises occurring over the second half of the nineteenth century, which triggered foundational debates over the merits of banking crisis interventions. Hawkish governors subsequently internalized the dictum advanced in 1866 by the Bank of England that "long-term benefits derived from refusing to rescue insolvent institutions may outweigh the temporary fruits of cooperation" (Schneider 2022). The moralistic undertones of prominent hawks such as Richard Koch at the Reichsbank were echoed in France but opposed by the Banca d'Italia's Giacomo Grillo, who objected to the idea of "self-correcting" economic forces.[22]
- Central bank governors during the 1920–70 period were preoccupied with policy debates on re-establishing the prewar gold standard. Advocates of a transition to free or managed-float currency regimes—"doves/pragmatists" in the FKSS (2023) classification—downplayed the adverse effects that such regimes would have on price stability. Bonaldo Stringher, the Banca d'Italia governor, personified this belief set during three decades (1900–30) in office, stubbornly opposing the deflationary demands of the government during the

1920s (Segreto 2019) but swiftly though selectively accommodating the 1927–28 banking crisis via LLR (Molteni and Pellegrino 2022). Meanwhile, governors favoring a return to fixed exchange rates were classic "hawks" who regarded emergency assistance to the financial sector not just as morally wrong but also as a threat to price stability (Meyer 1954). Junnosuke Inoue, the Bank of Japan governor during the 1920s, was one of these representative "hawks."

- During the 1970s and early 1980s, central bank governors across all seventeen advanced economies took part in the debates on inflation (Timberlake 1993). In this context, even "dovish/pragmatist" governors could be receptive to certain elements of monetarism without wholly accepting them. An example in this category was the Australian Reserve Bank governor Robert (Bob) Alan Johnston (1982–89), who experimented with monetary targets in the early phase of his tenure. Prior to the Australian crisis of 1989, Johnston adopted a similarly middle-ground attitude, mimicking the poet Arthur Hugh Clough: "Thou may not kill, but needst not strive officiously to keep alive." We see here how a moderate stance on price stability coincided with pragmatic attitudes on bank support.[23] "Hawks," on the other hand, were converts to Milton Friedman's ideas and favored tight control over inflation via the money-supply channel, a stance that led them to reject emergency lending to banks during crises if it violated money growth targets (Meltzer 1998; White 2012). Characteristically, Rolf Kullberg of the Bank of Finland (1983–92) repeatedly voiced dire warnings about the moral hazard implications of lax financial conditions prior to the Finnish banking crisis of the 1990s, when he justified his long hesitation to provide support to banks by the need to wait until they "capitulate and submit [themselves] to the Bank" on punitive terms (Sulkunen 2015).

- Finally, from the 1990s, governors focused on the designs of new inflation-targeting regimes (Goodfriend 2005) and the onset of the "great moderation." These debates again exemplify the coincidence of price and currency stability beliefs on the one hand and emergency crisis attitudes on the other. In Japan, the Governor of the Bank of Japan Yasushi Mieno sounded warnings about inflated land values on the eve of a financial crisis, motivating his deployment of the hawkish "Mieno Shock" program (Brierley and Hadfield 1990). Similarly, Mervyn King, who served as Governor of the Bank of England from 2003 to 2013—having spent years building a personal "arch-inflation hawk mythology" (*Herald* 2003)—resisted the deployment of emergency liquidity to British banks in 2007–8, long after peer institutions including the European Central Bank (ECB) had approved them, highlighting the moral hazard implications: "The provision of large liquidity facilities penalises those financial institutions that sat out the dance, encourages herd behaviour and increases the intensity of future crises" (King 2007). Jean-Claude Trichet (president of the ECB 2003–11), on the other hand, was representative of "dove/pragmatist" beliefs. Though he had been hawkishly inclined earlier in his career, by 2003, markets identified him with a "pragmatic and flexible policy stance" (Johnson et al. 2003). Prior to the beginning of the GFC, Trichet explicitly rejected a formalistic leaning against asset price bubbles, advocating a pragmatic stance on moral hazard dynamics and, in principle, approving official financial sector support (Trichet 2003a; Trichet 2003b).

Governor Beliefs, Central Bank Action, and Crisis Outcomes

Did the ex ante beliefs of governors actually affect central bank policies during financial crises? Were they strong enough to drive consequential choices, or did central bank committees counterbalance and dilute their ideological predispositions? FKSS (2023) shows that, under hawkish governors, central banks were significantly less likely to expand their balance sheets in response to financial crises. While hawks also reacted to financial crises by expanding balance sheets, they did so less often than their more dovish colleagues.

The differentiated effects of governors' preconceived ideological leanings on central bank policies also appear to have altered macroeconomic outcomes. Figure 10.7 shows average trajectories

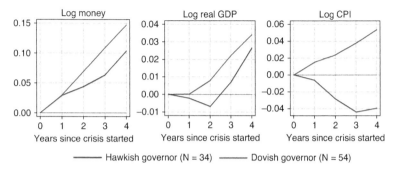

FIGURE 10.7. Macroeconomic Dynamics after Financial Crises by Governor Classification.

Notes: Postcrisis average trajectories for central bank assets, real GDP per capita, and consumer prices by ex ante governor beliefs estimated by the following local projections: $y_{i,t+b} - y_{i,t+1} = \alpha_{i,b} + \beta_b g_{i,t+1} + \varepsilon_{i,t+b}$ for $b = 2, 3, 4$ where $g_{i,t}$ is a binary indicating a hawkish governor, $y_{i,t}$ and stands for each of the three different outcome variables. Sample of eighty-nine financial crises that occurred since 1870 in seventeen advanced economies with an operating central bank and available macroeconomic data, excluding 1914–18, 1939–45, the German hyperinflation, and the Spanish Civil War. Averages purged of country-fixed effects. Source: FKSS (2023).

for the money aggregate (M2), real GDP per capita, and consumer prices since the start of a crisis split by ex ante governor beliefs, controlling for country-fixed effects. In the raw data, more dovish policy stances were indeed associated with vigorous money growth, quicker economic recoveries, and less deflation.

To test these patterns rigorously, FKSS (2023) estimates instrumental variables in local projections (*LP–IV*) for the macroeconomic effects of balance sheet expansions induced by preexisting central bank governors' beliefs. The empirical strategy is based on the notion that, ceteris paribus, hawkish governors are less likely to engage in balance sheet expansions than their dovish colleagues when facing a similar crisis. This will induce variation in liquidity injections that is exogenous to the crisis situation itself. Based on this exclusion restriction, we estimate expected changes of macro variables from a total of seventy-eight crisis observations using local projections for horizons *b = 2, 3, 4*, counting the years since the start of the crisis:

First stage: $m_{i,t+t} = a_i + bg_{i,t+1} + cx_{i,t+1} + e_{i,t+1}$ (1)

Second stage: $y_{i,t+h} - y_{i,t+1} = \alpha_{i,h} + \beta_h \hat{m}_{i,t+1} + \gamma_h x_{i,t+1} + \varepsilon_{i,t+h}$ (2)

where $y_{i,t}$ denotes a macroeconomic aggregate to be evaluated in natural logarithm to interpret differences as approximate growth rates. The binary variable $m_{i,t}$ takes a value of one if there has been an exceptional expansion—defined as annual central bank asset growth of 15% or more—during at least one of the preceding two years. Importantly, monetary policy $m_{i,t+1}$ will be instrumented by the binary variable $g_{i,t}$ indicating that the current central bank governor holds hawkish beliefs. Country-fixed effects $\alpha_{i,h}$ absorb time-invariant heterogeneity across countries while controls $\gamma_h x_{i,t+1}$ capture macro-financial dynamics prior to the crisis. FKSS (2023) shows that results hold qualitatively for various alternative control vectors.

The first stage relationship of equation (1) is statistically and quantitatively significant. Using our governor classifications, FKSS (2023) shows that hawkish governors have been roughly 36% less likely to conduct a balance sheet expansion either during a crisis year or one year after that. The first stage F-statistic for a test of instrument exclusion is 18.9, with results robust to the inclusion of governor-biographical and macro-institutional controls.

In FKSS (2023), we demonstrate that liquidity support during financial crises substantially cushioned negative effects on output. With liquidity support, real GDP per capita started to grow on average during the second year after a crisis outbreak and exceeded counterfactual levels of macroeconomic activity by more than +7% at medium-term horizons. Correspondingly, these estimates imply large gains in terms of *cumulative* real aggregate income, amounting to +21% over the projection horizon.

Moreover, balance sheet expansions led to persistent growth of broad money aggregates and typically prevented protracted deflation. Without central bank interventions, it is estimated that financial crises without liquidity support were followed on average by three years of falling prices. By contrast, deflation was typically avoided altogether when the central bank provided liquidity. These operations typically did not cause runaway inflation, however. On average, prices increased by +20% over four years, implying annual inflation of about 4.6%.

Our evidence corroborates the literature that has posited positive real effects from liquidity support, such as Richardson and Troost (2009). Based on the identification of exogenous variation in central bank balance sheet expansions, this evidence stands in contrast to previous assessments, including Bordo et al. (2001) and Honohan and Klingebiel (2003), which took a negative view on the real macroeconomic effects of liquidity support. Estimates are qualitatively robust to a range of alternative control setups, sample restrictions, and measurement choices, such as a continuous balance sheet expansion variable.

What if public knowledge about governors' beliefs changes pre-crisis dynamics? Kuttner and Posen (2010) show that financial markets react to the announcement of central bank governor appointments. Possibly, markets not only price in new trajectories of rates and inflation but also change the way they operate: The mere anticipation of dovish crisis management could encourage financial risk-taking ex ante. Accordingly, dovish governors might face not just more but crucially more severe financial crises, violating the instrument's exclusion restriction. Yet such mechanisms would load the dice against finding positive macroeconomic effects under dovish crisis management, because doves would face systematically worse situations. That is, the *LP–IV* estimates would be conservative, making it harder for FKSS (2023) to find anything.

Moral Hazard Effects Dominate the Long Term

Concerns that public policy for financial stabilization may encourage riskier behavior by market participants are not new. There are several empirical cross-country studies on the moral hazard effects of deposit insurance (Cordella and Yeyati 2003; Duchin and Sosyura 2014; Anginer and Demirguc-Kunt 2018). However, systematic evidence on the moral hazard effects of central bank liquidity support is limited. FKSS (2023) asks: Do short-term gains from balance sheet expansions incur long-term costs in the form of financial instability? This is a relevant concern, particularly because for many hawkish central bankers since 1870, the effects of balance sheet expansions on future financial sector risk-taking lay at the heart of their refusal to act more aggressively.

Moral hazard implies financial investments by market participants who expect the central bank to bear private liquidity risk or even bail out insolvent institutions. When such behavior becomes widespread, low-risk premia and easy leverage can fuel credit expansions of the detrimental type (Kirti 2018; Greenwood et al. 2022). If dovish central bank policy precipitated such financial fragility in the past, one should find a link between crisis intervention and subsequent credit booms gone bad.

On this basis, FKSS (2023) systematically explored the moral hazard channel for its crisis sample and found that the data reveal a clear pattern. After financial crises without liquidity support, credit booms generally occurred with a moderate and stable probability. Around 25% of country-years belong to a credit boom episode, a fraction only marginally higher than observed across our entire post-1870 sample. By contrast, the probability of credit booms rose after a crisis with liquidity support, peaking fifteen years after the crisis, with more than 50% of country-years experiencing a credit boom episode. Importantly, the discrepancy in credit boom probability is almost entirely driven by credit booms that turned sour. Such booms occasionally occur after crises without liquidity support: 4.3% of observations over a twenty-year window. However, after crises with liquidity support, the probability of "bad booms" sharply rises, with the probability averaged over a twenty-year window almost doubling to 8.4% relative to the no-expansion scenario. These differences are statistically significant across a variety of model constraints and specifications, controlling for confounding factors.

Overall, therefore, the data do not allow one to reject concerns about moral hazard. The worries about long-run moral hazard voiced by "hawkish" governors may have had a certain justification. This implies that governors in financial crises face a trade-off between short-run financial stability gains and long-run financial stability risks. Those findings tally with the recent literature on LLR operations and bank behavior, highlighting the moral hazard problem (Drechsler et al. 2016b; Anginer and Demirguc-Kunt 2018; Acharya et al. 2022).

Conclusion

Despite academic recognition of the importance of central bank balance sheets, their long-run empirical evolution, their actual size, and the precise economic effects of their deployment have, so far, not been studied systematically. FKSS (2023) fills this gap. We suggest that balance sheets have not simply traced transaction volumes in economies or any other specific macroeconomic variable and that the classical gold standard era was characterized by a surprising degree of balance sheet elasticity. The long-run evidence suggests that, while central bank balance sheets have indeed assumed unprecedented proportions relative to output in recent years, they continue to lag relative to total financial assets and total public debt.

While a willingness to expand balance sheets in times of geopolitical stress existed as early as the seventeenth century, FKSS (2023) shows that the expansion of central bank balance sheets did not yet constitute a systematic response to financial crises in Walter Bagehot's lifetime (1826–1877). Rather, this role evolved gradually until the post-1945 era, when investors could increasingly expect meaningful central bank liquidity support in the event of financial distress. How much support and with what consequences? Using the policy orientation of the key decision makers responsible for deploying central bank balance sheets in crisis times—typically central bank governors, but sometimes other officials at the central bank or Treasury—the ongoing work in FKSS (2023) suggests that one can address these questions empirically. FKSS (2023) shows that the deployment of liquidity support during financial crises contributes in a statistically significant and economically relevant way to a faster return to trend inflation, trend real GDP growth, higher stock prices, and stronger real investment. It does not appear to make a difference whether such liquidity support focuses on a particular asset type. Such results stand in contrast with the more skeptical findings of Bordo et al. (2001) and Honohan and Klingebiel (2003).

FKSS (2023) also adds an important qualification, however. For a long time, many economists and central bankers suspected that balance sheet expansions during financial crises could give rise to moral hazard—a concern that demonstrably motivated hawkish governors in the past to reject balance sheet expansions. We find evidence that such a sting in the tail exists. The time until the next systemic financial crisis is significantly shorter after major balance sheet expansions.

This paper summarizes insights from ongoing work by the authors, specifically, the working paper titled "The Safety Net: Central Bank Balance Sheets and Financial Crises, 1587–2020," abbreviated FKSS (2023) throughout this summary. Readers are advised to consult FKSS (2023) for all data, results, discussions, and exercises. We thank Barry Eichengreen for discussing FKSS (2023) and both the organizers and attendees of the Hoover Monetary Policy Conference 2023 for very helpful additional comments.

References

Acharya, Viral, Rahul Chauhan, Raghuram Rajan, and Sascha Steffen. 2022. "Liquidity Dependence: Why Shrinking Central Bank Balance Sheets Is an Uphill Task." Presented at the Jackson Hole Economic Policy Symposium sponsored by the Federal Reserve Bank of Kansas City, Jackson Hole, Wyoming (August).

Acharya, Viral, and David Skeie. 2011. "A Model of Liquidity Hoarding and Term Premia in Inter-bank Markets." *Journal of Monetary Economics* 58, no. 5 (July): 436–47.

Aksoy, Cevat G., Barry Eichengreen, and Orkun Saka. 2022. "The Political Scar of Epidemics." National Bureau of Economic Research Working Paper 27401, May.

Anginer, Deniz, and Asli Demirguc-Kunt. 2018. "Bank Runs and Moral Hazard: A Review of Deposit Insurance." World Bank Policy Research Working Paper 8589 (September).

Ashcraft, Adam, James McAndrews, and David Skeie. 2011. "Precautionary Reserves and the Interbank Market." *Journal of Money, Credit, and Banking* 43, Supplement 2 (October): 311–48.

Bagehot, Walter. (1873) 1962. *Lombard Street: A Description of the Money Market.* Reprint, Homewood, IL: Richard D. Irwin.

Bailey, Andrew, Jonathan Bridges, Richard Harrison, Josh Jones, and Aakash Manodi. 2020. "The Central Bank Balance Sheet as a Policy Tool: Past, Present, and Future." Bank of England Staff Working Paper 899 (December).

Balletta, Francesco. 2008. *La circolazione della moneta fiduciaria a Napoli nel Seicento e nel Settecento, 1587–1805.* Naples: Edizioni scientifiche italiane.

Balletta, Francesco, Luigi Balletta, and Eduardo Nappi. 2018. "The Investments of the Neapolitan Public Banks: A Long Run View (1587–1806)." In *Financial Innovation and Resilience: A Comparative Perspective on the Public Banks of Naples (1462–1808),* edited by Lilia Costabile and Larry Neal, 95–123. London: Palgrave Macmillan.

Baron, Matthew, Emil Verner, and Wei Xiong. 2021. "Banking Crises without Panics." *Quarterly Journal of Economics* 136, no. 1 (February): 51–113.

Behr, Patrick, and Weichao Wang. 2020. "The (Un)intended Effects of Government Bailouts: The Impact of TARP on the Interbank Market and Bank Risk-Taking." *Journal of Banking and Finance* 116 (July): 1–19.

Benmelech, Efraim, and Nittai Bergman. 2012. "Credit Traps." *American Economic Review* 102, no. 6 (October): 3004–32.

Benmelech, Efraim, Ralf R. Meisenzahl, and Rodney Ramcharan. 2016. "The Real Effects of Liquidity during the Financial Crisis: Evidence from Automobiles." *Quarterly Journal of Economics* 132, no. 1 (April): 317–65.

Bernanke, Ben. 2020. "The New Tools of Monetary Policy." *American Economic Review* 110, no. 4 (April): 943–83.

Bernanke, Ben, Brian Sack, Vincent Reinhart, Benjamin Friedman, and Lars E.O. Svensson. 2004. "Monetary Policy Alternatives at the Zero Bound: An Empirical Assessment." Brookings Papers on Economic Activity 2 (December).

Bindseil, Ulrich. 2004. *Monetary Policy Implementation: Theory—Past—Present.* Oxford: Oxford University Press.

———. 2019. *Central Banking before 1800: A Rehabilitation.* Oxford: Oxford University Press.

Bleck, Alexander, and Xuewen Liu. 2018. "Credit Expansion and Credit Misallocation." *Journal of Monetary Economics* 94 (April): 27–40.

Bolton, Patrick, Tano Santos, and Jose Scheinkman. 2011. "Outside and Inside Liquidity." *Quarterly Journal of Economics* 126, no. 1 (October 22): 259–321.

Bordo, Michael, and Harold James. 2007. "From 1907 to 1946: A Happy Childhood or a Troubled Adolescence?" In *The Swiss National Bank 1907–2007,* edited by Ulrich Kohli, 29–107. Zurich: NZZ Libro.

Bordo, Michael D., Barry Eichengreen, Daniela Klingebiel, and Maria Soledad Martinez-Peria. 2001. "Is the Crisis Problem Growing More Severe?" *Economic Policy* 16, no. 32 (April 1): 52–82.

Bordo, Michael D., and Klodiana Istrefi. 2023. "Perceived FOMC: The Making of Hawks, Doves, and Swingers." *Journal of Monetary Economics* 136 (May): 125–43.

Borio, Claudio, and Anna Zabai. 2018. "Unconventional Monetary Policies: A Re-appraisal. In *Research Handbook for Central Banking,* edited by Peter Conti-Brown and Rosa M. Lastra, 398–444. Northampton, MA: Edward Elgar Publishing.

Brierley, David, and Peter Hadfield. 1990. "Turmoil in Tokyo." *Sunday Times* (London), April 8.

Broadberry, Stephen, Bruce Campbell, Alexander Klein, Mark Overton, and Bas van Leeuwen. 2015. *British Economic Growth, 1270–1870.* Cambridge: Cambridge University Press.

Browning, Reed. 1971. "The Duke of Newcastle and the Financing of the Seven Years' War." *Journal of Economic History* 31, no. 2 (June): 344–77.

Brunnermeier, Markus K. 2009. "Deciphering the Liquidity and Credit Crunch 2007–2008." *Journal of Economic Perspectives* 23, no. 1 (Winter): 77–100.

Caballero, Ricardo, and Arvind Krishnamurthy. 2008. "Collective Risk Management in a Flight to Quality Episode." *Journal of Finance* 63, no. 5 (October): 2195–230.

Calomiris, Charles W. 2011. "Banking Crises and the Rules of the Game." In *Monetary and Banking History: Essays in Honour of Forrest Capie*, edited by Geoffrey Wood, Terence C. Mills, and Nicholas Crafts, 88–131. New York: Routledge.

Carlson, Mark, and David C. Wheelock. 2015. "The Lender of Last Resort: Lessons from the Fed's First 100 Years." In *Current Federal Reserve Policy under the Lens of Economic History: Essays to Commemorate the Federal Reserve System's Centennial*, edited by Owen F. Humpage, 49–101. Cambridge: Cambridge University Press.

Clapham, Sir John. 1958. *The Bank of England: A History*, vol. 1, *1694–1797*, 2nd ed. Cambridge: Cambridge University Press.

Clodfelter, Micheal. 2017. *Warfare and Armed Conflicts: A Statistical Encyclopedia of Casualty and Other Figures, 1492–2015*. Jefferson, NC: McFarland & Company.

Cochrane, John H. 2022. "UK Finance Fable Update." *The Grumpy Economist* (blog), October 14.

Cordella, Tito, and Eduardo Levy Yeyati. 2003. "Bank Bailouts: Moral Hazard vs. Value Effect." *Journal of Financial Intermediation* 12, no. 4 (October): 300–30.

Costabile, Lilia, and Eduardo Nappi. 2018. "The Public Banks of Naples between Financial Innovation and Crisis." In *Financial Innovation and Resilience: A Comparative Perspective on the Public Banks of Naples (1462–1808)*, edited by Lilia Costabile and Larry Neal, 17–53. London: Palgrave Macmillan.

Del Negro, Marco, Gauti Eggertsson, Andrea Ferrero, and Nobuhiro Kiyotaki. 2017. "The Great Escape? A Quantitative Evaluation of the Fed's Liquidity Facilities." *American Economic Review* 107, no. 3 (March): 824–57.

Dell'Ariccia, Giovanni, Enrica Detragiache, and Raghuram Rajan. 2008. "The Real Effect of Banking Crises." *Journal of Financial Intermediation* 17, no. 1 (January): 89–112.

Diamond, Douglas W., and Philip H. Dybvig. 1983. "Bank Runs, Deposit Insurance, and Liquidity." *Journal of Political Economy* 91, no. 3 (June): 401–19.

Dimand, Robert W. 2020. "J. Laurence Laughlin versus Irving Fisher on the Quantity Theory of Money, 1894 to 1913." *Oxford Economic Papers* 72, no. 4 (October): 1032–49.

Dimsdale, Nicholas, and Ryland Thomas. 2017. "A Millennium of Macroeconomic Data." OBER Dataset—Bank of England.

Dincecco, Mark. 2011. *Political Transformations and Public Finance: Europe, 1650–1913*. Cambridge: Cambridge University Press.

Drechsler, Itamar, Thomas Drechsel, David Marques-Ibanez, and Philipp Schnabl. 2016a. "Who Borrows from the Lender of Last Resort?" *Journal of Finance* 71, no. 5 (October): 1933–74.

———. 2016b. "Who Borrows from the Lender of Last Resort?" *Journal of Finance* 71, no. 5 (October): 1933–74.

Duchin, Ran, and Denis Sosyura. 2014. "Safer Ratios, Riskier Portfolios: Banks' Response to Government Aid." *Journal of Financial Economics* 113, no. 1 (February 19): 1–28.

Edvinsson, Rodney. 2014. "The Gross Domestic Product of Sweden Within Present Borders, 1620–2012." In *Historical Monetary and Financial Statistics for Sweden*. Vol. 2, *House Prices, Stock Returns, National Accounts and the Riksbank Balance Sheet, 1620–2012*, edited by Rodney Edvinsson, Tor Jacobson, and Daniel Waldenström, 101–82. Stockholm: Riksbank and Ekerlids Förlag.

Engen, Eric M., Thomas Laubach, and David L. Reifschneider. 2015. "The Macroeconomic Effects of the Federal Reserve's Unconventional Monetary Policies." In *Finance and Economics Discussion Series 2015-5*. Washington, DC: Board of Governors of the Federal Reserve System.

Ferguson, Niall, Martin Kornejew, Paul Schmelzing, and Moritz Schularick (FKSS). 2023. "The Safety Net: Central Bank Balance Sheets and Financial Crises, 1587–2020." CEPR Press Discussion Paper No. 17858 (January 31).

Ferguson, Niall, Andreas Schaab, and Moritz Schularick. 2014. "Central Bank Balance Sheets: Expansion and Reduction since 1900." CESifo Working Paper Series No. 5379 (June): 1–51.

Fregert, Klas. 2014. "The Riksbank's Balance Sheet, 1668–2011." In *Historical Monetary and Financial Statistics for Sweden*. Vol. 2, *House Prices, Stock Returns, National Accounts and the Riksbank Balance Sheet, 1620–2012*, edited by Rodney Edvinsson, Tor Jacobson, and Daniel Waldenström, 339–93. Stockholm: Riksbank and Ekerlids Förlag.

Fregert, Klas, and Lars Jonung. 1996. "Inflation and Switches between Specie and Paper Standards in Sweden 1668–1931: A Public Finance Interpretation." *Scottish Journal of Political Economy* 43, no. 4 (September): 444–67.

Fusco, Idamaria. 2007. *Peste, demografia e fiscalità nel regno di Napoli del XVII secolo*. Milan: Franco Angeli.

Gagnon, Joseph E., Matthew Raskin, Julie Remache, and Brian Sack. 2011. "The Financial Market Effects of the Federal Reserve's Large-Scale Asset Purchases." *International Journal of Central Banking* 7, no. 1 (March): 3–43.

Garriga, Ana Carolina. 2016. "Central Bank Independence in the World: A New Data Set." *International Interactions* 42, no. 5 (March 20): 849–68.

Gertler, Mark, and Peter Karadi. 2011. "A Model of Unconventional Monetary Policy." *Journal of Monetary Economics* 58, no. 1 (January): 17–34.

Gohlmann, Silja, and Roland Vaubel. 2007. "The Educational and Occupational Background of Central Bankers and Its Effect on Inflation: An Empirical Analysis." *European Economic Review* 51, no. 4 (May): 925–41.

Goodfriend, Marvin. 2005. "Inflation Targeting in the United States?" In *The Inflation Targeting Debate*, edited by Ben Bernanke and Michael Woodford, 311–50. Chicago: University of Chicago Press.

Green, E. H. H. 1988. "Rentiers versus Producers? The Political Economy of the Bimetallic Controversy c. 1880–1898." *English Historical Review* 103, no. 408 (July): 588–612.

Greenwood, Robin, Samuel G. Hanson, Andrei Shleifer, and Jakob Ahm Sorensen. 2022. "Predictable Financial Crises." *Journal of Finance* 77, no. 2 (April): 863–921.

Guerrieri, Veronica, and Robert Shimer. 2014. "Dynamic Adverse Selection: A Theory of Illiquidity, Fire Sales, and Flight to Quality." *American Economic Review* 104, no. 7 (July): 1875–1908.

Heckscher, Eli F. 1954. *An Economic History of Sweden*. Cambridge, MA: Harvard University Press.

Herald (Scotland). 2003. "King's First Outing as Governor Surprises Market. Rate Cut Taken as Sign That Hawkish Image Is Softening," July 10.

Hill, B. W., and L. S. Sutherland. 1971. "The Change of Government and the 'Loss of the City,' 1710–1711." *Economic History Review* 24, no. 3 (August): 395–413.

Honohan, Patrick, and Daniela Klingebiel. 2003. "The Fiscal Cost Implications of an Accommodating Approach to Banking Crises." *Journal of Banking and Finance* 27, no. 8 (August): 1539–60.

Johnson, Jo, Tony Major, and George Parker. 2003. "Trichet Gets Green Light for ECB." *Financial Times*, June 19.

Johnston, Robert. 1985. "Prudential Supervision of Banks" address to the Victorian Division of the Securities Institute of Australia and the Institute of Chartered Accountants, on February 2, 1985, in Melbourne. Published in *Reserve Bank of Australia Bulletin* no. 1 (March): 571–75.

Joyce, Michael, Ana Lasaosa, Ibrahim Stevens, and Matthew Tong. 2011. "The Financial Market Impact of Quantitative Easing in the United Kingdom." *International Journal of Central Banking* 7, no. 3 (September): 114–61.

King, Mervyn. 2007. "Turmoil in Financial Markets: What Can Central Banks Do?" Paper submitted to the Treasury Committee (September 12). http://img.thisismoney.co.uk/docs/king_letter.pdf.

Kirti, Divya. 2018. "Lending Standards and Output Growth." International Monetary Fund Working Paper No. 2018/23 (January 26).

Kuttner, Kenneth D., and Adam S. Posen. 2010. "Do Markets Care Who Chairs the Central Bank?" *Journal of Money, Credit, and Banking* 42, nos. 2–3 (March–April): 347–71.

Malmendier, Ulrike, and Jessica A. Wachter. 2022. "Memory of Past Experiences and Economic Decisions." Unpublished manuscript, prepared for the *Oxford Handbook of Human Memory*. https://eml.berkeley.edu/~ulrike/Papers/Memory Handbookv17.pdf.

Martin, Antoine. 2009. "Reconciling Bagehot with the Fed's Response to September 11." *Journal of Money, Credit, and Banking* 41, nos. 2–3 (March–April): 397–415.

Meltzer, Allan H. 1998. "Monetarism: The Issues and the Outcome." *Atlantic Economic Journal* 26, no. 1 (March): 8–31.

Metrick, Andrew, and Paul Schmelzing. 2021. "Banking-Crisis Interventions, 1257–2019." National Bureau of Economic Research Working Paper 29281 (September): 1–47.

Meyer, Eugene. 1954. "From Laissez Faire with William Graham Sumner to the RFC." *Public Policy* 5: 3–27.

Mishra, Prachi, and Ariell Reshef. 2019. "How Do Central Bank Governors Matter? Regulation and the Financial Sector." *Journal of Money, Credit, and Banking* 51, nos. 2–3 (March–April): 369–402.

Molteni, Marco, and Dario Pellegrino. 2022. "The Establishment of Banking Supervision in Italy: An Assessment (1926–1936)." *Business History* (published online October 28).

Monnet, Eric, and Damien Puy. 2020. "Do Old Habits Die Hard? Central Banks and the Bretton Woods Gold Puzzle." *Journal of International Economics* 127 (November): no. 103394.

Reinhart, Carmen M., and Kenneth S. Rogoff. 2009. *This Time Is Different: Eight Centuries of Financial Folly*. Princeton, NJ: Princeton University Press.

Richardson, Gary, and William Troost. 2009. "Monetary Intervention Mitigated Banking Panics during the Great Depression: Quasi-Experimental Evidence from a Federal Reserve District Border, 1929 to 1933." *Journal of Political Economy* 117, no. 6 (December): 1031–73.

Romer, Christina, and David Romer. 2018. "Phillips Lecture—Why Some Times Are Different: Macroeconomic Policy and the Aftermath of Financial Crises." *Economica* 85, no. 337 (January): 1–40.

Sayers, R. S. 1957. "The Development of Central Banking after Bagehot." In *The Development of Central Banking after Bagehot*, edited by R. S. Sayers, 8–19. Oxford: Oxford University Press.

Schneider, Sabine. 2022. "The Politics of Last Resort Lending and the Overend & Gurney Crisis of 1866." *Economic History Review* 75, no. 2 (May): 579–600.

Schularick, Moritz, and Alan M. Taylor. 2012. "Credit Booms Gone Bust: Monetary Policy, Leverage Cycles, and Financial Crises, 1870–2008." *American Economic Review* 102, no. 2 (April): 1029–61.

Scott, William Robert. 1912. *The Constitution and Finance of English, Scottish and Irish Joint-Stock Companies to 1720*. Cambridge: Cambridge University Press.

Segreto, Luciano. 2019. "Stringher, Bonaldo." In *Dizionario Biografico degli Italiani*, 94. Rome: Istituto della Enciclopedia Italiana.

Shafik, Minouche. 2016. "Small Is Beautiful, but Big Is Necessary." Speech given at Bloomberg Markets Most Influential Summit in London, September 28.

Shizume, Masato. 2020. "The Historical Evolution of Monetary Policy (Goals and Instruments) in Japan: From the Central Bank of an Emerging Economy to the Central Bank of a Mature Economy." In *Handbook of the History of Money and Currency*, edited by Stefano Battilossi, Youssef Cassis, and Kazuhiko Yago, 923–52. Singapore: Springer.

Simmons, Beth A. 1996. "Rulers of the Game: Central Bank Independence during the Interwar Years." *International Organization* 50, no. 3 (Summer): 407–43.

Sims, Eric, and Jing Cynthia Wu. 2021. "Evaluating Central Banks' Tool Kit: Past, Present, and Future." *Journal of Monetary Economics* 118 (March): 135–60.

Smets, Frank, and Simon M. Potter. 2019. "Unconventional Monetary Policy Tools: A Cross-Country Analysis." Committee on the Global Financial System Papers no. 63 (October): 1–85.

Sulkunen, Pekka Juhani. 2015. "What Is Neo-liberalism? Justifications of Deregulating Financial Markets in Norway and Finland." SIFO-National Institute for Consumer Research Project Note no. 6 (June): 1–48.

Thornton, Henry. (1802) 1939. *An Enquiry into the Nature and Effects of the Paper Credit of Great Britain*. Reprint, London: George Allen & Unwin Ltd.

Timberlake, Richard H. 1993. *Monetary Policy in the United States: An Intellectual and Institutional History*. Chicago: University of Chicago Press.

Trichet, Jean-Claude. 2003a. "Asset Price Bubbles and Their Implications for Monetary Policy and Financial Stability." In *Asset Price Bubbles: The Implications for Monetary, Regulatory, and International Policies*, edited by William C. Hunter, George G. Kaufman, and Michael Pomerleano, 15–22. Cambridge, MA: MIT Press.

———. 2003b. "Financial Stability." Speech delivered at the Forum Financier Belge, Brussels, November 26. Printed in *BIS Review* 53 (2003). https://www.bis.org/review/r031205a.pdf.

van Dillen, J. G. 1934. "The Bank of Amsterdam." In *History of the Principal Public Banks*, edited by J. G. van Dillen, 79–124. The Hague: Martinus Nijhoff.

van Ommeren, Emile, and Guilia Piccillo. 2021. "The Central Bank Governor and Interest Rate Setting by Committee." CESifo Economic Studies 67, no. 2 (June): 155–85.

van Zanden, Jan Luiten, and Bas van Leeuwen. 2012. "Persistent but Not Consistent: The Growth of National Income in Holland, 1347–1807." *Explorations in Economic History* 49, no. 2 (April): 119–30.

Volcker, Paul A. 2004. "Foreword." In *Too Big to Fail: The Hazards of Bank Bailouts*, by Gary H. Stern and Ron J. Feldman, vii–x. Washington, DC: Brookings Institution Press.

Webb, Stephen B. 1985. "Government Debt and Inflationary Expectations as Determinants of the Money Supply in Germany, 1919–23." *Journal of Money, Credit, and Banking* 17, no. 4 (November): 479–92.

White, Lawrence H. 2012. *The Clash of Economic Ideas: The Great Policy Debates and Experiments of the Last Hundred Years*. Cambridge: Cambridge University Press.

Wu, Jing Cynthia, and Fan Dora Xia. 2016. "Measuring the Macroeconomic Impact of Monetary Policy at the Zero Lower Bound." *Journal of Money, Credit, and Banking* 48, nos. 2–3 (March–April): 253–91.

Notes

1. Romer and Romer (2018) have recently reached a more benign assessment of the impact of monetary policy on output during financial crises. However, they use only a post-1970s event sample and investigate only policy rate reductions.

2. Across this literature, Ferguson et al. (2014) is the only one concerned with aggregate long-run balance sheet trends but focused on a restricted historical sample and also did not isolate the causal effects of balance sheet expansions.

3. For summaries of studies and the posited financial and macroeconomic effects, see, for instance, Borio and Zabai (2018) or Smets and Potter (2019).

4. Following Dincecco (2011)'s classification, who posits a completion of fiscal centralization for England in the year 1066, which is echoed in related literature.

5. Clapham (1958) in addition reports a GBP 20,000 loan to an anonymous private debtor extended by the Bank in 1711, with Bindseil (2019) interpreting the event as an early LLR instance.

6. In nominal terms, the key expansion years for total BoE assets at the time are 1720 (+19.5% year-on-year), 1723 (+24.1%), and 1724 (+19.1%). None of these years technically qualifies as a "major" expansion event along the FKSS (2023) definitions.

7. Dincecco (2011) posits a fiscal centralization for Sweden only by the year 1840, almost eight centuries after the English centralization. The 1668 and 1719 statutes explicitly formalized ownership of the Riksbank by the Riksdag, and contained a pledge by the King to respect the Bank's independence, see Fregert and Jonung (1996).

8. Fregert and Jonung (1996) provide both real (goods-based) and nominal Riksbank balances for the period to distinguish the effects of the currency devaluation: on their goods-based real Riksbank basis, balances tripled during the period of 1750–9, with the Riksbank essentially constituting the sole source of financing for both the Russian and the Seven Years' War after attempts to tap private markets failed. For the private sector, Fregert and Jonung (1996) highlight the Hat Party policy of protectionism and state subsidies for the merchant community underpinning generous emergency lending.

9. See the detailed chronology and context of lending interventions in Metrick and Schmelzing (2021).

10. As analyzed further in FKSS (2023), a liquidity provision event can be neutral with regard to the overall central bank balance sheet size if "risky" assets held by the private sector are swapped for "safe" assets held by the public sector or if lending is sterilized.

11. While we focus on summary statistics here, FKSS (2023) provides full historical context for the "top 25" largest historical expansion events, and respective sources, to illustrate our classification rationale.

12. FKSS (2023) counts 140 country-years in this category, and the average year-on-year nominal expansion in this category across country-years

stands at 55.9%. In this group, the German hyperinflation year of 1922 represents a significant outlier. Reichsbank nominal total assets in 1922 were expanding at 1186% year-on-year, mainly driven by sharply rising commercial bill discounting activity. Webb (1985, 480–83) argues the Reichsbank behaved passively through this phase, effectively letting the market decide its balance sheet size.

13. For all exercises involving the pre-1870 period, they use banking crisis definitions in Metrick and Schmelzing (2021). Twin crises—as long as they include a banking crisis event as classified by these chronologies—are part of our "financial crisis" sample.

14. "War or revolution" events are repeatedly associated with a "sovereign default" classification in financial crisis chronologies: for instance, Germany 1943, which Reinhart and Rogoff (2009) classify as a sovereign default event; unless also accompanied by a quantitatively dominant banking crisis, these events remain in the "war or revolution" category despite these overlaps.

15. FKSS (2023) noted that even major previous natural or health-related disasters, such as the 1918–19 Spanish influenza, the 1957–58 "Asian flu," or the 1906 San Francisco Earthquake, did not typically engender a measurable monetary policy response. We would also consider events such as the 9/11 balance sheet expansion in the US under this category, but the YOY growth for 2001 does not pass our 15% threshold: see Martin (2009, 400).

16. For the long-run evolution in "bank stress," see Metrick and Schmelzing (2021). For wars, conflict deaths per million population for the seventeen-country sample stands at 122.5 per country-year between 1650–1945, dropping to 2.12 for 1946–2020; 90.5% of country-years since 1946 are fully conflict-free, all on the Clodfelter (2017) basis.

17. FKSS (2023) generally focuses attention on banking crises, as opposed to other types of financial crises for which chronologies exist: it notes that the association between currency crises and major balance sheet expansions is less firm, using chronologies distinguishing between currency and banking crises to confirm the general patterns, including Reinhart and Rogoff (2009).

18. Excluded is the German hyperinflation episode of 1922–23.

19. Existing empirical evidence on the effectiveness of liquidity provisions is mixed and either deals with the post-2007 experience (e.g., Wu and Xia 2016, Smets and Potter 2019, and Bernanke 2020), selected historical case

studies (e.g., Richardson and Troost 2009 and Benmelech et al. 2019), or suffers from the simultaneity of crisis severity and liquidity injection (e.g., Bordo et al. 2001, Honohan and Klingebiel 2003, and Dell'Ariccia et al. 2008).

20. Our rationale relies on existing literature, e.g., Simmons (1996), who showed that during the interwar period central banks systematically tried to steer against government policies. Consistent with such views, the "political leanings" of the nominating government as identified by Van Ommeren and Piccillo (2021) do not accord consistently with the market reactions analyzed by Kuttner and Posen (2010).

21. The governor coding focuses on the most relevant single decision maker in the monetary executive: at times, this person does not have to be the central bank governor—or the finance minister—but rather a different person within the central bank. In a total of nine cases, either central bank independence indices or historical sources indicate clear constraints on the central banks' independence. These cases are discussed further in FKSS (2023).

22. The economic debate during the Third Republic was deeply influenced by moral hazard concerns, with Banque de France governors Pierre Magnin and Georges Pallain subscribing to Clément Juglar's dictum that "a crisis for a nation is the operation made necessary to re-establish an equilibrium broken by speculation" (Bordo and James 2007, 81).

23. Johnston's quote in Johnston (1985).

DISCUSSANT REMARKS

Barry Eichengreen

The chapter by Niall Ferguson, Martin Kornejew, Paul Schmelzing, and Moritz Schularick exploring the trade-off between stabilizing financial market intervention on the one hand and encouraging additional risk-taking on the other could not be more timely, given recent events surrounding, inter alia, Silicon Valley Bank. For purposes of their analysis, the authors assemble a remarkable four-hundred-year-long dataset on central bank balance sheets and their correlates. They have undertaken a monumental task of historical and empirical financial reconstruction for which we, meaning both the disciplines of economics and history, will be eternally grateful. This is not meant as a backhanded compliment; it is not meant to minimize their other contributions. But there is much more in these pages than additional crunching of existing datasets. This chapter will be widely cited, in part but not exclusively because of its invaluable new data.

In addition to important data, the chapter reports important findings, of which I would highlight three. First, the authors document that the circumstances in which central banks expand their balance sheets have changed over time, away from war finance, their traditional charge, and toward financial rescues, their recent preoccupation. Second, they find that liquidity support during financial crises tends to be stabilizing. Third, such support also raises the probability of future boom-bust cycles; it is a source of moral hazard.

The first finding, about changing motivations, is well known to historians though no less important for that fact. Central banks were originally created as financiers to the sovereign and the state.

And what is more important to sovereigns and states than the ability to wage defensive (and sometimes offensive) wars? The second finding of stabilizing effects on financial markets confirms the modern conventional wisdom about the importance of the central bank's lender-and-liquidity-provider-of-last-resort functions. And the third finding about boom-bust cycles confirms economic intuition, namely that financial market participants respond to incentives, if not always in socially desirable ways.

A number of the ancillary patterns documented in the chapter should reassure the "balance-sheet alarmists" amongst us. The authors' longtime series suggest that fiscal dominance is not, in fact, more of a problem now than in the past. They show that central bank balance sheets in recent years are not unprecedentedly large relative to the financial sector. To be sure, central bank balance sheets have grown relative to gross domestic product. But this is entirely because—some might say that it is a byproduct of the fact that—financial sectors have grown.

Along with praise, I have questions about the chapter, some of which are also posed by the authors themselves, others not. To start, what exactly is a central bank? The authors answer: a central bank is an institution established under the provisions of a central banking law. But what exactly constitutes a central banking law? They suggest that a central bank is an institution with a monopoly of note issuance. But if we adopt this definition, we are led to disqualify what is commonly thought of as the first central bank, the Swedish Riksbank (est. 1668), which lacked this monopoly privilege for much of the nineteenth century. Is a central bank an institution with special responsibility for accommodating the government's financial needs? Then, what responsibilities and needs exactly? Ultimately, the authors default to defining a central bank as an institution "occupying a position as 'bank among banks.'" I, for one, am not sure what this means. At this point, it is perhaps appropriate to invoke Justice Potter Stewart.

It makes a difference in practice. Thus, the authors count the Banque de France (est. 1800) as a central bank. But they do not count the Banque Générale (est. 1716, later the Banque Royale) or the Caisse d'Escompte (est. 1776), which carried out some of the same functions. The present example is French, but the problem is general. All scholars who work on central banking face this dilemma. The authors have, on balance, made sensible judgment calls. But they are, nonetheless, judgment calls.

The authors categorize balance sheet expansions as related to war (broadly defined), financial crises and rescues, and a small residual category labeled "other." This categorization is not entirely straightforward; it's not hard to cite ambiguous episodes that resist categorization. Take the Federal Reserve's balance sheet expansion in the spring and summer of 1932. Was this a response to the 1931 banking crisis (a financial-rescue-related expansion) or a response to congressional pressure to help struggling farmers (an "other" balance sheet expansion)? My reading is that the "second banking crisis"—the wave of US bank runs following the UK's departure from gold in September 1931—had largely dissipated by the spring of 1932 and that the Fed was motivated to act by congressional pressure in an election year. Which way do the authors classify this episode? The answer is unclear (they don't tell us in the chapter). This makes it somewhat difficult to assess the reliability of the three-way categorization.

I also have questions about the utility of pushing back the analysis fully four hundred years. If the authors' key point is that liquidity operations, while stabilizing in the short run, foment moral hazard and fuel boom-bust episodes in the long run, then I'm not sure how much mileage is added by the first two hundred years of data, since those earlier balance sheet operations were not liquidity related (central banks only acknowledging their lender-of-last-resort responsibilities and functions in the second half of the nineteenth century). I'm a believer that, to paraphrase the authors, a long-run historical view is useful for both policymakers and researchers as a complement to studies focusing on the past decade. This is especially true when studying relatively rare events such as financial crises, as the authors note. But how long is the long run when there are fundamental regime changes in the midst of the sample period?

Speaking of early recognition of lender-of-last-resort responsibilities, what about Bagehot's rule? Shouldn't moral hazard effects and the likelihood of boom-bust cycles depend on whether or not emergency liquidity was provided at a penalty rate? Might we want to distinguish balance sheet expansions accompanied by penalty rates from other balance sheet expansions?

The authors instrument their measure of liquidity support with a dummy variable for the "preexisting ideological beliefs of central bank governors." But is the identification of preexisting beliefs straightforward? Subsequent historical analyses and biographies are among the inputs used to characterize ideological beliefs. Might contributors to that literature have been influenced by subsequent actions actually taken?

In any case, is it really the governor who takes the decision (as opposed to a committee of board members, or the government itself when the central bank lacks legal, financial, and practical independence)? In the 1920s, Daniel Crissinger and then Roy Young served as chairmen of the Federal Reserve Board, while Benjamin Strong served as governor of the Federal Reserve Bank of New York. Who was more important in shaping the Fed's views toward the financial system? Starting in 1930, Eugene Meyer served as chairman of the Federal Reserve Board. But George Harrison served as governor of the New York Fed. Who was more important in framing the Fed's views of the desirability of lender-of-last-resort operations? The authors approvingly cite an influential article by Gary Richardson and William Troost comparing lender-of-last-resort operations in different Federal Reserve

Districts in 1931–2.[1] Was the decision to expand Federal Reserve Bank balance sheets in 1931–2 taken by Eugene Meyer and colleagues at the board or by the heads of the St. Louis and Atlanta Feds—William McChesney Martin Sr. and Eugene R. Black, respectively? Richardson and Troost suggest the latter.

There is much to like in this important chapter and much more still to be done.

Note

1. Gary Richardson and William Troost, "Monetary Intervention Mitigated Banking Panics during the Great Depression: Quasi-Experimental Evidence from a Federal Reserve District Border, 1929 to 1933," *Journal of Political Economy* 117, no. 6 (December 2009): 1031–73.

GENERAL DISCUSSION

MICHAEL BORDO (INTRODUCTION): I have been involved in these conferences for over ten years, and they keep getting better every year. This is a session in economic history on the evolution of central bank balance sheets in mitigating financial distress. The background is the Global Financial Crisis of 2007–8, leading to a massive response by the Federal Reserve, which expanded its balance sheet in unprecedented amounts and in novel ways. Such expansions in the past were only done during major wars. The Global Financial Crisis was followed by quantitative easing in 2009, which led to an even more massive expansion in the Fed's balance sheet. A similar response followed the onset of the COVID-19 pandemic in 2020. Similar policies were followed in other countries.

The massive fiscal and monetary expansions that occurred from 2020 to 2022 led to an upsurge in inflation, which is still problematic. Moreover, quantitative easing and balance sheet expansion has created new challenges for the conduct of monetary policy and a call to return to something like the "bills only" policies that were followed in the past. Also, the lender-of-last-resort and credit policies that were followed in 2020 were largely sterilized and did not impact the Fed's balance sheet. They may have prevented market meltdowns, but they may produce distortions and disincentives further down the road.

This very ambitious and interesting paper takes on extremely important topics: the impact of central bank balance sheet policies, most notably lender-of-last-resort and financial-stability policies on the economy, and the extent to which these policies have led to moral hazard. A major contribution of this paper is the impressive database the authors put together on the balance sheets of seventeen countries that goes back four hundred years and the narratives that go along with it. In addition to its historical depth, the paper develops an interesting identification strategy to isolate the independent effect of balance sheet policy on the economy. In sum, the paper has important lessons for the conduct of monetary policy.

*   *   *

BORDO: Thanks a lot. Did you want to say something, or should I just go for questions?

NIALL FERGUSON: Well, there are a few things that I could quickly react to, and maybe Paul [Schmelzing] can address some too. Barry [Eichengreen], thank you for an admirably thorough referee's report, which will be enormously useful to us as we revise the paper.

I think that the case of France is interesting, because there was such a discontinuity there and there's more continuity in the other cases. France had long, long periods without anything resembling a central bank until the Banque de France was created, not least because John Law had blown the entire system up with the Mississippi Bubble.

The paper does have an "other" category. I think the [slide presentation] deck doesn't reflect that. The standout cause of crisis is war and then financial crisis, but we have this kind of "other" category. I think we probably should put that in the main body rather than a footnote because clearly there are, as you rightly say, some political cases that don't fit into either bucket.

It's true that the paper has two different time frames, one of which is the long run, going back to the very origins of public banks. There's just no getting away from the fact that this is two papers pretending to be one, and that second paper is really a post-1866 paper.

And I couldn't agree more with you about the importance of adherence or nonadherence to Bagehot's rule about a penalty rate, and what is clearly differentiating about recent central bank balance sheet expansion is that there is no penalty rate. And that would shock [Walter] Bagehot if he were commenting on Bloomberg TV these days.

I'll add one more point. I'm eager to read the [Didac] Queralt book *Pawned States*, because of my own history of the Rothschilds. You cited yourself, so I'll do it. The history of the Rothschild bank shows that the Rothschild bank was much bigger than really any of the institutions that we're talking about in the nineteenth century, including the Bank of England, which Bagehot represents as absolutely central. But when one gets down into the weeds of nineteenth-century financial history, it becomes clear that private-sector actors are, in fact, really, really powerful in the game. Maybe that's also true today. I sometimes wonder if Jamie Dimon [CEO of JPMorgan Chase] is, in fact, the master of the financial system more than Jay Powell is. Paul, do you want to add anything on the specific data points that Barry raised?

PAUL SCHMELZING: Yeah, just briefly; also, thank you very much for these great comments. On the definition of central banks, I would just add that it's an art, not a science. We rely on some of the most recent books on central banks over time, like Ulrich Bindseil's book. And we're going beyond the idea that if it walks and quacks like a duck, it's a duck, in our framework.

Then I would just point to ongoing research on policy interventions over time that I did with Andrew Metrick, for instance, which looks at both the private-sector and the public-sector responses to financial distress. And based on that work, we can, in a more refined way, analyze which banks have previously been co-opted by policymakers in the private sector and have been endowed with at least implicit monopolies to react during distress episodes. And so, we are picking the banks that were seen by policymakers or markets over time, even if they were privately owned, to have a central place in the financial sector. And we can weigh that against the other policy options that obviously they had even in the seventeenth or eighteenth century. We can show that, say, they chose to activate rules-based interventions as opposed to liquidity or capital injection interventions in a crisis context. But we can balance the private-sector with the public-sector response from that angle and pick relevant actors.

Just on the national biographies, that's, of course, a very fair point that we naturally in these sources will have biases from these dictionaries and elsewhere. We do try to address that and check with the contemporary precrisis sources and newspapers, like the interviews you saw, to adhere to these ex post narratives. And we have a couple of cases in there. I don't expect people to read page 126 or wherever it is there. But we do throw out cases where it's glaringly obvious to contemporaries that someone else rather than the governor is in charge. Australia during the 1930s is, I think, one of the examples where contemporaries are convinced it's the vice governor calling the shots and the existing governor is really a passive observer of events.

And other than that, on the Richardson-Troost paper, we do focus on the aggregate level, but we are very much aware of the regional-level dynamics that are going on. And we face a similar problem, obviously, with the ECB [European Central Bank] dynamics these days, where interventions might happen on the country level, say in Spain or Italy, that are not necessarily always captured by the aggregate ECB balance sheet. And so, we're looking at the aggregate level to capture aggregate effects on the macroeconomy to really compare apples with apples. We think this is the cleanest way possible. And in the case of the Fed, if

I'm not mistaken, the Federal Reserve balance sheet includes the Atlanta Fed and the regional bank liquidity injections in the 1930s when we capture it at the aggregate data level. And so, we would capture if other regional central banks acted in concert with the Atlanta Fed and raised the aggregate level to an extent that crosses our threshold.

BORDO: I am going to take some questions. I'd like people to identify themselves, and before we do that, I'll just take one chairman's prerogative here—and I could ask a lot of questions—but Niall, you mentioned this, but economic science is evolving over time over this whole period, and that affects the glasses you're looking through, right? Well, how do you really pick that up? I mean, you said it's changing, but in a sense, that could really affect that chronology, and how you pick these guys out and classify them. So it's just something to think about. Let's see. Jeff Lacker.

JEFFREY LACKER: Thank you. Jeff Lacker, Shadow Open Market Committee. So first, let me commend the authors for a truly prodigious compilation of material that will be useful to your work and others' and to many others in the future, I'm sure. You identify the central bank balance sheet size with lender-of-last-resort operations. Now there are two definitions of the phrase "lender of last resort." Well, let me say, at least two. One is what might be thought of as the classic meaning of Walter Bagehot and, more importantly, Henry Thornton before him, of unsterilized lending that expands the central bank balance sheet to offset a drain out of a fractional reserve banking system to avoid a monetary contraction. And this is the sense in which [Milton] Friedman and Schwartz, particularly Anna Schwartz, adopt what's thought of as the narrower definition. And, relevant to 1932, whether it's lending or purchases of securities is immaterial. So they would have classified, I think, 1932's open market operations by the Fed as a lender-of-last-resort expansion of Fed liabilities.

Now, there's a broader definition that's around, and it's very common. It's probably the more common usage, which is "any central bank lending," whether sterilized or not. And this definition typically thinks of unsterilized open market purchases that expand the balance sheet as not lender-of-last-resort operations. And the second definition, as I said, seems to be more common.

Now, when you think about expanding the financial safety net, it's the lending that kind of matters whether or not it expands the balance sheet. So, there's a bit of a disconnect here. Your measure of balance sheet size includes lender-of-last-resort operations in the first sense, which includes government securities purchases, but it also includes those government securities purchases that arguably wouldn't engender the same sort of moral hazard problem. And your measure misses sterilized lending, which would, of course, have the same sort of effect as a financial rescue and the like. But these are often called "lender of last resort." This is bound to affect the size of the safety net, the scale and scope of the part of the finance sector that's viewed as likely to be rescued by a central bank, as does other non–balance sheet actions like the capital forbearance in the 1980s for large banks. And in addition, FDIC [Federal Deposit Insurance Corporation] rescues are sort of right out, right? They're just not in your measure. So, my first question is, do these distinctions seem important? They seem important, but do they affect the interpretation of your results?

My second question has to do with central bank intervention in credit markets over time itself having had a conditioning effect on the political system and sort of gradually shifting and desensitizing the political system to large central bank interventions that over time could have sort of softened up the political system for it and tilted their preferences—tilted their Overton window and shifted their preferences about the type of central banker they wanted to choose. So, is that a sort of an endogeneity in the choice of central bankers and their ideologies that would affect the interpretation of the results? I couldn't tell from reading the paper. So those are my two questions. Thank you.

BORDO: We will get a couple more questions. Andy Levin and Chris [Erceg].

ANDREW LEVIN: I'm Andrew Levin from Dartmouth College. So, really fascinating work. I just wanted to follow up on a couple of things Barry and Mike both said. It seems important that the central bank should be run by a team of experts instead of having all of the power concentrated in any single person. When Bagehot wrote his classic book [*Lombard Street: A Description of the Money Market*], the governor of the Bank of England only served for two years, but then he didn't leave the bank. Each of those who had previously served as governor stayed and formed a standing committee called the Committee of Treasury. And Bagehot writes, "The influence of the Committee of Treasury is always considerable, though not always the same. They form a cabinet of mature, declining, and old men just close to the executive, and for good or evil, such a cabinet must have much power." Okay, so I think what Bagehot was trying to say is that the governor did not have absolute authority, that there was a team of experts, seasoned veterans, who were kind of making sure that things stayed on an even keel. Now, that may not be true for some of the other central banks that you're looking at over this period. But you have this fascinating historical data set, so it will be informative to look at the extent to which each central bank is run by a single person or by a team of experts who help ensure that sensible decisions are made.

BORDO: Chris.

CHRISTOPHER ERCEG:[1] Thanks, that was a really excellent paper and discussion. So I just want to build on various comments. And in particular, I'd like to note that the rationale, as well as the design of interventions, matter both for their effectiveness and to limit moral hazard risks. In that vein, it matters whether they're conducted to serve financial stability goals and whether they're temporary and targeted. Of course, these are difficult aspects to get at, but I was wondering if you could at least exploit the duration dimension and investigate whether longer-lived interventions, in fact, have created moral hazard problems.

BORDO: Please give them an answer.

FERGUSON: In a way, these questions are like a research agenda for further work, because clearly we can slice and dice the material a good deal more than we have. This has been a lumping exercise, and next comes the splitting. You know, one thing that we didn't talk about, but you could equally well have asked is, "What about the other side of the balance sheet?" And that's something that is highly relevant when we're comparing recent events with the past because of innovations like interest on excess reserves. But I think in an exercise like this, we're lumping. And we're consciously taking everything, including the narrow and broad definitions of lender of last resort, and we're throwing it in with war finance. We're throwing it in with just about anything that causes central bank balance sheets to expand, the emphasis being the heterogeneity of rationales, the different ways in which these institutions have worked over time. And I think the next step is to get more precise.

In answer to Andy's point, you know, history is really just all about saying, "It's complicated." Every decision that we want to attribute to the president of the United States, on close inspection, is, in fact, the result of an interagency battle that is waged in the bureaucratic jungle that we call the Beltway. In that sense, all decision making in history should not be taken to be the work of the person at the top of the org chart. It almost never is. And I think what was rewarding about this exercise for me was that it forced us to look at all the central banks over a long period of time and get at least enough acquainted with the biographies of the central bankers to see just how diverse [the history] is. I mean, there were, of course, towering figures at the central banks of the twentieth century, the "lords of finance." But as Barry pointed out, it wasn't actually the Fed chairman who called the shots. So, I think this is an argument for digging deeper.

Bagehot's well worth rereading. I remember rereading Bagehot prior to one of the first of these conferences that I attended and realizing with horror that Bagehot would have been against the Taylor rule. In fact, implicitly, the whole of *Lombard Street* is a critique of the Taylor rule before it was even invented.

And finally, I think that what's really interesting, Chris, is precisely that we can get a sense of the duration of intervention. I'll hand it over to Paul on this, because we can certainly provide more precision. Can't we?

SCHMELZING: If I could just add one more thought on the other two questions. It's very much the case that we use a broader definition of lender of last resort among competing definitions. And we certainly don't distinguish what exact type of assets—from a risk profile, for instance—are purchased in each individual instance. So the aggregate size of the balance sheet can stay flat. However, you can swap risky assets for safe assets, and that might make a big, big difference for financial markets. We do have that data on a more granular level, as shown on the government side. We can at least distinguish between safe assets and "unsafe" assets, and it did not affect any of our main results. So that makes us confident that it's these aggregate dynamics that are decisive in the end.

And then I think a couple of questions go toward the idea that it might not really be the governor who's de facto in charge. There might be a lot more going on. Or does the executive, the government itself, mainly influence? And obviously, I should add that we do not consider, say, the Reichsbank during the 1930s as an independent central bank, where the governor has the autonomy to expand the balance sheet or not. So, we use some of the independence series that people have come up with. But we also rely on some research. Beth Simmons wrote a famous article, I think, on the interwar dynamics, where she shows that the governors systematically opposed the nominating government policy down the line once they were appointed. And a couple of other studies suggested that actually, the opposite is true, that once central bankers are appointed, they have a mind of their own, and they are not easily adhering to some sort of implicit dealmaking here.

On the duration, I'll just say this is a point very well taken. And at least for, you know, the second part of the sample, we should have a pretty good idea and work out in more nuanced ways some of the other attributes of these expansions. So that's a point very well taken. So, thanks for that.

BORDO: Do you have something that can be fast?

KRISHNA GUHA: I'll keep it very quick. Krishna Guha, Evercore Partners. I was struck looking at the long historical series that of course you're covering periods of very different monetary regimes. You've got pre–gold standard. You've got the gold standard. You've got post–gold standard Bretton Woods floating rates. One might have expected that there would be some breaks in behaviors associated with these regimes. That didn't seem to come across in your work. And I just wanted to ask, a) is that right, b) were you surprised, and c) are there any conclusions you draw from that?

FERGUSON: Well, this is a longer-answer type of question than we've got time for. But I think it's fair to say that we've been for some time skeptics about the clarity of these monetary orders. Paul has a paper (which I'm not sure was ever published) on the messiness of exchange regimes in practice; that many of these stories that we tell ourselves about monetary orders are stories; that what economists call "stylized facts," we historians call "fictions." And the realities are quite different when one actually scrutinizes the monetary regimes in practice. And Barry, of course, has written brilliantly on how the gold standard actually worked. So we weren't really expecting this to be a big sort of predictor of regime change. Paul, do you want to add anything to that?

SCHMELZING: No, I think you captured it very nicely. I mean, I would just add, yes, I think we pointed out some of the regime change narratives that one can draw from the data, certainly. I mean, the 2008–9 inflection relative to GDP is jumping into your eyes. It's glaringly obvious that something qualitatively has changed relative to output dynamics. But the point is, this paper, for the first time, I think, allows us to look at the question of whether there have been regime changes or not, because so much of the overwhelming debate has focused on 2008 and 2009 and has tried to draw structural conclusions and secondary implications from the policy actions that we've seen. And many of these other charts that Niall has shown put doubt on the idea that there was a big inflection point in 2008–9. So that's something we tried to stress in the first part of the paper, that this idea that something unprecedented happened in 2009 is only true in a very qualified sense.

BORDO: Okay, I think that's it. I'd like to thank you, everybody.

Note

1. The views expressed in this discussion are those of the author and do not necessarily represent the views of the IMF, its Executive Board, or IMF management.

FORECASTING INFLATION AND OUTPUT

11

The Fed: Bad Forecasts and Misguided Monetary Policy

Mickey D. Levy

The Fed failed to forecast the sharp rise in inflation in 2021–22 and significantly underestimated the federal funds rate necessary to achieve its inflation forecasts. These forecasting mistakes contributed to the biggest monetary policy error and the highest inflation since the 1970s. The Fed's misleading forward guidance on the future course of monetary policy and subsequent aggressive rate increases contributed to the sizable asset-liability mismatch of commercial banks, a key source of the recent banking crisis. The Fed's forecasting errors provide important lessons and suggest corrective action.

This chapter details the Fed's projections of inflation and interest rates in its quarterly Summary of Economic Projections (SEPs) and assesses the potential sources of the errors. It then considers the consequences of the Fed's mistakes and concludes with recommendations for improving the Fed's quarterly projections and conduct of monetary policy.

The Fed's Summary of Economic Projections

The Fed began publishing its quarterly SEPs during the Great Financial Crisis in 2009 to improve transparency into its views of the economy and inflation. In 2012, it introduced its dot plots, the Federal Open Market Committee (FOMC) participants' estimates of the appropriate monetary policy interest rate, along with longer-run estimates of the unemployment rate, real GDP growth, and the federal funds rate based on its 2% inflation objective. From 1980 to 2008, the Fed provided semiannual projections for inflation, real GDP, and the unemployment rate as mandated by the Full Employment and Balanced Growth Act of 1978. Those projections presumed that the Fed followed the appropriate monetary policy but did not include estimates of its policy rate.

Before analyzing the Fed's quarterly inflation projections, it is important to understand how they are developed, their conditionality, and their limitations. Each FOMC member projects real GDP (measured from fourth quarter to fourth quarter), the unemployment rate (average for the fourth quarter), and inflation (as measured by the personal consumption expenditures [PCE] price index [headline and core excluding food and energy] fourth quarter to fourth quarter). This is conditional on their estimate of the "appropriate monetary policy" that would achieve their economic and inflation projections. These conditional aspects of the SEPs are frequently overlooked by the media and financial market participants. The quarterly SEPs show the median projection of the FOMC participants, the range, and the central tendency that eliminates the three outside projections. Compiling the inflation projections of the individual FOMC members who may have different economic forecasts and varying assumptions of appropriate monetary policy involves an aggregation problem. There are similar aggregation problems with the median FOMC estimates of the federal funds rate.

While these SEP economic and inflation projections are conditional on the FOMC participants' estimates of the federal funds rate, those rate projections are not binding policy commitments (Bernanke 2016). Nevertheless, the interest rate estimates are widely perceived to be forward guidance on future monetary policy, and the Fed knows the median estimate and the "dots" of all participants are closely scrutinized. This may influence the Fed's projections, particularly as it seeks to steer market expectations and tries to avoid jarring changes in policy or forward guidance. Historically, the Fed has projected inflation to glide toward its 2% target, which makes sense since the appropriate monetary policy is supposed to be the interest rate consistent with the Fed achieving its inflation mandate. As inflation rose in 2021, the Fed may have been reticent to project that high inflation would persist, because it did not want the public to believe it may have sent the wrong signal. Nevertheless, one can argue that there was a lapse in the FOMC members' attention to the conditionality of its SEP projections.

Individual FOMC participant projections and interest rate estimates may be influenced by different views of the economy and other factors, as well as institutional factors. Historically, projections of the seven Fed governors have not strayed too far from the senior Fed board staff forecasts, which heavily influence the median projections of the nineteen FOMC members. Federal Reserve Bank presidents who historically have expressed more divergent views may also have felt constrained in their projections. In 2021–22, potential outliers may have shied away from projecting much higher inflation and dots, fearing that it might reduce their influence and credibility within the FOMC. Consider if an FOMC member had estimated in June 2021 that inflation would rise to 5% or that it would be appropriate to raise the federal funds rate to 5%.

The Fed's Inflation Projections

Table 11.1 displays the Fed's SEP projections for PCE inflation (headline and core excluding food and energy) beginning in September 2020. As a reference, columns 1 and 2 show the year-over-year inflation rate that was available when the Fed published its SEP. In each September SEP, the Fed rolls forward its projections another year; table 11.1 does not include the Fed's projections for 2025.

The key observation is that as inflation accelerated in 2021, the Fed adjusted up its inflation projection for 2021 to arithmetically

TABLE 11.1. FOMC's Summary of Economic Projections (SEPs) of PCE Inflation.

SEP Projection	Actual Inflation		2021		2022		2023		2024	
Made in:	(1)	(2) Core	(3)	(4) Core	(5)	(6) Core	(7)	(8) Core	(9)	(10) Core
September 2020	1.0	1.3	1.7	1.7	1.8	1.8	2.0	2.0	—	—
December 2020	1.2	1.4	1.8	1.8	1.9	1.9	2.0	2.0	—	—
March 2021	1.5	1.5	2.4	2.2	2.0	2.0	2.1	2.1	—	—
June 2021	3.6	3.1	3.4	3.0	2.1	2.1	2.2	2.1	—	—
September 2021	4.2	3.6	4.2	3.7	2.2	2.3	2.2	2.2	2.1	2.1
December 2021	5.0	4.1	5.3	4.4	2.6	2.7	2.3	2.3	2.1	2.1
March 2022	6.1	5.2	—	—	4.3	4.1	2.7	2.6	2.3	2.3
June 2022	6.3	4.9	—	—	5.2	4.3	2.6	2.7	2.2	2.3
September 2022	6.3	4.6	—	—	5.4	4.5	2.8	3.1	2.3	2.3
December 2022	6.0	5.0	—	—	5.6	4.8	3.1	3.5	2.5	2.5
March 2023	5.3	4.7	—	—	—	—	3.3	3.6	2.5	2.6

Note: PCE inflation (yr/yr) is the unrevised measure available at the time of each quarterly FOMC meeting.

Source: Data from Board of Governors of the Federal Reserve System, quarterly Summary of Economic Projections.

reflect its rise to date, and projected that inflation would quickly fall back toward the Fed's 2% target in 2022 (columns 5 and 6) and remain anchored (columns 7–10).

Through the June 2021 SEP, when inflation had already accelerated to 3.6% (3.1% on core inflation), the Fed projected core inflation would fall back to 2.1% in 2022 and 2023. In September 2021, the Fed acknowledged mild persistence of inflation, projecting core PCE inflation would be 2.3% in 2022 and 2.2% in 2023. In December 2021, facing an acceleration of inflation (to 5.0% and 4.1% on core), the Fed raised its 2022 projection of core inflation to 2.7% in 2022 and 2.3% in 2023. As described below, it is striking that throughout 2021 the Fed projected the appropriate federal funds rate to remain at zero, which involved an increasingly negative real policy rate. The quarterly SEPs in 2022, beginning in March, highlight how the Fed acknowledged that inflation would persist and that it was in catch-up mode. The Fed continued to project rapid declines in inflation by year-end 2022 (compare columns 5–6

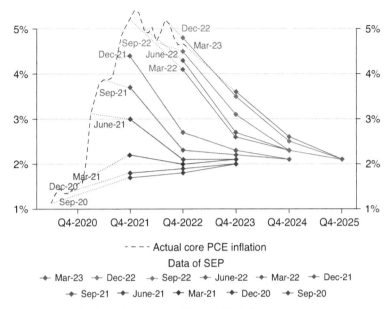

FIGURE 11.1. The Fed's Projections of Core PCE Inflation.

Notes: Forecasts are for Q4/Q4 percentage change in core PCE inflation for years ending 2021, 2022, 2023, 2024, and 2025; lines between forecasts of annual inflation are for visual convenience and not part of Fed's forecasts; dotted line is from last inflation observation available to Fed at time of SEP.

Source: Board of Governors of the Federal Reserve System, quarterly Summary of Economic Projections.

with columns 1–2) while acknowledging that inflation would persist significantly above its 2% target in 2023 and 2024 (columns 7–10), and it projected increasingly higher interest rates.

Figure 11.1 illustrates the sequencing of the Fed's SEP projections from September 2020 through March 2023, with each quarterly estimate (horizontal axis) shown from the level of inflation (vertical axis) at the time of the projection. It highlights the Fed's stubborn assessment that inflation would fall sharply as inflation rose higher and higher. Note that the projections are for fourth-quarter (Q4) year-over-year inflation, and the lines connecting the observations are for visual purposes.

The range of inflation projections for 2021 and 2022 of the FOMC participants was surprisingly narrow. As inflation rose in 2021, all FOMC members continued to project that inflation would fall sharply toward 2% in 2022, and the outliers were far too optimistic. In the September 2021 SEP, the highest FOMC participant-projected inflation would be 3% in 2022 (2.8% for core inflation). Actual PCE inflation ended up being 5.7% and 4.8% on core. As inflation pressures mounted into 2022, the range of FOMC participant projections widened, but the highest projection did not catch up to actual Q4 to Q4 2022 inflation until the December 2022 SEP.

The FOMC's Interest Rate Projections

The Fed's federal funds rate projections are the FOMC participants' year-end estimates of the policy rate they think is appropriate to achieve their inflation projection and economic conditions (unemployment rate and real GDP). Each quarterly SEP also includes a chart showing the "dots" of each participant's year-end estimate and charts of the participants' perceived risks around the median projections of inflation, real GDP, and the unemployment rate.

While the dot plots illustrate the array of interest rate estimates of the FOMC participants, each member's dot is not linked to their projections of the economy and inflation. While the median dot in each quarterly SEP involves an aggregation problem, the dots provide an assessment of the participants' estimates of the appropriate monetary policy and how the Fed expects it will have to adjust interest rates.

Table 11.2 shows the Fed's Q4 to Q4 inflation projections and the median and range of estimates of the year-end federal funds rate for 2021–24. Columns 1, 4, and 7 are the Fed's quarterly inflation projections, while columns 2, 5, and 8 show the median dot of the FOMC participants. Columns 3, 6, and 9 show the ranges of the participants' estimates. Columns 2 and 3 highlight how the

TABLE 11.2. FOMC Projections of Inflation and Estimates of the Federal Funds Rate.

	2021			2022			2023		
SEP Forecast Made in:	(1) Fed Infl Project*	(2) Median "Dot"**	(3) FOMC Range**	(4) Fed Infl Project	(5) Median "Dot"**	(6) FOMC Range**	(7) Fed Infl Project	(8) Median "Dot"**	(9) FOMC Range**
Sept 2020	1.7	0.1	0.1–0.1	1.8	0.1	0.1–0.6	2.0	0.1	0.1–1.4
Dec 2020	1.8	0.1	0.1–0.1	1.9	0.1	0.1–0.4	2.0	0.1	0.1–1.1
Mar 2021	2.4	0.1	0.1–0.1	2.0	0.1	0.1–0.6	2.1	0.1	0.1–1.1
June 2021	3.4	0.1	0.1–0.1	2.1	0.1	0.1–0.6	2.2	0.6	0.1–1.6
Sept 2021	4.2	0.1	0.1–0.1	2.2	0.3	0.1–0.6	2.2	1.0	0.1–1.6
Dec 2021	5.3	0.1	0.1–0.1	2.6	0.9	0.4–1.1	2.3	1.6	1.1–2.1
Mar 2022	—	—	—	4.3	1.9	1.4–3.1	2.7	2.8	2.1–3.6
June 2022	—	—	—	5.2	3.4	3.1–3.9	2.6	3.8	2.9–4.4
Sept 2022	—	—	—	5.4	4.4	3.9–4.6	2.8	4.6	3.9–4.9
Dec 2022	—	—	—	5.6	4.4	4.4	3.1	5.1	4.9–5.6
Mar 2023	—	—	—	—	—	—	3.3	5.1	4.9–5.9

* PCE inflation forecast is the % change, Q4 to Q4, for the year indicated.
** The median "dot" is the median FOMC member estimate of the federal funds rate at year-end that would achieve the member's forecasts of the economy and inflation. The range is the low and high estimate of all FOMC members.
Source: Board of Governors of the Federal Reserve System, quarterly Summary of Economic Projections.

Fed persistently estimated an appropriate federal funds rate of 0%–0.25% throughout 2021 and 2022, even as inflation surged and the Fed's inflation projections in 2022 and 2023 edged up. In the June 2021 SEP, when core inflation had risen to 3.1%, the Fed estimated the policy rate of 0%–0.25% through 2022 and 0.6% by year-end 2023. In December 2021, when inflation had risen to 5.0%, the Fed nudged its estimate of the appropriate policy rate to 0.9% at year-end 2022 and 1.6% in 2023. *That is, the Fed estimated that maintaining the federal funds rate well below the inflation rate it projected would reduce inflation sharply in 2022 and 2023.*

In its March 2022 SEPs, in response to mounting inflation pressures, the Fed dramatically raised its projections of inflation and interest rates. Although it raised its estimated policy rate to 1.9% for year-end 2022, this was still well below the 4.4% inflation that it projected. However, it raised its policy rate estimate to 2.8% for year-end 2023, a touch above its 2023 inflation forecast of 2.7%. In subsequent SEPs, the Fed dramatically raised its estimates of the federal funds rate, signaling that it would be appropriate to maintain a positive real interest rate.

Figure 11.2 illustrates the evolution of the FOMC's median projections of inflation and estimates of the federal funds rate (median and range) for each year 2021–24. Each quarterly SEP is shown on the horizontal axis, and the FOMC's projections of inflation and interest rate estimates are on the vertical axis. (Note that the Fed's projections are discrete quarterly observations, and the lines connecting them are visual aids.) This highlights the seeming inconsistencies between the Fed's estimates of the appropriate federal funds rate and its projections of sharply declining inflation.

Assessing the Fed's Projections

The Fed was caught flat-footed by the rise in inflation. It presumed inflation would stay low, as it did in the decade following the Great Financial Crisis, even though it never adequately explained why inflation had remained subdued. Based on the earlier sustained low inflation, the Fed overestimated its inflation-fighting credibility and relied too much on its ability to manage inflationary expectations. Mirroring its projections prior to the pandemic and throughout 2020, the Fed projected that inflation would rise gradually to 2% and stay there. In 2021, when inflation rose and inflationary expectations became unanchored from 2%, the Fed's focus was on the economic recovery and health-related concerns, and it brushed aside the rise in inflation and kept rates at zero, and continued its purchases of Treasuries and mortgage-backed securities even though the housing market was booming. Its projections in 2020 and 2021 were largely invariant to the massive fiscal and monetary policy responses to the pandemic or the rise in inflationary expectations.

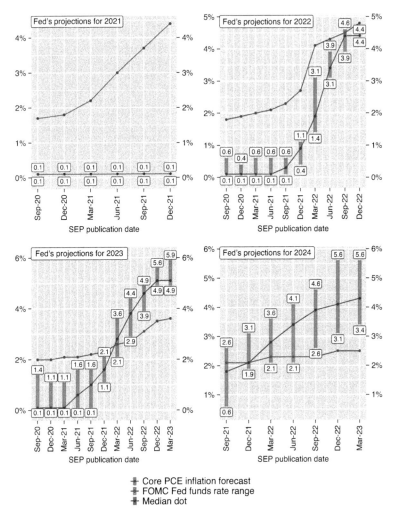

FIGURE 11.2. FOMC Member Projections of Core PCE Inflation and Estimated Dots, 2021–24.

Note: Projections of inflation are Q4/Q4 percentage change for year indicated while Fed funds rate estimate is for year-end.

Sources: Board of Governors of the Federal Reserve System, quarterly Summary of Economic Projections; Bureau of Economic Analysis.

During the period analyzed, the Fed's projections of the real economy were much more accurate than its inflation projections. Although the rebound from the pandemic contraction was much faster than the Fed projected in its 2020 SEPs, beginning in March 2021, the Fed overestimated real GDP growth and appropriately revised its projections downward as the pace of growth ebbed. The unemployment rate fell significantly faster than the Fed projected in 2020, but its unemployment rate projections beginning in March 2021 were reasonably close to the conditions that unfolded. This makes the Fed's inflation projection errors more puzzling.

The Fed's delayed policy response to the rising inflation resulted in the federal funds rate reaching its largest negative real value in modern history and one of the largest deviations from the Taylor rule. The inconsistencies between the Fed's projections of inflation and its estimates of the appropriate interest rate suggest that the Fed mistakenly attributed all of the rise in inflation to a temporary negative supply shock, which proved incorrect. This led to confusing communications, misleading forward guidance, and a loss of credibility.

The Fed's forecasting failures stemmed from a confluence of modeling and analytical errors, human and institutional errors, and a striking absence of risk management. Many of the Fed's errors are a blend of these categories of errors. Of note, the Fed did not heed important lessons from history.

Modeling and Analytical Errors

The Fed's large FRB-US macromodel failed to forecast the inflationary impacts of the unprecedented fiscal and monetary policy stimulus responses to the pandemic. The Fed's heavy reliance on managing inflationary expectations and forward guidance was flawed analytically and implemented poorly. The Fed's monetary policy focus was nominal rather than real interest rates. It continued to rely on a Phillips curve framework, which also contributed to misguided forecasts. Its new strategic framework also contributed to misguided policies.

The FRB-US is basically a dynamic stochastic general equilibrium model of the economy with neo-Keynesian features and Phillips curve influences, and heavily influenced by inflationary expectations. In the model, monetary policy affects aggregate demand through interest rates and financial conditions. Money supply indirectly affects financial conditions but is not explicit or central. The model presumes that inflationary expectations are anchored to the Fed's 2% longer-run inflation target, such that increases in inflation above 2% naturally tend to regress back to 2%. The magnitude and duration of fiscal stimulus impulses are muted by model specifications.

The failure of the FRB-US to forecast the inflationary impacts of the unprecedented fiscal stimulus and excessive monetary accommodation is striking. The fiscal responses to the pandemic—the CARES Act ($2.3 trillion, enacted March 2020), the Coronavirus Response and Relief Supplemental Appropriations Act ($900 billion, December 2020), and the American Rescue Plan Act ($1.9 trillion, March 2021)—totaled $5.1 trillion in additional deficit spending, over 27% of real GDP. This was three times higher than the 9% decline in real GDP. In comparison, President Obama's fiscal response to the Great Financial Crisis (GFC), the American Recovery and Reinvestment Act ($831 billion, January 2009), increased deficit spending by close to the same amount as the decline in real GDP.

Lawrence Summers highlighted this forecasting failure at last year's Hoover Monetary Policy Conference (Summers 2023). Summers simulated the FRB-US model and found that a $2 trillion deficit spending shock raised inflation by 0.7 percentage points, far below what he argued a simple output-gap framework would have predicted. The FRB-US forecasts are also inconsistent with outcomes generated with standard estimates of the fiscal policy multipliers (Tulip 2014), particularly with the Fed's highly accommodative zero interest rates and asset purchases, including the purchase of approximately one-half of all new Treasury bonds issued. The Fed's modeling did not reflect the historical link between budget deficits accommodated by easy monetary policy and inflation (Bordo and Levy 2020).

The fiscal stimulus primarily involved the government's transfer payments, which generated spikes in disposable personal income and financial cushions for businesses that boosted spending and retained labor. This supported spending, but households saved a sizable portion, generating a surge in personal savings estimated at $2.5 trillion, or 13.4% of disposable personal income, well above prepandemic levels. At the same time, M2 surged 40%.

By Q4 2020, nominal GDP had rebounded to its prepandemic level while real GDP was modestly below. Fueled further by the $1.9 trillion American Rescue Plan of March 2021, nominal GDP rose 12.2% in the next year through Q4 2021, well above its prepandemic path (see figure 11.3), and real GDP also handily exceeded its prepandemic level.

The fiscal stimulus and surge in aggregate demand seemed to receive inadequate attention at the Fed. The enactment of President Biden's $1.9 trillion deficit spending legislation (10% of GDP) in March had little impact on the Fed's projections. In its June SEPs, the Fed revised its inflation projections for 2021 (but not 2022), but this increase primarily reflected the inflation that had already occurred. Real GDP growth was revised upward for Q4 to Q4 2021, which primarily reflected the unanticipated strong 6.3% annualized growth in Q1, while the unemployment rate projection was unchanged. The minutes of the June 2021 FOMC meeting barely mentioned the fiscal stimulus (the word "fiscal" appeared only three times in the lengthy minutes). In the Staff Economic Outlook section, the only mention of fiscal policy was

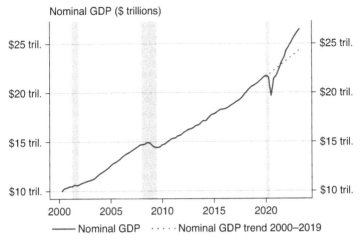

FIGURE 11.3. Nominal GDP, 2000–2020.
Sources: Data from Bureau of Economic Analysis; Haver Analytics; Berenberg Capital Markets.

that "the effects of the fiscal stimulus on economic growth were starting to unwind," and there was no mention of fiscal policy in the Participants' Views section (Board of Governors of the Federal Reserve System 2021a). The minutes did not include mention of the surge in bank deposits, money supply, or other indicators of the monetary policy transmission mechanism.

The Fed acknowledged the pickup in aggregate demand in its July 2021 semiannual report to Congress but emphasized supply bottlenecks as the source of inflation (Board of Governors of the Federal Reserve System 2021b). Two observations are appropriate. Even if the FRB-US model was unable to capture the magnitudes of the negative pandemic shock and unprecedented fiscal and monetary stimulus, the historical link between episodes of high deficits accommodated with monetary ease and inflation should have provided ample warning.

Second, the Fed was too quick to attribute the rise in inflation to transitory supply shocks and to presume that the supply bottlenecks would reverse more quickly than the positive shock to demand. The

Fed first used the term "transitory" in referring to the base effect of the year-over-year inflation in Spring 2021 as measured from the monthly declines in the PCE price index in March–April 2020. The transitory argument quickly shifted to insufficient supply as product demand surged and anecdotal evidence of supply chain bottlenecks became apparent. The overemphasis on supply shortages was a shift in interpretation from the post–Great Financial Crisis (GFC) period when the Fed attributed the low inflation to insufficient aggregate demand and prescribed more monetary stimulus. This asymmetric view that downplayed monetary stimulus of demand delayed the Fed's interest rate increases, following a long history of falling behind the curve (Bordo and Levy 2023a).

The role of the Phillips curve in the Fed's projections and policy decisions seemed inconsistent. By June 2021, the unemployment rate had declined dramatically from its 14.7% peak in May 2020 but was 5.9%, well above the Fed's 4.0% estimate of the longer-run natural rate of unemployment. This supported the Fed's assessment that labor market slack was consistent with low inflation. Summers and others argued that different labor market measures indicated that the non-accelerating inflation rate of unemployment (NAIRU) had increased significantly, suggesting tight labor markets. However, at the same time, the FOMC projected that the unemployment rate would fall to 3.8% in 2022 and 3.5% in 2023, and inflation would decline to 2.1%, and it was appropriate for the Fed to keep inflation below the inflation it was projecting (see table 11.3). The Staff Economic Outlook section of the FOMC meeting minutes (Board of Governors of the Federal Reserve System 2021a) mentioned the pickup in demand but concluded by saying, "a flat Phillips curve would cause inflation to revert to relatively low levels despite (a) strengthening economy." The Fed continued to estimate its policy rate below the inflation it projected in its December 2021 SEPs, even though the unemployment rate had fallen to 4% and anecdotal evidence of tight labor markets had become widespread.

TABLE 11.3. Summary of Economic Projections in June and December 2021.

	June 2021 SEP				December 2021 SEP				
	2021	2022	2023	Long Run	2021	2022	2023	2024	Long Run
Unemployment rate	5.5	3.8	3.5	4.0	4.3	3.5	3.5	3.5	4.0
PCE inflation	3.4	2.1	2.2	2.0	5.3	2.6	2.3	2.1	2.0
Fed funds rate	0.1	0.1	0.6	2.5	0.1	0.9	1.6	2.1	2.5
Ex ante real funds rate	-3.3	-2.0	-1.6	0.5	-5.2	-1.7	-0.7	0.0	2.0

Source: Board of Governors of the Federal Reserve System, quarterly Summary of Economic Projections.

The Fed's reliance on managing inflationary expectations was flawed and not adhered to with appropriate consistency. The importance of managing inflationary expectations was elevated in the post-GFC decade as the Fed acknowledged that the Phillips curve had flattened and had become a less reliable predictor of inflation. As former Fed vice chair Richard Clarida stated in his assessment of the Fed's new strategic plan in August 2020, "With regard to inflation expectations, there is a broad agreement among academics and policymakers that achieving price stability on a sustained basis requires that inflationary expectations be well anchored at the rate of inflation consistent with the price stability goal. This is especially true in the world that prevails today, with flat Phillips curves in which the primary determinant of actual inflation is expected inflation" (Clarida 2020).

The Fed's presumption that it can manage inflationary expectations requires that it have a credible framework for predicting inflation and reducing it to its 2% target and that it will take appropriate steps to reinforce its inflation-fighting credibility. Mervyn King and others have been critical of central bankers' heavy reliance on managing inflationary expectations (King 2021). Financial markets will question the Fed's expectations if they are not well grounded and supported by appropriate monetary policy. That is what happened in 2021–22. The Fed's framework for keeping inflation and inflationary expectations anchored to zero was not well grounded or supported by policies, and both market and survey-based expectations of inflation rose above 2%, defying the Fed's projections and public statements.

When inflation and inflationary expectations rose decidedly above 2% in 2021, the Fed did not take appropriate monetary policy action. Market-based expectations based on ten-year Treasury TIPS [Treasury Inflation-Protected Securities] remained reasonably anchored to 2% and gave the Fed confidence that it maintained inflation-fighting credibility, but shorter-duration breakevens and market-based surveys indicated much higher inflationary expectations. The Fed became concerned in the second half of 2021 when market-based expectations rose from 2.5 to 3%, and survey-based inflationary expectations shot above 5%, suggesting that expectations had become unanchored (University of Michigan 2021; Federal Reserve Bank of New York 2021a). Yet despite these signals that challenged the Fed's inflation-fighting credibility, the Fed delayed tapering its asset purchases and raising rates and continued to rely on forward guidance to manage expectations. Both market-based and survey-based measures of inflation rose further in early 2022.

Inflationary expectations receded in the second half of 2022 only when the Fed aggressively raised rates and supported them with public statements that it would raise rates further to achieve its 2% inflation target (Powell 2022). This highlighted the ineffectiveness of the Fed's efforts to manage inflationary expectations through forward guidance rather than actual adjustments in monetary policy. Policy actions speak louder than words, revealing a serious flaw in the Fed's analytical framework.

Human and Institutional Errors

Poor judgment, misguided assessments of data, and a failure to heed the lessons of history have contributed to the Fed's errors. The Fed's *presumption* that inflation would stay low drove its thinking and policies. Fed members and staffers had become influenced by the post-GFC decade when inflation stayed low even as the Fed maintained low rates and an enlarged balance sheet. These perceptions, which were incorporated into the Fed's modeling of inflation, were the basis for Fed staff research and underpinned the Fed's new strategic plan.

Increases in inflation above 2% were treated as temporary anomalies that would unwind naturally or could readily be unwound. The notion that *inflation should have stayed low* likely contributed to the Fed's misinterpretation of the data in 2021. The Fed "leaned against the data" and allowed its interpretation of the rising inflation to be influenced by its forward guidance (Doh, Gruber, and Song 2022). Even as aggregate demand accelerated sharply and detailed Bureau of Labor Statistics data showed that price increases had become pervasive across a broad array of goods and services, the Fed stuck with its transitory supply shortage argument and suggested that the inflation was primarily due to sharp price increases of select goods (Levy 2021).

Once the Fed came around to acknowledge that high inflation would persist, its estimates that it could lower inflation through maintaining a negative real federal funds rate seemed to rely on the transitory argument and were puzzling. The federal funds futures began pricing in Fed rate increases well above the Fed's estimates, challenging the Fed's forecasts, and they proved correct. There are concerns that this dented the Fed's credibility (Reis 2022).

As the Fed's forecasting errors persisted, it did not seem to seriously consider alternative outcomes. Finally, after being renominated to a second term as Fed chair, Powell stated in testimony to the Senate Banking Committee on November 30, 2021, that "it is time to retire the term transitory" and acknowledged that inflation had been more persistent than earlier presumed, and suggested that the Fed should speed up the tapering of its asset purchases and move up its anticipated rate increases (Powell 2021). Other FOMC members quickly supported this notion, distancing themselves from the "transitory" rationale, suggesting that inflation would remain higher in 2022 than they had projected earlier and that rate increases would be forthcoming.

In keeping with tradition, the Fed has been reticent to admit mistakes, but Fed governor [Christopher] Waller's refreshing candor in a recent interview with CNBC's senior economics reporter Steve Liesman provides important insights (Council on Foreign Relations 2023):

> **Liesman:** Are you at all humbled in your certainty about the trajectory of inflation by what happened a year ago?
>
> **Waller:** Yeah . . . 2022 really was—it was a humbling experience. When you sat in April or May of 2021 and you saw this inflation you said . . . this can't persist for very long . . . and inflation will come right back down. And that story held from April until September of 2021. Inflation was monthly coming down. It looked transitory. And then October, November, December of 2021, it just exploded. So once that happened, we had to quickly change pace and say, you know, this story, this belief, it's just not there. So, you know, it was a mistake.
>
> **Liesman:** But what was the mistake? Was the mistake being too, you know, locked into your view? Or was the mistake that you were simply low in terms of your trajectory on inflation?
>
> **Waller:** *The mistake in my mind, that we made, was we bet the farm on the transitory story.* And any risk management model, you would have said, what if it doesn't go away? What should you be doing to get ready for that event, if it doesn't go away?

These comments highlight the Fed's poor judgment and risk management. Facing significant uncertainties and high inflation that rose further above its expectations, the Fed was remiss not to consider alternative scenarios and how monetary policy would respond to outcomes that differed from its baseline projections. In 2012, the Fed conducted an internal exercise that considered participant views on appropriate monetary policy responses under alternative economic scenarios. Some Fed members provided constructive follow-up comments, but the Fed did not conduct further scenario analysis exercises (Board of Governors of the Federal Reserve System 2012). That is unfortunate, as uncertainties have persisted and evolved. Formally incorporating scenario analysis into its quarterly forecasting exercises and policy deliberations would have improved the Fed's risk management, monetary policy responses, and communications (Bordo, Levin, and Levy 2020).

The lack of dispersion of forecasts among FOMC members suggests that the Fed's institutional nature and structure may have influenced and constrained the FOMC participant projections and contributed to policy errors. The range of projections in the SEPs shows that no participant came anywhere close to anticipating the rise in inflation. The Fed's estimates of the appropriate interest rate were equally off the mark. Through December 2021, not one Fed member projected that a positive real federal funds rate would be necessary to reduce inflation through 2023, and through the December 2022 SEP, no Fed member projected that a positive real federal funds rate was appropriate for 2022. Such projected outcomes were inconsistent with historical experience: every time the Fed raised rates to reduce inflation pressures in modern history, it raised its policy rate above inflation (Bordo and Levy 2023a). No Fed member dissented from the FOMC's policy decisions to keep rates anchored to zero in 2021. Of the several dissents in 2022, one argued to raise rates more slowly and one to raise rates more quickly.

The Fed's organization and governance skews power toward the chair and the Board of Governors and away from the Federal Reserve bank presidents. The economic and financial forecasts developed by the board's large and well-trained economics staff carry substantial weight. This institutional centrifugal force leads the governors to align their forecasts with staff forecasts. Historically, the Reserve banks have been the sources of important ideas and research innovations, and some Federal Reserve bank presidents have been outliers (Bordo and Prescott 2019). In recent years, outlier positions taken by Federal Reserve bank presidents seem to have diminished. Why have Federal Reserve bank presidents been so *reserved*? To what extent do internal pressures discourage them from articulating alternative views and analytical frameworks?

A related issue is how the anecdotal evidence gathered by the Federal Reserve banks affects the FOMC projections and policy deliberations. When inflation accelerated sharply in mid-2021, the Fed's Beige Book prepared for the July 2021 FOMC meeting reported: "Pricing pressures were broad-based. . . . While some contacts felt that pricing pressures were transitory, the majority expected further increases in input costs and selling prices in the coming months." (Board of Governors of the Federal Reserve System 2021c). As noted earlier, in contrast to this assessment of stronger demand and broadening inflation pressures, in its semiannual *Monetary Policy Report* to Congress, the Fed chose to emphasize supply chain bottlenecks (Board of Governors of the Federal Reserve 2021b). Did Reserve bank presidents express views different from the board consensus, and if so, did they receive proper attention?

Like so many organizations, the Fed has a "circle the wagons" mentality in which FOMC members are encouraged (feel pressure) to support the institution's views and not deviate very much. Certainly, policy deliberations include outlying views, but the Fed discourages official dissents.

Certainly, the Fed was not alone in its overly optimistic inflation forecast, as most private-sector forecasters were also caught by surprise (Waller 2023). The Blue Chip Economic Indicators and the Survey of Professional Forecasters missed with forecasts that were similar to the Fed's SEPs (Wolters Kluwer 2021). This is not surprising since many private-sector forecasters take their cues from the Fed (and many of them have been trained at the Fed). Financial markets were also slow to forecast higher inflation in 2021, as reflected in market-based measures such as breakevens on the TIPS and sustained low bond yields. Still, survey-based inflationary expectations (University of Michigan 2021; Federal Reserve Bank of New York 2021a) were much more accurate. Some alternative measures, such as the Federal Reserve Bank of New York's Underlying Inflation Gauge, also projected that high inflation would persist (Federal Reserve Bank of New York 2021b). The Fed's projection misses were consistent with its history of being fairly accurate when real growth and inflation remain in narrow ranges but inaccurate when conditions change significantly or rapidly. Analogously, in periods of stable inflation, professional forecasters have a better track record of forecasting inflation than consumer surveys, while consumer surveys have better track records when inflation is changing rapidly (Goodspeed 2022).

The Fed's New Strategic Plan

The new strategic framework contributed to and reinforced the Fed's misguided projections and delayed its response to the rise in inflation (Levy and Plosser 2022). The Fed's presumption that inflation would stay low like it did following the GFC fueled its concern about the risk of a collapse in inflationary expectations that would drive interest rates to the effective lower bound and constrain monetary policy. The contractionary impact of the pandemic accentuated these concerns. The Fed's new strategic plan, rolled out in August 2020, institutionalized asymmetries into its interpretation of its inflation and employment mandate and its conduct of policy. The new plan involved an overly complex flexible average inflation targeting (FAIT) plan that favored higher inflation to make up for earlier sub-2% inflation but was absent any numeric range of acceptable inflation. It also prioritized its employment mandate and enhanced it to "maximum inclusive employment." While these provisions encouraged discretionary activist policy, the plan eschewed preemptive tightening in response to anticipated higher inflation. By de-emphasizing preemptive monetary policy, the Fed rejected a key strategy that had been instrumental in keeping inflation low during the Great Moderation (Taylor 1993; Goodfriend 1997).

When inflation rose above 2% in 2021, the Fed viewed it as a positive step associated with the economic recovery from the pandemic. As the robust recovery in employment and supply shortages tightened labor markets, the Fed said it would delay tapering its asset purchases, and thereby delay raising interest rates, until it saw "substantial progress" toward its employment mandate. The Fed did not provide any guidance on how it would evaluate substantial progress. The Fed's new strategy of de-emphasizing preemptive monetary tightening contributed to the delays in raising interest rates.

Misreading History

Among the Fed's key misreads of history, the presumption that inflation would stay low failed to take into consideration the stark differences between the pandemic and the GFC. The economic recovery from the GFC was sluggish, despite monetary and fiscal stimulus. Nominal GDP did not accelerate materially beyond 4% and averaged 4% annually during the 2009–19 expansion, which resulted in 2.2% real growth and 1.6% PCE inflation. The Fed's primary explanation for the persistently low inflation—that the Phillips curve was flatter than earlier presumed—seemed more of an *ex post* observation that provided little insight into why aggregate demand and inflation may have stayed low. In contrast, aggregate demand surged following its sharp but brief pandemic contraction.

Besides the much larger magnitude of the fiscal response to the pandemic, several other factors may explain the sizable differences between the economic responses during the GFC and the pandemic. First, changes in the Fed's operating procedures during the GFC may have dampened the monetary policy transmission channels and constrained aggregate demand. The Fed began paying interest on excess reserves and tightened capital and liquidity standards for banks, which may have encouraged banks to hold reserves created by the Fed's quantitative easing rather than make loans (Plosser 2018; Ireland 2019). Bank lending may have also been deterred by heightened regulatory scrutiny and the Fed's imposition of rigorous stress tests. Second, following the GFC, weak financial conditions constrained the economic recovery. The banking system was crippled and undercapitalized. Household finances were impaired, and the housing sector was severely damaged. The Fed's qualitative easing post-GFC generated a spike in bank reserves but no lasting impact on the growth of M2. For years into the recovery, bank credit to households or businesses fell and mortgage debt outstanding receded. These factors, not the flatter Phillips curve, explain the post-GFC weak demand and low inflation.

The Fed adjusted far too slowly to the starkly different post-pandemic conditions. Banks remained well capitalized and were not impaired. Consumer balance sheets were healthy, supported by government transfer payments, and businesses were flush with cash. There was pent-up demand. The private sector responded strongly to the artificially low rates and excessive fiscal and monetary stimulus, housing boomed, and aggregate demand rebounded strongly.

The Fed understated the importance of other valuable benchmarks from history. Major wars have typically involved deficit financing accommodated by monetary ease that subsequently resulted in inflation, and the government's pandemic spending was very warlike (Hall and Sargent 2023). There are interesting parallels between the post–World War II inflation period and the pandemic.

In 2021, the Fed disparaged any parallels to the inflation of the 1970s, even though some lessons were instructive. Understating the unprecedented fiscal stimulus, sustaining a negative policy rate, and allowing a wide shortfall from Taylor rule estimates proved costly.

Observations on the Recent Bank Stresses

The recent bank failures and financial stresses naturally followed the Fed's projections, forward guidance, and monetary policy. Banks' poor risk management is to blame, but the Fed's actions were complicit. Its extended zero-rate policy and ultralow bond yields fueled a surge in asset prices and risk-taking. The government's excessive fiscal transfer payments and personal and business savings inundated banks with deposits. The Fed's projections and forward guidance that it would not need to raise rates very much likely encouraged commercial banks to extend the duration of their asset portfolios. This generated high profits in 2020–21, but realities hit in 2022 as the Fed raised rates aggressively and bond yields rose sharply.

Commercial banks' asset-liability mismatches proved costly. The failure of Silicon Valley Bank (SVB) stemmed from its uniquely concentrated exposure of its deposits (and its startlingly high portion of uninsured deposits) and assets to high-tech and venture capital. It was a poster child for bad risk management. However, its asset-liability mismanagement was not unique, as banks hedged only a very minor portion of their long-duration asset holdings against higher interest rates (Jiang et al. 2023). The FDIC estimated that at year-end 2022, commercial banks faced a cumulative $620 billion in losses from their asset-liability mismatches (FDIC 2023; see figure 11.4). History shows that periods of Fed tightening following delayed exits from easing always have jarring financial effects and should not have been surprising (Bordo and Levy 2023b).

The Fed's failures to appropriately supervise banks in an important sense were an extension of the Fed's own poor risk manage-

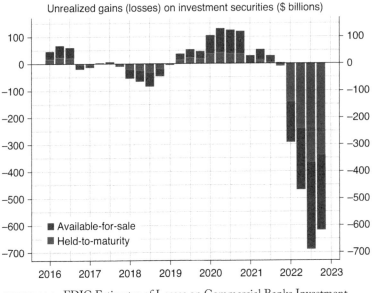

FIGURE 11.4. FDIC Estimates of Losses on Commercial Banks Investment Securities.

Sources: FDIC; Haver Analytics.

ment. Why did the Fed's bank supervisors overlook the risks of sharply higher interest rates and bond yields following a period when the Fed maintained artificially low interest rates and purchased assets that had kept bond yields hovering near record lows and then raised rates rapidly? Readily available data showed that banks had extended the duration of their portfolios and carried sizable asset-liability mismatches. Fed supervisors seemed to have conducted their jobs using the same perspective as the FOMC, ignoring simple rules of risk management. This is perplexing since scenario analysis is a critical element of bank stress testing.

The Fed supervisors should have uncovered the risks, regardless of banks' asset size or whether they were designated systematically important financial institutions and subject to stress tests. Some observers argue that if the stress tests had been performed on a wider array of medium-sized banks, SVB's problems would have been identified and addressed. That may be the case, but it seems unlikely. The Fed's annual stress tests involved the same themes as when they were introduced in 2009, involving severely negative scenarios of the *real economy* and *lower* interest rates. In its 2022 stress test scenarios issued in February 2022, the Fed's severely adverse scenario involved a severe global recession, heightened stress on commercial real estate and corporate debt markets, and interest rates falling to zero (Board of Governors of the Federal Reserve System 2022). Whether SVB would have failed this stress test or its faulty risk management would have been revealed is uncertain. Like the FOMC, the Fed's supervisors were fighting the last battle. Finally, in 2023, the Fed introduced an "experimental scenario" that involved higher rates (Board of Governors of the Federal Reserve System 2022 and 2023). The Fed's recent review of its supervision and regulation of SVB stated that it will enhance future stress tests and include tests of interest rate sensitivity (Board of Governors of the Federal Reserve System 2023).

The bottom line is that if the Fed had more experience relying on risk management and had incorporated scenario analysis in its conduct of monetary policy, its supervision of banks would improve.

Concluding Remarks

The Fed's aggressive interest rate increases since mid-2022 and sizable upward revisions to its projections have been necessary and positive steps, and inflation has begun to recede from its peak. However, the magnitude and persistence of the forecasting and policy errors raise many questions and suggest room for improvement. It would be insufficient for the Fed to say, "We're on top of the issue now, so don't worry about it."

The Fed must assess the sources of its errors and establish a plan for corrective action. The Fed would benefit from a formal internal introspection—an "after-action review"—that includes outside participants with diverse perspectives. Shortfalls in the FRB-US model must be addressed, particularly its failure to adequately capture the fiscal stimulus and the failure of its financial conditions parameters to capture the extent of the Fed's monetary accommodation and the surge in money. The Fed must reestablish symmetry in its mindset about its 2% inflation target and correct the flaws and eliminate the asymmetries in its strategic framework. Its FAIT must be replaced with a simpler, symmetric low-inflation objective with numeric guidelines around it. Preemptive monetary policy must be reinstituted. The assessment held by some Fed members that the strategic plan is sound, but implemented incorrectly in 2021–22 is clearly inconsistent with the outcome and a misguided interpretation that is prone to future mistakes. The shortcomings of the Fed's heavy reliance on the managing of inflationary expectations through forward guidance require scrutiny. The Fed must improve the quarterly SEPs. This involves clarifying the conditionality of the inflation projections and establishing consistency with the Fed's interest rate estimates using the Taylor rule and other guidelines. The SEPs should include alternative scenarios to improve risk management. They should also include estimates of its balance sheet changes, which the Fed identifies as important components in its monetary policy tool kit. The Fed also needs to encourage diverse views among FOMC participants and take steps to avoid inadvertent institutional dampening of alternative views on the economy, inflation, and appropriate policies. It must also consider ways to make better use of anecdotal evidence gathered by district banks. The Fed needs to address its unhealthy relationship with financial markets, which may improve its communications strategy. The objective is to improve the Fed's conduct of monetary policy.

References

Bernanke, Ben. 2016. "Federal Reserve Economic Projections: What Are They Good For?" The Brookings Institution, November 28.

Board of Governors of the Federal Reserve System. 2012. Minutes of the Federal Open Market Committee Meeting, April 24–25.

———. 2021a. Minutes of the Federal Open Market Committee Meeting, June 15–16.

———. 2021b. *Monetary Policy Report* (*Monetary Policy Report* submitted to Congress on July 9, 2021, pursuant to section 2B of the Federal Reserve Act).

———. 2021c. Beige Book: Summary of Commentary on Current Economic Conditions by Federal Reserve District, July.

———. 2022. Stress Test Scenarios, February.

———. 2023. "Review of the Federal Reserve's Supervision and Regulation of Silicon Valley Bank." April.

Bordo, Michael D., Andrew T. Levin, and Mickey D. Levy. 2020. "Incorporating Scenario Analysis into the Federal Reserve's Policy Strategy and Communications." National Bureau of Economic Research Working Paper 27369, June.

Bordo, Michael D., and Mickey D. Levy, 2020. "Do Enlarged Deficits Cause Inflation: The Historical Record." National Bureau of Economic Research Working Paper 28195, December.

———. 2023a. "The Fed's Monetary Policy Exit Once Again Behind the Curve." In *How Monetary Policy Got Behind the Curve—and How to Get Back*, edited by Michael D. Bordo, John H. Cochrane, and John B. Taylor, 141–79. Stanford, CA: Hoover Institution Press.

———. 2023b. "Fed Rate Increases from Behind the Curve: Financial Stresses Current and Historical." Shadow Open Market Committee, April 21.

Bordo, Michael D., and Edward S. Prescott. 2019. "Federal Reserve Structure, Economic Ideas, and Monetary and Financial Policy." National Bureau of Economic Research Working Paper 26098, July.

Clarida, Richard H. 2020. "The Federal Reserve's New Monetary Policy Framework: A Robust Evolution." Peterson Institute for International Economics, August 31.

Council on Foreign Relations. 2023. "C. Peter McColough Series on International Economics with Christopher J. Waller." January 20.

Doh, Taeyoung, Joseph Gruber, and Dongho Song. 2022. "Leaning against the Data: Policymaker Communications under State-Based Forward Guidance." Federal Reserve Bank of Kansas City Working Paper 22-11, September.

Federal Deposit Insurance Corporation (FDIC). 2023. "Remarks by FDIC Chairman Martin Gruenberg on the Fourth Quarter 2022 Quarterly Banking Profile." February 28.

Federal Reserve Bank of New York. 2021a. "Survey of Consumer Expectations: Median One-Year Ahead Expected Inflation." June–December.

Goodfriend, Marvin. 1997. "Monetary Policy Comes of Age: A 20th Century Odyssey." Federal Reserve Bank of Richmond *Economic Quarterly* 83, no. 1 (Winter): 1–22.

Goodspeed, Tyler. 2022. "Trust the Experts: Relative Performance of Inflationary Expectations, 1946–2022." Hoover Institution Economics Working Paper 22120, October.

Hall, George J., and Thomas J. Sargent. 2023. "Financing Big US Federal Expenditures Surges: COVID-19 and Earlier US Wars." In *How Monetary Policy Got Behind the Curve—and How to Get Back*, edited by Michael D. Bordo, John H. Cochrane, and John B. Taylor, 253–91. Stanford, CA: Hoover Institution Press.

Ireland, Peter. 2019. "Interest on Reserves: History and Rationale and Risks," *Cato Journal* 39, no. 2 (Spring/Summer): 327–37.

Jiang, Erica, Gregor Matvos, Tomasz Piskorski, and Amit Seru. 2023. "Limited Hedging and Gambling for Resurrection by US Banks during the 2022 Monetary Tightening?" Social Science Research Network, April 3.

King, Mervyn. 2021. "The King Canute Theory of Inflation." Bloomberg.com, November 23.

Levy, Mickey D. 2021. "Rising Inflation: Granular Data Analysis Shows Broadening Dispersion of Price Increases." Berenberg Capital Markets, November.

Levy, Mickey D., and Charles Plosser. 2020. "The Murky Future of Monetary Policy." Hoover Institution Economics Working Paper 20119, October. Republished in Federal Reserve Bank of St. Louis *Review* 104, no. 3 (Third Quarter 2022): 178–88.

Plosser, Charles I. 2018. "The Risks of a Fed Balance Sheet Unconstrained by Monetary Policy." In *The Structural Foundations of Monetary Policy*, edited by Michael D. Bordo, John H. Cochrane, and Amit Seru, 1–16. Stanford, CA: Hoover Institution Press.

Powell, Jerome H. 2021. US Congress, Senate, Committee on Banking, Housing, and Urban Affairs. *Coronavirus and CARES Act: Statement of Jerome H. Powell, Chair of the Federal Reserve Bank*. 117th Cong., 2nd sess., November 30.

———. 2022. "Monetary Policy and Price Stability." Remarks at Reassessing Constraints on the Economy and Policy," a Federal Reserve Bank of Kansas City Economic Symposium, August 26.

Reis, Ricardo. 2022. "The Burst of High Inflation in 2021–22: How and Why Did We Get Here?" Bank for International Settlements Working Paper 1060, December.

Summers, Lawrence H. 2023. "A Labor Market View on Inflation." In *How Monetary Policy Got Behind the Curve—and How to Get Back*, edited by Michael D. Bordo, John H. Cochrane, and John B. Taylor, 17–32. Stanford, CA: Hoover Institution Press.

Taylor, John B. 1993. "Discretion versus Policy Rules in Practice." *Carnegie-Rochester Conference Series on Public Policy* 39: 195–214. Amsterdam: North-Holland.

Tulip, Peter. 2014. "Fiscal Policy and the Inflation Target." Reserve Bank of Australia Research Discussion Paper 2014-02, March.

University of Michigan. 2021. "University of Michigan Expected Inflation Rate." Surveys of Consumers, June–December.

Waller, Christopher J. 2023. "Reflections on Monetary Policy in 2021." In *How Monetary Policy Got Behind the Curve—and How to Get Back*, edited by Michael D. Bordo, John H. Cochrane, and John B. Taylor, 333–40. Stanford, CA: Hoover Institution Press.

Wolters Kluwer. 2021. *Blue Chip Economic Indicators*, January–December.

DISCUSSANT REMARKS

Steven J. Davis

The Fed made large forecasting and policy errors in 2021 and 2022. In his excellent contribution to this volume, Mickey Levy skillfully documents several of these errors. Some examples:[1]

- No Federal Open Market Committee (FOMC) member "came anywhere close to anticipating the rise in inflation" that emerged in 2021–22.
- "As inflation accelerated in 2021, the Fed adjusted up its inflation projection for 2021 to arithmetically reflect its rise to date and projected that inflation would quickly fall back toward the Fed's 2% target in 2022."
- Through December 2021, the Fed projected that negative real federal funds rates would yield sharply reduced inflation in 2022 and 2023.
- "Once the Fed came around to acknowledge that high inflation would persist, its estimates that it could lower inflation through maintaining a negative real federal funds rate seemed to rely on the transitory argument and were puzzling. The federal funds futures began pricing in Fed rate increases well above the Fed's estimates, challenging the Fed's forecasts, and they proved correct."

Levy traces the forecasting and policy errors to deeper analytical, institutional, and strategic errors:

- *Modeling and analytical errors* These include an overreliance on managing inflation expectations and forward guidance; a presumption—baked into the FRB-US model—that inflationary expectations are strongly anchored at the Fed's target rate; and early insistence that the inflation rise in 2021 reflected temporary, self-reversing factors.

- *Human and institutional errors*   These include inadequate risk management, misguided data assessments, failure to heed important lessons from history, and a circle-the-wagons mentality that fosters groupthink in analysis and decision making.
- *The Fed's new strategic plan*   Rolled out in August 2020, this plan involved a new flexible average inflation target, a new emphasis on "maximum inclusive employment," and a tilt away from preemptive tightening in response to anticipations of above-target inflation.

I largely share Levy's assessment of the Fed's errors in this period. Rather than delineate my points of agreement and my reservations, I will focus on deeper tensions that color the Fed's forecasting enterprise, influence its choice of headline economic models, and push the Fed to discount models and narratives that question its credibility and the potential for inflation expectations to become de-anchored. I will argue that the Fed faced incentives to commit the types of forecasting and policy errors it actually made.

I will further argue that circumstances in 2021–22 intensified the Fed's incentives to shade its projections and discount contrary models and narratives, contributing to avoidable policy errors. Finally, I will argue that conformist pressures for groupthink inside the Fed and the outward emanations of Fed thinking, models, narratives, and perspectives also reduce the quality of decision making about monetary policy. In the last part of my remarks, I propose reforms that aim to reduce the negative incentive effects associated with the Fed's forecasting enterprise, the concerns about groupthink, and the potential of all of the above to undermine the quality of the Fed's decisions about monetary policy.

The Basic Incentive Problem

By making projections about inflation and its own policy actions, the Fed creates incentives that influence its forecasting enterprise and can contribute to policy errors. Consider two propositions:

1. Expected inflation affects actual inflation.
2. Fed projections influence expected inflation.

These propositions are noncontroversial inside the Fed and not much contested outside the Fed. The first proposition holds in any macroeconomic model with an expectational Phillips curve equation. The second is implicit in the view that it's useful for the Fed to publish its projections.

When the Fed believes these two propositions, it has an incentive to shade its inflation projections to achieve its policy goals at lower cost. In particular, if inflation exceeds the desired level—or threatens to do so in the near future—the Fed has an incentive to shade its inflation projections to the downside to lower expected and actual inflation with less need for raising the trajectory of its policy rate.

Of course, if the Fed distorts its projections, it risks undermining its credibility as a forecaster and its reputation for honest communications. In normal times, credibility and reputation concerns may suffice to prevent any distortion in the Fed's projections. I return to this point shortly and argue that 2021 and 2022 were not normal times in this respect. Before doing so, I set forth a fuller statement of the incentive problems that surround the Fed's public projections for inflation, output, and its policy rate.

Most or all FOMC members subscribe to three propositions:

1. Expected inflation affects actual inflation.
2. Explicit forward guidance, Fed projections, and the Fed's headline economic models all influence expected inflation or have the potential to do so in some circumstances.
3. The future conduct of monetary policy influences future inflation.

The restatement of the second proposition recognizes that the Fed's projections and its choice of which economic models to favor in forming its projections also effectively function as forward guidance.[2] As an immediate corollary to the third proposition, expectations about the future conduct of monetary policy influence expected future inflation. Thus, the third proposition implies that the Fed also has incentives to distort projections of its own policy rates. As before, there is a trade-off between the Fed's desire to meet near-term policy goals at least cost and the desire to preserve its credibility and reputation.

Notable Circumstances in 2021 and 2022

The US macroeconomic landscape exhibited some notable circumstances in 2021 and 2022—circumstances that were unusual in recent American history.[3] First, inflation had recently begun to exceed the desired rate after many years at or below the desired rate. Second, as inflationary pressures emerged in 2021, there was genuine uncertainty about the persistence of undesirably high inflation absent tighter monetary policy. Third, and related, there was genuine uncertainty about the extent and duration of monetary tightening required to bring inflation back to a desired level.

Pandemic-related disruptions in the global supply chain contributed to uncertainty about the economic outlook and appropriate monetary policy. In particular, economists disagreed about the extent to which supply chain disruptions drove the initial inflation surge and the extent to which the resolution of those disruptions would moderate inflation pressures. In addition, they disagreed about the inflation effects of the tremendously expansive fiscal policy actions the US government undertook in the wake of the pandemic. They also disagreed about the risks of inflation expectations becoming de-anchored, which fed into disagreements about the urgency of the need for policy rate hikes to restrain inflation. The surprise nature of the inflation surge for goods and services raised concerns that catch-up wage inflation would propagate the initial surge, possibly setting in motion a hard-to-contain wage-price spiral. All of these unusual circumstances, some lacking close historical precedents, contributed to an unusually uncertain outlook for inflation in 2021 and 2022.

These circumstances raised the stakes for monetary policy and intensified Fed incentives to distort its projections in a manner that lower inflation at the least cost. Specifically, they intensified Fed incentives to double down on a narrative that stresses the transitory, self-correcting nature of the then-recent inflation surge. To do otherwise would validate narratives that stress the prospects for persistent inflation, which, in turn, would raise inflation expectations and the cost of achieving the Fed's policy objectives.

FOMC members also perceived another feature of the economic environment during this period that influenced their thinking. Here, I will quote Richard Clarida (2020), speaking about the Fed's new strategic plan in his capacity as vice chairman of the Federal Reserve:

> With regard to inflation expectations, there is broad agreement among academics and policymakers that achieving price stability on a sustained basis requires that inflationary expectations be well anchored at the rate of inflation consistent with the price-stability

goal. *This is especially true in the world that prevails today, with flat Phillips curves in which the primary determinant of actual inflation is expected inflation.* [emphasis added]

This passage makes it clear that the Fed saw the anchoring of inflation expectations as especially vital in 2020, a view that I believe still held inside the Fed in 2021 and 2022. This view means that it was especially risky, in the eyes of the Fed, to validate inflation narratives that ran counter to its claim that inflation expectations were firmly anchored. This view also helps explain the Fed's focus on managing inflation expectations. If you approach the conduct of monetary policy through the lens of a Phillips curve and you further believe that economic slack has little impact on inflation, then monetary policy can materially influence inflation only through its impact on inflation expectations. It's either that or pray for favorable supply shocks.[4]

The Fed's Choice of Headline Models

The incentives to distort the Fed's forecasting enterprise extend to its choice of headline economic models. Consider the reaction if, in 2021 or early 2022, the board staff had moved to feature models that lack a strong anchor for inflation expectations. FOMC members would have seen such a move as contributing to the risk that inflation expectations would become de-anchored and, further, as casting doubts on the credibility of monetary policy. They would have viewed such a move as harming their efforts to achieve the Fed's mandate at least cost.

This incentive perspective is consistent with the design of the FRB-US model. As Levy remarks, "The [FRB-US] model presumes that inflationary expectations are anchored to the Fed's 2% longer-run inflation target, such that increases in inflation above 2% naturally tend to regress back to 2%. The magnitude and duration of fiscal stimulus impulses are muted by model specifications." Summers (2023) also highlights the limited responsiveness of inflation to fiscal stimulus in the FRB-US model in his contribution to the 2022 edition of this conference.

It would be naïve, in my view, to see the strongly anchored nature of inflation expectations in the FRB-US model as the product of a purely disinterested scientific analysis. That model design feature is influenced by the institutional objectives of the Fed, especially those of the Board of Governors and its professional staff. Similar remarks pertain to the Fed's propensity in 2021 and early 2022 to discount narratives that stress loosely anchored inflation expectations or otherwise question the Fed's ability to keep inflation near its desired level.

Moreover, it is hard for an institution like the Fed to divorce its internal deliberations, analysis, and policy decisions from its public-facing projections, favored narratives, and choice of headline economic models. A theorist might imagine the Fed advancing one view in public and holding other distinct views that actually drive its internal deliberations and policy decisions. In practice, incentives that distort the Fed's public-facing projections and choice of headline models will also influence its internal thinking and policy choices.

Inadequate Attention to Risk Management

Levy quotes Fed governor Christopher Waller, who offers his characterization of the Fed's errors in an interview with CNBC's senior economics reporter Steve Liesman on January 20, 2023:

> **Waller:** *The mistake in my mind, that we made, was we bet the farm on the transitory story.* And any risk management model, you would have said, what if it doesn't go away? What should you be doing to get ready for that event, if it doesn't go away?

But sound risk management would have lent credibility to contrary inflation narratives, potentially de-anchoring inflation expectations and raising the cost of achieving the Fed's mandate. In other words, the Fed's desire to shape the narrative around the inflation outlook created internal pressures that pushed it away from sound risk management.

Fed Groupthink and Its Outward Emanations

Any big organization that exercises a strong influence on the careers of its employees will create, deliberately or inadvertently, pressures for groupthink and conformity of (expressed) views. Levy puts the point this way: "Like so many organizations, the Fed has a 'circle the wagons' mentality in which FOMC members are encouraged (feel pressure) to support the institution's views and not deviate very much. Certainly, policy deliberations include outlying views, but the Fed discourages official dissents."

Levy also observes that "many private-sector forecasters take their cues from the Fed (and many of them have been trained at the Fed)." Thus, groupthink that originates inside the Fed emanates outward to the broader community of researchers and analysts who think and write about monetary policy. It's worthwhile to expand on this point.

The Federal Reserve System employs more than four hundred PhD economists at the Board of Governors and well in excess of two hundred others at the twelve regional Federal Reserve banks.[5] Grim (2009) argues that "a very significant majority" of professional monetary economists in the United States work for the Fed or did so earlier in their careers. He also describes other channels through which the Federal Reserve System and individual Fed economists exercise influence in the economics profession, including the power to invite (or disinvite) speakers to high-profile conferences and the role of Fed economists in the review process for scholarly journals. In this regard, Grim remarks, "At the Journal of Monetary Economics, a must-publish venue for rising economists, more than half of the editorial board members are currently on the Fed payroll—and the rest have been in the past." Grim's concept of "on the Fed payroll" appears to include consultants as well as employees. Nevertheless, the grounds for concern are clear.

Let me clarify the nature of (my) concerns about groupthink and its potential to discourage fruitful lines of thinking and analysis, with detrimental effects on the conduct of monetary policy. Consider, first, the extensive dialogs that occur between economists and policymakers inside the Fed system and those in academia and the private sector who have expertise in monetary policy and central banking. These dialogs with outside experts can push against groupthink. To its credit, the Fed recognizes the value of these dialogs and does much to facilitate them. Still, there is room for improvement. I offer a concrete suggestion below.

Second, it's essential to preserve intellectual space for contending perspectives to surface within the Federal Reserve System, to ground these perspectives in analysis and evidence, and to ensure that the leading perspectives—i.e., the ones that drive the conduct of monetary policy—are subject to vigorous critiques. Historically, the regional Federal Reserve banks served an important role in this regard. They are now less inclined to play that role, according to several conference participants who reacted to my remarks in private conversations. If true, that is a serious problem.

It is insufficient if a few isolated economists inside the Federal Reserve System critique the dominant models and narratives that drive FOMC decisions. To fully develop such critiques, and to adequately develop alternative models and narratives, requires institution-level resources. The regional Federal Reserve banks are natural homes for these types of contrarian research activities.

Third, there is the matter of the Fed's extensive reach, its financial resources, its impact on the career development of hundreds of economists, its role in the editorial review process for research papers on monetary policy and macroeconomics, and the Fed's capacity to offer desirable platforms for the presentation and dissemination of research and policy analysis. Fed "clout" in these various respects surely influences the expression of views and scholarly research on monetary policy, central banking, and macroeconomics.

The Fed's influence in this regard is not necessarily nefarious. Indeed, Fed economists have tremendous expertise in monetary policy, the financial system, and the workings of the broader economy. It's appropriate to tap that expertise to understand the economy and formulate better policies. But the potential for groupthink pressures that originate within the Fed to emanate outwards and shape professional opinions and the direction of research more broadly is a concern. In this respect, the Fed is not just another big organization. It is also large relative to the broader intellectual and professional ecosphere within which it operates.

Incentives and Beliefs

It's not my view that FOMC members misrepresented their beliefs in their public projections, nor do my arguments about incentives and institutional pressures rest on that view. Instead, my view is that humans have a tendency to believe that which is comfortable, familiar, and aligned with their incentives and goals. For the Fed in 2021 and early 2022, that meant the belief that inflationary impulses from supply-chain disruptions and fiscal policy actions would be modest in size, that the resulting inflation would be short lived, that inflation expectations were and would remain well anchored, and that the Fed could manage inflation expectations to achieve its policy goals. There were sound reasons to question those beliefs, but they remained tenable for some time in the face of the uncertainty and unusual circumstances that prevailed in 2021 and early 2022. Institutional pressures for conformist thinking inside the Fed system reinforced the very human tendency to maintain comfortable beliefs until they were clearly falsified by the accumulation of evidence and the course of events.

My remarks above about the Fed's shading of projections should be understood in this light. In particular, the shading is relative to what disinterested, equally informed experts would think, absent the incentives and groupthink pressures that I describe. Similarly, my remarks above about the Fed's preference for models with strongly anchored inflation expectations and its tendency in 2021 and early 2022 to discount contrary models and narratives should be understood in that light.

Incentives Are Not Destiny: Proposals for Reform

Recognition and acknowledgment are the first steps in addressing incentive problems and their consequences. Further steps require institutional change, which is typically hard. I now sketch a few proposed reforms that aim to reduce the force of the incentive problems described above, mitigate the force of conformist pressures inside the Fed, and help contain their negative consequences.

Discontinue the Fed's Public-Facing Projection Enterprise

I start with the Fed's quarterly Summary of Economic Projections, a central object of analysis in Levy's paper. In light of my remarks above, it's reasonable to ask whether the Fed should simply stop publishing numerical forecasts for the economic outlook and its policy rate.

One argument for stopping flows directly from the incentive perspective developed above. Briefly, the argument runs as follows: When the Fed publishes numerical forecasts, it creates incentives to shade those forecasts to help achieve its policy goals in a least-cost manner. Because it's hard to divorce the Fed's public forecasts from its internal thinking and deliberations, the incentives for the Fed to shade its forecasts also undermine the quality of its decision making about monetary policy.

Uncertainty about the economic outlook, especially for inflation, intensifies the incentives for the Fed to shade its public forecasts, as described in my discussion of the 2021–22 period. The premium on sound monetary policy is likely to be especially high when there is great uncertainty about the economic outlook. Thus, it is not much of a retort to claim that the incentive problems manifest mainly, or only, in unusual circumstances.

There are other arguments for stopping as well. For example, Summers (2023) argues that the Fed should drop its specific numerical targets for forward guidance and "return to a more modest framework with broad objectives clearly stated," because the inevitable forecast errors associated with specific projections undermine the Fed's credibility. In addition, "When the Fed gives specific forward guidance, it feels constrained to follow through on it, and so it diverts policy from what would otherwise be the more optimal path." His argument differs from mine, but I see his points as essentially additive to the concerns that flow from my incentive analysis.

In short, there is a plausible case against the Fed's current practice of issuing specific numerical forecasts for the future paths of inflation, output, and the policy rate. I have not studied the issue with enough care to hold a firm view on the matter. I do think the time is ripe for a reconsideration of the Fed's public-facing forecasting enterprise. Dropping specific numerical forecasts altogether ought to be one option on the menu of possible reforms.

Improve the Fed's Public-Facing Projection Enterprise

Another possibility is to improve the Fed's current approach to its public-facing forecasts. That approach strikes me as suboptimal, to put it softly.[6] So, I now offer a proposal for improving the Fed's current approach. The key idea is to replace projections conditional on each FOMC member's estimate of the "appropriate monetary policy" (the current approach) with *projections conditional on specified trajectories for the policy rate and other policy instruments*. The specific elements of my proposal are as follows:

- Board staff to specify a baseline monetary policy trajectory, a materially looser policy trajectory, and a materially tighter one. Each monetary policy trajectory is to include, at a minimum, a path for the Fed's policy rate over the projection horizon.
- Each voting and nonvoting FOMC member to supply projections for inflation, output, and unemployment conditional on each of the three policy trajectories specified by the board staff. (Governors can default to the board staff's projections if they wish.)
- In forming projections, all unspecified shocks and policies that might influence inflation and real activity over the projection horizon to be held constant across the specified policy trajectories. (Of course, FOMC members will differ in their unstated assumptions about these other shocks and policies.)
- Publish each FOMC member's set of projections.
- Identify the source of each set of projections.
- The regional Fed banks can specify additional policy trajectories, if they wish, and provide projections conditional on those trajectories.

This proposal offers several advantages relative to the Fed's current approach. First, it clarifies the monetary policy assumptions behind the economic projections. In contrast, the current approach involves projections conditioned on a vague and unspecified notion of "appropriate monetary policy." Second, it simplifies the aggregation of projections, because each set of projections is conditioned on explicit trajectories for monetary policy. Third, it reveals what each FOMC member believes about the output, unemployment, and inflation effects of deviations from the baseline policy trajectory. Extracting that information from the Fed's current projections is impossible. Fourth, revealing each FOMC member's projections strengthens their incentives to prepare well-grounded projections and defend them publicly. Fifth, by advancing three rather than one policy rate trajectory, my proposal dilutes the Fed's incentives to shade its projections.

My proposal also creates more space for the regional Feds to dissent from the board's view by presenting materially different projections for the economic outlook, conditional on the board's specified policy trajectories, or by advancing alternative policy trajectories and corresponding economic projections. These are softer forms of dissent than voting against the FOMC majority's instructions regarding the federal funds target rate. Hence, dissent may surface more often. Dissents would also be more informative, because they could be related directly to the dissenter's projections and changes in those projections over time.

I recognize that this proposal raises new issues. One thorny matter is whether and how fully to articulate the auxiliary assumptions that underpin the conditional projections. Should the board staff also articulate its assumptions about the fiscal policy trajectory that underpins its projections for inflation, output, and unemployment? Should the board staff articulate other assumptions, e.g., regarding the outlook for energy supplies? Should individual FOMC members articulate their assumptions in this regard? There is a challenging trade-off here between simplicity of presentation and precision about the assumptions behind the projections. A clear picture of this trade-off may emerge only after a period of experimentation. The opportunity for the regional banks to specify alternative trajectories is a natural vehicle for such experimentation.

Another issue is whether it's practical to compel individual-level FOMC members to hold their auxiliary assumptions constant across the board-specified trajectories. That's reasonably straightforward for professional economists armed with an explicit model. It may be hard for others to implement and for the public to understand.

Yet another issue is whether the Board or the regional banks, should be encouraged to specify policy trajectories (and attendant economic projections) for multiple scenarios with respect to fiscal policy and shocks. The advantage of that approach is to help communicate the uncertain and contingent nature of future monetary policy actions. The disadvantage is a further increase in the complexity of the economic projections and the greater communication challenges that come with that complexity.

A New Federal Reserve Forum

The Fed should sponsor an annual conference that highlights tail risks for monetary policy and central banking, advances nonstandard scenario analyses, considers emerging and latent threats to sound monetary policy, and draws lessons from historical episodes. Unlike the many forums for research and policy analysis that the Fed already sponsors and organizes, the agenda for this new forum should be externally driven. Specifically:

- The scientific committee should be composed of outside experts who are not currently or recently (say, within five years) employed by the Board of Governors or the regional Federal Reserve banks.
- Paper authors should be drawn mainly from outside the Fed system.
- Discussants should be drawn mainly from inside the Fed system.
- Substantial cash prizes should be awarded for the most thought-provoking, innovative, and informative papers—as judged by the scientific committee, with input from discussants, conference participants, and anyone else who wants to offer an assessment.

These conference elements aim to encourage outside economists to consider monetary policy issues and to encourage Fed economists to engage with the ideas, analysis, and evidence that the conference brings to the table.

Sponsorship by one or more regional Federal Reserve banks (a coalition of the willing) would be sufficient to launch and fund this enterprise and to see that it receives attention inside and beyond the Fed system. This new forum should not require board approval. Indeed, it's preferable if one or more of the regional Federal Reserve banks takes the lead in this effort.

Promote the Analysis of Tail Risks inside the Fed, including at the Board

Separate business-as-usual forecasting from assessing recession risks, major inflation threats, financial crisis risks, and the implications of unprecedented shocks. These assessments call for different skills, methods, and data than business-as-usual forecasting. Moreover, standard model-based forecasts typically rest on small perturbations to highly stable systems. That may be suitable for projecting conditional mean outcomes under normal economic conditions, but it's less useful for assessing extreme tail risks and the implications of major shocks and developments that lack close precedents. Historical analyses, case studies, and the analytical evaluation of tail-risk scenarios are all potentially useful in these respects. Perhaps these nonstandard types of analyses already attract much intellectual energy at the Board of Governors and adequately inform the FOMC's deliberations about monetary policy. My impression is that they do not.

Foster Contrarian Thinking at the Regional Federal Reserve Banks

The regional Federal Reserve banks are natural homes for nurturing nonconformist thinking. They should be encouraged to play that role. However, the regional banks also face pressures to conform to the perspectives that dominate thinking and policy analysis by the Board of Governors. Here, I consider one important source of conformist pressure.

The appointment of a Federal Reserve bank president is subject to the approval of the Federal Reserve Board of Governors.[7] Moreover, "The chair of the Board of Governors' Committee on Federal Reserve Bank Affairs meets regularly with the search committee chair [for a new president] throughout the search process regarding the candidate pool, with a particular focus on ensuring it is broad and diverse. The search committee interviews a range of potential candidates and forwards to the Board of Governors a list of finalist candidates, all of whom are interviewed by the governors."

It makes perfect sense for the Board of Governors to play an advisory role in vetting Federal Reserve bank presidents. Granting the Board of Governors a veto role in the selection process is much more problematic. That veto role is a powerful tool for extending conformist pressures and groupthink at the Board throughout the entire Federal Reserve System. Even if one believes that the Board of Governors has exercised its veto role with a light hand in the past, there is no assurance it will continue to do so. One alternative is to make the appointment of a Federal Reserve bank president subject to the approval of Congress or, in the event that Congress fails to approve or disapprove a proposed appointment within a reasonable time span, to revert to approval or disapproval by the Board of Governors.

References

Clarida, Richard H. 2020. "The Federal Reserve's New Monetary Policy Framework: A Robust Evaluation." Peterson Institute for International Economics, August 31.

Grim, Ryan. 2009. "Priceless: How the Federal Reserve Bought the Economics Profession," *Huffington Post*, May 9, 2009, updated on May 13, 2013.

Reis, Ricardo. 2023. "The Burst of High Inflation in 2021–22: How and Why Did We Get Here?" In *How Monetary Policy Got Behind the Curve—and How to Get It Back*, edited by Michael D. Bordo, John H. Cochrane, and John B. Taylor, 203–26. Stanford, CA: Hoover Institution Press.

Summers, Lawrence H. 2023. "A Labor Market View of Inflation." In *How Monetary Policy Got Behind the Curve—and How to Get It Back*, edited by Michael D. Bordo, John H. Cochrane, and John B. Taylor, 17–32. Stanford, CA: Hoover Institution Press.

Notes

1. See chapter 11 as well as tables 11.1 and 11.2.
2. In his comments from the floor at the conference, Jeff Lacker points out that the Fed's Summary of Economic Projections was built to influence inflation expectations. See panel discussion for the section Forecasting Inflation and Output.
3. See Reis (2023) for a much fuller discussion of these circumstances.
4. I am neither endorsing nor disputing the flat-Phillips-curve view here. Nor am I taking a stand on whether the Phillips curve is a useful tool in thinking about monetary policy. Instead, I am describing nettlesome incentives that confront the Fed when FOMC members hold the flat-Phillips-curve view.
5. The figure for the Federal Reserve Board of Governors website comes from the Federal Reserve "Meet the Economists" web page, https://www.federalreserve.gov/econres/theeconomists.htm (accessed on June 11, 2023). The figure for the regional Federal Reserve Bank is my assessment. The Federal Reserve Banks of Chicago, New York, and San Francisco jointly employ nearly 150 PhD economists. Information on how many at each bank can be similarly accessed from each bank's website. All were accessed on June 11, 2023.
6. Before reading Levy's paper, I had no occasion to think about how the Fed forms and communicates its projections. So, perhaps I fail to appreciate some subtle virtues in the Fed's current approach. By the same token, I have not been socialized to see the current approach as a sensible one. As it turns out, I do not.
7. See "How Is a Federal Reserve Bank President Selected?" at https://www.federalreserve.gov/faqs/how-is-a-federal-reserve-bank-president-selected.htm, accessed June 19, 2023.

GENERAL DISCUSSION

JAMES WILCOX (INTRODUCTION): When the COVID-19 pandemic struck in 2020, forecasters could hardly be expected to know how much their forecast-error distributions had changed. As it happened, both inflation and employment were higher than generally forecasted and by considerable amounts. Before and after COVID struck, the Fed seems to have stayed with its view that the Phillips curve had become quite flat. Indeed, for at least twenty years before the pandemic, the responses of inflation to swings in unemployment did seem weak, if not completely gone. Booms in the 2000s, the 2010s, and even the Great Recession changed the core inflation rate remarkably little. We have yet to fully understand what accounts for any flattening of the pre-COVID Phillips curve.

Not surprisingly, perhaps, having concluded they faced a quite-flat Phillips curve, the Fed and many others attributed most of the postpandemic inflation to energy shocks and supply-chain disruptions. Those higher inflation rates would be transitory, subsiding as the ripples of those shocks faded.

Fifty years ago, Milton Friedman concluded that, in the fifty years before that, the Fed almost invariably acted "too much too late." One reason for acting too late, then and now, might be underestimating the steepness of Phillips curves. Underestimating how steep Phillips curves were, or are, might also lead to interest rate hikes that prove to be "too much." Alternatively, "too much too late" might also result from underestimating how fast Phillips curves shift.

The Fed's oft-stated target for inflation is 2%. FOMC [Federal Open Market Committee] members' forecasts for long-run inflation are apparently well anchored at 2%. Many private-sector analysts also forecast longer-run inflation of 2%.

But, in 2020, the Fed announced its revised policy strategy, which has come to be known as flexible average inflation targeting, or FAIT. (My personal policy is to neither attribute nor to succumb to "fate.") The revised policy added the term "average." But [Federal Reserve] Chairman Jay Powell has made it clear that his averaging applies primarily, and likely only, to past inflation rates below 2%. As a result, the Fed, forecasters, and financial markets now seem to have well-anchored expectations that the average that the Fed uses for its average-inflation target will omit the first half of the 2020s, when inflation has been, and very likely will average, far above 2%.

To the extent the FAIT policy is credible, it would be surprising if expectations of genuinely average inflation, and expectations of inflation at a point in the distant future, are anchored at 2%. Anchored perhaps, but not as low as 2%. As for the revised policy achieving its goals, so far, FAIT has been anything *but* "accompli."

This morning, Peter [Blair] Henry argued that extinguishing moderate inflation may be quite costly in equity valuations, economic growth, and time. In telecom, transportation, and package deliveries, completing the "last mile" can be vastly more expensive; so, too, perhaps, for eventually reducing embedded US inflation, for example from 4% down to 3% and then to 2%. If so, Fed transparency and credibility would be well served by alerting the public that the "last mile" on the road to 2% inflation may be long and costly.

Our presenter in this session, Mickey Levy, is well known to audiences at Hoover Monetary Policy conferences. He has a long record of research and papers on Federal Reserve policies and their effects. Mickey is the chief economist for Berenberg Capital Markets LLC and a visiting scholar here at Hoover.

He is a long-standing member of the Shadow Open Market Committee and has often testified in Congress about macroeconomic and financial matters. Mickey also served on the Financial Research Advisory Committee of the US Office of Financial Research. For the fifteen years prior to joining Berenberg, Mickey was the chief economist for Bank of America.

As the lead discussant for Mickey's paper, we are fortunate to hear from Steven Davis. Steve Davis is a senior fellow here at Hoover Institution after having had a distinguished career at the University of Chicago Booth School of Business. Steve belongs to NBER [National Bureau of Economic Research] and advises the Congressional Budget Office, as well as Brookings Papers on Economic Activity. In addition to his other research, we know him well for his research associated with the Economic Policy Uncertainty project and the [Atlanta Fed, Chicago Booth, and Stanford University] Survey of Business Uncertainty. Along with other important activities, Steve co-organizes the annual Asian Monetary Policy Forum.

Speaking of uncertainty, we turn now to our presenter, Mickey Levy, who is well known for leaving very little uncertainty about his assessment of Fed policies.

* * *

WILCOX: Thank you, Mickey. And thank you, Steve. We'll now take questions from the floor, and as usual, please identify yourselves. Rich?

RICHARD CLARIDA: Richard Clarida, Columbia University. Mickey has written, as one might expect, a thoughtful and provocative paper. I have several observations and will try to be brief.

I think Mickey's paper tries to explain too much. It ignores the fact that there are ten countries in the G10, and all ten of them failed to hike rates before inflation exceeded the target rate, and eight of them failed to hike rates before core inflation exceeded the target, the two exceptions being Switzerland and Norway. So, to me, this indicates there was something about the shocks—to aggregate and sectoral supply and to aggregate demand—or about central bankers' interpretation of the shocks that led them to choose to fall behind the curve. That's omitted from the paper, which is very Fed-specific.

My second point, which Steve also touched on in his fine discussion, relates to the nature of the Fed's inflation forecast miss in 2021. Speaking for myself, throughout 2021, I was looking for private-sector forecasts of inflation at the high end and trying to look at appropriate policy under a plausible worst-case scenario. I'll give you one data point. In April of 2021, the *Wall Street Journal* surveyed seventy-five economists. This was after the American Rescue Plan Act of 2021 passed. It's on the web; you can go look up every individual forecast. And the median forecast post–American Rescue Plan in 2021 for inflation was 2.1%, and the most hawkish pessimistic forecast was 2.7%. So there was an epic forecast missed here. It may be because many private-sector forecasters are former Fed staff. The inflation swap markets are different. Investing in inflation swaps is just about getting expected inflation right. And in 2021, they were not pricing in the surge in inflation that we actually got. Moving on to counterfactuals, I would observe that it's hard to do counterfactuals right. Hindsight is 2020, which is too easy, but I can think of at least two approaches that make sense. One is to look at the policy path indicated by a Taylor-type rule. And that exercise has been done and is regularly updated by [David H.] Papell and [Ruxandra] Prodan, which was featured in my talk.

What you see is that had the Fed been following a Taylor-type rule, lift-off would have commenced by the September 2021 FOMC meeting. The Fed's new framework did lay out particular thresholds for lift-off, and those were met by December 2021.

So, given the nature of the shocks, it would not have mattered if the policy had been outsourced either to a Taylor rule or to a mechanical application of the new framework. Clearly, the Fed got aggregate supply wrong. Wage inflation skyrocketed, with an unemployment rate of 5% and millions of fewer workers than had been employed prepandemic. Broad-based price inflation picked up when the level of GDP was two percentage points below the then-prevailing estimate of potential. So there was a huge supply shock in play. Aggregate demand was excessive relative to available aggregate supply.

Fast-forward to today. We are now two-plus years into the reopening and the surge in global inflation. Core inflation in every G10 country save Switzerland is running well above inflation targets, and central banks are scrambling to hike rates into restrictive territory to bring inflation back to its target. Moreover, as for inflation expectations, by most measures, they have remained reasonably well anchored, which was not the case in the 1970s. Thank you.

WILCOX: Jim Bullard? Identify yourself just to make sure . . .

JAMES BULLARD: Jim Bullard, St. Louis Fed. I just want to emphasize that we should put 2021 into some context. There was basically no inflation in the first quarter, nor was any inflation expected. Vaccines came in the second quarter. I wanted to see how the vaccines would proceed and whether they would be successful. By the time we got to July 1, you did have some inflation. The vaccine seemed to be pretty successful. The pandemic did not end cleanly there. There were other things happening in the second half of 2021. So I think that you have to have some context about the crisis that was going on.

My main point is that, as my colleague Chris Waller detailed at this conference last year, moves were made in a hawkish direction during the fall of 2021. It's just that they're not visible in these charts, because the projected date of ending the asset purchases was way off in 2024. That was reeled in during the fall of 2021. Ideas that we would raise the policy rate sooner rather than later were taking hold. This was pushing the two-year [Treasury bond] yield up, as I emphasized last year. While hawkish moves were being made, the pandemic hit was very strong, and [it was widely feared] that this was going to be the Great Depression—that the economy was going to be very, very sluggish for a very long time, and inflation was going to be very low for a very long time. All of that was being upset in 2021. And we were bringing the change to monetary policy, but it didn't manifest itself in lift-off until March 2022. Then we started to move very rapidly in 2022 with the policy rate. I just want to say that some things were being done in the fall of 2021.

WILCOX: Next is Andy, followed by John Cochrane. Andy?

ANDREW LEVIN: Of course, I agree with everything Mickey says. Chris [Erceg] and I were kind of musing about Steve's recommendations, which seem exactly the opposite of what Jordi Galí, Mike Woodford, and Lars Svensson have previously advocated. In a macro model, having an exogenous nominal interest rate tends to be problematic, so those issues can be considered further.

On the broader issues, think about a team of medical doctors, the patient, and the patient's family. I think it's a useful analogy to think about these communication issues. Because if we follow Steve's assessment of incentives, then the team of doctors will be constantly telling the patient, "Oh, don't worry, everything's gonna be fine. Just relax." Of course, there are times when the patient is really stressed and the doctors simply need to provide some reassurance. But there are also situations where the patient gets worried in the middle of the night, like, "Maybe the doctor's not telling me everything." And if they feel like the physicians are not telling them the whole truth, that can also be very problematic. Now that the fact of the matter is, in the medical world, you have to prepare the patient for the possibility that they might need chemotherapy or surgery. And that's much easier if you tell them further ahead, to say, "There's a risk here. We hope it won't be necessary, but just a heads-up that could be coming." Or even that you need to take this very unpleasant medicine for a few weeks, but you'll get past it. And I think that's what was missing, Steve, from your incentive story. Here is the other side of this, which was the old idea of, we're going to warn the public that we may need to raise rates a lot, and there's going to be some short-term pain, but it's going to be worth it, because we all want price stability over time. And I think the problem the Fed is still facing now is they haven't clearly told the public, Congress, or the markets that the possibility is still out there. And it makes me worry that it's going to get harder and harder for the team of physicians to convey that message. At that point, there will be a public outcry, "Why didn't you give us any warning?"

WILCOX: Thank you. Next is John Cochrane, followed by Jeff Lacker.

JOHN COCHRANE: Thank you, this is great. This is a really important panel, because we need to figure out what the heck went wrong.

I want to expand on some of the conceptual issues. I'll phrase these points as statements, but you can take them as questions and disagree.

Of course, yes, the Fed's mistake was repeated by central banks around the world and by industry analysts. So, conceptual problems are common to lots of people. Here's a list of additional conceptual problems I think that went wrong.

First, demand versus supply. To central bankers, demand and output are practically synonyms. Supply is, at best, vaguely out there somewhere. So, if this event came from supply shocks, then where is the team of central bank economists monitoring supply? They're not there. If there were going to be supply shocks, maybe we needed such a team.

Second, fiscal issues. Five trillion bucks of fiscal stimulus. Why did this not show up anywhere in the Fed's forecasting and assessment of surging inflation? I have heard quietly some of the answers: to say so would be political, and the Fed can't get involved in politics. But nonetheless, $5 trillion is going to show up in inflation somewhere. Saying there won't be inflation and acting as if there won't be inflation because we can't talk about its fiscal source is not the right answer!

Third, the Phillips curve came up a lot here. I think we're making some mistakes in how we think about it. In this discussion, as well as in much of the Fed, the Phillips curve is taken as a causal reaction: Output or employment and expected inflation determine current inflation. It's just a correlation. But maybe the Phillips curve is how inflation determines output. The Phillips curve is also not the whole model. Lots of other equations in our models have output, inflation, and interest rates in them. You can't just think in terms of the Phillips curve as if it were a complete model of the economy.

I think forecasters also look too short term in this Phillips curve theorizing. Inflation is driven by expected inflation. That should remind you how finance works. Today's price is tomorrow's expected price, plus the dividend. If you're looking at a one-day horizon, you say to yourself, talk up tomorrow's price, and that will raise today's price. But iterate that forward. Stock prices are not just about tomorrow's price. In the end, they are the present value of dividends. I think looking a few more steps ahead of the game would be useful in thinking about inflation, too.

Even thinking about expected inflation driving inflation, expected inflation is not an exogenous variable. It's just determined by speeches. It comes from a regime—"anchored." Anchored by what? Anchored by more speeches about how important anchoring is? I notice the Fed is unwilling to really answer the question, "Anchored by what?" The answer has to be, if it comes to it, we will replay 1980, if necessary, no matter how hard that might be. Here, stating projections in terms of time rather than data is a mistake—which comes down to the whole Taylor rule theme. To say, "Expectations should be anchored, because if it comes to it, we will replay 1980," the Fed must say how it will respond to inflation that it hopes will not happen, not "Here's what we're going to do next month into next year."

Steve had a couple of important points, which I want to emphasize using slightly different language. First, I've learned something at Hoover by hanging out with the military people, who are fascinating. The Fed says, "Here's what we expect the economy will look like, so here's what we're going to do for the next year or so." No self-respecting military person would ever say, "Here's what we expect the enemy to do. So here's our plan. We're sticking to it." No, they go through a hundred different iterations of: "If they come on the left flank, here's what we do. If they come on the right flank, here's what we do." Where is the Fed's monetary policy risk management? [Former professional boxer] Mike Tyson has said what happens if you just make a plan and go into battle with it: "Everybody has a plan until they get punched in the mouth." Similarly, the military red-teams plans. (The "red" is an allusion to the Communist enemy. What would they do?) A group is designated to poke holes in plans and is rewarded for doing a good job. The Fed does not do red-team or devil's-advocate planning. I gather from people inside the Fed that disagreeing is not good for your career. We need to change that. Likewise, in the military, if they lose a battle, there's an inquest. How did we miss this? Right here on this panel, we are starting to ask this question. But where is the inquest inside the Fed? Where's the court martial? After Pearl Harbor, they didn't just say, "Well, it was a supply shock. Who coulda known?"

Now, I don't know what happened. I don't know how to forecast inflation either, and evaluating what's happening to the economy in real time is very hard. Maybe it's impossible to do better. But even that knowledge would radically change procedures. Managing monetary policy as if forecasts and shock assessments are meaningful, if in fact they are not, is a big mistake.

WILCOX: Jeff Lacker, followed by Volker.

JEFFREY LACKER: Jeff Lacker, Shadow Open Market Committee. So, Mickey and I've been talking for months, so I knew what was coming in this paper. But it's wonderfully documented and dissected. And I think incredibly useful. Steve Davis, your theory rings true. It's definitely the case for me that the Fed always felt like Andy Levin's old-time paternalistic doctor that thought that the best thing for the patient was that they not know what risks were out there. And to that point, the phrase "risk management" within the Fed—and I think you'll find this in the transcripts in the early 2000s—was a synonym for raising rates based on some probabilistic assessment of possibilities, not what John [Cochrane] was talking about in terms of military planning. So the SEP [Summary of Economic Projections], I think, deserves to be dismembered and rebuilt from scratch. The SEP—I just rediscovered this through looking into the origin of the consensus statement in 2012—was introduced without dots and with a two-year horizon, and it was done as a shortcut to an inflation target. The idea, the expectation, the hope at the board was that everyone would submit 2%, or at least the same number, for the last year the inflation was forecasted. That failed. They added a third year. That failed. And so, they added a final column of long-run projections. And the dots were added later to provide a vehicle for portraying policies "lower for longer" in order to pull the yield curve down, again to influence expected inflation. So the SEP was sort of built around trying to influence expected inflation, and I think it needs to be rebuilt now.

There's always been a hesitancy about letting staff forecasts out into the wild. And I can't imagine them being comfortable taking that step. But I'm sure something better can be constructed.

Finally, I'll point out something I haven't heard in any of the coverage about SVB [Silicon Valley Bank], but my understanding of the early days of the stress test is that the macroeconomic assumptions were vetted at the most senior levels. A perspective brought to bear on those assumptions was how it might get out and how it might reflect on what the Fed thought about what was going to happen. So, the assumptions were chosen as an adverse but not that bad scenario. I've always wondered about the stress test assumptions that showed no rate increases, as to whether last year the Fed was reluctant to really put into a stress test those stresses that they could see were coming in the banking sector. So again, thank you both for your great contributions.

WILCOX: Volker?

VOLKER WIELAND: I want to add two points from a European perspective. First, definitely keep the survey of projections [issued by] the FOMC. I've always recommended that the ECB [European Central Bank] also publish such forecasts. It's worse if the central bank is not transparent in this regard. The advantage of the SEP is that these individual forecasts are public. This allows criticism and makes the central bank somewhat vulnerable.

The second point refers to the experience in early 2021 when I was still a member of the German Council of Economic Experts, involved in preparing a forecast. So, in February 2021, you could see the first upward inflation surprise. I gave some interviews to German newspapers emphasizing the distribution of the survey of professional forecasters collected by the ECB. I was quoted as saying, "There is a significant risk that inflation could be 3% for the next three years." When I discussed with my colleagues as we had to make our forecasts, they all said, "Look, but the ECB says it's temporary." So we came out with a very moderate forecast. But based on these distributions, board members of the ECB could have discussed these risks publicly and said, "We forecast that the inflation surge is temporary, but there is a significant risk that it is not temporary, and then we would react to that." That would have sent a very different message. But nobody did that. The ECB continued to say it's a purely transitory effect until November 2021. So, I think looking at such risk scenarios and talking about them should be incentive compatible. Because if you make a mistake, and you've never alerted to the risk of such a mistake, you're worse off.

WILCOX: We have a question. And then, after this question, we'll let Mickey and Steve reply, since we're running short on time.

TERRY ANDERSON: Terry Anderson, senior fellow at the Hoover Institution. I'm not a macroeconomist. But I am a political economist, a public choice economist, if you will. And so when I hear that the Fed should, or that "we" should, replace projections, or that "we" should allow regionals to do such and such, I think, well, who is "we," or how do "we" make this happen? And I think, Steven, you jumped over one of your suggestions that we probably need institutional change. So my question is the same one I asked last year of one of the panels: How can this institutional change come about? How can people at the Hoover Institution, or people in audiences like this, help bring about the necessary policy changes? It won't do to just say "the Fed should" or "Congress should." So, what are the institutional underpinnings of the bad incentives you described?

WILCOX: Mickey? Would you like to respond?

MICKEY LEVY: Sure. Let me start by responding to Jim Bullard and Rich Clarida. Yes, there were extraordinary circumstances, with unprecedented negative supply and demand shocks, followed by unprecedented monetary and fiscal stimulus and concerns about healthcare. Yet, the inflation data started to show this dramatic acceleration in spring 2021. By June 2021, inflation had risen above 3%. In the Fed's Beige Book prepared for the

July FOMC meeting, nearly every one of the twelve district banks identified mounting evidence of a sharp acceleration in demand, higher business operating costs, and business flexibility for raising prices. These observations reflected a combination of supply and demand factors underlying the rise in inflation. This was reflected in the sharp acceleration in nominal GDP. Yet, a month later, the Fed's semiannual report to Congress basically only talked about the supply side and understated the inflationary impact of the strong demand.

Rich, to your point, it's extremely difficult to forecast. But this is an interesting issue, because the vast majority of Wall Street and professional forecasters were either trained at the Fed or they're heavily influenced by the Fed. Moreover, the normal operation of professional forecasters is to ask, What's the consensus? And to determine whether to be above or below and not to deviate very much. This exercise, rather than thinking conceptually, dominates most forecasting. In this way, the private sector is guilty of groupthink. And as I emphasized, the prevalent view, like the Fed's, was that inflation would stay low, as it did following the Great Financial Crisis.

Most of you commented about uncertainty and the failure to manage expectations. In May and June of 2020, Mike Bordo, Andy Levin, and I were finishing a paper on dealing with uncertainty and urging the Fed to use scenario analysis and incorporate it into their thinking and policy deliberations. We were holed up during the pandemic in our remote sites having lengthy discussions about the median path of the economy and inflation, alternative high paths and the low paths, and how the Fed would respond under different scenarios. We argued back and forth, and the discussions were very instructive. Since publishing the paper, about every six months Andy would say, "We need to update that paper." We all got busy and never prepared an update, but that type of scenario analysis would be just as important today and a valuable contribution to the Fed's projections and policy debate.

I applaud Steve's initiative in his suggestions for thinking about how to change the SEPs. The current SEPs are the Fed's best forecasts and, based on incentives, could be the Fed's optimal forecasts. There are many ways the Fed can improve upon its SEP projections, and it should put a high priority on doing so.

Inflationary expectations and the ability to manage them are critically important to anchoring inflation. But to be credible, inflationary expectations have to be embedded in a model and a framework that can credibly achieve the inflation objective. As John Cochrane emphasizes, it takes more than just giving speeches to anchor inflationary expectations to a long-run target. The current monetary policy is necessary.

Fast-forward to today. At last year's Hoover Monetary Policy Conference, the Fed had just begun hiking rates, and the Fed funds rate was 0.75%. Now the Fed has raised rates above core inflation, and monetary policy is much better aligned with the Fed's objective of reducing inflation. So far, the economy has been resilient, and a soft landing in the economy is possible. I would absolutely applaud the Fed if that were to pass. But now is the critical time to conduct a serious reassessment of monetary policy and learn from the mistakes made in the last couple of years so that these big mistakes aren't made in the future.

WILCOX: Steve, we'll give you the last word here.

STEVEN DAVIS: Thanks. Let me start with Terry Anderson's remark about institutional change. One of the virtues of the Fed's rather unwieldy decentralized structure is the dozen somewhat independent regional Feds. Most of my proposals could be taken up by one or two Feds. "A coalition of the willing" within the Fed system is all that's needed to launch the new conference, for example. Announcing projections conditional on specified policy trajectories could be done by a handful of the regional

Feds. You don't need the [Board of Governors]' acquiescence for that. I agree that getting the board to buy into the kind of suggestions I made is unlikely. But historically, some regional Feds have played this kind of iconoclastic or outsider role—the St. Louis Fed and the Minneapolis Fed come to mind. So, I do think it's more than wishful thinking to believe that institutional change within some part of the decentralized Fed system can happen. Fed bank presidents have their own career concerns that are somewhat different from those of people at the board. Bank-level innovation within the Fed system has happened in the past and can happen again.

Regarding Andy Levin's remarks: I wasn't quite sure where you were coming from, Andy. I was trying to offer an explanation of why the doctor had not been fully forthcoming and honest with the patient. I agree that more honesty would be good.

To John Cochrane's remarks, I agree that there are important conceptual issues to consider. John mentioned fiscal policy in this regard. At last year's conference, [former Treasury secretary] Larry Summers pointed out that the FRB-US model is structured in a way that yields modest inflationary effects even from a giant fiscal stimulus. To my way of thinking, that's an example of how the incentives facing the Fed shape its analytical framework and influence its views about the economic outlook. Summers used a different analytical framework that supported a different perspective on the economic outlook.

Turning to John's comments about regimes and speeches, my only quibble is I don't actually think expectations are all about what regime we're in, because nobody's completely sure what regime we're in. There are many examples of central bankers giving speeches that move markets, and the only reasonable interpretation I can come up with is that they've somehow shifted expectations even within a given monetary policy regime. But otherwise, I'm quite sympathetic to John's comments.

To Rich's remarks, one of the things I like about the incentive story that I advanced is that it's not US-specific. It was a fundamental problem facing leading central banks around the world, and it diffused to the private sector, as I briefly tried to explain. I'll stop there.

WILCOX: Okay, well, we've exceeded our time limit by the optimal amount. And so we'll stop here. But let's thank our panelists.

TOWARD A MONETARY POLICY STRATEGY

12

The Monetary-Fiscal Policy Mix and Central Bank Strategy

James Bullard

Introduction

US monetary and fiscal policy response to the pandemic created too much inflation. To eliminate the excess inflation, the monetary-fiscal response must be countered by returning to the prepandemic policy mix that delivered low and stable inflation. I will argue that this is already happening. The fiscal stimulus is receding, and monetary policy has been adjusted rapidly in the last year to better align with traditional central bank strategy. Accordingly, the prospects for continued disinflation are good but not guaranteed.

The Fiscal-Monetary Response

Think of the pandemic as a global war that induced large-scale deficit spending combined with accommodative monetary policy (Hall and Sargent 2022; Bullard 2023a). The spirit of the macroeconomic policy response to the pandemic was to err on the side of too much rather than too little. This could be thought of as risking a high-inflation regime, as the monetary authority did not attempt to offset the inflationary impulse unleashed by the fiscal authority.

Figure 12.1 portrays monetary and fiscal policy responses to the pandemic. Deficit spending was used for transfer payments to disrupted workers and businesses. This shows up at the aggregate level as a sharp increase in personal savings relative to trend

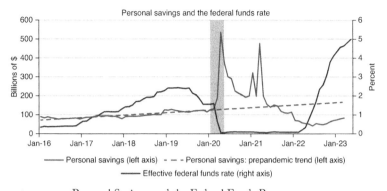

FIGURE 12.1. Personal Savings and the Federal Funds Rate.
The monetary and fiscal response to the pandemic shock. The gray shaded area indicates a US recession.

Sources: Bureau of Economic Analysis; Federal Reserve Bank of New York; author's calculations. Last observations: March 2023 and May 2023.

(Abdelrahman and Oliveira 2023). Fiscal action of this magnitude is unprecedented in US postwar macroeconomics. Meanwhile, the monetary policy reaction to the pandemic was to lower the policy rate sharply, accommodating the deficit spending.

In macroeconomic historical context, this combination of policies often leads to substantial inflation. Table 12.1 reports various measures of underlying inflation—that is, measures of inflation that downplay the most extreme price movements—from the Atlanta Fed's Underlying Inflation Dashboard.[1] The inflationary effects of the monetary-fiscal response are apparent in the elevated readings for all the measures in April 2022. The inflation has also been persistent—the last column shows that five of the nine underlying inflation measures are higher today than a year ago. Core personal consumption expenditures (PCE) is the measure preferred by the Federal Open Market Committee (FOMC); it is now 4.6%, down from 5% a year ago. However, all these measures would be down if a clear disinflationary path were established in the US economy.

TABLE 12.1. Various Measures of Underlying Inflation.
The inflationary effects of the monetary-fiscal response are apparent in the elevated readings for all the measures in April 2022, and inflation has remained persistent. Figures are year-on-year percentage changes.

Measure of Underlying Inflation	April 2022	March/April 2023
Core CPI	6.1	5.5
Cleveland Fed median CPI	5.4	7.0
Cleveland Fed trimmed-mean CPI	6.2	6.1
Atlanta Fed sticky CPI	4.9	6.5
Core PCE	5.0	4.6
Market-based core PCE	4.9	4.7
Dallas Fed trimmed-mean PCE	3.9	4.7
San Francisco Fed cyclical core PCE	6.3	7.9
Cyclically sensitive inflation	5.5	6.7

Source: Federal Reserve Bank of Atlanta Underlying Inflation Dashboard. Last observations: April 2023 (CPI-based measures) and March 2023 (PCE-based measures).

The Switch to Disinflationary Policy

According to the literature, what is now required is a switch back to the prepandemic monetary-fiscal regime that featured inflation near its target. Sargent (1982)—one of the best papers of twentieth-century macroeconomics—shows how inflation ended *on the day* that monetary and fiscal reform occurred in four hyperinflationary economies after World War I. These are dramatic examples of how a credible change of regime happening at the same time for monetary and fiscal policy can end even very high inflation with little or no other macroeconomic consequences. Although the current US monetary-fiscal regime change is not happening all at once, it is happening nonetheless.

With regard to fiscal policy, the fiscal impulse has been fading, and personal saving is now below the prepandemic trend line. However, these effects have not dissipated completely, as the area above the trend line in figure 12.2 is still more than $400 billion larger than the area below the trend line.

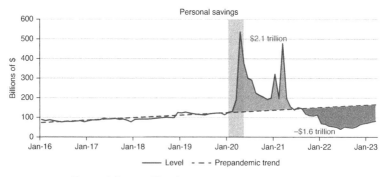

FIGURE 12.2. Personal Savings Trends.
Excess savings are diminishing but have not yet dissipated. Savings in excess of the prepandemic trend added up to about $2.1 trillion, whereas savings are currently below trend for a cumulative shortfall of about $1.6 trillion. The gray shaded area indicates a US recession.
Sources: Bureau of Economic Analysis; author's calculations. Last observation: March 2023. See Abdelrahman and Oliveira (2023) for details.

Sufficiently Restrictive Monetary Policy

On the monetary policy side, we have to switch to a sufficiently restrictive monetary policy more consistent with the prepandemic policy. I will assess whether monetary policy is sufficiently restrictive by looking at the recommendations of Taylor-type policy rules.

Monetary policy rules are useful because they provide an explicit recommendation for the value of the policy rate given current macroeconomic conditions. Taylor-type rules have been evaluated in a large amount of literature and have been argued to characterize close-to-optimal monetary policy in commonly used macroeconomic models. The literature also takes "long and variable lag" effects into account. Policy rules help pin down different arguments about the appropriate level of interest rates.

A Taylor-type monetary policy rule (Taylor 1993 and 1999) with generous assumptions will give us a minimal recommended value for the policy rate given current macroeconomic conditions. Less generous assumptions will give us an upper bound for a desirable target range for the policy rate. The recommended "zone" is the area between the lower and upper bounds. I will ignore balance sheet policy in these calculations.

I will consider the following rule:

$$R_t = max\left[R^* + \pi^* + \varphi_\pi(\pi_t - \pi^*) + min(ygap_t, 0), 0\right]$$

where R_t is the recommended policy rate; R^* is the real interest rate; $\pi^* = 2\%$ denoting the inflation target; π_t is inflation measured from one year earlier; φ_π describes the reaction of the policymaker to deviations of inflation from target; and $ygap_t$ is the output gap. The term $min(ygap_t, 0)$ is meant to capture that the FOMC's "policy decisions must be informed by assessments of the shortfalls of employment from its maximum level."[2] The max operator reflects the zero lower bound on the nominal interest rate. The output gap, $ygap_t$, can be constructed by applying Okun's law to deviations of the unemployment rate, u_t, from the median Summary of Economic Projections (SEP) longer-run value, u_t^{LR}:

$$ygap_t = -2\left(u_t - u_t^{LR}\right)$$

Given that the unemployment rate is below the median SEP longer-run value, the last term in the rule is currently equal to 0.[3]

In the first version of the Taylor-type rule outlined above, I use the most generous assumptions (those that tend to recommend a lower value of the policy rate). These assumptions are:

1. The Dallas Fed trimmed-mean PCE inflation rate is used as the inflation rate.
2. An approximate prepandemic value for the real interest rate (R^*) is −50 basis points.
3. The relatively low value of 1.25 is used for the parameter describing the reaction of the policymaker to deviations of inflation from target.

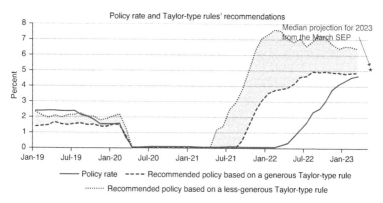

FIGURE 12.3. Policy Rate and Taylor-Type Rules' Recommendations.
The sufficiently restrictive zone for the policy rate spanned 4.85% to 6.40% in
March 2023. The actual policy rate in May 2023 was 4.99% (average of daily
values up to May 10).

Sources: Bureau of Economic Analysis; Bureau of Labor Statistics; Federal Reserve Bank
of Dallas; Federal Reserve Bank of New York; FOMC's March 2023 SEP; author's calculations. Last observations: March 2023 and May 2023.

For a less generous specification, I use:

1. Core (excluding food and energy) PCE inflation as the inflation
   measure.
2. A higher value for the real interest rate (R^*) of +50 basis points.[4]
3. A parameter value describing the reaction of the policymaker to
   deviations of inflation from target that is closer to the literature
   standard of 1.5 (see Taylor 1993 and 1999).

Figure 12.3 portrays the recommended zone for the policy rate,
as well as the actual policy rate. Monetary policy settings were
about right prepandemic, as shown in the figure. Monetary policy
was behind the curve in 2022, i.e., the actual policy rate was below
the zone (Bullard 2023b). However, monetary policy is now at the
low end of what is arguably sufficiently restrictive, given current
macroeconomic conditions. Note that the zone itself can move in
reaction to incoming data.

The policy rate was adjusted only partially toward the recommended policy rate during 2022, a phenomenon referred to as "policy inertia" in the literature. In my view, inertia involves a judgment by the FOMC concerning the pace of adjustment and its possible risks, weighed against the gains from returning the economy as quickly as possible to the balanced growth path with 2% inflation. Inertia has not been included in the calculations here, as the desire has been to locate a recommended level of the policy rate independently of the judgment call on policy inertia.[5]

The Prospects for Disinflation

So far, core PCE inflation has declined only modestly from the peak levels observed last year. However, an encouraging sign that the switch to prepandemic monetary-fiscal policy is working comes from market-based inflation expectations. As illustrated in figure 12.4, these expectations were near 2% in the first quarter of 2021, before any inflation had appeared or was widely expected. After moving higher in the last two years, inflation expectations have now returned to levels consistent with 2% inflation.

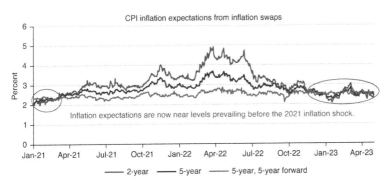

FIGURE 12.4. CPI Inflation Expectations from Inflation Swaps.
Inflation expectations have returned to levels consistent with the inflation target.
Sources: Bloomberg; author's calculations. Last observation: May 11, 2023.

Conclusion

The monetary and fiscal policy response to the pandemic created too much inflation. Historically speaking, we know that the combination of monetary accommodation and fiscal stimulus creates a lot of inflation across many times and places, typically in the aftermath of wars. To bring inflation back under control, we have to return to the prewar or prepandemic monetary and fiscal policy. I have argued this is happening. The fiscal stimulus, on the dimension that it matters for this issue, is receding, and monetary policy has been adjusted rapidly. Therefore, I think the prospects for continued disinflation are reasonably good.

References

Abdelrahman, Hamza, and Luiz E. Oliveira. 2023. "The Rise and Fall of Pandemic Excess Savings." *Federal Reserve Bank of San Francisco Economic Letter* 11, May 8.

Bullard, James. 2023a. "Credible and Incredible Disinflations," remarks delivered at The Credibility of Government Policies: Conference in Honor of Guillermo Calvo, Panel Discussion: Back to 2% Inflation? Columbia University, New York, February 24.

———. 2023b. "Is the Fed 'Behind the Curve'? Two Interpretations." In *How Monetary Policy Got Behind the Curve—and How to Get Back*, edited by Michael D. Bordo, John H. Cochrane, and John B. Taylor, 313–24. Stanford, CA: Hoover Institution Press.

Federal Open Market Committee (FOMC). 2023. "Statement on Longer-Run Goals and Monetary Policy Strategy," adopted effective January 24, 2012, as reaffirmed effective January 31, 2023.

Hall, George J., and Thomas J. Sargent. 2022. "Financing Big US Federal Expenditures Surges: COVID-19 and Earlier US Wars." Unpublished manuscript, June 12.

Papell, David H., and Ruxandra Prodan. 2023. "Policy Rules and Forward Guidance following the COVID-19 Recession." *SSRN Electronic Journal,* April 14, 2022 (Revised May 3).

Sargent, Thomas J. 1982. "The Ends of Four Big Inflations." In *Inflation: Causes and Effects,* edited by Robert E. Hall, 41–97. Chicago: University of Chicago Press.

Taylor, John B. 1993. "Discretion versus Policy Rules in Practice." *Carnegie-Rochester Conference Series on Public Policy* 39: 195–214. Amsterdam: North-Holland.

———. 1999. "A Historical Analysis of Monetary Policy Rules." In *Monetary Policy Rules*, edited by John B. Taylor, 319–48. Chicago: University of Chicago Press.

Notes

1. Available at https://www.atlantafed.org/research/inflationproject/underlying-inflation-dashboard.
2. See FOMC (2023).
3. The March 2023 unemployment rate was 3.5%; the median longer-run unemployment rate in the March 2023 SEP was 4.0%.
4. According to the March 2023 SEP, the median longer-run value for PCE inflation is 2.0%, while the median longer-run value for the federal funds rate is 2.5%. This implies a longer-run value for the real rate of 50 basis points.
5. See Papell and Prodan (2023) for an analysis of the role of policy inertia.

13

On the Assessment of Current Monetary Policy

Philip N. Jefferson

Good afternoon, everyone. Thank you to the organizers for inviting me to speak. It is a pleasure to be here. I welcome hearing diverse views on how to best conduct monetary policy, and this conference is certainly providing an invigorating debate on that topic.

Before I begin, I want to address quickly some news from this morning. I am deeply honored by the trust President Biden and Vice President Harris have shown me with the nomination to be the next vice chair of the Federal Reserve Board of Governors. I am humbled by this extraordinary opportunity and thankful to my colleagues, friends, and family for their support.

Turning back to the conference, as I join this debate, let me remind you that the views I will express today are my own and are not necessarily those of my colleagues in the Federal Reserve System.

The title of the conference, "How to Get Back on Track: A Policy Conference," is potent. Its intent and ambiguity are striking. First, the title presupposes that US monetary policy is currently on the wrong track. Second, the web page for this conference advances a puzzling definition of the phrase "on track." How so? According to the Hoover web page, "A key goal of the conference is to examine how to get back on track and, thereby, how to reduce the inflation rate *without* slowing down economic growth" (emphasis added).[1] As this audience knows, there are macroeconomic models that permit disinflation with *no* slowdown in economic growth, but the assumptions underlying these models are very strong.[2] It's not clear, at least to me, why such a strict metric would be used to assess real-world monetary policymaking. Third, the definition of "on track" in the title contrasts with more commonplace definitions such as "achieving or doing what is necessary or expected," as offered by a standard reference such as the Merriam-Webster dictionary.[3] My view is that this commonplace definition provides a more practical lens through which to assess real-world policymaking.

Against this semantic backdrop, I will begin my remarks with my perspective on the current inflation and economic situation. Then, I will consider credit conditions in response to the recent bank stress events. Next, I will offer some normative thoughts about strategic monetary policymaking in highly uncertain environments. Finally, I will argue that if you are willing to widen your lens to include a more commonplace definition, then it is possible to conclude that current monetary policy is, in fact, "on track."

Current inflation is still high. Figure 13.1 illustrates this point. Personal consumption expenditures (PCE) inflation, the black line, stands at 4.2%, and core PCE inflation, the red line, stands at 4.6% for year-end March 2023.

Overall, news on inflation so far this year has been mixed. The good news is that food and energy prices both fell in March, and total PCE inflation slowed to 4.2% from 5% in February. Since peaking in June 2022, inflation has declined about 2.75 percentage points—with nearly all the step-down explained by falling energy prices and slowing food prices. The bad news is that there has been little progress on core inflation.

To understand why, I find it useful to separately analyze three large categories that together make up core PCE (figure 13.2): goods excluding food and energy, the red line; housing services, the black line; and services excluding housing and energy, the blue dashed line. The drivers of inflation in each of these sectors differ somewhat, and understanding the different causes and how they

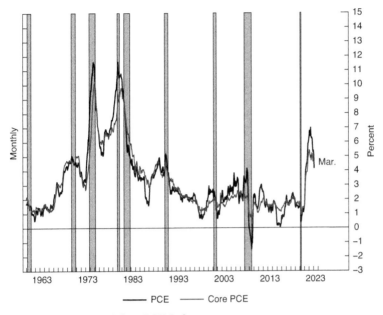

FIGURE 13.1. PCE and Core PCE Inflation.

Notes: Twelve-month percentage change in the personal consumption expenditures (PCE) price index. *Core* refers to the price index excluding food and energy. The gray shaded bars indicate periods of business recession as defined by the National Bureau of Economic Research. The nine shaded recession periods extend from April 1960 through February 1961, December 1969 through November 1970, November 1973 through March 1975, January 1980 through July 1980, July 1981 through November 1982, July 1990 through March 1991, March 2001 through November 2001, December 2007 through June 2009, and February 2020 through April 2020.

Source: Bureau of Economic Analysis, Personal Consumption Expenditures Price Index.

affect the different components can help predict the future course of inflation.

Core goods inflation, the red line in figure 13.2, has come down since its peak of 7.6% in February 2022, but the most recent news has been discouraging. Outside of used motor vehicle prices, which fell unexpectedly in March, disinflation in core goods prices is occurring at a slower pace than expected. Supply and demand imbalances in the goods sector seem to be resolving less quickly than expected. Core housing services inflation, the black line in

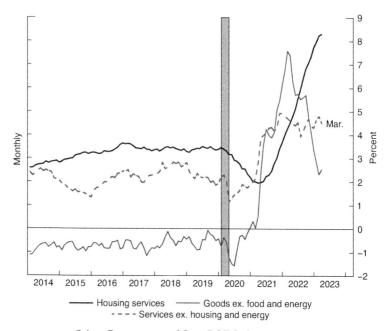

FIGURE 13.2. Select Components of Core PCE Inflation.

Notes: Twelve-month percentage change in select categories of the personal consumption expenditures (PCE) price index. The gray shaded bar indicates a period of business recession as defined by the National Bureau of Economic Research. The shaded recession period extends from February 2020 through April 2020.

Source: Bureau of Economic Analysis, Personal Consumption Expenditures Price Index.

figure 13.2, surged over the past couple of years as demand in the housing sector underwent a major shift during the pandemic. The latest monthly readings have started to slow, though that is not yet evident in the twelve-month changes shown here. The recent slowing was presaged by a flattening out of rents on new leases to new tenants since the middle of last year. In contrast, core services excluding housing inflation, the blue dashed line in figure 13.2, has not shown much sign of slowing.

Turning to labor markets, the April 2023 employment report data continue to point to a strong labor market amid improvements in labor supply, with the prime-age labor force participation rate exceeding its prepandemic level. Wage growth has continued to run ahead of the pace consistent with 2% inflation and current trends in productivity growth. Wage gains are welcome as long as they are consistent with price stability. Over the twelve months ended in March 2023, the employment cost index (ECI) for total hourly compensation for private-sector workers rose 4.8%, down only a little from its peak of 5.5% last June.

Despite strong growth in consumption spending, gross domestic product (GDP) grew modestly at an annual rate of 1.1% in the first quarter of 2023 as inventory investment slowed down substantially, similar to the below-trend pace of growth in 2022. Looking ahead, last quarter's growth in consumer spending seems unsustainable. Indeed, after rising very steeply in January 2023, consumer spending ticked down in February and was flat in March. Moreover, I expect slower consumer spending growth over the remainder of the year in response to tight financial conditions, depressed consumer sentiment, greater uncertainty, and declines in overall household wealth and excess savings.

The tightening in financial conditions we have seen in response to our monetary policy actions is likely to be augmented by the effects on credit conditions from recent strains in the banking sector. The US banking system is sound and resilient. The Federal Reserve, working with other agencies, has taken decisive actions to protect the US economy. Nevertheless, it is reasonable to expect that recent stress events will lead banks to tighten credit standards further.[4] Even though it is too early to tell, my view is that these incremental credit restraints will have a mild retardant effect on economic growth, because the recent bank failures were isolated and addressed swiftly by aggressive macro- and microprudential policy actions.

Nevertheless, I acknowledge that there is significant uncertainty around the amount of tightening of credit conditions in the coming year in response to the bank stress and the magnitude of the effect that tightening might have on the US economy. Therefore, there is some downside risk that the incremental effect of the credit shock is larger than I expect.

The pandemic aftermath, geopolitical instability, and banking sector stress have contributed to a highly uncertain economic environment. Additionally, the numerous postpandemic "surprises" in inflation, employment, and economic growth suggest that the underlying structure of the US economy may be in flux. More simply, the data-generating process for the postpandemic US macroeconomy is less clear.

Due to the proximity of the pandemic and its unprecedented disruptions of economic and social activity, there are currently insufficient postpandemic data to identify the parameters and stable relationships that characterize the possible new structure of the economy. Given this observation, what is a reasonable monetary policymaking strategy? The answer to this question is likely to be different for each monetary policymaker.

I want to share with you a few strategic principles that are important to me. First, policymakers should be ready to react to a wide range of economic conditions with respect to inflation, unemployment, economic growth, and financial stability. The unprecedented pandemic shock is a good reminder that under extraordinary circumstances, it will be difficult to formulate precise forecasts in real time. Our dual mandate from Congress is especially helpful here. It provides the foundation for all our policy decisions. Second, policymakers should clearly communicate monetary policy decisions to the public. Our commitment to transparency should be evident to the public, and monetary policy should be conducted in a way that anchors longer-term inflation expectations. Third—and this is where I am revealing my passion for econometrics—policymakers should continuously update their priors about how the economy works as new data become available. In other words, it is appropriate to change one's perspective as new facts emerge. In this sense, I am in favor of a Bayesian approach to information processing.

While these principles do not constitute a complete monetary policymaking framework, I think they are useful when thinking about the features of such frameworks.

By way of concluding, I would like to return to the question of whether current monetary policy is "on track" but allow for the wider defining lens of "achieving or doing what is necessary or expected." The national unemployment rate was 3.6% in March 2022, when the current monetary policy tightening cycle began. Today, after 500 basis points of tightening the policy rate, the national unemployment rate stands at a near-record low of 3.4%. At its recent peak, total PCE inflation was 7% in June 2022. Currently, it is 4.2% in March 2023. Is inflation still too high? Yes. Has the current disinflation been uneven and slower than any of us would like? Yes. But my reading of this evidence is that we are "doing what is necessary or expected" of us.

Furthermore, monetary policy affects the economy and inflation with long and varied lags, and the full effects of our rapid tightening are still likely ahead of us. We are balancing the directives of the dual mandate given to us by the US Congress. This is not an easy task in these uncertain times, but I can assure you that my colleagues on the Federal Open Market Committee and I take it quite seriously and with great humility. It is in this sense that I believe that we are well "on track."

Thank you.

References

Croushore, Dean. 1992. "What Are the Costs of Disinflation?" Federal Reserve Bank of Philadelphia *Business Review* (May/June): 3–15.

Goodfriend, Marvin, and Robert G. King. 2005. "The Incredible Volcker Disinflation," *Journal of Monetary Economics* 52, no. 5 (July): 981–1015.

Sargent, Thomas J. 1983. "Stopping Moderate Inflations: The Methods of Poincaré and Thatcher." In *Inflation, Debt, and Indexation*, edited by Rudiger Dornbusch and Mario Henrique Simonsen, 54–96. Cambridge, MA: MIT Press.

Tetlow, Robert J. 2022. "How Large Is the Output Cost of Disinflation?" Finance and Economics Discussion Series 2022-079, Board of Governors of the Federal Reserve System, November.

Notes

1. See this conference's web page at https://www.hoover.org/events/how -get-back-track-policy-conference.
2. Estimates of the cost of disinflation depend on the model used to measure it. Classical models, in which rational expectations play a dominant role in determining the cost of disinflation, show low cost, while Keynesian models, in which slack in the economy is needed to reduce inflation, show high cost. See, for example, Sargent (1983), Croushore (1992), Goodfriend and King (2005), and Tetlow (2022) for a comparison of the cost of disinflation across macroeconomic forecasting models.
3. See the definition for "track" at Merriam-Webster, https://www.merriam -webster.com/dictionary/on%20track.
4. The April 2023 Senior Loan Officer Opinion Survey on Bank Lending Practices (SLOOS) shows that banks, especially small and midsize banks, reported further tightening in credit standards on loans to businesses and households over the past three months, following widespread tightening in previous quarters. The April 2023 SLOOS is available on the Board's website at https://www.federalreserve.gov/data/sloos/sloos-202304.htm.

14

The Fed Should Improve Communications by Talking about Systematic Policy Rules

Jeffrey M. Lacker and Charles I. Plosser

Introduction

The Federal Reserve is facing the most challenging inflationary surge in more than a generation. Inflation began to rise in the second half of 2020 and has remained elevated well above its long-run target of 2%. The price index for personal consumption expenditures (PCE) rose 6.0% for 2021 and 5.3% for 2022.[1] These are the highest rates seen since the end of the Great Inflation in the early 1980s.

After more than a year of asserting that the elevated inflation would be short lived, the Federal Reserve began tightening in March 2022, and the stance of monetary policy shifted dramatically. By December 2022, the Federal Open Market Committee (FOMC) had raised the federal funds rate target by 400 basis points to a range of 4.25 to 4.50% and had begun shrinking the balance sheet.[2] The monetary policy outlook changed as well. The median federal funds rate deemed appropriate by FOMC participants for the fourth quarter of 2023 was 4.6% in September 2022 and 5.1% in March 2023, up from 1.0% in September 2021. Many FOMC participants have explicitly stated their resolve to reduce inflation, even at the cost of weaker economic activity and job markets. Several have emphasized that stopping short of bringing inflation back down to the target in the interest of ameliorating the short-term costs would be more costly in the long run.

Bringing inflation back to the Fed's 2% target will require reducing spending growth and cooling off the labor market. At the time of this writing, May 2023, that process has only just begun. Signs of slowing are apparent in housing markets and, to a lesser extent, in consumer spending. Nevertheless, much of the fight against inflation remains ahead. Despite the decline in job openings in recent months, the labor market is still generally quite tight, with unemployment rates and initial claims still low. Wage rates are still advancing at inflationary rates. Consumer and business expectations for inflation over the next year or so remain elevated, and inflation is showing a breadth and persistence that it lacked when the surge began.

While near-term inflation expectations are relatively high, increases in measures of expected inflation at longer horizons have been more modest—a relatively bright spot in the economic outlook. The stability of longer-term inflation expectations suggests that consumers and firms believe the FOMC will likely bring inflation back down to near its 2% target within a few years. It is unclear, however, how well the public understands what might be required to achieve that goal. Financial market projections for the path of the federal funds rate have risen significantly since early 2022 as inflation readings persistently exceeded expectations and the FOMC raised its projections. And yet, in the summer of 2022, market participants, for a time, priced in a Fed "pivot" to easing for the first half of 2023, anticipating that weakness in real activity would, in turn, induce an early policy reversal. It was a misperception that FOMC participants sought to dispel in public communications, including Chairman Jerome Powell's succinct and forceful statement of resolve at Jackson Hole (Powell 2022).

Speculation about a "pivot" to a less restrictive policy outlook reemerged after public statements by FOMC participants before the November 2022 FOMC meeting seemed to suggest reducing the rate of increase in the federal funds rate target from 75 basis points per meeting to 50 basis points. The statement issued following that meeting included new forward guidance language that was taken as signaling *both* a reduced pace of tightening and a generally less restrictive medium-term policy path than had been anticipated.[3] Bond and equity prices rose quickly on the statement's release, consistent with market participants viewing the policy outlook as more accommodative. Chairman Powell pushed back forcefully at the press conference after the meeting, taking pains to separate the pace of rate increases from the question of how high the Fed would ultimately raise the policy rate, stating that the latter was higher than had been thought at the September meeting. He emphasized that "we have some ground left to cover here and cover it we will."[4] Financial markets reversed course.

The gyrations in public perceptions of the Fed's likely policy course were the result of significant gaps in the FOMC's communications and could have been avoided. While the committee foreshadows the future level of interest rates participants view as likely to be appropriate in its quarterly release of the Summary of Economic Projections (SEP), it has provided only vague guidance on the *determinants* of the ultimate level interest rates will reach. The November FOMC statement stated it intends "to attain a stance of monetary policy that is *sufficiently restrictive* to return inflation to 2% over time." (emphasis added) By itself, this provides no analytical guidance at all and places tremendous weight on the indeterminant qualitative phrase "sufficiently restrictive."[5]

Fed officials generally define "restrictive" as an interest rate setting above "the neutral rate," but some have struggled to coherently convey the meaning of "neutral." At times, the neutral federal funds rate has been identified with the median longer-run projection of 2.5% for the federal funds rate in the FOMC's SEPs. For example, after the July 2022 FOMC meeting, Chairman Powell stated that the committee believed that the federal funds rate target (then 2.25 to 2.50%) was "at" neutral in this sense.[6] But the interest rate that moderates the incentive of businesses and consumers to delay or advance spending is clearly the ex ante real interest rate—that is, the nominal rate minus the expected inflation rate.[7] The neutral or "natural" rate that divides expansive from restrictive policy is thus a real, inflation-adjusted interest rate.[8] A 2.5% longer-run federal funds rate, with a longer-run inflation projection of 2.0%, thus delivers a neutral real federal funds rate of one-half. When inflation is running over 5%, 2.5% is decidedly not a "neutral" rate setting but is instead quite expansionary. Federal Reserve Bank of New York president John Williams corrected the record in an interview with the *Wall Street Journal* one month later.[9]

In the months following the committee's introduction of the phrase "sufficiently restrictive," the media and financial markets devoted considerable attention to deciphering its meaning. Fed officials are regularly asked about what level of the federal funds rate they view as sufficiently restrictive. To what principles should they look for their assessments of when to pause rate hikes? How should they explain their assessments? How should they respond to complaints they are "overdoing it" or are risking inflation becoming "entrenched"? How should they convince the public that they have indeed raised rates to a level sufficient to bring inflation down to their 2% target?

Fortunately, there is a well-established framework in monetary economics that provides much-needed guidance. Systematic monetary policy rules, such as those proposed by John Taylor relating the Fed's interest rate settings to measures of inflation and real activity, can capture the patterns of policy response that have successfully reduced inflation in the past. They are grounded in historical experience and performance across a range of compelling economic models, and thus, their prescriptions provide sound guidance for monetary policy. In 2014, one of us (Plosser 2014) publicly called for the Federal Reserve to take a step toward a more systematic policy framework by regular public reporting and discussion of the likely behavior of interest rate policy based on a few

Taylor-style rules. The Federal Reserve began reporting on such rules in its semiannual *Monetary Policy Report* (MPR) to Congress in July 2017. The Federal Reserve, however, almost never references the prescriptions emanating from these rules in its regular communications to the public about policy.[10]

The FOMC can and should routinely reference the implications of such a range of monetary policy rules when publicly discussing the likely future path of interest rates. This would not require taking the step of committing to any one particular rule. Policymakers could simply note that the successful pursuit of the Fed's mandate is likely to require policy settings that are broadly aligned with the magnitude of various rule prescriptions. Talking about policy rule prescriptions in this way would guide public expectations about how high interest rates might need to rise to restore price stability and how that path is likely to depend on incoming data. Policy rule prescriptions provide an empirically grounded basis for estimating what level of interest rates will be "sufficiently restrictive." Also, referencing policy rules would provide a benchmark to dampen the perception that Fed policy decisions are arbitrary or motivated by distributional considerations or political pressures. Greater use of policy rules in communications, thus, could bolster the credibility of the Federal Reserve's resolve and thereby reduce the costs of disinflation.

Systematic Monetary Policy Rules

Since John Taylor's seminal paper proposing simple rules as a method of encapsulating the conduct of monetary policy over time, a large research literature has studied the properties of various versions of such rules (Taylor 1993; Taylor and Williams 2010; Teryoshin 2023). In particular, research has examined how policy has behaved in the past and looked for versions of policy rules that delivered successful outcomes in practice and across a range of empirically grounded models of inflation and real activity.

While there are a variety of desirable policy rules, they share a few basic properties. One is that the policy rate rises more than one-for-one with inflation, a feature known as the "Taylor principle" (Taylor 1999; Woodford 2001). The intuition for this result rests on two ideas. One is that expected inflation often closely tracks lagged inflation, so increases in realized inflation typically signal commensurately higher expected inflation. The other is that the interest rate net of expected inflation (the ex ante *real* interest rate) summarizes the stance of monetary policy since it represents the incentive to substitute away from current spending by delaying outlays. When inflation rises, spending restraint is called for; thus, real interest rates should rise. Thus, the policy rate—which is a nominal interest rate—should increase by more than the increase in expected inflation—otherwise, real interest rates fall, and consumers and firms have an enhanced incentive to spend more to avoid imminent price hikes. This is what happened in 2021; real interest rates fell significantly as the Fed held the federal funds rate near zero while inflation and expected inflation rose.

Another property of successful rules that is important for success is that the policy rate should respond to a measure of real resource utilization, rising when activity is relatively strong (for example, when unemployment is low) and falling when activity is relatively weak (for example, when unemployment is high), all else constant (Goodfriend and King 1997). This property reflects the fact that strong real activity is associated with heightened pressure on aggregate supply, in which case it is desirable to raise real interest rates to encourage consumers and firms to postpone spending, and vice versa when real activity is weak.

A wide range of research has shown the value of simple monetary policy rules that embody these principles (Taylor and Williams 2010). These rules perform well in a wide variety of models and are often more robust than a rule that is fully optimal in a specific model. Such rules capture the behavior of central banks during periods of good economic outcomes fairly well, such as during the Great Moderation. During periods of poor performance, such as the Great Inflation of the 1960s and 1970s, central bank behavior deviates from the principles underlying good rules. For these reasons, many economists have urged the Federal Reserve to make greater use of such monetary policy rules in the formulation and communication of monetary policy (Levin 2014; Plosser 2014; Taylor 2017; Hetzel 2019; Ireland 2020).[11] In fact, the Federal Reserve's semi-annual *Monetary Policy Report* to Congress routinely includes a section discussing the prescriptions of several specific policy rules in the current environment.[12] Prescriptions of these monetary policy rules are routinely compiled and have been shared with committee participants before each FOMC meeting since 2004. And Chairman Powell has noted that the committee is aware of policy rule prescriptions, but their influence on policy is seldom publicly discussed.

However, by its own account, the Fed diverged significantly from policy rule prescriptions in late 2021. In the Fed's June 2022 MPR, all versions of the Taylor rule are shown prescribing lift-off for the federal funds rate target in the second or third quarter of 2021 and a federal funds rate ranging between 4% and 7% for the first quarter of 2022.[13] The reason reflected not just the increases in inflation but the rapid fall in the unemployment rate from the peak of 14.7% in April 2020 to 6.0% by April 2021. Thus the FOMC found itself far behind the curve in confronting inflation, necessitating the rapid response witnessed since the spring of 2022.[14] Papell and Prodan (2023) compare real-time Taylor rule prescriptions to the FOMC's policy settings and economic projections from September 2020 through March 2023; they also demonstrate how far behind the Fed was in late 2021 and early 2022.

The FOMC has rapidly raised the policy rate as it recognized that it was far behind the curve. As a result, the gap is shrinking between the prescriptions of systematic policy rules and the actual policy stance. We can see this in table 14.1, which displays

TABLE 14.1. Policy Rule Prescriptions Using March 2023 FOMC Economic Projections.

Federal Funds Rate	Q4 2022	Q1 2023	Q4 2023	Q4 2024	Q4 2025
Taylor (1993)	8.42	7.24	4.15	2.88	2.28
Taylor (1999)	8.79	7.69	3.85	2.50	1.90
Taylor (1999) with core inflation	7.51	7.38	4.30	2.65	1.90
Median FOMC projections			5.10	4.30	3.10
Actual federal funds rate	3.65	4.51			

Economic Data and Projections	Actuals		Median FOMC Projections		
PCE price index*	5.69	4.86	3.30	2.50	2.10
Core PCE price index*	4.84	4.65	3.60	2.60	2.10
Unemployment rate	3.60	3.50	4.50	4.60	4.60

Note: FOMC projections for the average federal funds rate for the fourth quarter of 2023, made in March 2023, are below the prescriptions of representative Taylor rules, under the assumption that economic data on inflation and unemployment are consistent with FOMC projections.

* Year-over-year percentage change

Sources: FRED, Federal Reserve Bank of St. Louis; Federal Open Market Committee, Summary of Economic Projections, March 22, 2023 (authors' calculations).

prescriptions for the federal funds rate over the next two years from three widely investigated policy rules: Taylor's 1993 and 1999 rules and Taylor's 1999 rule using core inflation instead of headline inflation.[15]

The reported calculations use the median projections for inflation and unemployment from the FOMC's March 2023 Summary of Economic Projections. The average federal funds rate for the first quarter of 2023 is well below the range of these policy rule prescriptions, indicating that the Fed is still catching up to where policy ought to be.

As Chairman Powell emphasized in the lead-up to the December 2022 FOMC meeting, the medium-term path of the federal funds rate is more important than the size of the rate increase at any specific meeting.[16] Looking ahead to the fourth quarter of 2023, the median federal funds rate projections from the March 2023 FOMC meeting are higher than the prescriptions of policy rules shown in table 14.1. Recall that the federal funds rate projections are based on median participant projections for inflation and unemployment. FOMC participants projected a relatively rapid decline in inflation for 2023. Specifically, the median projection for the four-quarter percent change in the price index for personal consumption expenditures falls to 3.3% as of the fourth quarter of 2023 from 5.7% for the fourth quarter of 2022. For the core version of that index, the four-quarter percent change is projected to fall to 3.6% versus 4.8% for Q4 2022. As a result, the policy rules also would be expected to decline from their peak, and all three versions of the Taylor rule do so.

Alternative assumptions about the course of inflation and unemployment lead to different policy rule prescriptions. If we instead assume, for example, that inflation persists through the end of 2023 at the four-quarter rate registered for the first quarter—holding the projected unemployment rate path the same as in the March 2023 SEPs—we get higher recommended policy paths, as shown in table 14.2. Since inflation has proven surprisingly persistent over

TABLE 14.2. Policy Rule Prescriptions with More Persistent Inflation.

Federal Funds Rate	Q4 2022	Q1 2023	Q4 2023	Q4 2024	Q4 2025
Taylor (1993)	8.42	7.24	6.49	4.08	2.28
Taylor (1999)	8.79	7.69	6.19	3.70	1.90
Taylor (1999) with core inflation	7.51	7.38	5.88	4.15	1.90
Median FOMC projections			5.10	4.30	3.10
Actual federal funds rate	3.65	4.51			

Economic Data and Projections	Actuals		Alternative Projections		
PCE price index*	5.69	4.86	4.86	3.30	2.10
Core PCE price index*	4.84	4.65	4.65	3.60	2.10
Unemployment rate	3.60	3.50	4.50	4.60	4.60

Note: The prescriptions of representative Taylor rules for the fourth quarter of 2023 are higher than FOMC projections under the assumption that inflation does not fall.

* Year-over-year percentage change

Sources: FRED, Federal Reserve Bank of St. Louis; Federal Open Market Committee, Summary of Economic Projections, March 22, 2023 (authors' calculations).

the past year, continually exceeding the FOMC's projections, this would appear to be a plausible scenario.

In this persistent inflation scenario, the three policy rules recommend a federal funds rate between 5.9 and 6.5%—2 to 2.5 percentage points *higher* by the fourth quarter of 2023 than in the more favorable inflation scenario envisioned by the FOMC. The March 2023 SEP median federal funds rate projection, at 5.1%, lies well below these three prescriptions. While the March SEP projected policy path is in line with or a bit above the systematic policy rules under the assumption that inflation subsides rapidly in the coming year, more persistent inflation could necessitate a significantly higher rate path. Systematic policy rules provide a transparent and well-grounded method of conveying the way in which the policy path responds to economic outcomes.

If, in addition to inflation proving more persistent than the FOMC projected in March 2023, the unemployment rate failed to rise as sharply as it envisioned, policy rules would prescribe even higher federal funds rate paths. Table 14.3 shows the implications of assuming that disinflation occurs one year later than the FOMC projects, as in table 14.2, *plus* the unemployment rate remains at 3.5% through the fourth quarter of 2023.

In this scenario, these three policy rules recommend a federal funds rate of between 7.2 and 7.7% for the fourth quarter of 2023. Again, systematic policy rules provide a transparent and well-grounded method of conveying how the policy path responds to economic outcomes.

The shift in policy rule prescriptions in response to alternative assumed paths for inflation and unemployment illustrates how useful it would be to reference such rules in FOMC communications. As forecasts of future inflation and unemployment vary with incoming data, policymakers could point to such rule prescriptions as indicative of how the outlook for the policy rate path might need to evolve. Indeed, data received between the

TABLE 14.3. Policy Rule Prescriptions with Persistent Inflation, Tight Labor Market.

Federal Funds Rate	Q4 2022	Q1 2023	Q4 2023	Q4 2024	Q4 2025
Taylor (1993)	8.42	7.24	7.24	4.15	2.28
Taylor (1999)	8.79	7.69	7.69	3.85	1.90
Taylor (1999) with core inflation	7.51	7.38	7.38	4.30	1.90
Median FOMC projections			5.10	4.30	3.10
Actual federal funds rate	3.65	4.51			
Economic Data and Projections	Actuals		Alternative Projections		
PCE price index*	5.69	4.86	4.86	3.30	2.10
Core PCE price index*	4.84	4.65	4.65	3.60	2.10
Unemployment rate	3.60	3.50	3.50	4.50	4.60

Note: The prescriptions of representative Taylor rules for the fourth quarter of 2023 are much higher than FOMC projections under the assumption that inflation does not fall and unemployment does not rise.

* Year-over-year percentage change

Sources: FRED, Federal Reserve Bank of St. Louis; Federal Open Market Committee, Summary of Economic Projections, March 22, 2023 (authors' calculations).

September and November 2022 FOMC meetings led to upward revisions in inflation forecasts. In the press conference following the November 2022 meeting, Chairman Powell said that he believed the projected federal funds rate path would have been higher had one been compiled.[17] If market participants had been conditioned by past FOMC communications to connect, even loosely, the expected federal funds rate path to a range of policy rule prescriptions, the confusion and whipsaw movements in financial asset prices on the afternoon of November 2, 2022, might have been avoided. The FOMC would not have had to place so much weight on the phrase "sufficiently restrictive." Policy rule prescriptions would provide a natural reference point for what the FOMC means by that phrase. They would also provide a quantitative sense of how policy is "data dependent."

One last point deserves emphasis. The notion that making use of monetary policy rules requires handing over interest rate settings to a specific algebraic formula for setting the federal funds rate is a straw man. In the current circumstances, such a claim serves to preserve discretion and evade discussion of the magnitude of policy tightening that is likely needed to restore price stability. The FOMC could make much greater use of a range of monetary policy rules in public commentary about future policy without turning the federal funds rate over to an algorithm. The goal would be not to make pinpoint promises about the future path of rates but to convey likely paths, the associated uncertainty, and dependence of the path on the evolution of the economy.

The Case for Referencing Monetary Policy Rule Prescriptions in FOMC Communications

The Federal Reserve should make more extensive references to systematic monetary policy rules in communicating about monetary policy. Doing so would have been particularly constructive in the current tightening cycle, which began in March 2022. For example, in public speeches, testimony, and press conferences, Fed speakers should have pointed to rule prescriptions for the federal funds rate path under plausible near-term paths for macroeconomic variables. They could have noted that such prescriptions are derived from historical evidence on how the Fed responded in the past when it successfully reduced inflation. They could have noted that success in restoring price stability would likely require an FOMC response in line with the prescriptions of such rules. In this way, Fed speakers would be providing a transparent scientific grounding for how high and how rapidly the Fed might have to raise interest rates. Individual policymakers could cite particular rules they find compelling or desirable on methodological grounds, just as they do now with regard to particular price indices. But there is no need to select a personal favorite; they could simply cite the prescriptions from the representative collection of rules included in the MPR to Congress.[18]

Bolster Credibility

Public reference to rule prescriptions in discussing the monetary policy outlook would yield a number of benefits. First and foremost, it would help bolster the credibility of the Fed's commitment to price stability. Fed officials have made a special point of conveying their resolve to ensure that inflation returns soon to its 2% target, even if that means some economic hardship. Perhaps the major risk to the economic outlook in mid-2022 to late 2022 was the possibility that the Fed might come to be seen as not maintaining that resolve in the event that the economy actually does slip into recession. Overall, labor market conditions are still exceptionally tight, despite emerging pockets of weakness. But when labor market conditions weaken, as they must if the Fed is to slow spending enough to get inflation back under control, calls will emerge from many quarters for the Fed to suspend its fight against inflation and forestall a contraction. Indeed, we are already seeing complaints that the Fed is running the risk of "overshooting" or "overdoing it." Since monetary policy operates famously with "long and variable lags," current data alone will not say whether Fed policy has overshot or undershot.

The FOMC will likely decide to stop increasing or start reducing the federal funds rate before twelve-month inflation actually has returned to target. Doing so will immediately raise the question of how the committee decided to stop where it did. The choice runs the risk of appearing relatively arbitrary unless the committee can provide a compelling rationale. The rhetoric of "risk management," describing monetary policy as balancing perceived probabilities of various future developments, is vague and opaque and leaves it open to second-guessing. The compelling guide to monetary policy is the historical evidence of what has led to successful disinflations in the past—exactly the information that is encoded in monetary policy rules. Anchoring communication about a policy pivot in systematic policy rules will reduce the risk of compromising the Fed's credibility.

On the other hand, resisting premature calls for easing will be essential to avoiding the stop-go policy pattern of the 1970s, in which recessions prompted policy easing before inflation had fully subsided. As the public came to understand this propensity, inflation became more entrenched and harder to suppress. Indeed, several FOMC members, including Chairman Powell, repeatedly have noted that while the current policy tightening does run a risk of inducing a recession, that risk is preferable to allowing inflation to persist, necessitating even more costly action down the road. Monetary policy rules also capture how the Fed avoided overresponding to weakening economic activity during regimes in which policy was relatively successful. Again, aligning policy with such regimes can help the Fed navigate a recession without sacrificing credibility.

Bolstering the Fed's credibility can, in turn, reduce the costs of restoring price stability. Reducing doubts about the Fed's commitment would reduce uncertainty about inflation at longer horizons and thus keep longer-run inflation expectations better anchored. Expectations of imminent disinflation would also dampen pricing pressures in the short run, helping the Fed's cause. Well-anchored inflation expectations would reduce the likelihood that the Fed needs to take costly measures to re-establish its credibility.

Clarity about the Policy

The relatively small increase in measures of longer-run inflation suggests that at present, consumers and firms believe that the Fed is likely to follow through on its commitment to do what is required to bring inflation back down to target within a few years. And yet a lack of clarity is apparent regarding what it will take. As noted earlier, the expected interest rate path has fluctuated significantly over the last year, inducing significant swings in financial asset prices, as markets conjectured an early Fed easing next year in response to weakening economic activity. At present, the public seems to be operating without a clear understanding of the principles governing how high rates will need to go to accomplish the Fed's avowed objective. To better anchor its expectations, the Fed should direct its attention to the historical evidence on the characteristics of successful monetary policy practices and the implications for the likely magnitude of tightening required by the current inflationary surge. Explicitly referencing the prescriptions of systematic monetary policy rules can do that.

Transparent Data Dependence

Another benefit of framing monetary policy by referencing monetary policy rules is that it would convey the way the policy rate path is likely to vary with incoming economic data. Fed officials often describe their policy as "data-dependent" without providing much information on just how the policy will vary with future data. The outlook for inflation has varied significantly in recent quarters, but the Fed has struggled to convey to the markets how the federal funds rate path will likely be affected. Indeed, in his contribution to this conference, Mickey Levy (see chapter 11) documented the magnitude of the upward revisions to the Fed's inflation projections during this tightening cycle and the accompanying revisions to the federal funds rate outlook. The Fed initially projected a relatively rapid disinflation but has had to revise its outlook as inflation proved more persistent than expected. The projections of the federal funds rate path have been revised upward as well. When inflation first emerged in 2021, the FOMC could have prepared the public for scenarios—reasonably plausible at the time—in which inflation fails to subside as rapidly as it projected.[19] The Fed could have cited systematic monetary policy rules that imply that all else equal, the federal funds rate would be correspondingly higher. Framing monetary policy in terms of historically successful rules would help participants draw a quantitative connection between scenarios in which inflation proves more persistent than they expect and higher policy rates. Such an approach would improve upon the vague "risk management" approach in which that connection is obscured.

On the other hand, policy rules would also help clarify the circumstances in which the committee would cease raising rates. Speculation has been widespread about the FOMC's contemplation of a pause in rate increases to "take a look around" to see what effect rate increases were having. Pausing rate increases before inflation has fully returned to target makes sense, given the long and variable lags that have long been known to characterize how changes in the stance of monetary policy affect the economy. But how is the public to predict when such a pause might take place? And how would the committee justify the point at which it chooses to pause? Monetary policy rules provide the natural answers. They provide prescriptions for how high interest rates should be for any given *actual* inflation rate and real activity measure in order to successfully disinflate. Such relationships implicitly build in historical lags in how future outcomes connect to current data and policy settings. While there may be a range of prescriptions, depending on the particular version, their connection to historical periods of monetary policy success can provide a relevant anchor. Without such an anchor, the choice of when to pause could well be perceived as arbitrary, leaving the Fed vulnerable to accusations of favoritism or political influence.

Similarly, grounding policy setting in monetary policy rules would help anchor discussions about when incoming data might reveal enough weakening to warrant the Fed reversing course and easing policy. It would quantify how much weakness would justify a cut in interest rates without jeopardizing price stability. Indeed, policy rule prescriptions supported the need for monetary stimulus at the moment the pandemic hit in early 2020. Further down the road, monetary policy rule prescriptions would help the Fed avoid the chronic problem of delaying the exit from monetary ease (Bordo and Levy 2022).[20]

Constructive Forward Guidance

Referencing historically successful monetary policy rules would be a constructive method for the FOMC to provide forward guidance. The traditional method involving qualitative or quantitative committee statements about future interest rate settings or asset purchases has encountered a number of pitfalls. One stems from the ambiguity in such statements about whether the committee was conveying information about its reaction function or its economic outlook. The committee often intended the former, seeking to encourage the belief that it would hold rates "lower for longer" than market participants had believed, only to find that the forward guidance announcement led market participants to believe that the FOMC was more pessimistic about the outlook than they had thought. Emphasizing the implications of systematic policy rules that the committee is likely to need to emulate would convey information about the Fed's reaction function without implicating the committee's economic outlook.

Another pitfall in traditional forward guidance practice is the tension it creates with the notion that policy will be "data dependent." Emphasizing systematic rule-like behavior is a natural way for the Fed to stress its reaction function or data dependence. Framing decision making in this manner is far more appropriate and likely to be more effective than the Fed's halting and confusing steps to offer forward guidance as if it were some kind of independent tool. Referencing systematic policy rules would help integrate communication about forward guidance with the usual meeting-to-meeting policy-setting process.

Framing forward guidance in terms of systematic policy rules would also alleviate the problem that arises when being seen as complying with past forward guidance conflicts with the policy response indicated by incoming data.[21] This tension was evident in late 2021 when forward guidance about the sequencing of asset purchase tapering and rate increases delayed the lift-off that incoming data indicated was urgently needed. Monetary policy rules build in responsiveness to incoming economic data in a way that is more continuous than the process of invoking an "escape clause." Explaining policy as a systematic pattern of response or reaction function is likely to be as close to a credible commitment as the Fed can achieve while describing the future outlook for policy. It would be more easily understood by the public as well.

Improved Clarity and Precision of Communications

Referencing monetary policy rules would also allow the Fed to avoid confusion about elusive abstract concepts such as "the neutral rate" when discussing the likely future path of interest rates. The media and financial markets, and at times Fed officials, have identified "the neutral federal funds rate" with the longer-run projection for the federal funds rate in the FOMC's SEP. In this context, a neutral interest rate corresponds to the concept, attributed to Knut Wicksell, of a "natural" interest rate that prevails in a hypothetical equilibrium without inflation or deflation, the idea being that rates above that restrain the economy while rates below that provide stimulus.[22] In the September 2022 SEP, participants' longer-run federal funds projections ranged from 2.3 to 3.0%, with a median of 2.5%. In the same SEP, every participant projected inflation to be at 2.0% in the longer run. But inflation now is running above 5%, and inflation expectations are above 2%. FOMC participants thus project the real federal funds rate to be between 0.3 and 1.0% in the longer run, with a median of 0.5%. The natural interest rate varies continually over time with economic conditions, a point emphasized by Marvin Goodfriend and Robert King (1997), as well as Michael Woodford (2003). And it certainly varies with the expected rate of inflation; as noted above, it is the ex ante real interest rate that moderates the incentive of consumers and firms to delay current spending. The 2.5% median SEP projection for the nominal federal funds rate in the longer run, when inflation has settled at 2%, is irrelevant as a benchmark for gauging the current stance of monetary policy when inflation is above 5%.

Some Federal Reserve officials have referred to the FOMC's longer-run projections for the nominal federal funds rate as the "neutral" rate and have talked about rates above that as "restrictive." For example, after the July 2022 FOMC meeting, Chairman Powell stated that the committee believed the funds rate target— then 2.25 to 2.50%—was "at" neutral in the sense that it matched up with the longer-run federal funds rate projections in the SEP.[23] With inflation running at 5% or more, a federal funds rate of 2.5% implies a real, inflation-adjusted rate of negative 2.5% or below— quite stimulative by historical standards. In an interview a month later, Federal Reserve Bank of New York president John Williams provided a very different analysis, describing the neutral rate as a longer-run *real* federal funds rate of about one-half and stating that the nominal interest rate minus what inflation is expected to be over the next year needed to rise above that.[24] Williams's approach represents an application of the Taylor principle, and it would be just a small further step to appeal to the historical record embodied in monetary policy rules as the appropriate benchmark for assessing the stance of monetary policy.

Conclusion

The Fed is facing many challenges. Some, if not most, are self-inflicted. The changes it made to its strategic framework in

August 2020 contributed to an inflationary bias in its approach to policy and significant confusion on the part of the public. It constituted a significant departure from the past. This left the Fed unprepared and somewhat confused when faced with the inflationary consequences of the pandemic and the aggressive stimulus provided by monetary and fiscal policies during and following the crisis.[25] Its policy response was at first denial, blaming inflation on exogenous and transitory forces beyond its control. The result was surging inflation and public questioning of the Fed's commitment to price stability. Belatedly, it reversed course. It forcefully reaffirmed its commitment to price stability and began to tighten policy assertively. Better late than never. However, despite the messages and near-term actions, there is much ambiguity and uncertainty over the path of policy going forward.

The hard work of restoring price stability has just begun. Reducing inflation will require a sustained effort to restrain aggregate nominal demand. That will slow economic growth and soften the labor market. More difficult challenges will arise as the slowdown becomes more apparent. The Fed will come under increasing pressure to back off its fight against inflation and turn its attention to promoting economic expansion and employment growth in particular. As the slowdown continues, political pressure will undoubtedly grow for the Fed to reverse course. This is when the real test of the Fed's resolve will arise. Federal Reserve officials have expressed their determination to resist the urge to ease prematurely or too quickly, which would only prolong high inflation. Maintaining its stated resolve will be easier if the Fed describes what it believes will be necessary and what principles will guide its decisions in more objectively grounded, quantitative terms. Such efforts will give the public a better understanding of the Fed's underlying reaction function and, thus, how its policy will evolve as the economy evolves. Such efforts will help minimize the extent to which speculation about the Fed's intentions drives financial market volatility.

In this essay, we argue that there is a well-established framework that can provide much-needed guidance, enhance transparency, and improve communication and accountability. Economists have learned that simple policy rules, such as those suggested by John Taylor that describe how interest rates should be set in response to changes in inflation and real activity, provide good results in a wide range of models. Such rules are also grounded in historical experience; central bank behavior aligned with desirable simple rules has yielded good economic outcomes, while significant departures from the set of desirable rules have led to monetary instability and adverse economic outcomes. That is, the prescriptions of simple policy rules provide important and useful guidance for monetary policy in a wide range of economic conditions.

Referencing systematic policy rules that are grounded in historical experience can be a constructive way for the Fed to communicate about the likely path of monetary policy. In the current environment, referencing the prescriptions of such rules can provide valuable information to the public about how high rates might need to go and the conditions that might give rise to a pivot in policy or a reduction in rates. Such references would not constitute rigid commitments but would be more informative to markets and the public than the subjective, discretionary, "trust me" approach that largely describes current practice. Moreover, referencing systematic policy rules can bolster the Fed's credibility—so crucially important now—by making policy more transparent and understandable. Doing so can only help reduce the costs of restoring price stability.

References

Bordo, Michael D., Andrew T. Levin, and Mickey D. Levy. 2020. "Incorporating Scenario Analysis into the Federal Reserve's Policy Strategy and Communications." National Bureau of Economic Research Working Paper 27369, June.

Bordo, Michael D., and Mickey D. Levy. 2022. "The Fed's Delayed Exits from Monetary Ease: The Fed Rarely Learns from History." Shadow Open Market Committee, February 11.

Bullard, James. 2022a. "Is the Fed 'Behind the Curve'? Two Interpretations." Presented at the Hoover Monetary Policy Conference, Hoover Institution, Stanford University, May 6.

———. 2022b. "Getting into the Zone." Presented at the Regional Economic Development Update, Louisville, Kentucky, November 17.

Goodfriend, Marvin, and Robert King. 1997. "The New Neoclassical Synthesis and the Role of Monetary Policy." In *NBER Macroeconomics Annual 12*, edited by Ben S. Bernanke and Julio J. Rotemberg, 231–83. Cambridge, MA: MIT Press.

Hetzel, Robert L. 2019. "Rules vs. Discretion Revisited: A Proposal to Make the Strategy of Monetary Policy Transparent." Mercatus Working Paper, June 25.

Humphrey, Thomas M. 1986. "Cumulative Process Models from Thornton to Wicksell." Federal Reserve Bank of Richmond *Economic Review* (May/June): 18–25.

Ireland, Peter. 2020. "Monetary Policy Rules: SOMC History and a Recent Case Study." Shadow Open Market Committee, March 6.

Lacker, Jeffrey M. 2019. "Forward Guidance: A Comment." *Journal of Monetary Economics* 102 (April): 24–28.

Levin, Andrew T. 2014. "The Design and Communication of Systematic Monetary Policy Strategies." *Journal of Economic Dynamics and Control* 49 (December): 52–69.

Levy, Mickey D., and Charles I. Plosser. 2022. "The Murky Future of Monetary Policy." Federal Reserve Bank of St. Louis *Review* 104, no. 3 (Third Quarter): 178–88.

Papell, David H., and Ruxandra Prodan. 2022. "Policy Rules and Forward Guidance following the COVID-19 Recession." *SSRN Electronic Journal,* April 14 (Revised May 3, 2023).

Plosser, Charles I. 2013. "Forward Guidance." Presented at the Stanford Institute for Economic Policy Research, Stanford, California, February 12.

———. 2014. "Systematic Monetary Policy and Communication." Presented at the Economic Club of New York, New York, June 24.

Powell, Jerome H. 2022. "Monetary Policy and Price Stability." Presented at "Reassessing Constraints on the Economy and Policy," an economic policy symposium sponsored by the Federal Reserve Bank of Kansas City, Jackson Hole, Wyoming, August 26.

Taylor, John B. 1993. "Discretion versus Policy Rules in Practice." *Carnegie-Rochester Conference Series on Public Policy* 39: 195–214. Amsterdam: North-Holland.

———. 1999. "A Historical Analysis of Monetary Policy Rules." In *Monetary Policy Rules*, edited by John B. Taylor, 319–48. Chicago: University of Chicago Press.

———. 2017. "Rules vs. Discretion: Assessing the Debate over the Conduct of Monetary Policy." National Bureau of Economic Research Working Paper 24149, December.

Taylor, John B., and John C. Williams. 2010. "Simple and Robust Rules for Monetary Policy." National Bureau of Economic Research Working Paper 15908, April.

Teryoshin, Yevgeniy. 2023. "Historical Performance of Rule-Like Monetary Policy." *Journal of International Money and Finance* 130 (February): 102766.

Wall Street Journal. 2022. "Transcript: WSJ Q&A with New York Fed President John Williams," August 30.

Woodford, Michael. 2001. "The Taylor Rule and Optimal Monetary Policy." *American Economic Review* 91, no. 2 (May): 232–37.

———. 2003. *Interest and Prices: Foundations of a Theory of Monetary Policy.* Princeton, NJ: Princeton University Press.

Notes

The authors are grateful for comments by Mickey Levy and Andrew Levin. A previous version of this paper was presented at the November 10, 2022, meeting of the Shadow Open Market Committee.

1. The corresponding values for the core PCE are 5.1% for 2021 and 4.6% for 2022. The consumer price index rose 7.2% for 2021 and 6.4% for 2022.

2. The federal funds rate target reached 4.75 to 5.0% in March 2023. The balance sheet reached $8.9 trillion in March 2022 and shrunk to about $8.6 trillion as of December 2022. By March 2023, the balance sheet remained at about $8.6 trillion.

3. "In determining the pace of future increases in the target range, the Committee will take into account the cumulative tightening of monetary policy, the lags with which monetary policy affects economic activity and inflation, and economic and financial developments." FOMC Statement, November 2, 2022.

4. "We think there's some ground to cover before we meet that test [referring to 'significantly restrictive'] and that's why we say that ongoing rate increases will be appropriate. And, as I mentioned, incoming data between the meetings, both a strong labor market report but particularly the CPI report, do suggest to me that we may ultimately move to higher levels than we thought at the time of the September meeting." (Board of Governors of the Federal Reserve System, Transcript of Chairman Powell's Press Conference, November 2, 2022, 5–6)

5. The reliance on vague guidance such as "lower for longer" is not uncommon in Fed speak. Unfortunately, such phrases provide no quantitative guidance or conditionality that could help inform financial markets and the public.

6. "So I guess I'd start by saying we've been saying we would move expeditiously to get to the range of neutral. And I think we've done that now. We're at—we're at 2.25 to 2.5 [percent], and that's right in the range of what we think is neutral." Chairman Powell, Transcript of Chairman Powell's Press Conference, July 27, 2022, 5.

7. Note that near-term inflation expectations—over one year or so—are the ones most relevant to decisions to delay or advance current spending, independent of inflation expectations at longer horizons.

8. The natural rate concept is attributed to the early twentieth-century economist Knut Wicksell. See Woodford (2003) and Humphrey (1986), though the latter notes the much earlier contribution of Henry Thornton and Thomas Joplin.

9. "And I think that, to me, that's one of the benchmarks. That we need to get the interest rate relative to where inflation is expected to be over the next year, into a positive space and probably even, you know, higher than the longer-run neutral level—which I think is around a ½ percent on real interest rates." See *Wall Street Journal* (2022).

10. One noteworthy exception is James Bullard, president of the Federal Reserve Bank of St. Louis, who has highlighted policy rule prescriptions in public presentations since mid-2022. See chapter 12 of this volume and Bullard (2022 and 2022b).

11. Such economists include many members of the Shadow Open Market Committee.

12. The most recent *Monetary Policy Report* was submitted to the Board of Governors of the Federal Reserve System in March 2023. The section on

monetary policy rules was inexplicably omitted from the February 2022 *Monetary Policy Report*.

13. Board of Governors of the Federal Reserve System, *Monetary Policy Report*, June 2022, 46–48.

14. Even in the March 2023 *Monetary Policy Report* (pp. 42–44), the actual federal funds rate is shown to be substantially below the rates recommended by most of the selected policy rules.

15. The Federal Reserve Bank of Cleveland posts prescriptions from seven different Taylor rules for three different published economic forecasts: https://www.clevelandfed.org/indicators-and-data/simple-monetary-policy-rules#background. The Federal Reserve Bank of Atlanta website has a Taylor rule utility in which users can display prescriptions for up to three alternative rules using alternative rule parameters and alternative measures of inflation and real activity: https://www.atlantafed.org/cqer/research/taylor-rule.

16. "To be clear, let me say again the question of when to moderate the pace of increases is now much less important than the question of how high to raise rates and how long to keep monetary policy restricted, which really will be our principal focus." Chairman Powell, Transcript of Chairman Powell's Press Conference, November 2, 2022, 6.

17. "Our message should be—what I'm trying to do is make sure that our message is clear, which is that we think we have a ways to go, we have some ground to cover with interest rates before we get to, before we get to that level of interest rates that we think is sufficiently restrictive. And putting that in the statement and identifying that as a goal is an important step. And that's meant to put that question, really, as the important one now going forward. I've also said that we think that the level of rates that we estimated in September—the incoming data suggests that that's actually going to be higher, and that's been the pattern." Chairman Powell, Transcript of Chairman Powell's Press Conference, November 2, 2022, 20.

18. The MPR reports monetary policy rule prescriptions only up through the most recent quarter of reported economic statistics; the MPR submitted on March 3, 2023, for example, only displays predictions through the fourth quarter of 2022. The MPR also reports the most recent SEP, however (December 2022), including FOMC participants' projections of the end-of-year values of variables that appear on the right-hand-side of policy rules. It would be a simple matter for the MPR to also display the

results of applying rules to the median or central tendency projections in the SEP.

19. The FOMC would do well to make more extensive use of scenario analysis, both in policy setting and in communications; see Bordo, Levin, and Levy (2020) and Levin (2014).

20. As noted earlier, the policy rules reported in the MPR recommended a lift-off of the federal funds rate in Q2 or Q3 of 2021, well before the Fed acted at the very end of Q2 of 2022.

21. The FOMC generally expresses forward guidance as predictions of what a future committee will want to do, rather than as commitments to do what the committee might not otherwise want to do when the time comes. Nevertheless, forward guidance is often perceived, outside the committee and within, as commitments in the latter sense. See Lacker (2019) and Plosser (2013).

22. See Woodford (2003) and Humphrey (1986). The latter notes the much earlier contributions of Henry Thornton and Thomas Joplin.

23. "So I guess I'd start by saying we've been saying we would move expeditiously to get to the range of neutral. And I think we've done that now. We're at—we're at 2.25 to 2.5 [percent], and that's right in the range of what we think is neutral." Chairman Powell, Transcript of Chairman Powell's Press Conference, July 27, 2022, 5.

24. See note 9 above.

25. See Levy and Plosser (2022) for an early critique of the Fed's new regime.

GENERAL DISCUSSION

JOHN TAYLOR (INTRODUCTION): We're at our next-to-last session, a very important one, "Toward a Monetary Policy Strategy." We have four excellent speakers, two current and two former [Federal Open Market Committee] members. And what more could we ask for? We'll have a good discussion.

Anyway, we're going to start with Jim Bullard, who's president of the St. Louis Federal Reserve Bank, Philip Jefferson, a governor on the Federal Reserve Board, and Jeff Lacker, and Charlie Plosser. We'll go in that order. So, take it away, Jim.

* * *

TAYLOR: Thank you. We have time for a few questions or comments. Right here first, Mickey, and then behind you. Go ahead, Mickey. Here comes a mic down the aisle. Thank you.

MICKEY LEVY: Jim, your piece is about monetary policy and fiscal policy, and I want to toss out a caution about overstating the extent to which fiscal policy stimulus is diminishing. Certainly, fiscal stimulus is far less than it was in 2020 and 2021, but three points are important. First, President Biden's Infrastructure Investment and Jobs Act of 2021, which authorized $1 trillion of spending, is starting to flow into the economy. It had a large impact on government consumption and investment (the "G" in "GDP") in Q4 2022 and Q1 2023, and these increases will continue for many years. One hundred percent of the infrastructure spending is calculated directly in GDP, and many private-sector jobs are [being] created. Fiscal analysis historically suggests that government investment spending generates a higher multiplier than transfer payments. Second, of the $5 trillion in budget spending, half a trillion was federal grants to state and local governments. Virtually all of that was saved by state and local governments that were benefiting from surging tax receipts. Right now, with the exception of the Federal Reserve, state and local governments are the second largest holder of US Treasuries, about $750 billion more than prepandemic levels. That is over 3% of GDP. We know that eventually it will be spent or used to lower taxes, and will stimulate economic activity, long after it was recorded as increases in the federal budget deficit. Third, the cost-of-living adjustments [COLAs] involve increases in deficit spending that add to disposable income and aggregate demand. The social security COLA alone adds $100 billion to disposable income this year. Most of the spending on Medicare, Medicaid, and SNAP programs is indexed to inflation. This adds up to a tremendous increase in nominal disposable income. Accordingly, I caution on stating that fiscal policy has turned restrictive, based on diminishing deficits.

TAYLOR: Quick response?

JAMES BULLARD: Sure. I think that the composition of government spending is important for this purpose. If you think that the infrastructure spending is legitimately public capital and that that's improving the productive capacity of the country—something we could definitely have a whole conference on—that's a different animal than borrowing money and putting it directly into bank accounts of households.

On the state and local matter, I agree with you. One of the things that I've found anecdotally and from talking to people across the district and across the country is that state and local governments are flush. They have a lot of spending. So, it's like you poured a lot of federal spending, you put it out to the state and local governments, but they don't really have the infrastructure to be able to spend it at that rate. So, it's trickling out, and I think that will come out over time. So, I agree with that.

Cost-of-living adjustment is also an issue, but I think the more immediate issue for monetary policy is the transfer payments.

TAYLOR: Yes, could you please say your name?

CHARLES SIGULER: Hey there. Charlie Siguler. We talk a lot about forward projections and trying to make all sorts of forward assumptions. And yet the Fed gets, on a weekly basis, data on the M2 money supply. Yet we hardly hear about it. And in recent data, there's been nothing normal about it. And two years ago, there was nothing normal about it. So I just want to sort of highlight a couple of things. From January 1, 2020, through December 31, 2021, the money supply grew by 40%, which was the highest two-year growth in history. There may be something in the 1700s that Niall Ferguson may see, but in the data that I looked at, there's nothing. At the same time, bank deposits grew by 36%, to the tune of about $4 trillion. Both money supply and bank deposits peaked in the same month last year, April 2022, and they've both been in decline since this. Now there's a year-over-year decline in M2 and bank deposits, which is the first time that I've seen this has ever happened. Most recent data shows that M2 is declining by 4.1% annualized, which is an all-time low in terms of percentage growth. So just trying to sort through all this. And there are a lot of extremes going on here, and with these fluctuations, I just wonder if these extreme gyrations reflect or are affecting financial and price stability, and is M2 something that the Fed should be looking at more closely?

TAYLOR: You're not jumping out of this one. You owe me to answer.

BULLARD: I will say this about M2. I come from the "monetarist bank" and sort of grew up as a monetarist. So I'm very sympathetic. It's been hard to relate money growth to inflation empirically. The standard thinking—around the St. Louis Fed anyway—over the years has been that there's just too much other noise going on in the economy at low levels of inflation and low rates of money growth. It's hard to relate money growth to inflation in that circumstance. Recently, you had an outsize movement in M2. Sure enough, you got inflation right behind it. So maybe monetarism will be reinvigorated by this episode. If you subscribe to this theory, this bodes well for disinflation ahead.

TAYLOR: Go ahead.

JEFFREY LACKER: Yeah. I'd recommend a recent piece by Peter Ireland in *Forbes*, or at least on their website, arguing that we need to relearn monetarism, to play on a senior official who said we unlearned it.

TAYLOR: Okay, we have Bill Nelson, and then Krishna [Guha]. Then we've got to stop. Bill?

WILLIAM NELSON: Bill Nelson, Bank Policy Institute. So I have two questions for the panel. The first is, to what extent do the FOMC [Federal Open Market Committee] and the Fed bear some responsibility for the financial turmoil we've been experiencing owing in large part to the sharp rise in interest rates that we've witnessed? I mean, I'll acknowledge up front that first and foremost, the problems were the responsibility of really awful bank risk management. And we learned a lot about regulation—improvements to regulation and supervision. But, you know, it's also true that a central bank that is behind the curve raises rates just as much as one that's not behind the curve—but actually by more, and more rapidly—and that financial stability consequence is one of the important reasons not to fall behind the curve. But it's worse than that. Sorry. You know, there was also . . . I mean, the Fed was actively communicating to the markets. You know that the neutral policy was 2.5% at a time when inflation was running at 8%. So for example, this is from the July 2022 FOMC meeting where Chair [Jerome] Powell said: "We've been saying we would move expeditiously to get to the range of neutral, and I think we've done that now. We're at two and a quarter to two and a half, and that's right in the range of what we think is neutral." And there were plenty of commentators—well, some commentators, and I was one of them—saying that's dangerous advice, because it's going to cause intermediate and longer-term rates to be too low.

And the second question, which is related to that, is, I'm curious from each of the panelists to know your current spot estimate of the nominal neutral federal funds rate.

TAYLOR: So, let's go to Andy and Krishna.

ANDREW LEVIN: Over the past several years I've been concerned about the lack of dissenting votes on FOMC decisions. By comparison, the Bank of England has been facing lots of tough decisions and there's been dissent on both sides. And meanwhile, the FOMC has been circling the wagons. Sometimes a dissenter might be wrong, and sometimes they might be right. But it takes courage to cast a dissenting vote.

I'm also concerned that the [federal] funds rate is currently at the very bottom of the "comfort zone." Is that the right policy stance for effective risk management? Should we be at the bottom, or maybe at the top, or somewhere in the middle? And that underscores the merits of using the Taylor rule as a benchmark.

TAYLOR: So, Krishna, and then we have the response.

KRISHNA GUHA: Thanks very much. Krishna Guha, Evercore Partners [formerly of] the New York Fed. Quick comment and quick question. The quick comment is, when we talk about the market and where the market's misunderstanding things, I think it's illustrative to point out that were the world to evolve along the lines envisaged in the FOMC's SEP [Summary of Economic Projections], then, in fact, according to standard Taylor rule specifications, the [federal] funds rate should be somewhere between two and a half and three at the end of 2024. That's what your first slide showed. And so, it's not necessarily obvious that the market is wildly mispriced. The market may, however, be too optimistic about the prospects of achieving that inflation path, which you rightly illustrated yourselves in the second set of slides.

My question has to do with the multiple forms of tightening that are taking place at the moment. So, we have three forms of tightening underway. There's monetary tightening through the classic interest rate channel, there's balance sheet tightening, and there's some hard-to-quantify credit tightening taking place. So, if we were to try to integrate this into a Taylor-type rule, would it be reasonable to enter in some additional terms for those other forms of tightening? And if not, how should we integrate these into our thinking?

TAYLOR: Phil, do you want to take this?

PHILIP JEFFERSON: Yeah. These last three questions are, to me, closely related, okay? One was about trying to assess the impact of . . . let's call it the credit shock, okay? The one prior to that had to do with balancing the dual mandate. The one before that was from Bill, asking about what was the neutral rate. So, in my mind, these questions are kind of all related to one another in some way. And I think that is what makes monetary policy quite challenging. Because I do take the dual mandate very seriously. For those of you who may not know about my background in terms of my scholarship, I've written extensively on poverty and inequality from a neighborhood in Washington, DC, where I've seen very disparate incomes for people in this society. So I care very much about how the labor market performs because, for most people in the US economy, their standing in the labor market will very much determine their station in life. So that's something I'm very mindful of.

But I also am aware that inflation is the most insidious of social diseases. And so, it's important to try to get it down so that people can go about their lives in a way where inflation is in the background.

So, what makes saying what the neutral rate is in this environment so difficult is that we have multiple things going on. Okay? We do have the credit shock and its impact, and that can impact your thinking. I think it's a matter of public record that before the banking shocks occurred, I would guess—and Bill, Jim, please correct me—if people on the FOMC had one view of what that neutral rate might have been, or the terminal rate if you want to think about it in that way, the credit shock may have had some impact on their thinking. So, whether or not anyone wrote down a Taylor rule that included the impact of the credit tightening, we can't say for sure. But I think in terms of policymakers' thinking, it certainly weighs in. So, you know, I don't have a definite answer to these three questions, but I want you to know that these are the considerations that we're all trying to balance as we're looking or thinking about the appropriate setting of the main policy rate.

TAYLOR: Thank you. Jeff, then we have to stop.

LACKER: So, to Bill Nelson. We did cite the Powell statement you quoted in our paper, and we noted that a month and a half later, in August, John Williams, head of the New York Fed, gave an interview to the *Wall Street Journal* where he lays out the right way to think about the neutral rate. The neutral rate depends on how you define it. Like Wicksell or the SEP? You know, those are two different things.

Is the market off base? The question is: What's going to get inflation down to where it's going in the SEP? And the Taylor rule says, well, you know, given what we've seen now, we're not there. It's sort of like a miracle happens in the next three quarters or two quarters.

So, the concern about credit tightening is interesting. The Taylor rule summarizes, given inflation and unemployment, where the rate should be. Now, times when the Fed's had to tighten to reduce inflation, it's almost always been associated with some credit tightening, virtually every time, right? So, you would only want to adjust the Taylor rule for credit tightening, you would only want to forego rate increases that you would otherwise undertake on the basis of Taylor rules, if you thought the credit tightening was worse than it was typically in the past at times such as 1990, the early 1990s, 2001, and 1982. So, it doesn't seem to me like that's warranted now.

TAYLOR: I think we have to stop after that. Is that okay? Maybe the last word for Jim. Go ahead.

BULLARD: Okay, so I agree with Philip Jefferson. The unemployment rate is very low, at a fifty-year low. The inflation tax is high. This hurts the population in the lowest segment of the income distribution the hardest. They have less ability to adjust to inflation. I think that's our opportunity to get inflation down now, if we can get rid of the inflation tax while the labor market is strong. On Krishna Guha's question, I agree that the market's optimistic. They're not necessarily wrong. I like to interpret that as they have a lot of confidence in the FOMC. [*Laughter*] I think there are multiple forms of tightening going on. You have to put that in a model. You can't just put that in your Taylor rule.

On the financial stability question posed by Bill Nelson—Did the Fed contribute to the financial turmoil?—I think we did communicate fairly effectively that we were going to raise rates quickly. I think that by and large, the financial sector agreed that we were going to have to do this. You just can't expect every entity in the whole country to adjust appropriately. Some probably are going to get burned on this, but I think overall it's been pretty good. I will say financial stress metrics are actually still quite low. So, we're not in the situation that we were in March–April of 2020, and we're certainly not in the situation that we were in 2008. So far, so good. Hopefully, we'll get good results out of this.

TAYLOR: Okay, thank you, panel.

LATIN AMERICAN INFLATION

15

Latin American Inflation and Chile's Market-Oriented Reforms

Sebastian Edwards

When John Taylor called me to contribute a chapter to this book, I immediately agreed and offered to talk about inflation in Latin America. Then, he found out that my new book on Chile (*The Chile Project: The Story of the Chicago Boys and the Downfall of Neoliberalism*) had just been released by Princeton University Press, and he said, "Well, why don't you talk about Chile?" So, since Chile *is* in Latin America and has an interesting inflation history, I will merge the two topics and divide my remarks into two parts. I'll start by talking about inflation in Latin America in general and then zoom into Chile, which is, or was—I'm going to argue that it still is—the brightest star in Latin America, thanks to the market reforms that were implemented with the help of the "Chicago Boys."[1]

Latin America's Inflation Challenges

Latin America has a bad reputation when it comes to inflation. And I will show you that even now, in mid-2023, it's not fully deserved. In fact, Latin America has recently been doing quite well when it comes to inflation. So here are the data on most Latin American countries (see figure 15.1).

I don't have the Caribbean, so it's just Latin America, with two exceptions, Argentina and Venezuela. They are not included in the figure because their inflation is just too high. Both points would be off the chart. Argentina has 110% inflation. So, it would be in

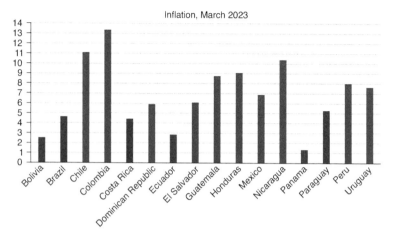

FIGURE 15.1. Annual Inflation Rate in Selected Latin American Countries, March 2023.
The red bars are countries that have, in May 2023, an inflation rate below that of the United States. The figure excludes Argentina and Venezuela.
Source: Trading Economics.

the "high inflation" category, according to the definition in Peter Blair Henry's chapter (see chapter 8). Venezuela has around 400% inflation, but we think the data may be doctored. So, we don't know what the rate of inflation is in Venezuela.

The red bars are countries that have, as this is written in May 2023, an inflation rate below the United States. This is the first time in my career that Brazil has a lower inflation rate than the United States. And the basic reason for that is that it has an independent central bank, which is run by a University of California–Los Angeles graduate, Roberto Campos Neto. We trained him well, yet the president of Brazil, Luiz Inácio Lula da Silva (Lula), wants to get rid of him. And Campos Neto is standing firm and will not allow that to happen and will not step down. They may want to change the law, but it would be a big scandal.

Let me note, before proceeding, that those that don't have inflation as low as the United States don't have very high inflation rates. Only a few countries have double digits, and in most of them, inflation is coming down. Chile had 13%, and two days ago, the new data for April were announced, and it's now 9.9%. So, it made it to single-digit inflation.

Now, what unifies the six countries that have lower inflation than the United States? What do they have in common? They have very high real interest rates, and they follow the Taylor rule in a very strict fashion. And it's not a "generous" Taylor rule. It's a "strong" Taylor rule. So let me give you the numbers. For Brazil, the real interest policy rate, using the ongoing inflation to subtract from the nominal rate, is 9.5%. And that very high real interest rate explains why Lula wants to get rid of Campos Neto. And this is one of the reasons why Brazil has a 4.6% rate of inflation right now and has had an incredibly stable exchange rate. If you remember, during Lula's first presidency, Brazil's currency depreciated quickly.

Let me now focus on the rest of the low-inflation countries. Bolivia has a 2% real interest rate. Costa Rica is at 4%, Ecuador at 6%, and Paraguay at 3%.

Some of these countries have another attribute in common: they don't have a currency of their own. They use the US dollar. And one of the countries with a currency of its own, Bolivia, has a fixed exchange rate. Bolivia is interesting for many reasons. It suffered from hyperinflation in the 1980s and was able to defeat it through a pretty orthodox program. Bolivia also has the third-largest deposit of lithium in the world. And lithium is a big deal right now. So, many people may not know where Bolivia is located within Latin America, but I know for a fact that Chinese lithium companies are rounding Bolivia nonstop and making all sorts of offers to the government. So, Bolivia has a fixed rate and an inflation rate of 2.2%. But—this is the interesting part for economists—it is facing a speculative attack on the currency. And our models—remember our models on speculative attacks went out of fashion because very few countries now have fixed exchange rates? We are going to be able to apply these models

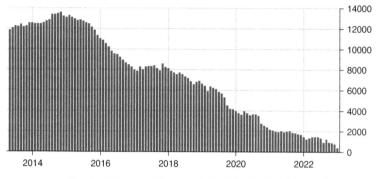

FIGURE 15.2. Foreign Exchange Reserves in Bolivia (in $US Millions), 2013–22.
Foreign exchange reserves in Bolivia decreased to $372 million in January 2023 from $709 million in December 2022.
Source: Central Bank of Bolivia.

again to Bolivia. In figure 15.2, I show the international reserves of Bolivia.

They went from $14 billion, which is a lot of money for a small and poor country like Bolivia, to about $300 million. And any day now, there is going to be a big devaluation and a currency crisis. And how has the Bolivian government dealt with this issue? Badly. The first thing that they did was force the pension funds, with individual savings accounts invested in diversified portfolios, to buy government paper. And now they have decided to sell all the gold the central bank holds on its balance sheet. If you look at the assets, you have gold and special drawing rights (SDRs). But you cannot really sell the SDRs. So, they are selling all the gold to keep the boliviano fixed. But the devaluation will come, and those of us who really like these devaluation speculative attack models will see the whole process in real time.

Let me address the main issues in terms of inflation in Latin America before I move to the case of Chile. One question is, of course, what we have been discussing during many of the sessions in this conference, "r-star." And as I showed you, most Latin American central banks, many being independent, have had no problem raising the policy rate. They understand the Taylor rule and that the parameters don't have to be the same across countries. In countries with traditionally high inflation, it makes sense to use, instead of one and a half, maybe two or two and a half in front of the divergence between their target rate and actual inflation. Their target rate is not quite 2%. It's 3% or a band that goes from 2 to 4%.

A second question, which is very pertinent for Argentina, is whether to dollarize. We had that discussion back in the late 2000s when John Taylor was with the US Treasury department. Taylor and the IMF [International Monetary Fund] were very tough with Argentina while being quite supportive of Brazil and Uruguay at that time. Argentina is again thinking of dollarizing. And the question is if they do dollarize, at what exchange rate? Now you would say that the market exchange rate is the right rate. Well, it's not that easy, because they have multiple exchange rates. They have six different exchange rates. And the spread between the market-determined and the official rate, which is the export rate, the rate at which exporters must sell their dollars to the government, is one to two. Its free rate (known as the "blue dollar") is almost 500 pesos to the dollar, the free and the official rate is 260 pesos to the USD.

Ecuador is currently dollarized and El Salvador is dollarized and uses Bitcoin as the other official currency. Of course, Panama has been dollarized since 1904.

Another important issue in Latin America when it comes to inflation is the pass-through coefficient. If the exchange rate depreciates, how much of that is passed through onto prices? And that, of course, affects inflation. A discussion that economists have in Latin America all the time is whether the central bank should add the exchange rate to the Taylor rule as an additional term. Some argue that the deviation between the exchange rate and the exchange rate supported by fundamentals, or equilibrium rate, should be a third term in the Taylor rule. I think many of us have looked into the issue and concluded that the exchange rate is already in the standard Taylor rule through the actual rate of inflation. And adding it as an additional explicit term would make things more complicated to explain and communicate to people, because it is particularly difficult and controversial to determine if the exchange rate is out of sync with the fundamentals.

Let me move to a third issue, capital and exchange controls. This question has been dormant in the last few years, and in most countries in the region, we now have fairly high capital mobility. The exceptions, of course, are Argentina and Venezuela. But in Chile, you can walk into a bank and say I want to buy $3 million and transfer the money to John Taylor. I would have to give them my details because of drug trafficking and so forth; I would have to give them my tax ID number, address, and whatever. But I could move $3 million with absolutely no problems. But the capital controls issue will come back again. Since John Lipsky left a few years ago, the IMF has become more sympathetic toward capital controls. And I think that is, in most cases, a mistake.

A fourth important issue concerns remittances and monetary policy. I just wrote an evaluation of the Central Bank of Guatemala. One of the most important issues is that they monetize remittances that are 15% of GDP. Given the magnitude of these flows, it is very difficult to sterilize them fully. And this, of course, puts pressure on an exchange rate that appreciates in real terms. Therefore, exporters get really mad. And it's very difficult to convince the Guatemalans that this scenario, with very high and stable remittances, is the new state of the world, the "new normal" for Guatemala. It is likely that in the future, more Guatemalans will migrate to the US. They're going to send more money into the country, and that will put additional pressure on the exchange rate. But this is an issue that very few people in the advanced world face. It is, however, very important in a number of Latin American countries, and there is a need to think of policy measures to deal with it.

The final inflation-related issue I want to mention is the revival, in some quarters, of Modern Monetary Theory (MMT). What is interesting is that MMT-type policies have a long tradition in Latin America. I will deal with this in my remarks on the Chilean market-oriented reforms. Needless to say, MMT has had very negative consequences in Latin America and has been behind most (if not all) of the region's experiences with runaway inflation.

The Chilean Market-Oriented Reforms and Inflation

Let me now move to the Chilean part of my inflation story. And it's a fascinating case study. This section is based on my recent book, *The Chile Project*, where I tell the story of the revolution the "Chicago Boys" put together in Chile. And how they transformed a very mediocre country into the brightest star in the Latin American sky.

And as you can see in figure 15.3, Chile moved from being at the bottom of the Latin American region in income per capita in the 1980s to number one. In 1989, when the seventeen-year dictatorship led by General Augusto Pinochet came to an end, Chile had an identical income per capita (in purchasing power parity rates, or PPP) to Ecuador and Costa Rica. Today, income per capita in Chile is twice as high as in Ecuador and 50% higher than in Costa Rica. This is a true miracle. And it was built based on market reforms, wholesale privatization, and the opening up of the economy. Import tariffs in Chile, for all practical purposes right now, are at zero. The Chicago Boys model was used at almost every level. And this is why I label the model as "neoliberal." Notice that I am not using the word "neoliberal" in a bad or pejorative sense. It's true that "neoliberal" has acquired a very bad reputation as a word, but I do believe that if we define it in a clear way, we can use the term in serious analysis. Therefore, I define "neoliberal" as using markets at every possible level. That's what Chile did. And that's

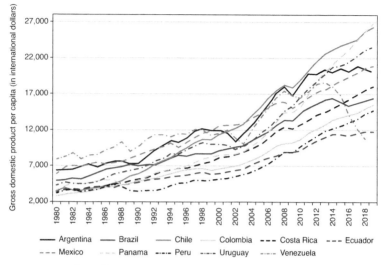

FIGURE 15.3. Gross Domestic Product Per Capita in Selected Latin American Countries, 1980–2019.
Gross domestic product per capita is in international dollars.
Source: The World Bank.

what's behind this miracle. A particularly important component of the policies that generated the miracle was the individual pension savings accounts.

Figure 15.4 shows Arnold (Al) Harberger, who has been called the godfather of the Chicago Boys, with Sergio de Castro, the leader of the group. In figure 15.5, we have the four most important members of the team that modernized the Chilean economy: Sergio de Castro, Sergio de la Cuadra, Pablo Baraona, and Alvaro Bardón.

Milton Friedman had a great influence on the Chilean reforms. He visited Chile twice, and during his first trip in 1975, he met with General Pinochet. That visit was very controversial and haunted Friedman for the rest of his life. The left really took it out on him. He was verbally attacked when he received the Nobel Prize; people in the audience shouted and tried to shut down the event. After 1975, everywhere Friedman went, demonstrators accused him of

FIGURE 15.4. Some of the Chicago Boys.
Sergio de Castro (left) and Arnold Harberger (right).
Source: Rolf Lüders's personal collection.

being an accomplice of Pinochet's and blamed him for supporting human rights violations.

In that first visit—and I'm going to get back to that—Friedman recommended a shock treatment to deal with inflation. And people like Naomi Klein and even Joseph Stiglitz and Paul Krugman criticized Friedman because of the shock treatment in Chile. The second time Friedman went to Chile was in 1981 when Chile was

FIGURE 15.5. More Chicago Boys.
From left to right: Chicago Boys Sergio de Castro, Sergio de la Cuadra, Pablo Baraona, and Alvaro Bardón, circa 1978.
Source: *La Tercera* photo archive.

trying to bring inflation down to a single digit using an exchange-rate-based approach, which failed. And I'll get back to that.

Now, as a parenthesis around that time, John Lipsky lived in Chile and almost ran the country. He was the IMF resident representative. So, any major policy move had to be cleared with him.

In figure 15.6, I show the Chilean six-month annualized inflation, a metric that has recently become quite popular when discussing US inflation.

As can be seen, inflation peaked at 1,600% in September 1973, the month the military deposed the socialist president, Salvador Allende. This is pretty much hyperinflation.

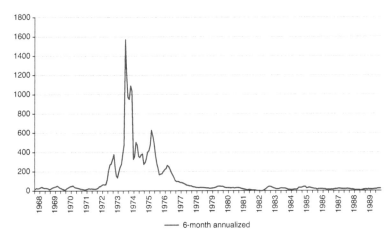

FIGURE 15.6. Six-Month Annualized Inflation in Chile, 1968–89.
Six-month annualized change in consumer price index (CPI). The y-axis repre-
sents annualized percentage increase in CPI.
Source: Central Bank of Chile.

The data on inflation in figure 15.6 may be divided into six distinct phases: (a) 1968–71, when inflation averaged approximately
20% per annum; (b) 1971 to September 1973, when the country moved toward hyperinflation; (c) October 1973–May 1975,
when it declined to about 400% and got stuck at that level; (d)
May 1975–June 1978, with a slow decline to 40%; (e) June 1978–
June 1982, when it declined further under an exchange-rate-based
stabilization program, and at the end of this period, inflation was
9%; and (f) June 1982–December 1990. After a major currency
crisis in June 1982, inflation hovered around 20%. In 1991, outside
the graph, inflation targeting was adopted, allowing Chile to have
3% inflation. Chile returned to democratic rule in March 1990.

The first segment (1968–71) is, in some ways, related to Friedman.
During this period, the economy was fully indexed. There was full
backward-looking indexation with a monetary policy that accommodated whatever inertia there was. And you may not know this,
but Friedman became enamored of indexation when Brazil put it

in place, big time, in the 1960s. And in the Friedman papers at the Hoover Institution Library & Archives, there is a presentation by Friedman on Brazil's indexation; he was fascinated by it. As I noted, inflation in Chile during this first period was about 20% on average. About once a year, maybe once every eight months, every price, every contract, and the exchange rate were adjusted by past inflation. And it was sort of stable at 20%. The problem with this system is that it has no anchor, and any shock brings you to a different plateau.

The second period (1971–73) corresponds, as noted, to the socialist government. And this is MMT big-time, with the addition of nationalization and wholesale expropriation of arable land, manufacturing firms, all banks, and all insurance companies. This is the period when Salvador Allende, the socialist president, nationalized the copper mines that were then owned by Kennecott Copper Corporation and Anaconda Copper Mining Company, two large mining multinationals based in the US. The government decided the expropriated companies would receive compensation based on book value in 1955. However, there was a wrinkle. "Excessive profits" obtained by the American companies since 1955 would be subtracted from book value. "Excessive profits" were defined as over and above 12%, accrued since 1955. As it turned out, when these calculations were done, the American companies owed money to Chile! During this period, the public sector deficit, broadly defined to include losses of state-owned enterprises (including newly nationalized firms), reached the astonishing figure of 30% of GDP. This extremely large deficit was fully financed through money creation by the central bank. Inflation was 1,600% at the end of the government in September 1973.

The third phase (1973–75) is very interesting and characterized by money targeting with huge fiscal dominance. So, what happened? What's the story? When the military took over, the economy was in shambles. There were shortages, black markets, multiple exchange

rates, output declines, and all these companies that had been nationalized by the socialists. At first, the military didn't want to privatize all these companies. They were very nationalistic and initially
favored a model where the armed forces ran companies considered
"strategic."

However, most of these companies were losing tons of money
and feeding the deficit. This had been reduced relative to the
Socialist regime, but it was still 10% of GDP and fully financed
by the central bank printing money. When Friedman visited in
March 1975, inflation was stuck at 400%. And what he found out
is what I just mentioned: the central bank was financing the losses
from companies being run by generals, colonels, and admirals. Now
the armed forces owned a steel mill, and they owned the brewery.
And this is when Friedman said, "You guys need a shock treatment." And he recommended they cut government expenditures
by 25% overnight. That was done, and inflation came down fairly
quickly, as you can see from figure 15.6.

However, once again, it got stuck, this time at around 30%. And
that's when there was a change in strategy, and we move to the
next phase, 1978–82. At that point, Columbia University's Robert
Mundell and University of Chicago's Harry Johnson took over
from Friedman intellectually, and Chile fixed the exchange rate to
eliminate inflation. The evolution of the peso to the USD exchange
rate is reflected in figure 15.7.

Between 1975 and 1979, there was a crawling peg or a mini
devaluation system. In mid-1979, however, the exchange rate was
completely fixed at 39 pesos per dollar. But inflation continued
at 20% per year for several months. So, the real exchange rate
strengthened, and the peso became seriously overvalued. A decline
in the price of copper in the global market did not help. A very
large current account deficit developed, and in mid-1982, there was
a big crisis and, as you can see from figure 15.7, a big devaluation.

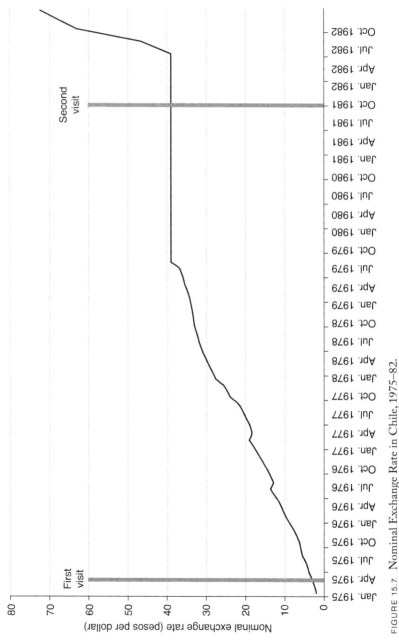

FIGURE 15.7. Nominal Exchange Rate in Chile, 1975–82.

The line corresponds to the nominal exchange rate between the Chilean peso and the US dollar in monthly frequency. The mark "First visit" is Milton Friedman's first visit in March 1975, and "Second visit" is Milton Friedman's second visit in October 1981.

During the next inflation phase, there was a lot of pragmatism. A second generation of Chicago Boys took over economic and monetary policy. They implemented real exchange rate targeting with fiscal adjustment, and they privatized a massive number of companies. Now the military didn't own the so-called strategic firms—this was, of course, a very big political struggle. And now the Chicago Boys were able to bring down inflation gradually. In 1992–93, Chile adopted inflation targeting. It was one of the first nations to do so after New Zealand, and inflation started coming down very, very slowly.

When Friedman went to Chile for the second time in October 1981, the current account deficit was almost 12% of GDP. He was asked, "Do you support the fixed exchange rate?" His answers were noncommittal. He didn't say that he supported it, nor did he criticize the policy. A few months after this second visit, it was impossible to defend the fixed rate any longer, and the peso was devalued (see figure 15.7). The devaluation crisis of 1982 was profound and resulted in a rate of unemployment exceeding 25%. That's after the devaluation. Figure 15.8 shows Friedman giving a press conference during his second visit in October 1981.

Was Chile a neoliberal country? Was this a model where markets were used profusely? The answer is "yes." However, it is important to notice that in Chile, there were different phases and that the "neoliberal" model evolved through time. During the early years of the Chicago Boys, the policy was middle-of-the-road. I think it is fair to say that neoliberalism began in 1979 when Pinochet announced major reforms to education, health, pensions, and the judiciary. He also announced a new constitution. The speech was called the "Seven Modernizations" and included individual private accounts for pensions, school vouchers, and vouchers for health services. In addition, there was total privatization, lowering import tariffs to 3%, and absolute fiscal consolidation. But the one thing they didn't do was privatize infrastructure or the corporate company.

FIGURE 15.8. Milton Friedman Talks to the Media.
Milton Friedman gives a press conference in Chile in November 1981.
Source: *La Tercera* photo archive.

University of Chicago economist Gary Becker had significant intellectual influence during this process, although he never advised the government. In figure 15.9, we can see Becker with some of the second-generation Chicago Boys in Chile.

After the 1982 currency crisis, the policy stance evolved into what I have called "pragmatic neoliberalism." The main goal was to consolidate market orientation and expand privatization, establish the rule of law, provide a robust legal framework for foreign investment, and encourage exports through a competitive exchange rate.

The third phase of Chile's neoliberalism began in 1990, with the return to democracy and the first center-left government from the Concertación coalition. The government led by President Patricio Aylwin took important steps toward expanding the privatization process and further opening the economy. What's very interesting is that many of the newly elected leaders and cabinet members had been in exile, in prison, or tortured by the military. And despite that, they maintained the model. They not only maintained it, but they also deepened it. And they say, well, they didn't say they were

FIGURE 15.9. Another Visitor from Chicago.
From left to right: Carlos Cáceres, Gary Becker, Hernán Büchi, and
Juan Andrés Fontaine, Chile, 2007.
Source: Collection of Carlos Cáceres.

neoliberals, but acted and privatized the rest of the firms, the companies that had not been privatized, and expanded the scope of
markets. They also improved and expanded social programs. And
that's what I have called "inclusive neoliberalism." It was during
this phase—from 1990 through 2015, approximately—that Chile
really took off and climbed to first place on the Latin American
scorecard. The Chicago Boys set up the policies and institutions
that allowed the economy to grow at a very fast clip for twenty-
five years. But the actual growth spurt took place after the return
to democratic rule and under left-of-center administrations. Yes,
they were left of center, but their policies were largely neoliberal
until 2015 or so.

Around 2015, the model started to face diminishing returns. And
the rate of growth went from 7% to 5% to 4% to 3% to 2%, and people
became unhappy. And there were riots in 2019. Demonstrators set

twenty metro stations on fire, destroyed public and private property, attacked motorists, harassed anyone looking bourgeois, and looted supermarkets, department stores, banks, and pharmacies. The police used heavy-handed tactics and were accused of violations of human rights. On November 15, 2019, politicians from most political parties agreed that a possible way out was to have a national conversation about a new "social pact." This new agreement was to be enshrined in a new constitution. A constitutional assembly was elected in 2021. Most members were from the far left and proceeded to draft a radical constitution that introduced drastic changes to Chile's traditional political system and institutions. They went so far and became so disconnected from the people that in an "exit referendum" to approve or reject the draft, the "reject" option won by a landslide. At this point, a new constitutional council is working on a draft that will be submitted to the people in December 2023. Of course, we don't know yet what this new proposal will look like, but my guess is that it will move the country closer to a social democracy. Several new rights will be enshrined in the constitution, but the economic system will continue to be unabashedly capitalistic but not as market oriented as in the 1990s.

An open question is whether the magic of the miracle propelled by the Chicago Boys will return. Although skeptical, I believe that if social and political middle ground is found, the country can return to robust growth.

References

Edwards, Sebastian. 2023. *The Chile Project: The Story of the Chicago Boys and the Downfall of Neoliberalism*. Princeton, NJ: Princeton University Press.

Edwards, Sebastian, and Alejandra Cox Edwards. 1991. *Monetarism and Liberalization: The Chilean Experiment*. Chicago: University of Chicago Press.

Note

1. "The Chicago Boys" were Chilean economists who were educated at the University of Chicago and had a great influence on the market reforms that were implemented in Chile. Arnold Harberger, who has been called the godfather of the Chicago Boys, had an important influence on this group. Sergio de Castro, Sergio de la Cuadra, Pablo Baraona, and Alvaro Bardón were important exponents (see figures 15.4 and 15.5).

GENERAL DISCUSSION

JOHN TAYLOR (INTRODUCTION): Thank you so much for coming. It's a great event. I have to say the debate back and forth just seems so healthy and reasonable, and I have enjoyed it tremendously. So, thank you all for doing that. Thanks for being here. This is our thirteenth or fourteenth conference, I don't know, but we keep doing them, and they seem successful. Tonight, we're very happy to have Sebastian [Edwards], who is talking about inflation in Latin America. We haven't focused enough on Latin America. So we'll hear about Chile, especially, and other countries in our neighborhood. So thank you, Sebastian.

* * *

STEVEN DAVIS: Chile had an extraordinary policy reform experience that extended over decades, as you just described. Two questions: First, can you give us some insight into the social and political circumstances that made it possible for those reforms to come about? Second, why, given the picture you showed us of Chile's remarkable economic success, haven't other Latin American countries followed in its footsteps?

SEBASTIAN EDWARDS: Okay, so the first one, the way it works is, why was it possible to do it? Because it was a very strict dictatorship. And there were very significant political costs up front. And as you saw, it was very hard to bring inflation down. It was not a point carrier type of system where from one day to the next, you had no inflation. And the shock treatment was very significant. And the exchange rate crisis brought open unemployment to 26%. That does not include emergency employment programs,

401

people just cleaning the parks, and so on. So it was possible to do it because of that. And when the pragmatists took over and the exchange rate was finally allowed to fluctuate, Chile took off. And it started growing at 6%, 7%. And that's when the elections came, and the Left was elected. And the economists from the Left, who had criticized—as John Lipsky was reminding me yesterday, had spent seventeen years criticizing—the Chicago Boys, and the first thing they said is, we're going to continue with these policies. So there's nothing more seductive than success. And they were able to see that things were [succeeding]. And they kept this system for many years now.

Now, why didn't other countries in Latin America follow? Many countries did. And the Chilean pension fund system with individual savings accounts was adopted by Mexico, the Mexico affordance. It was adopted by Argentina. It was adopted by Peru. It was adopted by Colombia. So many, many countries adopted similar policies. Brazil is the one country that has been very reluctant. And the reason is that Brazil thinks in some ways, with good reason, that they are very different. They don't speak Spanish. They are not as good at soccer as the Argentinians, but almost. [*Laughter*] But every time I go to Brazil, and I tell the Brazilians to look at Chileans, their answer is very simple: we export manufactured goods [valued at] about two times Chile's GDP; there's nothing we can learn from that "Mickey Mouse" country.

That's a Brazilian answer. It may be one way or not. . . . So Brazil hasn't done it.

Why did people become unhappy? One problem that happened was that. . . . Let me say something. How do I summarize this whole Chilean story? We went through this amazing miracle. And then it seems to be unraveling, and people are having a revolt and an insurgency. And I think that there was success and neglect. Success is this, and the neglect is that people like us neglected defending the market system. We declared victory. We won the war of ideas. And now we can go and do our thing. And the Chicago Boys joined boards, went to the private sector, and started making a lot of money. And who continued to fight the war of ideas? No one. And they didn't realize that the opponents licked their wounds, regrouped, read Antonio Gramsci, an Italian Marxist, and came back and convinced the young generation that this was very unfair, that they can assist them, that it was very unequal, and so on and so forth. So, I think that one of the lessons is that we have to understand that the war of ideas never ends.

TAYLOR: Thank you.

EDWARDS: Thank you, John.

ABOUT THE CONTRIBUTORS

ANAT R. ADMATI is the George G.C. Parker Professor of Finance and Economics at Stanford Graduate School of Business, where she is faculty director of its Corporations and Society Initiative, and a senior fellow at Stanford Institute for Economic Policy Research. Her current interests lie in the interaction of business, policy, and law. Her insights have been featured in media outlets including the *New York Times*, *Washington Post*, *Wall Street Journal*, *Bloomberg*, *Financial Times*, CNN, and PBS. In 2014, Admati was named by *Time* magazine as one of the one hundred most influential people in the world and by *Foreign Policy* as among one hundred global thinkers. She is the coauthor, with Martin Hellwig, of *The Bankers' New Clothes: What's Wrong with Banking and What to Do about It* (Princeton University Press 2013; expanded ed. forthcoming 2024). Admati holds a BSc from the Hebrew University, an MA, MPhil, and PhD from Yale University, and an honorary doctorate from University of Zurich. She is a fellow of the Econometric Society and a past board member of the American Finance Association. She has served on editorial boards and on the FDIC's Systemic Resolution Advisory Committee and the CFTC's Market Risk Advisory Committee.

MICHAEL D. BORDO is a Board of Governors Professor of Economics and director of the Center for Monetary and Financial History at Rutgers University. He is the Ilene and Morton Harris Distinguished Visiting Fellow at the Hoover Institution. He has held previous academic posts at the University of South Carolina and Carleton University in Ottawa, Canada, and was visiting professor at Cambridge, Princeton, and Harvard Universities and others. Bordo was also a visiting scholar at the International Monetary Fund, the Federal Reserve Banks of St. Louis, Cleveland, and

Dallas, the Federal Reserve Board of Governors, the Bank of Canada, the Bank of England, and the Bank for International Settlements. He is a research associate of the National Bureau of Economic Research and a member of the Shadow Open Market Committee. He has a BA from McGill University, an MSc in economics from the London School of Economics, and a PhD from the University of Chicago. He has published eighteen books on monetary economics and monetary history, most recently *The Historical Performance of the Federal Reserve: The Importance of Rules* (Hoover Institution Press, 2019). He is editor of a series of books for Cambridge University Press: *Studies in Macroeconomic History*.

JAMES BULLARD was recently named inaugural dean of the Mitchell E. Daniels, Jr. School of Business at Purdue University. He was previously (and at the time of this conference) president and CEO of the Federal Reserve Bank of St. Louis, in which role he oversaw the Federal Reserve's Eighth District and participated on the Federal Open Market Committee. As a noted economist and policymaker, Bullard makes Fed transparency and dialogue a priority on the international and national stage as well as on Main Street. He serves on the board of directors of Concordance Academy of Leadership, and he is a past board chair of the United Way USA. Bullard is coeditor of the *Journal of Economic Dynamics and Control*, a member of the editorial advisory board of the *National Institute Economic Review*, and a member of the Central Bank Research Association's senior council. He is an honorary professor of economics at Washington University in St. Louis, where he also sits on the advisory council of the economics department and the advisory board of the Center for Dynamic Economics. A native of Forest Lake, Minnesota, Bullard received his doctorate in economics from Indiana University Bloomington.

ANUSHA CHARI is a professor of economics and finance at the University of North Carolina at Chapel Hill, where she was inaugural director of the Modern Indian Studies Initiative. She serves as chair of the American Economic Association's Committee on the Status of Women in the Economics Profession. She is also a research associate in the National Bureau of Economic Research's International Finance and Macroeconomics Program, a research fellow at the Center for Economic and Policy Research, and a nonresident senior fellow at the Brookings Institution. She is an associate editor at the *Journal of International*

Economics and the *Journal of Economic Perspectives*. She holds a PhD in international finance from the Anderson School at UCLA and BAs in philosophy, politics, and economics from Balliol College at Oxford, and in economics from the University of Delhi. She has served on the faculties of the University of Chicago's Booth School of Business, the University of Michigan, the Haas School of Business at the University of California–Berkeley, and Harvard University. Chari was a special advisor to the Indian prime minister's Economic Advisory Council. Her research is in the fields of open-economy macroeconomics and international finance.

RICHARD H. CLARIDA is the C. Lowell Harriss Professor of Economics and International Affairs at Columbia University. He previously served as vice chairman of the Board of Governors of the Federal Reserve, as assistant secretary of the US Treasury for economic policy, and as chairman of the Columbia University Department of Economics. Earlier in his career, he taught at Yale University and served as senior staff economist for President Ronald Reagan's Council of Economic Advisers. He has also consulted for several prominent financial firms, including the Global Foreign Exchange Group at Credit Suisse First Boston and Grossman Asset Management, and has been a global advisor with PIMCO. He is a member of the Council on Foreign Relations and was a member of the National Bureau of Economic Research, where he edited *G7 Current Account Imbalances: Sustainability and Adjustment* (University of Chicago Press, 2007) and coedited the *NBER International Seminar on Macroeconomics*. He is also coeditor, along with Jeff Fuhrer, of the volume *Recent Developments in Monetary Policy, Fiscal Policy, and Financial System Design: A Conference to Honor Ben Friedman, Special Supplemental Issue of the International Journal of Central Banking* (January 2012). Clarida received his BS from the University of Illinois and his MA and PhD from Harvard University.

JOHN H. COCHRANE is the Rose-Marie and Jack Anderson Senior Fellow at the Hoover Institution. He is also a research associate of the National Bureau of Economic Research and an adjunct scholar of the Cato Institute. Before joining Hoover, Cochrane was a professor of finance at the University of Chicago's Booth School of Business and previously taught in its economics department. He served as president of the American Finance Association and is a fellow of the Econometric

Society. He writes on asset pricing, financial regulation, business cycles, and monetary policy. He has also written articles on macroeconomics, health insurance, time-series econometrics, financial regulation, and other topics. His books include *The Fiscal Theory of the Price Level* (Princeton University Press, 2023) and *Asset Pricing* (Princeton University Press, 2001, rev. 2005). Cochrane frequently contributes essays to the *Wall Street Journal*, *National Review*, *Project Syndicate*, and other publications. He maintains the *Grumpy Economist* blog. Cochrane earned a bachelor's degree in physics at MIT and his PhD in economics at the University of California–Berkeley.

STEVEN J. DAVIS is a senior fellow (adjunct) at the Hoover Institution and William H. Abbott Distinguished Service Professor of International Business and Economics at the University of Chicago Booth School of Business. He is a research associate of the National Bureau of Economic Research, economic adviser to the US Congressional Budget Office, visiting scholar at the Federal Reserve Bank of Atlanta, elected fellow of the Society of Labor Economists, senior adviser to the Brookings Papers on Economic Activity, and senior academic fellow of the Asian Bureau of Finance and Economic Research, where he also serves on the executive committee. Davis is cofounder of the Economic Policy Uncertainty project, the Survey of Working Arrangements and Attitudes, the WFH Map project, the Survey of Business Uncertainty, and the Stock Market Jumps project. He co-organizes the Asian Monetary Policy Forum, held annually in Singapore.

DARRELL DUFFIE is the Adams Distinguished Professor of Management and Professor of Finance at Stanford University's Graduate School of Business and a senior fellow, by courtesy, at the Hoover Institution. He is a research fellow of the National Bureau of Economic Research and a fellow of the American Academy of Arts and Sciences. Duffie is a past president of the American Finance Association and chaired the Financial Stability Board's Market Participants Group on Reference Rate Reform. He is an independent director of the Dimensional Funds, project advisor of the G30 Working Group on Treasury Market Liquidity, and a codirector of the Hoover Institution's Study of the Global Implications of China's Central Bank Digital Currency. Duffie's most recent book is *Fragmenting Markets: Post-Crisis Bank Regulations and Financial Market Liquidity* (De Gruyter, 2022).

SEBASTIAN EDWARDS is the Henry Ford II Professor of International Economics at the University of California–Los Angeles. From 1993 to 1996, he was chief economist for Latin America at the World Bank. He has advised numerous governments, financial institutions, and multinational companies and was codirector of the National Bureau of Economic Research's Africa Project. Edwards has published fifteen books, among them *Left Behind: Latin America and the False Promise of Populism* (University of Chicago Press, 2011), *American Default: The Untold Story of FDR, the Supreme Court, and the Battle over Gold* (Princeton University Press, 2018), and most recently, *The Chile Project: The Story of the Chicago Boys and the Downfall of Neoliberalism* (Princeton University Press, 2023). Edwards has been president of the Latin American and Caribbean Economic Association and is currently a member of the Scientific Advisory Council of the Kiel Institute for the World Economy. He also served on California governor Arnold Schwarzenegger's Council of Economic Advisers. He was awarded the 2012 Carlos Díaz-Alejandro Prize for his research on the Latin American economies. Edwards was educated at the Universidad Católica de Chile. He received an MA in economics and a PhD in economics from the University of Chicago.

BARRY EICHENGREEN is George C. Pardee and Helen N. Pardee Chair and Distinguished Professor of Economics and Political Science at the University of California–Berkeley. He is a research associate of the National Bureau of Economic Research, research fellow of the Centre for Economic Policy Research, fellow of the American Academy of Arts and Sciences, distinguished fellow of the American Economic Association, corresponding fellow of the British Academy, and life fellow of the Cliometric Society. He has held Guggenheim and Fulbright fellowships and been a fellow of the Center for Advanced Study in the Behavioral Sciences at Stanford University and the Institute for Advanced Study in Berlin. He was a senior policy advisor at the International Monetary Fund, president of the Economic History Association, and, for fifteen years, convener of the Bellagio Group. Among Eichengreen's awards are the Economic History Association's Jonathan Hughes Prize for Excellence in Teaching Economic History, the 2010 Schumpeter Prize, and the 2022 Nessim Habif Prize for Contributions to Science and Industry. He is a regular monthly columnist for *Project Syndicate*. His most recent book is *In Defense of Public Debt*, with Asmaa El-Ganainy, Rui Esteves, and Kris James Mitchener (Oxford University Press, 2021).

NIALL FERGUSON, MA, DPhil, FRSE, is the Milbank Family Senior Fellow at the Hoover Institution and a senior faculty fellow of the Belfer Center for Science and International Affairs at Harvard. He is the author of sixteen books, including *The Pity of War* (Basic Books, 1999), *The House of Rothschild* (Viking, 1998–9), *Empire* (Basic Books, 2003), *Civilization* (Penguin, 2012), and *Kissinger, 1923–1968: The Idealist* (Penguin, 2015), which won the Arthur Ross Book Award from the Council on Foreign Relations. As a filmmaker, he received an international Emmy for his 2009 PBS series *The Ascent of Money*. His book *The Square and the Tower* (Penguin, 2018) was a *New York Times* bestseller and was also adapted for PBS as *Niall Ferguson's Networld*. In 2020, he joined Bloomberg Opinion as a columnist. He is the founder and managing director of Greenmantle LLC, a New York–based advisory firm, a cofounder of Ualá, a Latin American financial technology company, and a trustee of the New-York Historical Society, the Centre for Policy Studies, and the University of Austin. His latest book, *Doom: The Politics of Catastrophe* (Penguin, 2021) was short-listed for the Lionel Gelber Prize. He is currently writing *Kissinger, 1969–2023*.

PETER BLAIR HENRY is the Class of 1984 Senior Fellow at the Hoover Institution, senior fellow at Stanford University's Freeman Spogli Institute for International Studies, and dean emeritus of New York University's Leonard N. Stern School of Business. Henry is the former Konosuke Matsushita Professor of International Economics at the Stanford Graduate School of Business, where his research was funded by a National Science Foundation CAREER Award. He is the author of *Turnaround: Third World Lessons for First World Growth* (Basic Books, 2013). A vice chair of the boards of the National Bureau of Economic Research and the Economic Club of New York, Henry also serves on the boards of Citigroup and Nike. In 2015, he received the Foreign Policy Association Medal, and in 2016, he was honored as one of the Carnegie Foundation's Great Immigrants. Henry leads the PhD Excellence Initiative, a mentorship program for exceptional students of color interested in pursuing doctoral studies in economics, a role for which he received the 2022 Impactful Mentor Award from the American Economic Association. Henry received his PhD in economics from MIT and bachelor's degrees from Oxford University and the University of North Carolina at Chapel Hill.

PHILIP N. JEFFERSON took office as the vice chair of the Board of Governors of the Federal Reserve System on September 13, 2023, for a four-year term, after taking office as a member of the board on May 23, 2022, to fill an unexpired term ending January 31, 2036. Most recently, Jefferson was vice president for academic affairs and dean of faculty and the Paul B. Freeland Professor of Economics at Davidson College. Previously, Jefferson served as chair of the Department of Economics at Swarthmore College, where he was the Centennial Professor of Economics. Prior to this position, Jefferson was an economist at the Board of Governors of the Federal Reserve System. Jefferson's other past roles include being president of the National Economic Association. He also served on the Vassar College Board of Trustees and the Board of Advisors of the Opportunity and Inclusive Growth Institute at the Federal Reserve Bank of Minneapolis. Jefferson received a BA in economics from Vassar College and an MA and a PhD in economics from the University of Virginia.

MARTIN KORNEJEW is a PhD candidate at the University of Bonn, expected to graduate in 2024. He was a visiting PhD student at the University of Chicago Booth School of Business and received his bachelor's and master's degrees in economics from the Free University of Berlin and the University of Kiel, visiting University College London and the University of Stockholm. He has served as a consultant at the World Bank and for the European Commission's Joint Research Centre. Kornejew's research focuses on institutions governing business investment and the resolution of financial distress. Drawing on various types of data from a wide array of sources and combining empirical with theoretical methods, he analyzes the economic ramifications of these institutions, both at the micro- and macroeconomic levels. Kornejew has received scholarships from the German Federal Ministry of Education and Research, the Bonn Graduate School of Economics, and the German Research Foundation via the University of Bonn's Research Training Group 2281 on the Macroeconomics of Inequality.

HARUHIKO KURODA was governor of the Bank of Japan from 2013 to 2023. He previously served as president of the Asian Development Bank from 2005 to 2013. He was also special advisor to the cabinet of Japanese prime minister Junichiro Koizumi, while also serving as professor at Hitotsubashi University in Tokyo, from 2003 to 2005. During his career at Japan's Ministry of Finance (1967–2003), Kuroda's responsibilities encompassed fields including international finance and tax policies. From 1999 to 2003, he represented the ministry as vice minister of finance for international affairs at numerous international monetary conferences, such as the Group of Seven (G7) and Group of Twenty (G20) meetings. Kuroda holds a BA in law from the University of Tokyo, and an MPhil in economics from the University of Oxford.

JEFFREY M. LACKER was president and CEO of the Federal Reserve Bank of Richmond from 2004 to 2017, having previously served as senior vice president and director of research. As president, he participated in meetings of the Federal Open Market Committee and served four rotations as a voting member; and led an organization of 2,700 employees over several states. In 2022, Lacker was named to the Shadow Open Market Committee and inducted into the Global Interdependence Center College of Central Bankers. Lacker was distinguished professor in the department of economics at the Virginia Commonwealth University School of Business (2018–22), was visiting scholar at the Swiss National Bank (1997), taught at the College of William and Mary (1992–93), and was assistant professor of economics at the Krannert School of Management at Purdue University (1984–89). Lacker received a bachelor's degree in economics from Franklin & Marshall College and a doctorate in economics from the University of Wisconsin. He serves on the boards of the Council for Economic Education, the Virginia Council for Economic Education, the World Affairs Council of Greater Richmond, and the Richmond Jewish Foundation, of which he is chair.

MICKEY D. LEVY is the chief economist for Berenberg Capital Markets LLC and a visiting scholar at the Hoover Institution. He is a long-standing member of the Shadow Open Market Committee. He is also a member of the Council on Foreign Relations and the Economic Club of New York. Levy is a past member of the Financial Research Advisory Committee of the Office of Financial Research. From 1998 to 2013, he was chief economist at Bank of America Corporation, where he was on the Executive Asset Liability and Finance committees. He conducts research on monetary and fiscal policies, their impacts, and how they influence economic and financial market performance. He has authored numerous papers on the Federal Reserve; the effectiveness of monetary and fiscal policies, and their interaction and influences on the business cycle; credit conditions; and inflation. He testifies frequently before the US Congress on various aspects of monetary policy and banking regulation, credit conditions and debt, fiscal and budget policies, and global capital flows.

JOHN LIPSKY is a senior fellow of the Foreign Policy Institute at Johns Hopkins University's School of Advanced International Studies. Most recently, he was first deputy managing director of the International Monetary Fund. Previously, he was vice chairman of JPMorgan Investment Bank, chief economist at JPMorgan Chase, chief economist and director of research at Chase Manhattan Bank, and chief economist at Salomon Brothers. Early in his career, he spent ten years at the International Monetary Fund. Currently, he is the chair of the National Bureau of Economic Research and the cochair of the Aspen Institute's Program on the World Economy. He is vice chair of the Center for Global Development and of the Bretton Woods Committee. He also serves on the advisory board of the Stanford Institute for Economic Policy Research, is a director of the American Council on Germany, and is a life member of the Council on Foreign Relations. He received his PhD in economics from Stanford University.

WILLIAM R. NELSON is an executive vice president and chief economist at the Bank Policy Institute, where he oversees research and analysis in support of the advocacy of the institute's member banks. Previously, he served as executive managing director, chief economist, and head of research at the Clearing House Association and chief economist of the Clearing House Payments Company. Prior to joining the Clearing House in 2016, Nelson was a deputy director of the Division of Monetary Affairs at the Federal Reserve Board, where his responsibilities included monetary policy analysis, discount window policy analysis, and financial institution supervision. Nelson earned a PhD, an MS, and an MA in economics from Yale University and a BA from the University of Virginia. He has published research on a wide range of topics, including monetary policy rules; monetary policy communications; and the intersection of monetary policy, lender-of-last-resort policy, financial stability, and bank supervision and regulation.

CHARLES I. PLOSSER served as president and CEO of the Federal Reserve Bank of Philadelphia from 2006 until his retirement in 2015. He has been a longtime advocate of the Federal Reserve's adopting an explicit inflation target, which the Federal Open Market Committee did in January 2012. Before joining the Philadelphia Fed in 2006, Plosser served as dean of the University of Rochester's Simon School of Business from 1993 to 2003. He has been a research associate of the National Bureau of Economic Research as well as a visiting scholar at the Bank of England. He is currently a visiting scholar at the Hoover Institution. Plosser served as coeditor of the *Journal of Monetary Economics* for two decades and cochaired the Shadow Open Market Committee with Anna Schwartz. His research and teaching interests include monetary and fiscal policy, long-term economic growth, and banking and financial markets. Plosser earned PhD and MBA degrees from the University of Chicago.

RANDAL QUARLES is chairman and founder of the Cynosure Group, a diversified investment firm focused on alternative assets. From October 2017 through October 2021, he was vice chairman of the Federal Reserve System, serving as the system's first vice chairman for supervision, charged with ensuring stability of the financial sector. From December 2018 until December 2021, he also served as the chairman of the Financial Stability Board, a global body established after the Great Financial Crisis to coordinate international efforts to enhance financial stability. Earlier in his career, Quarles was a longtime partner at the Carlyle Group, a leading global private equity firm, and previously a partner at the international law firm of Davis Polk & Wardwell, where he was cohead of its financial services practice. He has been a close advisor to every Republican Treasury secretary for the last thirty-five years, including as under secretary of the Treasury in the George W. Bush administration. He has represented the United States in meetings of the Group of Seven, the Group of Twenty, and the Financial Stability Forum and was also US executive director of the International Monetary Fund.

JOSHUA D. RAUH is the Ormond Family Professor of Finance at Stanford's Graduate School of Business and a senior fellow at the Hoover Institution. He formerly served as principal chief economist on the president's Council of Economic Advisers (2019–20) and taught at the University of Chicago's Booth School of Business (2004–9) and the Kellogg School of Management (2009–12). Rauh studies government pension liabilities, corporate investment, business taxation, and investment management. His research on pension systems and public finance has received national media coverage, and he has testified before Congress on these topics. He has received various awards recognizing his scholarship, including the Brattle Group Prize and the Smith Breeden Prize of the American Finance Association. His scholarly papers have appeared in journals such as the *Journal of Political Economy*, the *Quarterly Journal of Economics*, the *Journal of Finance*, the *Journal of Financial Economics*, the *Review of Financial Studies*, and the *Journal of Public Economics*. Before his academic career, he was an associate economist at Goldman Sachs in London. Rauh received a BA from Yale University and a PhD from the Massachusetts Institute of Technology, both in economics.

CONDOLEEZZA RICE is the Tad and Dianne Taube Director and the Thomas and Barbara Stephenson Senior Fellow on Public Policy at the Hoover Institution. She is also the Denning Professor in Global Business and the Economy at Stanford's Graduate School of Business and a founding partner of international strategic consulting firm Rice, Hadley, Gates & Manuel LLC. Rice served as the sixty-sixth US secretary of state (2005–9) and national security advisor (2001–5) in the George W. Bush administrations. She previously served on President George H. W. Bush's National Security Council staff and as Stanford University's provost. She has been on the Stanford faculty since 1981 and has won two of the university's highest teaching honors. In 2022, Rice became a part owner of the Denver Broncos as part of the Walton-Penner Family Ownership Group. Born in Birmingham, Alabama, Rice earned her bachelor's degree, cum laude and Phi Beta Kappa, from the University of Denver; her master's from the University of Notre Dame; and her PhD from the Graduate School of International Studies at the University of Denver, all in political science. Rice is a fellow of the American Academy of Arts and Sciences and has been awarded over fifteen honorary doctorates.

PAUL SCHMELZING is an assistant professor of finance at Boston College and a research fellow at the Hoover Institution. His research concentrates on current financial and macroeconomic topics within a long-run historical perspective, often deploying new archival financial sources. Areas include asset pricing, banking, and financial economics. On asset pricing, he is currently writing a book under contract with Yale University Press, reconstructing global real interest rates and capital market trends since the Renaissance. On banking, he is the coauthor, with Andrew Metrick, of the new Metrick-Schmelzing database on banking-crisis interventions, 1257–2020; this new resource proposes a new crisis-intervention classification and documents almost two thousand emergency policy responses during financial stress episodes over seven centuries. In the area of financial economics, he is currently researching long-run empirical dynamics in monetary economics and central bank balance sheets. He is a consultant for the International Monetary Fund and has also been a visiting scholar for the Bank of England since 2016. Schmelzing holds a PhD in history from Harvard and a BSc in economic history from the London School of Economics. Outside academia, he has gained a variety of professional experiences in finance and financial policy.

MORITZ SCHULARICK is president of the Kiel Institute for the World Economy and professor of economics at Sciences Po, Paris, where he was Alfred Grosser Chair from 2015 to 2016. He is an elected member of the Academy of Sciences of Berlin and a research professor at New York University. Previously, he taught at the Free University of Berlin, and was a visiting professor at the University of Cambridge. He is a recipient of the 2022 Leibniz Prize from the German Research Foundation and the 2018 Gossen Prize from the German Economic Association. He is a fellow of the Institute for New Economic Thinking, and a managing editor of Europe's most important policy journal, *Economic Policy*. His work on credit cycles, asset prices, and financial stability has provided the backdrop for so-called macro-prudential policies aimed at curbing credit booms and stability risks. With Niall Ferguson, he authored a number of influential papers on US-China relations, coining the term "Chimerica." His research spans macroeconomics, finance, international economics, and economic history and has been published in leading journals. His research is supported by major grants from the European Research Council, the German Research Foundation, and the Institute for New Economic Thinking.

AMIT SERU is a senior fellow at the Hoover Institution, the Steven and Roberta Denning Professor of Finance at Stanford's Graduate School of Business, a senior fellow at Stanford's Institute for Economic Policy Research, and a research associate at the National Bureau of Economic Research. Seru's primary research interest relates to financial intermediation and regulation. He was a coeditor of the *Journal of Finance*, department editor of *Management Science*, and associate editor of the *Journal of Political Economy*. He has received various National Science Foundation grants and the Alexandre Lamfalussy Senior Research Fellowship from the Bank for International Settlements (BIS). He has presented his research to US and international regulatory agencies, including BIS, the Consumer Financial Protection Bureau, the European Central Bank, the Federal Reserve, the Federal Deposit Insurance Corporation, the Financial Industry Regulatory Authority, the International Monetary Fund, and the Monetary Authority of Singapore. His research has been featured in leading economic journals and major media outlets. Seru earned a BE in electronics and communication and an MBA from the University of Delhi and a PhD in finance from the University of Michigan. He was formerly a tenured faculty member at the University of Chicago's Booth School of Business.

JOHN B. TAYLOR is the George P. Shultz Senior Fellow in Economics at the Hoover Institution, where he chairs the Economic Policy Working Group and cochairs the Technology, Economics, and Governance Working Group; and the Mary and Robert Raymond Professor of Economics at Stanford University. He also directs Stanford's Introductory Economics Center, and cochairs the Faculty Council of the Stanford Emerging Technology Review. He served as senior economist on the President's Council of Economic Advisers; as under secretary of Treasury for international affairs; as president of the Mont Pelerin Society; and on the G20 Eminent Persons Group on Global Financial Governance. Among his many awards are the US Treasury's Alexander Hamilton Award and Distinguished Service Award, the Medal of the Oriental Republic of Uruguay, the Truman Medal for Economic Policy, the Bradley Prize, and the Hayek Prize for his book *First Principles* (W. W. Norton, 2012). His most recent books are *Choose Economic Freedom: Enduring Policy Lessons from the 1970s and 1980s* (with George P. Shultz, Hoover Institution Press, 2020) and *Reform of the International Monetary System* (MIT

Press, 2019). Taylor received a BA in economics, summa cum laude, from Princeton and a PhD in economics from Stanford.

VOLKER WIELAND holds the Endowed Chair of Monetary Economics at the Institute for Monetary and Financial Stability at Goethe University of Frankfurt. He also serves as the institute's managing director. He was a member of the German Council of Economic Experts from 2013 to 2022. In 1995, Wieland received a PhD in economics from Stanford University. Before joining the Frankfurt faculty in 2000, he was a senior economist at the Board of Governors of the Federal Reserve System. His research interests include monetary and fiscal policy, business cycles, macroeconomic models, and economic dynamics. He has published in leading economic journals such as the *American Economic Review*, the *Journal of Monetary Economics*, and the *Review of Economics and Statistics*. He has served as managing editor of the *Journal of Economic Dynamics and Control* and has received several awards and grants. Furthermore, he has been a consultant to central banks and international institutions. Recently, he has been coordinating the creation of a public archive of macroeconomic models for comparative purposes, the Macroeconomic Model Data Base.

JAMES A. WILCOX is a professor of the Graduate School at the University of California–Berkeley, where he was previously professor of finance and of economic analysis and policy in the Haas School of Business. His research interests include banks' underwriting and lending, Fed policy and interest rates, consumer attitudes and spending, credit unions, Islamic banking, and nonfinancial corporations' internal capital markets. At the Haas School, he teaches courses on macroeconomics and on banking. Wilcox originated Fannie Mae's monthly Home Purchase Sentiment Index. He has served as the chief economist at the US Office of the Comptroller of the Currency, as a senior economist for monetary policy and macroeconomics on the President's Council of Economic Advisers, and as an economist on the Board of Governors of the Federal Reserve. He has been a visiting scholar at the Federal Reserve Banks of San Francisco and Atlanta. Wilcox is a member of the Financial Economists Roundtable and is a fellow of the Wharton Financial Institutions Center. He was a founding fellow of the Filene Research Institute and has been president of the International Banking, Economics, and Finance Association.

About the Hoover Institution's Economic Policy Working Group

The Economic Policy Working Group brings together experts on economic and financial policy at the Hoover Institution and elsewhere to study key developments in the US and global economies, examine their interactions, and develop specific policy proposals.

For twenty-five years starting in the early 1980s, the US economy experienced an unprecedented economic boom. Economic expansions were stronger and longer than in the past. Recessions were shorter, shallower, and less frequent. GDP doubled, and household net worth increased by 250 percent in real terms. Forty-seven million jobs were created.

This quarter-century boom strengthened as its length increased. Productivity growth surged by one full percentage point per year in the United States, creating an additional $9 trillion of goods and services that would never have existed. And the long boom went global, with emerging-market countries from Asia to Latin America and Africa experiencing the enormous improvements in both economic growth and economic stability.

Economic policies that place greater reliance on the principles of free markets, price stability, and flexibility have been the key to these successes. Recently, however, several powerful new economic forces have begun to change the economic landscape, and these principles are being challenged, with far-reaching implications for US economic policy, both domestic and international. A financial crisis flared up in 2007 and turned into a severe panic in 2008, leading to the Great Recession. The economic expansion that followed that Great Recession lasted for more than a decade but ended severely as the forces of the coronavirus pandemic hit the US and world economy in 2020, leading to another recession. This episode and the ongoing recovery raise fundamental questions about the role of economic policy. How we interpret and react to these forces—and in particular whether proven policy principles prevail going forward—will determine whether strong economic growth and stability return and again continue to spread and improve more people's lives or whether the economy stalls and stagnates.

The Economic Policy Working Group organizes seminars and conferences, prepares policy papers and other publications, and serves as a resource for policymakers and interested members of the public.

INDEX

Note: The letter f *following a page number denotes a figure; the letter* t *denotes a table.*

Hoover Monetary Policy Conference Volumes

Getting Monetary Policy Back on Track
Edited by Michael D. Bordo, John H. Cochrane, and John B. Taylor

How Monetary Policy Got Behind the Curve—and How to Get Back
Edited by Michael D. Bordo, John H. Cochrane, and John B. Taylor

Strategies for Monetary Policy
Edited by John H. Cochrane and John B. Taylor

Currencies, Capital, and Central Bank Balances
Edited by John H. Cochrane, Kyle Palermo, and John B. Taylor

The Structural Foundations of Monetary Policy
Edited by Michael D. Bordo, John H. Cochrane, and Amit Seru

Rules for International Monetary Stability: Past, Present, and Future
Edited by Michael D. Bordo and John B. Taylor

Central Bank Governance and Oversight Reform
Edited by John H. Cochrane and John B. Taylor

Across the Great Divide: New Perspectives on the Financial Crisis
Edited by Martin Neil Baily and John B. Taylor

Government Policies and the Delayed Economic Recovery
Edited by Lee E. Ohanian, John B. Taylor, and Ian J. Wright

The Road Ahead for the Fed
Edited by John D. Ciorciari and John B. Taylor